Strategic Intervention Teacher Guide

Grade 1

Harcourt School Publishers

www.harcourtschool.com

Copyright © by Harcourt, Inc.

All rights reserved. No part of this publication may be reproduced or transmitted in any form or by any means, electronic or mechanical, including photocopy, recording, or any information storage and retrieval system, without permission in writing from the publisher.

Requests for permission to make copies of any part of the work should be addressed to School Permissions and Copyrights, Harcourt, Inc., 6277 Sea Harbor Drive, Orlando, Florida 32887-6777. Fax: 407-345-2418.

STORYTOWN is a trademark of Harcourt, Inc. HARCOURT and the Harcourt Logo are trademarks of Harcourt, Inc., registered in the United States of America and/or other jurisdictions.

Printed in the United States of America

ISBN 10: 0-15-365497-X
ISBN 13: 978-0-15-365497-8

4 5 6 7 8 9 10 0877 16 15 14 13 12 11 10 09

If you have received these materials as examination copies free of charge, Harcourt School Publishers retains title to the materials and they may not be resold. Resale of examination copies is strictly prohibited and is illegal.

Possession of this publication in print format does not entitle users to convert this publication, or any portion of it, into electronic format.

CONTENTS

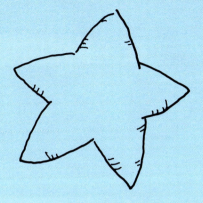

CONTENTS

INTRODUCTION

Research has shown the importance of building a strong foundation early in the process of learning to read. Most children will acquire the foundational skills needed for success in learning to read in kindergarten and grade 1. These requisite skills, which include academic language, concepts of print, phonemic awareness, letter names and sounds, letter-sound associations, and recognition of high-frequency words, all contribute to success in learning to read.

However, research also shows us that children enter school with a wide range of previous experiences with forms and functions of print. In addition, there are enormous individual differences in learning rates and learning needs that will affect children's progression in learning to read. Many children will have difficulty learning to read unless extensive additional instruction and practice is provided.

Intervention that addresses the learning needs of these children is paramount to effective prevention of reading difficulties. Intervention offered early and targeted to children who need it most will facilitate success. Intervention requires additional engaged academic time and support through strategic and systematic instruction in the foundational and requisite reading skills.

The *Strategic Intervention Resource Kit* provides additional intensive systematic teaching and practice to help children learn the skills and strategies important for proficient reading. Aligned with and correlated to the instructional goals and objectives of *StoryTown* Grade 1 program, the *Strategic Intervention Resource Kit* optimizes the learning opportunities and outcomes for children at risk. The additional targeted teaching and practice will help children build a strong foundation in the fundamental skills for successfully learning to read.

Components of the Strategic Intervention Resource Kit

The goal of this *Strategic Intervention Resource Kit* is to provide the scaffolding, extra support, and extra reading practice that struggling readers need to succeed. Each kit includes the following components:

- *Teacher Guide* with lessons directly aligned with and correlated to the lessons in the *StoryTown* Teacher Edition.
- *Interactive Reader* that provides accessible reading materials with built-in support for the child.
- *Practice Book* with a write-in, consumable text to provide direct application and practice of phonic elements and grammar skills.
- *Teacher Resource Book* with Copying Masters that include High-Frequency Word Cards and story strips to provide additional reinforcement of high-frequency words.
- *Assessment Book* to monitor progress and ensure success.
- *Photo Cards* with four-color illustrations to support instruction.
- *Sound/Spelling Cards* to support recognition of letter names and letter forms and to reinforce connecting letters to sounds.
- *Word Builders and Word Builder Cards* to demonstrate blending and word building. Children practice with these to develop blending and word building skills.
- *Write-On/Wipe-Off Board with Phonemic Awareness Disks* help make the abstract concept of phonemes more concrete. One side of the board has Elkonin boxes so children can track phonemes in two- and three-phoneme words or syllables in two- and three-syllable words. The other side provides a model of the uppercase and lowercase alphabet, space for writing or drawing with dry erase markers, and write-on lines to practice letter formation and handwriting.

Using the Strategic Intervention Teacher Guide

The *Strategic Intervention Teacher Guide* gives support for struggling readers in key instructional strands, plus prerequisite phonics skills and oral-reading fluency. Each five-day lesson plan includes the following resources:

- *Phonemic Awareness* instruction with activities to teach phonemic awareness skills.

- *Phonics and Spelling* lessons to systematically preteach and reteach basic phonics skills and connect spelling and phonics.

- *High-Frequency Words* lessons to preteach, reteach, and provide cumulative review and reinforcement of the high-frequency words taught, increasing the exposure to and experiences with words children should be learning.

- *Build Robust Vocabulary* lessons with Student-Friendly Explanations to enrich children's listening and speaking vocabularies and help children master the language of school.

- *Directed Reading Lessons* for the *Interactive Reader* selection to reinforce basic comprehension skill using questions and teacher modeling.

- *Fluency* lessons to develop and practice oral reading fluency.

- *Grammar and Writing* lessons to reinforce the lesson's grammar skill and provide support for key writing forms.

- *Comprehension* lessons to ensure that children get the in-depth instruction they need to reach grade-level standards.

Depending on your individual classroom and school schedules, you can tailor the instruction to suit your needs. The following pages show two options for pacing the instruction in this guide.

Grade 1 For Use with *StoryTown*

DAY 1

RETEACH

PHONEMIC AWARENESS
- Practice the phonemic awareness skill for Day 1.

PHONICS AND SPELLING
- Reteach the skill that was introduced on Day 1 in *StoryTown*.

HIGH-FREQUENCY WORDS
- Provide guided practice for the high-frequency words from the Student Edition selection.

COMPREHENSION
 Preteach the skill that will be introduced on Day 2 in *StoryTown*.

FLUENCY
- Begin fluency practice for the current week.

GRAMMAR/WRITING
- Reteach the grammar skill that was introduced on Day 1 in *StoryTown*.

DAY 2

RETEACH

PHONEMIC AWARENESS
- Practice the phonemic awareness skill for Day 2.

PHONICS AND SPELLING
- Provide guided practice for the phonics skill that is reviewed on Day 3 in *StoryTown*.

HIGH-FREQUENCY WORDS
- Review the high-frequency words for the current lesson.

FLUENCY
- Continue fluency practice.

READING
- Read the Student Edition selection.
  - Build Background
  - Monitor Comprehension
  - Have students answer the *Think Critically* questions

BUILD ROBUST VOCABULARY
- Preteach the robust vocabulary words that will be taught on Day 3 in *StoryTown*.

GRAMMAR/WRITING
- Reteach the grammar skill that is taught this week in *StoryTown*.

Grade 1 OPTION 2 : As a stand-alone program

DAY 1

PHONEMIC AWARENESS
- Practice the phonemic awareness skill for Day 1.

PHONICS AND SPELLING
- Reteach the phonics skill.

COMPREHENSION
 Teach the Focus Skill.

HIGH-FREQUENCY WORDS
- Provide guided practice for the high-frequency words from the Student Edition selection.

FLUENCY
- Begin fluency practice for the current week.

GRAMMAR/WRITING
- Reteach the grammar skill.

DAY 2

PHONEMIC AWARENESS
- Practice the phonemic awareness skill for Day 2.

PHONICS AND SPELLING
- Provide guided practice for the phonics skill.

HIGH-FREQUENCY WORDS
- Review all the high-frequency words for the current lesson.

FLUENCY
- Continue fluency practice.

READING
- Read the Student Edition selection.
  - Build Background
  - Monitor Comprehension
  - Have students answer the *Think Critically* questions

BUILD ROBUST VOCABULARY
- Teach the robust vocabulary words.

GRAMMAR/WRITING
- Reteach the grammar skill.

DAY 3

RETEACH

PHONEMIC AWARENESS
- Practice the phonemic awareness skill for Day 3.

PHONICS
- Preteach the phonics skill that will be introduced on Day 4 in *StoryTown*.

PHONICS AND SPELLING
- Provide guided practice of the phonics skill that is taught this week in *StoryTown*.

HIGH-FREQUENCY WORDS
- Review high-frequency words from the Student Edition selection.

COMPREHENSION
- Reteach the skill that is taught this week in *StoryTown*.

FLUENCY
- Continue fluency practice.

GRAMMAR/WRITING
- Reteach the writing form that is taught this week in *StoryTown*.

DAY 4

RETEACH

PHONEMIC AWARENESS
- Practice the phonemic awareness skill for Day 4.

PHONICS
- Reteach the phonics skill that was introduced on Day 4 in *StoryTown*.

PHONICS AND SPELLING
- Provide guided practice for the phonics skill that is taught this week in *StoryTown*.

HIGH-FREQUENCY WORDS
- Revlew high-frequency words.

COMPREHENSION
- Provide guided practice for the skill taught this week in *StoryTown*.

FLUENCY
- Continue fluency practice.

GRAMMAR/WRITING
- Reteach the writing form that is taught this week in *StoryTown*.

DAY 5

PRETEACH **FOR next week's *StoryTown* lesson**

HIGH-FREQUENCY WORDS
- Review the high-frequency words that were taught this week in *StoryTown*.

PHONEMIC AWARENESS
- Practice the phonemic awareness skill for Day 5.

PHONICS AND SPELLING
- Preteach the skill that will be introduced on Day 1 next week in *StoryTown*.

BUILD ROBUST VOCABULARY
- Preteach the robust vocabulary words that will be introduced on Day 1 next week in *StoryTown*.

GRAMMAR/WRITING
- Preteach the grammar skill that will be introduced on Day 1 next week in *StoryTown*.

DAY 3

PHONEMIC AWARENESS
- Practice the phonemic awareness skill for Day 3.

PHONICS
- Teach the secondary phonics skill.

PHONICS AND SPELLING
- Provide guided practice of the phonics skill.

HIGH-FREQUENCY WORDS
- Review high-frequency words from the Student Edition selection.

COMPREHENSION
- Reteach Focus Skill.

FLUENCY
- Continue fluency practice.

GRAMMAR/WRITING
- Introduce the writing form.

DAY 4

PHONEMIC AWARENESS
- Practice the phonemic awareness skill for Day 4.

PHONICS
- Reteach the secondary phonics skill.

PHONICS AND SPELLING
- Provide guided practice for the phonics skill.

HIGH-FREQUENCY WORDS
- Review high-frequency words.

COMPREHENSION
- Provide guided practice for the Focus Skill.

FLUENCY
- Continue fluency practice.

GRAMMAR/WRITING
- Reteach the writing form.

DAY 5

HIGH-FREQUENCY WORDS
- Review the high-frequency words for the current week.

PHONEMIC AWARENESS
- Practice the phonemic awareness skill for Day 5.

PHONICS AND SPELLING
- Teach the phonics skill.

BUILD ROBUST VOCABULARY
- Teach the robust vocabulary words.

GRAMMAR/WRITING
- Teach the grammar skill.

We Can Tap!

Rabbit can tap. Tap, tap!

LESSON 1

30+ Minutes

PHONEMIC AWARENESS
Phoneme Isolation

PHONICS AND SPELLING
Reteach Short Vowel /a/*a*

COMPREHENSION
Preteach Make Predictions

HIGH-FREQUENCY WORDS
Reteach *let's, now*

FLUENCY
Accuracy

GRAMMAR/WRITING
Reteach Sentences

Materials Needed:

Word Builders and Word Builder Cards

Write-On/ Wipe-Off Boards

Heading Out Student Edition pp. 4–5

Practice Book

p.3

Practice Book

Spelling Words

1. am	6. man
2. at	7. map
3. cat	8. tap
4. can	9. a
5. ran	10. the

Have children practice writing spelling words on their *Write-on/Wipe-off Boards.*

Phonemic Awareness

Phoneme Isolation   Tell children to listen for the /a/ sound as you say two words. Say: *cat, cup.* **Which word has the /a/ sound?** *Cat* **has the /a/ sound. Now you try.** Repeat with the words: *mitt/map, cab/cot, him/ham, tip/tap, mad/mop, run/ran.*

RETEACH

Phonics and Spelling

Short Vowel /a/*a*

Word Building   Place the *Word Builder Cards a* and *m* in the *Word Builder.* Ask children to say each letter name and the sound it stands for. Slide your hand under the letters as you blend the sounds—/am/. Then read the word naturally—*am.* Have children do the same. Continue building new words by asking children:

- **Which letter should I change to make *am* become *at*?** (Change *m* to *t*.)

- **Which letter should I add to make *at* become *cat*?** (Add *c* before *a* and *t*.)

Continue with the words *can, ran, man, map,* and *tap.* As words are built, write them on the board. Then have children read the list of words.

Read Words in Context   Write the following sentences on chart paper. Track the print as children read the sentences aloud. Finally, point to the underlined words at random and have children read them. *Dad looked <u>at the</u> <u>map</u>. I <u>can</u> <u>tap</u> and sing.*

PRETEACH

Comprehension

Make Predictions   Explain to children that using clues from a story and what they know from real life can help them predict what will happen next in a story. Say: **Matt is standing with his bike in front of his house. Soon he sees Meg coming down the street. She is riding her bike too. "I'm ready to go," she calls as she gets closer.** Ask children to predict what they think will happen next and tell why they think this. (Matt was waiting for Meg to come so they can ride bikes together. I think this because they both have their bikes and Meg says she's ready to go.)

Tell children as they read a story they can also use the title and the story pictures as clues to guess what will happen next.

RETEACH

High-Frequency Words

- **pp. 4–5** Write the words *let's* and *now* on the board.
  - Point to and read *let's*. Repeat, having children say *let's* with you.
  - Say: ***Let's* ride to the park.**
- Repeat the word and point to each letter as you spell it. Then have children say and spell *let's* with you. Have children reread the word.

Repeat for *now*. Use the following sentence: Now *I am ready to go swimming.*

Have children turn to page 4 of *Heading Out* and have them read aloud the words at the top of the page. Talk about the illustrations. Then guide children in choosing and circling the word that names each picture. (3. *tap*, 4. *cat*) Have children read aloud each word in the list on page 5. Ask volunteers to read the sentences aloud. Then have children choral-read the sentences. Guide them to read and trace the word that completes each sentence. (1. *now*, 2. *let's*)

RETEACH

Grammar/Writing

 Practice Book p.3

Sentences Write these sentences on the board:

> Pat can tap.
> Sam can wag.
> Cat can nap.

Read each sentence. Ask: **What kind of letter begins each sentence?** (a capital letter) **What is at the end of each sentence?** (a period) Remind children that a sentence tells a complete thought. Have children dictate sentences that tell what they can do. Use children's names to record, such as: *Missy can paint. Jorge can play ball.* Read the sentences. Have children underline the capital letter and circle the period in each one. Complete *Practice Book* page 3 together.

Fluency

 Photo Card

Accuracy Explain to children that when they read a story, it is important to read the words correctly in order to understand the story.

Use word cards and *Photo Cards* to form the following sentences in a pocket chart. *Cat has a [Photo Card gift]. Pam has a [Photo Card flower].*

Read the first sentence while tracking the print. Say: **Cat hat a gift.** Ask if the sentence makes sense. Have children point out the word you did not read with accuracy. (*has*) Then repeat the sentence and have children echo-read. Repeat for the second sentence.

30+ Minutes

DAY AT A GLANCE

Day 2

PHONEMIC AWARENESS
Phoneme Blending

PHONICS AND SPELLING
Reteach Short Vowel /a/*a*

HIGH-FREQUENCY WORDS
Reteach *help, now, let's*

FLUENCY
Accuracy

READING
"We Can Tap!"

BUILD ROBUST VOCABULARY
Preteach *attention, perform, supportive*

GRAMMAR/WRITING
Reteach Sentences

Materials Needed:

Word Builders and Word Builder Cards

Practice Book p.4
Practice Book

Copying Masters 1–2
Lesson 1 High-Frequency Word Cards

Heading Out Student Edition pp. 6–13

High-Frequency Words

help	let's
now	

Phonemic Awareness

Phoneme Blending Tell children they are going to play a guessing game. Then say: **I'm thinking of a word that names something you wear on your head. It is a /h/ /a/ /t/. What's my word? The word is** *hat.* **Now you try.** Continue with clues for the words: /h/ /a/ /m/ (*ham*), /m/ /a/ /d/ (*mad*), /n/ /a/ /p/ (*nap*), /p/ /a/ /n/ (*pan*), /m/ /a/ /p/ (*map*).

RETEACH

Phonics and Spelling

 Short Vowel /a/*a*

Word Building Use a *Word Builder* and *Word Builder Cards* and have children repeat each step after you. Build the word *can.* Blend the sounds to read the word—/kan/. Ask children to name each letter and tell whether it is a consonant or a vowel. Remind children that in words with the consonant-vowel-consonant pattern, the vowel is often short. Ask them what vowel sound they hear in *can.* (/a/; short *a*) Then have children say the word naturally—*can.* Lead children in building and reading new words by saying:

- **Change *c* to *f*. Read the word.** (*fan*)
- **Change *f* to *m*. Read the word.** (*man*)
- **Change *n* to *p*. Read the word.** (*map*)

Continue with the following words: *cap-lap-sap-sad.* As each word is built, write it on the board. Then have children read the list of words.

Practice Book p.4 **Read Words in Context** Ask children to turn to *Practice Book* page 4. Read the sentences aloud and have children echo read. Then ask volunteers to read each sentence aloud. Ask: **Who has two caps?** (Sam) **What can Sam give Pat?** (one cap) **Who has two bats?** (Pat) **What can Pat give Sam?** (one bat) Guide children to frame and read words that have the short *a* sound.

RETEACH

High-Frequency Words

Copying Masters 1–2 Display the *High-Frequency Word Cards* for *help, now,* and *let's.* Point to each card and read the word. Have children repeat. Distribute cards to children. Have them work with partners to play a game. Tell them to shuffle the cards and turn them face down. Have partners play a memory game by turning the cards over two at a time to match and read.

Reading

 pp. 6–13

Build Background: "We Can Tap!"

Read the title with children. Ask children if they have ever performed on a stage. Talk about what kind of act they did and how they felt about performing in front of an audience. Tell children they will be reading about a very special performance on a stage.

Monitor Comprehension: "We Can Tap!"

Have children turn to the first page of the story. Ask a volunteer to reread the title. Ask children to look at the picture on page 6 and think about what the selection will be about and what the character is doing. Guide children through the story as they read.

 pp. 6–7

Say: **I see a character on stage. Let's read to find out what this character can do.**

After reading the pages, ask: **Who is the character on stage?** (Rabbit) **CHARACTERS**

Ask: **What can Rabbit do?** (Rabbit can tap.) **Frame and read the words with the short *a* sound.** (*can, tap*) **NOTE DETAILS/APPLY PHONICS**

Ask: **Do you think there will be other performers? What do you think they will do?** (Possible response: Yes. They will probably dance or sing.) 🔄 **MAKE PREDICTIONS**

 pp. 8–9

Say: **A new character will perform next. Read to find out who it is.**

After reading the pages, ask: **Who performs after Rabbit?** (Turtle) **SEQUENCE**

Ask: **What can Turtle do on stage?** (He can tap too.) **NOTE DETAILS**

Say: **Look at the pictures of Turtle and Rabbit. How is Turtle's dance a little different from Rabbit's dance?** (Turtle takes off his hat.) **COMPARE AND CONTRAST**

pp. 10–11

Say: **Now a third performer comes on stage. Let's read to find out who this is and what he can do.**

After reading the pages, ask: **Who performs after Turtle?** (Skunk) **SEQUENCE**

What can Skunk do on stage? (Skunk can tap too.) **NOTE DETAILS**

Ask: **How is Skunk's dance a little different from Rabbit's and Turtle's?** (He dances with a cane.) **COMPARE AND CONTRAST**

Fluency

Accuracy Write these words on the board: *cat, tap, help, sad, map, now, can, man, let's*. Tell children that they know these words and some of the words will appear in the story they will read.

Explain that being able to recognize words quickly is an important part of reading. Point to the words in order and have children read them. Then point to the words at random and have children read them.

Ask: **How do you think the show will end?** (Possible response: Maybe they will all dance together.) **MAKE PREDICTIONS**

page 12 Say: **Look at the picture on this last page. Let's read to find out how the show ends.**

After reading the page, ask: **How does the show end?** (The three dance together.) **CONFIRM PREDICTIONS**

Ask: **How are the dancers all the same now?** (They all dance with canes and with their hats off.) **COMPARE AND CONTRAST**

Ask: **Why do you think the three decide to tap together at the end? Give a reason for your answer.** (Possible response: I think they tapped together because they can all tap and it makes a nice act to close the show.) **DRAW CONCLUSIONS**

page 13 **Answers to *Think Critically* Questions**
Help children read and answer the *Think Critically* questions on page 13. Answers are shown below.

1. ‹stage› **SETTING**
2. ‹Rabbit taps.› **SEQUENCE**
3. ‹All three tap.› **SEQUENCE**

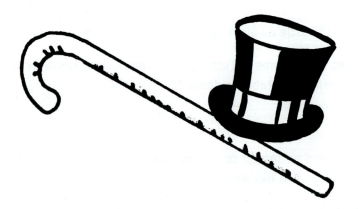

Build Robust Vocabulary

Introduce Robust Vocabulary   Read the student-friendly explanation for each word. Then discuss each word using the following examples.

Say: **If you were learning how to do something new, you would have to pay attention. Why should you pay attention to your art teacher?**

Say: **Some people perform in dance recitals on a stage. Have you ever performed in a show or in a play? What did you do?**

Say: **If you wanted to run in a race, it would be supportive of your friends to come watch and cheer you on. If your friend was in a play, what could you do to be supportive?**

Grammar/Writing

Sentences   Ask children to think about things they do at school. Model a sentence for children, such as *I can spell*. Write your sentence on the board or on chart paper without a capital letter or a period. Then have children dictate sentences that tell things they can do at school. Record their sentences in the same manner.

> i can read books
>
> i can paint
>
> i can add numbers
>
> i can sing new songs

Read each sentence while tracking the print. Have children echo-read. Guide children to correct the sentences by adding a capital letter and period to each sentence. Then reread the corrected sentences with children.

ROBUST VOCABULARY

Student-Friendly Explanations

attention If you pay attention, you listen or watch very carefully.

perform If you perform, you do something, like sing, dance, act, or read a poem for a group of people.

supportive If you are supportive of someone, you help them believe they can do something.

LESSON 1

30+ Minutes

DAY AT A GLANCE

Day 3

PHONEMIC AWARENESS
Phoneme Segmentation

PHONICS
Preteach Inflection -s

PHONICS AND SPELLING
Reteach Short Vowel /a/a

HIGH-FREQUENCY WORDS
Reteach now, let's

FLUENCY
Accuracy

COMPREHENSION
Reteach Make Predictions

GRAMMAR/WRITING
Reteach Labels

Materials Needed:

Write-On/ Wipe-Off Boards with Phonemic Awareness Disks

Word Builders and Word Builder Cards

Copying Masters 3–4

Lesson 1 Story Strips

Heading Out Student Edition pp. 6–12

Photo Cards

Spelling Words

1. am	6. man
2. at	7. map
3. cat	8. tap
4. can	9. a
5. ran	10. the

Phonemic Awareness

Phoneme Segmentation Have children use the three boxes on the *Write-on/Wipe-off Boards.* Tell children that the boxes stand for sounds in words. Say the word *cat* and ask: **What is the first sound in *cat*?** (/k/) Have children place a disk in the first box along with you. Have them name the second sound in *cat* (/a/) and place a disk in the second box. Then have them identify the last sound in *cat* (/t/) and place a disk in the third box. Point to each box in sequence as children say the word. **How many sounds do you hear in *cat*? I hear three.** Repeat with the words *hat, tap, pat, lap, sat, can.*

PRETEACH

Phonics

Inflection -s Write the following words on the board: *hat, map, can, bag.* Have children read the words aloud. Say: **The letter *s* can be added to each word to make a new word.**

Write: *hats, maps, cans, bags.* Say: **The letter *s* stands for the /s/ sound in the words *hats* and *maps*. The letter *s* stands for the /z/ sound in *cans* and *bags*.** Then write the words *fan, cap, mat, yam,* and *cab.* Guide children to add *-s* and read the new word.

RETEACH

Phonics and Spelling

Short Vowel /a/a

Build Words Use *Word Builders* and *Word Builder Cards* to form words. Have children listen to your directions and change letters in each word to spell a spelling word. Form *am* and have children read the word. Ask:

- **Which spelling word can you make by changing *m* to *t*?** (*at*)
- **Which spelling word can you make by adding *c* before *a* and *t*?** (*cat*)

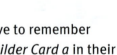

Follow a similar procedure with the following words: *cat* (*can*), *can* (*ran*), *ran* (*man*), *man* (*map*), *map* (*tap*). As the words are built, write them on the board. Then have children read the list of words.

Remind children that there are some other words they have to remember how to spell. Have children say *a.* Have them put *Word Builder Card a* in their *Word Builder,* picture the word *a* in their minds, and use the card to build the word. Write the word on the board. Follow the same procedure with *the.*

High-Frequency Words

now   let's

RETEACH
High-Frequency Words

 Duplicate and distribute *Copying Masters* 3–4 to each child. Explain that the sentences tell about the story "We Can Tap!" but some have missing words.

List the words *now* and *let's* on the board. Guide children to read aloud each story strip sentence and name the correct word on the board that makes sense in the sentence. Have children write the missing words in the blanks and read the completed sentences aloud. Help children cut apart the strips, read the completed sentences, and arrange them in story order.

RETEACH
Comprehension

  Make Predictions Review with children how to make predictions. Remind children to think about the story title, illustrations, and what they know. Have children look at page 6 in *Heading Out*. Ask: **What did you predict the story would be about from reading the title and looking at the picture?**

Ask children how they make predictions every day. Ask questions such as: **What do you predict the weather will be like today? What do you predict we will have for lunch today? What do you predict you will do on the playground at recess?** Guide children to explain the reason for each prediction.

RETEACH
Grammar/Writing

Labels Display *Photo Card ant*. Write the word *ant* on an index card and display the card under the *Photo Card*. Explain that this is a label. Tell children that labels name things and people in a picture or illustration, and they are short so that readers can quickly read and understand them. A label has one or two words, and words in labels should be spelled correctly. Point out that names in labels should begin with a capital letter.

Choose and display a variety of *Photo Cards*. Ask children to suggest labels for the *Photo Cards*. Spread the *Photo Cards* out. Write the labels on cards and help children place the labels near the cards named.

Fluency

Accuracy Remind children that it is important to read words correctly so a story makes sense. Explain that they should think about what word makes sense in the sentence and look for high-frequency words they know as they read.

Have partners read aloud "We Can Tap!" Offer feedback to help children read more accurately.

PHONEMIC AWARENESS
Phoneme Blending

PHONICS
Reteach Inflection -*s*

PHONICS AND SPELLING
Reteach Short Vowel /a/*a*

HIGH-FREQUENCY WORDS
Reteach help, now, let's

FLUENCY
Accuracy

COMPREHENSION
Reteach Make Predictions

GRAMMAR/WRITING
Reteach Labels

Materials Needed:

| Practice Book | Lesson 1 High-Frequency Word Cards | *Heading Out* Student Edition pp. 6–12 |

Phonemic Awareness

Phoneme Blending Tell children that they are going to play a game of "Fix It." Tell them you are going to say some words that are broken and they will put together sounds to figure out the words. Say: /r/ /a/ /g/. **What word does /r/ /a/ /g/ say? /r/ /a/ /g/ says** *rag*. **Now you try.** Continue with: /s/ /a/ /d/ (*sad*), /r/ /a/ /t/ (*rat*), /b/ /a/ /t/ (*bat*), /k/ /a/ /p/ (*cap*), /m/ /a/ /n/ (*man*).

RETEACH
Phonics

Inflection -*s* Remind children that -*s* can be added to a word to make a new word. Introduce the term *root word*. Write *tag* on the board. Say: **The word** *tag* **is a root word. I can add -*s* to** *tag* **to make the word** *tags*. Point out that the word *tags* ends with the sound /z/. Repeat the procedure with the word *tap*. Then list these words on the board: *dad, wag, cab, jam,* and *bat*. Read the words with children. Ask volunteers to come to the board, write the root word and add -*s,* then read the new word.

RETEACH
Phonics and Spelling

Practice Book p.5 **Short Vowel /a/*a***
Direct children's attention to page 5 of their *Practice Books*. Complete the page together.

Assess children's progress using the following sentences.

1. am — I **am** six years old.
2. at — Tim is **at** school.
3. cat — My **cat** is so soft.
4. can — **Can** we go to the park today?
5. ran — Tad **ran** around the track.
6. man — There is a **man** at the door.
7. map — I need a **map** to get to the beach.
8. tap — Let's **tap** and sing for the show.

High-Frequency

9. a — There is **a** dog in my yard.
10. the — I like **the** red bike the best.

Spelling Words

1. am	6. man
2. at	7. map
3. cat	8. tap
4. can	9. a
5. ran	10. the

RETEACH

High-Frequency Words

Copying Masters 1–2

Display *High-Frequency Word Cards* for this lesson's words—*help, now,* and *let's*—and the previously learned high-frequency words. Point to words at random and ask children to read them.

RETEACH

Comprehension

Make Predictions Show children the opening page of "We Can Tap!" in *Heading Out.* Remind children that they made predictions about this story. Remind children that they use clues from the story—the title, words, and illustrations—and what they know to make predictions.

Draw a three-column chart on the board as shown below. Guide children to recall what they predicted the story would be about. Record their predictions in the column labeled *During the Story.* Then reread "We Can Tap!" in *Heading Out.* Invite children to predict what the characters did before the story begins. Then have them predict what the characters might do next after the story ends. Record their predictions on the chart.

"We Can Tap!"		
Before the Story	**During the Story**	**After the Story**
	We predict the story is about animals dancing in a show.	

RETEACH

Grammar/Writing

Labels Review with children the characteristics of labels.

Labels

A label names someone or something.
A label is short. It has one or two words.
Words in labels should be spelled correctly.
Names in labels should begin with a capital letter.

Have children think of their favorite animal. Help them brainstorm ideas by talking about what animals they have for pets, or what animals they would like to see at a zoo. List ideas on chart paper. Have children choose an animal and draw a picture of it. Guide them to write labels for their pictures. Have children use the list you brainstormed together for spelling.

High-Frequency Words

help	let's
now	

Fluency

Accuracy Read aloud "We Can Tap!" in *Heading Out,* demonstrating fluent and accurate reading. Have children track the print as you read. Review any words children may have trouble with and read them together.

Have partners practice reading the story together to practice fluency. Offer feedback as you listen to them read.

30+ Minutes

DAY AT A GLANCE
Day 5

HIGH-FREQUENCY WORDS
Reteach *help, now, let's*

PHONEMIC AWARENESS
Onset and Rime

PHONICS AND SPELLING
Preteach Short Vowel /a/*a*

BUILD ROBUST VOCABULARY
Preteach *escape, fright, nearby*

GRAMMAR/WRITING
Preteach Word Order

Materials Needed:

Copying Masters 1–2

Sound/Spelling Card

Lesson 1 High-Frequency Word Cards

Sound/Spelling Card *Aa*

Word Builders and Word Builder Cards

Write-On/ Wipe-Off Boards

Practice Book p.6

Practice Book

High-Frequency Words

help	let's
now	

RETEACH

High-Frequency Words

Copying Masters 1–2 Display *High-Frequency Word Cards* for *help, now, let's,* and the other previously learned high-frequency words. Say the word *help,* ask a volunteer to point to *help,* and have children read the word aloud. Continue with the remaining high-frequency words. Repeat this activity several times to reinforce instant recognition.

Phonemic Awareness

Onset and Rime Have children name the words as you say them in parts. Model the first one. **Listen as I say this word in parts. /k/-at—The word I said was *cat*. Now you try some: /n/-ap, /r/-an, /s/-ack, /p/-an, /t/-ag, /h/-am, /b/-ag.**

PRETEACH

Phonics and Spelling

Sound/Spelling Card **d o t** **Short Vowel /a/*a***
Connecting Letter to Sound Remind children that they have learned the sounds for many letters of the alphabet. Have children say the alphabet in order as you point to the letters. Then say a letter name, such as "capital G," and have a volunteer identify the letter by pointing to it. Repeat for several letters. Next, point to various capital and lowercase letters and have children name them.

Have children say these words and listen for the beginning sound: *at, am, apple.* Elicit that each word begins with /a/. Then have children say these words and listen for the middle sound: *fan, cap, pad.* Elicit that each word has /a/ in the middle. Display *Sound/Spelling Card Aa.* Remind children that the letter *a* can stand for the sound /a/, the "short *a* sound." Have children say /a/ several times.

Give each child an *Aa Word Builder Card.* Say: **When I say a word that begins with /a/, hold up your card and say /a/. When I say a word that does not begin with /a/, hold your card behind your back.** Say these words: *add, an, on, ask, ant, in.* Remind children that many words have the short *a* sound in the middle. Say *map,* elongating the /a/ sound. Ask children to repeat the word and listen for /a/ in the middle. Say the following words, and have children hold up their *Aa Word Builder Card* if they hear /a/ in the middle: *fan, cap, sit, van, fox, pad.* Then say these words, and have children say *beginning* or *middle* to tell you where they hear the short *a* sound: *fan, had, at, add, cap, and, bad, pat.*

d o t **Word Blending** Demonstrate each step with *Word Builder Cards* and a *Word Builder* and have children repeat each step after you. Hold up *c* and say /k/. Hold up *a* and say /a/. Hold up *t* and say /t/.

- Place the letters *c, a, t* in the *Word Builder*.

- Point to *c*. Say /k/. Point to *a*. Say /a/. Prompt children to repeat after you.
- Slide *a* next to *c*. Run your hand under the letters as you blend the sounds, elongating them—/ka/.
- Point to *t* and say /t/.
- Slide *t* next to *ca*. Run your hand under *cat* as you blend the sounds, elongating them—/kat/.
- Read *cat* naturally.

Follow the same procedure with these words: *map, sad, mat*.

  Word Building Place the *Word Builder Cards h, a,* and *t* in the *Word Builder* and have children do the same. Slide your hand under the letters as you slowly blend the sounds to read the word—/hat/. Then read the word naturally—*hat*. Have children build and read new words. As they build each word, write it on the board. Say:

- **Change *t* to *d*. What word did you make?** (*had*)
- **Change *h* to *s*. What word did you make?** (*sad*)

Continue with the words *sat, bat,* and *bag*. Then have children read the words on the board. Direct children's attention to page 6 of their *Practice Books*. Complete the page together.

PRETEACH

Build Robust Vocabulary

Introduce Robust Vocabulary Read the student-friendly explanation for each word. Then discuss each word using the following examples.

Say: **The class hamster tried to escape from its cage. Which place would you want to escape from—a playground or a dark forest?**

Say: **A lion on the loose at the zoo would make me run in fright. Which would make you feel fright—a squirrel or a skunk? Tell why.**

Say: **The bookcase is nearby my desk in the classroom. What is nearby you in the classroom?**

PRETEACH

Grammar/Writing

Word Order Write these sentences on the board: *The man has a cat. The cat is fat.* Read the sentences with children. Explain that the sentences make sense because the words are in the right order.

Then write the words: *ran fast the cat.* Read the words and explain they do not make sense. Help children put the words in sentence order: *The cat ran fast.* Rewrite the sentence with correct capitalization and punctuation. Repeat with *has a cap the man* (*The man has a cap.*)

Spelling Words

1. hat	6. bag
2. had	7. at
3. sad	8. can
4. sat	9. help
5. bat	10. now

Have children practice writing spelling words on their *Write-on/Wipe-off Boards*.

VOCABULARY

Student-Friendly Explanations

escape To escape means to get away from someone or something.

fright If you feel fright, you are scared.

nearby If something is nearby, it is close to you.

DAY AT A GLANCE

Day 1

30+ Minutes

PHONEMIC AWARENESS
Phoneme Isolation

PHONICS AND SPELLING
Reteach Short Vowel /a/*a*

COMPREHENSION
Preteach Make Predictions

HIGH-FREQUENCY WORDS
Reteach *in, too, help*

FLUENCY
Accuracy

GRAMMAR/WRITING
Reteach Word Order

Materials Needed:

Photo Cards

Word Builders and Word Builder Cards

Write-On/Wipe-Off Boards

Heading Out Student Edition pp. 6–12 pp. 14–15

Practice Book p.7

Spelling Words

1. hat	6. bag
2. had	7. at
3. sad	8. can
4. sat	9. help
5. bat	10. now

 Have children practice writing spelling words on their *Write-on/Wipe-off Boards.*

LESSON 2

Phonemic Awareness

Phoneme Isolation   Display *Photo Cards add* and *bug.* Have children say the picture names after you and listen for the picture name with the /a/ sound. Say: ***Add, bug.* Which of these picture names has the /a/ sound? *Add* has the /a/ sound. Now you try.** Repeat with the *Photo Cards ant* and *box, hen* and *path,* and *sack* and *fish.*

RETEACH

Phonics and Spelling

Short Vowel /a/*a*
Word Building   Place the *Word Builder Cards h, a,* and *t* in the *Word Builder.* Ask children to say each letter name and the sound it stands for. Slide your hand under the letters as you blend the sounds—/hat/. Then read the word naturally—*hat.* Have children do the same. Ask:

- **Which letter should I change to make *hat* become *had*?** (Change *t* to *d*.)

- **Which letter should I change in *had* to make *sad*?** (Change *h* to *s*.)

Continue with the words *sat, bat,* and *bag.*

Read Words in Context   Write the following sentences on chart paper. Have children read each sentence silently. Then track the print as children read the sentences aloud. Finally, point to the underlined words at random and have children read them. *I had a bat in the bag. I can see the cat now. The cat sat on my hat. Sam is sad. Look at Pat tap. Help me, Dan!*

PRETEACH

Comprehension

Make Predictions   Remind children that good readers make predictions before and during reading. Sometimes these predictions don't happen. Have children turn to "We Can Tap!" in *Heading Out.* Ask children to read the title and look at the pictures on pages 6–7. Say: **Before we read "We Can Tap!" we made predictions about what the story would be about. We used the pictures and the title to predict that the story would be a story about animals that performed on stage. Our prediction was right.**

RETEACH

High-Frequency Words

pp.
14–15

Write the words *in, too,* and *help* on the board.

- Point to and read *in.* Repeat, having children say *in* with you.
- Say: **Dad is *in* the yard.**
- Repeat the word and then point to each letter as you spell it. Then have children say and spell *in* with you. Have children reread the word.

Repeat for the remaining words. Use the following sentences: *Meg will help Dad too. Matt can help Dad build a dog house.*

Have children turn to page 14 of *Heading Out* and have them read aloud the words at the top of the page. Talk about the illustrations. Then guide children in choosing and circling the word that names each picture. (3. *bag,* 4. *can*) Have children read aloud each word in the list on page 15. Ask volunteers to read the sentences aloud. Then have children choral-read the sentences. Guide them to read and trace the word that completes each sentence. (1. *in,* 2. *help,* 3. *too*)

RETEACH

Grammar/Writing

Photo Card   Practice Book p.7

Word Order   Remind children that the words that make up a sentence must be in a certain order to make sense. Write the words *ran* and *the* on index cards. Display the words with *Photo Card bug*: *ran the.* Guide children to rearrange the words and picture to make sense.

Write the sentence on the board without correct capitalization and punctuation: *the* [bug] *ran.* Ask children to read the sentence and correct the errors. Repeat with the following word cards and *Photo Cards: at the* [moon] *look. has a* [box] *the man.* Complete *Practice Book* page 7 together.

High-Frequency Words

in	help
too	

Fluency

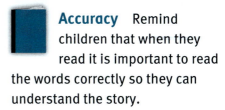
Accuracy   Remind children that when they read it is important to read the words correctly so they can understand the story.

Have children turn to "We Can Tap!" in *Heading Out.* Read aloud pages 6–7 and have children track the print. Point out that if you did not read the words correctly, the sentences would not make sense.

Have partners take turns reading each page aloud. Listen to partners read and provide feedback for improving their fluency.

PHONEMIC AWARENESS
Onset and Rime

PHONICS AND SPELLING
Reteach Short Vowel /a/a

HIGH-FREQUENCY WORDS
Reteach *in, too, no, help*

FLUENCY
Accuracy

READING
"Come In!"

BUILD ROBUST VOCABULARY
Preteach *cram, solution, strategy*

GRAMMAR/WRITING
Reteach Word Order

Materials Needed:

Word Builders and Word Builder Cards

Practice Book *p.8*

Lesson 2 High-Frequency Word Cards

Heading Out
Student Edition
pp. 6–12
pp. 16–23

High-Frequency Words

in	no
too	help

30+ Minutes

Phonemic Awareness

Onset and Rime   Tell children they are going to be detectives and say the word you are thinking about. Say: **I'm thinking of a word that names what a dog does with its tail. It is /w/-ag. What's my word? The word is** *wag.* **Now you try.** Continue with clues for the words: /b/ ag (*bag*), /l/ ap (*lap*), /k/ at (*cat*), /h/ am (*ham*), /h/ at (*hat*), /s/ ad (*sad*).

RETEACH

Phonics and Spelling

d o t   Short Vowel /a/a

Word Building   Use a *Word Builder* and *Word Builder Cards* and have children repeat each step after you. Build the word *map.* Blend the sounds to read the word—/map/. Then say the word naturally—*map.* Have children do the same. Lead children in building and reading new words. Say:

- **Change** *p* **to** *n.* **Read the word.** (*man*)
- **Change** *m* **to** *p.* **Read the word.** (*pan*)

m a p

m a n

p a n

Continue with the following words: *cat-can-fan, fat-pat-pad, at-sat-sand.*

Practice Book **p.8**

Read Words in Context   Ask children to turn to *Practice Book* page 8. Read each sentence aloud and have children echo-read. Then ask volunteers to read each sentence aloud. Ask: **What does Dan run for?** (his cap) **Is the cap in the van?** (no) **Is the cap on the mat?** (no) **Where does Dan find his cap?** (on his head) Call on volunteers to frame and read short *a* words. Then guide children to circle all words with short vowel *a.*

RETEACH

High-Frequency Words

Copying Masters **5–6**

Display the *High-Frequency Word Cards* for *in, too, no,* and *help.* Point to each card and read the word. Have children repeat. Then have children sit with a partner. Give each child a set of word cards. Have the partners mix the cards and place them face down to play a concentration game.

Reading

pp. 16–23

Build Background: "Come In!"

Read the title with children. Have children role play opening the door to invite a friend to come in. Then invite children to share different things they do with friends when they come over to visit.

Monitor Comprehension: "Come In!"

Have children turn to the first page of the story. Ask a volunteer to reread the title. Have children look at the picture on page 16. Have children predict whom the story will be about and what the characters might be planning to do. Then guide children through the story as they read.

pp. 16–17

Say: **The duck has come to the raccoon's house. Is he carrying something? Let's read to find out what the duck has.**

After reading the pages, ask: **What does the duck ask the raccoon?** (if he can come in) **What does the duck bring?** (apples) **What is the duck's name? Frame and read the word.** (*Dan*) NOTE DETAILS/APPLY PHONICS

Ask: **Why do you think Dan has gone to the raccoon's house with apples?** (Possible response: to have lunch) DRAW CONCLUSIONS

pp. 18–19

Say: **We know that Dan has brought apples to the raccoon's house. Let's read to find out who comes next.**

After reading the pages, ask: **Who asks to come in after Dan the duck? Frame and read the name.** (*Pam*) SEQUENCE/APPLY PHONICS

Ask: **What do you think the animals will do with the apples and bananas?** (Possible response: eat them) MAKE PREDICTIONS

pp. 20–21

Say: **Look at the pictures on these pages. We see another friend has arrived. Let's find out who it is and what he brings.**

After reading the pages, ask: **Who is the lizard? Frame and read his name.** (*Max*) CHARACTER/APPLY PHONICS

Ask: **Who all is at the raccoon's house now?** (Dan, Pam, and Max) SUMMARIZE

Ask: **What does Max bring?** (oranges) Ask: **What do you notice about the things Dan, Pam, and Max bring?** (They are all fruit.) NOTE DETAILS

Fluency

Accuracy Have children turn to "We Can Tap!" in *Heading Out.* Read the story aloud as children follow along, demonstrating accuracy. Then reread the story, but eliminate or mispronounce words. Ask which story was easier to understand.

Guide children to understand the importance of accuracy when reading and communicating. Then have children practice reading aloud pages of "We Can Tap!" with accuracy.

Say: **The animal friends are seated around a table. Let's read the ending of the story to see what the friends can do.**

After reading the pages, ask: **What can the friends do?** (They can help make some food to eat.) **NOTE DETAILS/DRAW CONCLUSIONS**

Ask: **Could this story really happen? Explain.** (Possible response: No, because animals do not act like people.) **REALITY/FANTASY**

Ask: **If you had been invited, what would you have brought?** (Possible response: pears, plums, or grapes) **EXPRESS PERSONAL OPINIONS**

Ask: **How do you think the friends feel? Why do you think that?** (Possible response: happy because they are smiling and helping) **CHARACTERS' EMOTIONS**

Ask: **If you invited three friends to come to your house, what would you do together?** (Possible response: play games and have a picnic) **PERSONAL RESPONSE**

Answers to *Think Critically* Questions

Help children read and answer the *Think Critically* questions on page 23. Answers are shown below.

1. ‹the lizard› **CHARACTER**
2. ‹bananas› **NOTE DETAILS**
3. ‹four friends seated at the table eating› **MAKE PREDICTIONS**

PRETEACH

Build Robust Vocabulary

Introduce Robust Vocabulary Read the student-friendly explanation for each word. Then discuss each word using the following examples.

Say: **If you cram too much into your backpack, it might be too heavy to carry. What will happen if you cram too many clothes into a suitcase?**

Say: **If I add 1 plus 1, the solution is 2. What would be a good solution if you forgot to pack your lunch?**

Say: **My strategy for the year is to teach you lots of new things. What plan or strategy do you use when you clean your room?**

RETEACH

Grammar/Writing

Word Order Ask children to dictate sentences that tell about favorite foods they like to eat. Explain you will write the words they say in different order.

> likes pizza Matt.
>
> eats peanut butter and jelly sandwiches Meg.
>
> likes tacos Janet.

Read aloud the first sentence as you track the print. Ask if the sentence make sense. Model how to write it correctly so it makes sense. Say: **The words don't make sense in the order they are in right now. I will change the order of the words so the sentence says:** *Matt likes pizza.* Point out the capital letter and the period at the end of the sentence. Follow this procedure with the remaining sentences, guiding children to put the words in an order that makes sense. Then track the print as you read each sentence. As you read, ask children if the order of the words makes sense.

Student-Friendly Explanations

cram When you cram many things into something, you fill it with too much.

solution If you have a solution to a problem, you know how to fix it. You have an answer.

strategy If you have a strategy for something, you have a plan.

DAY AT A GLANCE

Day 3

PHONEMIC AWARENESS
Phoneme Segmentation

PHONICS
Preteach Phonograms *-ap, -at*

PHONICS AND SPELLING
Reteach Short Vowel /a/*a*

HIGH-FREQUENCY WORDS
Reteach *in, too, help*

FLUENCY
Accuracy

COMPREHENSION
Reteach Make Predictions

GRAMMAR/WRITING
Reteach Sentences

Materials Needed:

Write-On/ Wipe-Off Boards with Phonemic Awareness Disks

Photo Cards

Word Builders and Word Builder Cards

Copying Masters 7–8

Lesson 2 Story Strips

Heading Out Student Edition pp. 16-22

Spelling Words

1. hat	6. bag
2. had	7. at
3. sad	8. can
4. sat	9. help
5. bat	10. now

Phonemic Awareness

Phoneme Segmentation   Have children use the three boxes on the *Write-on/Wipe-off Boards.* Tell children that the boxes stand for sounds in words. Have children repeat each step with their boards and disks. Show *Photo Card ant.* Say: *Ant.* **The first sound in *ant* is /a/.** Model placing a disk in the first box. Use this procedure for the second sound in *ant* (/n/), placing a disk in the second box, and the last sound in *ant* (/t/), placing a disk in the third box. Point to each box in sequence as children say the word. **How many sounds do you hear in *ant*? I hear three.** Repeat with *Photo Cards box, bug, hen, sack.*

PRETEACH

Phonics

Phonograms *-ap, -at*   Tell children that they are going to learn about word families. Write the words *lap* and *tap* on the board. Ask: **What letters are the same?** (*ap*) **What sounds are the same?** (/ap/) Explain: **These words belong to the same word family because they end with the same sound—/ap/.** Underline *ap* as children reread the words. Then begin a new list with *-at* words such as *at, sat,* and *mat.*

RETEACH

Phonics and Spelling

Short Vowel /a/*a*
Build Words   Use a *Word Builder* and *Word Builder Cards* to form words. Have children listen to your directions and change a letter in each word to spell a spelling word. Form *hat* and have children read the word. Ask: **Which spelling word can you make by changing the last letter?** (*had*)

Follow a similar procedure with the following words: *had* (*sad*), *sad* (*sat*), *sat* (*bat*), *bat* (*bag*), *as* (*at*), *Dan* (*can*).

Remind children that there are some other words they have to remember how to spell. Have children say *help.* Tell them to put *Word Builder Cards h, e, l, p* in their *Word Builders,* picture the word *help* in their minds, and build the word. Write the word on the board. Follow the same procedure with *now.*

High-Frequency Words

Copying Masters 7–8

Duplicate and distribute *Copying Masters* 7–8 to each child. Explain that the sentences tell the story "Come In!" but some have missing words.

List the words *in, too,* and *help* on the board. Have children read aloud each story strip sentence and name the correct word on the board that makes sense in the sentence. Have children write the missing words in the blanks and read the completed sentences aloud. Help children cut apart the strips, read the completed sentences, and arrange them in story order.

High-Frequency Words

in	help
too	

Comprehension

Making Predictions Review with children how to make predictions. Have children turn to "Come In!" in *Heading Out.* Say: **Think about the story title. What does the title "Come In!" tell you about this story? Think about illustrations and words. When you looked at the first few pictures in "Come In!" did you predict whether this story was about real or imaginary characters? Tell why.** Revisit the story pictures and have children recall if they were able to predict what would happen in this story as they read and tell what clues helped them to do this.

Grammar/Writing

Sentences Explain to children that they are going to learn about writing sentences. Write the following sentences on the board.

> Pam has a bag.
>
> Dad has a map.
>
> Max can rap.

Read the first sentence with children. Ask: **Who is this sentence about? What does it tell us about Pam?** Explain that good sentences give information and tell something about the person or thing. Point out the capital letter and period and explain that good sentences use capital letters and end marks correctly. Repeat the process with the remaining sentences.

Fluency

Accuracy Remind children that reading words correctly is important to understand a story.

Say: **If I'm reading and I come to a word I'm not sure about, I look at the letters and think about what word makes sense in the sentence. Once I figure out the word, I go back and read the sentence again more smoothly.**

Have partners read "Come In!" several times to practice reading with fluency. Provide feedback and encouragement as partners read.

DAY AT A GLANCE
Day 4

PHONEMIC AWARENESS
Onset and Rime

PHONICS
Reteach Phonograms *-ag, -and*

PHONICS AND SPELLING
Reteach Short Vowel /a/*a*

HIGH-FREQUENCY WORDS
Reteach *in, too, no, help*

FLUENCY
Accuracy

COMPREHENSION
Reteach Make Predictions

GRAMMAR/WRITING
Reteach Sentences

Materials Needed:

Practice Book

Lesson 2 High-Frequency Word Cards

Heading Out Student Edition pp. 6–12 pp. 16–22

Spelling Words

1. hat	6. bag
2. had	7. at
3. sad	8. can
4. sat	9. help
5. bat	10. now

Phonemic Awareness

Onset and Rime   Tell children that you are going to say some word parts and they should put them together to say the word. Say: **Listen as I do the first one: /t/-ap. What word did I say? I said the word** *tap.* **Now you try.** Continue with the words: /b/-at (*bat*), /t/-ag (*tag*), /p/-in (*pin*), /b/-us (*bus*).

RETEACH

Phonics

Phonograms *-ag, -and*   Write the words *rag* and *sag* on the board. Read the words with children. Ask how they are alike. (They end with the same two letters and sound—/ag/.) Explain that *rag* and *sag* are in the *-ag* word family. Repeat with *and* and *land.* Read the words and identify the word family. (*-and*) Work with children to write other words with *-ag* and *-and.* Read the list with children.

RETEACH

Phonics and Spelling

Short Vowel /a/*a*
Direct children's attention to page 9 of their *Practice Books.* Complete the page together.

Assess children's progress using the following sentences.

1.	hat	My dad wears a brown **hat**.
2.	had	We **had** chicken for dinner.
3.	sad	I was **sad** when we moved to a new home.
4.	sat	Mom and I **sat** at the table.
5.	bat	Hit the ball with my **bat**.
6.	bag	Put your lunch in this **bag**.

Review

7.	at	Look **at** the rainbow!
8.	can	We **can** ride our bikes.

High-Frequency

9.	help	I **help** my dad in the garden.
10.	now	Let's plant tulips **now**!

RETEACH

High-Frequency Words

Copying Masters 5–6

Display *High-Frequency Word Cards* for this lesson's words—*in, too, no,* and *help*—and the previously-learned high-frequency words. Point to words at random and ask children to read them.

RETEACH

Comprehension

Make Predictions Remind children that they made predictions before and during reading when they read "We Can Tap!" and "Come In!" in *Heading Out*. Remind children that they use two things to make predictions: clues from the story such as the title, words, and pictures from the story, and what they know from their own experiences. Have children form two teams: one for "Let's Tap" and one for "Come In!" Tell children you will make some predictions. Have the team that thinks the prediction is about their story tell why. For example: This story is an animal fantasy. (both stories) This story is about a group of friends who go visiting. ("Come In!") This story is about some friends who like to dance. ("We Can Tap!")

RETEACH

Grammar/Writing

Sentences Review with children characteristics of good sentences.

How to Write Good Sentences

Name who or what you are writing about.
Tell something about the person or thing.
Use capital letters and end marks correctly.

Have children look back at the sentences you wrote on Day 3. Point out the characteristics of good sentences. Have children think of a pet they want to write about. Write the list of ideas children dictate. Lead children in writing good sentences to tell about the pet. Ask for children's help in choosing the best words and using capitalization and punctuation. Read the sentences aloud and have children echo-read.

High-Frequency Words

in	no
too	help

Fluency

Accuracy Reread "Come In!" from *Heading Out*, modeling fluency and accuracy while children track the print. Then have each child select a page to practice reading aloud. Have everyone read the last page of the story in unison. Comment on children's ability to read accurately in order to make the story understandable for everyone.

DAY AT A GLANCE

Day 5

HIGH-FREQUENCY WORDS
Review *in, too, no*

PHONEMIC AWARENESS
Onset and Rime

PHONICS AND SPELLING
Preteach Short Vowel /i/*i*

BUILD ROBUST VOCABULARY
Preteach *especially, memorize, sensed*

GRAMMAR/WRITING
Preteach Naming Parts of Sentences

Materials Needed:

Lesson 2 High-Frequency Word Cards

Sound/Spelling Card *Ii*

Word Builders and Word Builder Cards

Write-On/ Wipe-Off Boards

Practice Book

High-Frequency Words

in	no
too	

High-Frequency Words

Copying Masters 5–6 Display *High-Frequency Word Cards* for *in, too, no,* and the other previously learned high-frequency words. Say the word *in,* ask a volunteer to point to *in,* and have children read the word aloud. Continue with the remaining high-frequency words. Repeat this activity several times to reinforce instant recognition.

Phonemic Awareness

Onset and Rime Have children name the words as you say them in parts. Model the first one. **Listen as I say this word in parts. /b/-ig—The word I said was *big*. Now you try some.** Continue with: /p/-in, /d/-ig, /s/-ip, /p/-ick, /t/-in, /n/-ap, /h/-ip, /w/-in, /s/-ad, /f/-in.

Phonics and Spelling

Sound/ Spelling Card **Short Vowel /i/*i***
Connecting Letter to Sound Say the words *in, ink,* and *inch* and have children repeat the words. Explain that all three words begin with the /i/ sound. Have children say /i/ several times. Display *Sound Spelling Card Ii,* say the letter name, and name the picture. Tell children that *i* can stand for the sound /i/, the sound they hear at the beginning of *igloo.* Tell children that this is the "short *i* sound." Point to the letter several times as children say /i/.

Have children use their *Word Builder Card* for *i.* Say: **When I say a word that begins with /i/, hold up your card and say /i/. An example of this would be *it*. When I say a word that does not begin with /i/, put your card behind your back.** Say these words: *ill, ink, igloo, ant, inch, apple.* Tell children that some words, like *pig,* have the sound /i/ in the middle. Follow the same procedure for the medial position with the following words: *fin, sit, can, big, dip,* and *sad.*

Word Blending Demonstrate each step with *Word Builder Cards* and a *Word Builder* and have children repeat each step after you. Hold up *w* and say /w/. Hold up *i* and say /i/. Hold up *n* and say /n/.

- Place the letters *w, i, n* in the *Word Builder.*

- Point to *w.* Say /w/. Point to *i.* Say /i/. Prompt children to repeat after you.

- Slide *i* next to *w.* Run your hand under the letters as you blend the sounds, elongating them—/wi/.

- Point to *n* and say /nn/.
- Slide *n* next to *wi*. Run your hand under *win* as you blend the sounds, elongating them—/wiiinn/.
- Read *win* naturally.

Follow the same procedure with these words: *wig, fin, sit.* Introduce words with double consonants and final blends: *mitt, kiss, list, wind.* Remind children that the double consonants stand for one sound. Point out the two consonants at the end of *list* and *wind* and guide children to blend the two consonant sounds.

  Word Building   Place the *Word Builder Cards i* and *n* in the *Word Builder* and have children do the same. Slide your hand under the letters as you read the word with children. Have children build and read new words. As they build each word, write it on the board. Say:

- **Add *p* to *in*. What word did you make?** (*pin*)
- **Change *n* to *g*. What word did you make?** (*pig*)

Continue with the words *big, dig,* and *did.* Then have children read the words on the board. Direct children's attention to page 10 of their *Practice Books.* Complete the page together.

Practice Book
p.10

Practice Book p.10

PRETEACH

Build Robust Vocabulary

Introduce Robust Vocabulary   Read the student-friendly explanation for each word. Then discuss each word using the following examples.

Say: **I feel especially nervous when I have to stand in front of a group. Would you feel especially nervous when buying a pet or taking a test?**

Say: **I had to memorize a new song for a show. What song or rhyme have you memorized? Can you tell us?**

Say: **I sensed that it would rain today, so I brought my umbrella. If you sensed that a new classmate was shy, what would you do?**

PRETEACH

Grammar/Writing

Naming Parts of Sentences   Write these sentences: *The pig digs in the sand. Jim likes cats. Sam has a map.* Read the sentences while tracking the print. Underline *The pig* in the first sentence. Explain that this is the naming part of the sentence because it tells who or what the sentence is about. Tell children that each sentence has a naming part. Repeat the procedure with the next two sentences.

Spelling Words

1.	in	6.	did
2.	pin	7.	had
3.	pig	8.	sat
4.	big	9.	no
5.	dig	10.	too

Have children practice writing spelling words on their *Write-on/Wipe-off Boards.*

VOCABULARY

Student-Friendly Explanations

especially   If something is especially important, it is very important.

memorize   If you memorize a poem, you learn it so you can say it without looking at the words.

sensed   If you sensed something, you had a feeling about it before you were even told about it.

LESSON 3

So Big!
by Steve Davis
illustrations by Vincent Nguyen

The truck is so big.

It can hold boxes.

Day 1

PHONEMIC AWARENESS
Phoneme Isolation

PHONICS AND SPELLING
Reteach Short Vowel /i/ *i*

COMPREHENSION
Preteach Classify/Categorize

HIGH-FREQUENCY WORDS
Preteach *so, hold*

FLUENCY
Punctuation

GRAMMAR/WRITING
Reteach Naming Parts of Sentences

Materials Needed:

Photo Cards

Word Builders and Word Builder Cards

Write-On/Wipe-Off Boards

Heading Out Student Edition pp. 16–22 pp. 24–25

Practice Book **p.11**
Practice Book

Spelling Words

1.	in	6.	did
2.	pin	7.	had
3.	pig	8.	sat
4.	big	9.	no
5.	dig	10.	too

Have children practice writing spelling words on their *Write-on/Wipe-off Boards.*

Phonemic Awareness

Phoneme Isolation   Display *Photo Cards fish* and *ant.* Have children say the picture names after you and listen for the /i/ sound. Say: ***Fish, bug.* Which picture name has the /i/ sound? *Fish* has the /i/ sound. Now you try.** Repeat with the *Photo Cards path* and *gift, sack* and *gift, fish* and *add.* Guide children to categorize the pictures into two groups with /i/ and /a/.

RETEACH

Phonics and Spelling

Short Vowel /i/ *i*

Word Building   Place the *Word Builder Cards i* and *n* in the *Word Builder.* Ask children to say each letter name and the sound it stands for. Slide your hand under the letters as you read the word *in.* Have children repeat the process. Continue building new words by asking children:

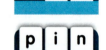

- **Which letter should I change to make *in* become *pin*?** (Add *p* before *i.*)

- **Which letter should I change to make the word *pig*?** (Change *n* to *g.*)

Continue with the words *big, dig,* and *did.*

Read Words in Context   Write the following sentences on chart paper. Have children read each sentence silently. Then track the print as children read the sentences aloud. Finally, point to the underlined words at random and have children read them. *Jim had jam in a sack. The pig can dig. No, I don't like that pin. I did see the cat too. The big man sat in the van.*

PRETEACH

Comprehension

Classify/Categorize   Say: **When you categorize things, you sort them and label them. Listen as I name some objects. Think about which objects belong in the same category: books, desk, chicken, crayon, cat, dog. Books, a desk, and a crayon belong together because they are all things you can find in class. A chicken, a cat, and a dog belong together in another category—things that are animals.** Guide children to sort the following items into two groups and to name the categories—*Things to Eat* and *Things to Wear:* shirt, pizza, bread, jeans, carrots.

High-Frequency Words

so	hold

High-Frequency Words

pp. 24–25

Write the words *so* and *hold* on the board.

- Point to and read *so*. Repeat, having children say *so* with you.
- Say: **The music is *so* loud!**
- Repeat the word and then point to each letter as you spell it. Then have children say and spell *so* with you. Have children reread the word.

Repeat for *hold*. Use the following sentence: *Please* hold *my hand*.

Have children turn to page 24 of *Heading Out* and have them read aloud the words at the top of the page. Talk about the illustrations. Then guide children in choosing and circling the word that names each picture. (3. *mitt*, 4. *big*)

Have children read aloud each word in the list on page 25. Ask volunteers to read the sentences aloud. Then have children choral-read the sentences. Guide them to read and trace the word that completes each sentence. (1. *so*, 2. *hold*)

Grammar/Writing

Practice Book p.11

Naming Parts of Sentences   Review that the naming part of a sentence tells who or what the sentence is about. Write the following sentences on the board.

> Dan has apples.
>
> Pam has bananas.
>
> Max has oranges.

Have children echo-read the sentences and identify the naming part. Then write: ___*is six*. ___*likes cats*. ___*can tap*. ___*has a cap*. Invite children to find a sentence about them and write the child's name. Read the sentences together and have children say the naming part. Complete *Practice Book* page 11 together.

Fluency

Punctuation Explain that good readers pay attention to end marks and other marks to help them read and understand sentences. Have children turn to "Come In!" in *Heading Out*.

Review that a period shows where a sentence ends, an exclamation point shows that a sentence should be read with excitement, and a comma means to pause before reading the next word.

Model reading the story with appropriate intonation and expression and have children echo-read each sentence.

DAY AT A GLANCE

Day 2

PHONEMIC AWARENESS
Phoneme Blending

PHONICS AND SPELLING
Reteach Short Vowel /i/*i*

HIGH-FREQUENCY WORDS
Reteach *so, hold, get, home, soon*

FLUENCY
Punctuation

READING
"So Big!"

BUILD ROBUST VOCABULARY
Preteach *capacity, haul, proud*

GRAMMAR/WRITING
Reteach Naming Parts of Sentences

Materials Needed:

Word Builders and Word Builder Cards

Practice Book p.12

Copying Masters 9–10
Lesson 3 High-Frequency Word Cards

Heading Out Student Edition pp. 6–12 pp. 26–33

Photo Cards

High-Frequency Words

so	home
hold	soon
get	

Phonemic Awareness

Phoneme Blending Tell children they are going to play a guessing game. Say: **Listen as I do the first one. I'm thinking of a word that means "very large." It is /b/-/i/-/g/. What's my word? The word is** *big.* **Now you try.** Continue with clues for the following words: /l/-/i/-/p/-/s/ (*lips*), /p/-/i/-/g/ (*pig*), /w/-/i/-/n/ (*win*), /b/-/i/-/b/ (*bib*), /f/-/i/-/n/ (*fin*), /w/-/i/-/g/ (*wig*), /p/-/i/-/n/ (*pin*).

RETEACH

Phonics and Spelling

Short Vowel /i/*i*
Word Building Use a *Word Builder* and *Word Builder Cards* and have children repeat each step after you. Build the word *in.* Run your hand under the letters as you read the word with children. Lead children in building and reading new words by saying.

- **Add** *p* **before** *in.* **Read the word.** (*pin*)
- **Change** *i* **to** *a.* **Read the word.** (*pan*)
- **Change** *n* **to** *st.* **Read the word.** (*past*)

Continue with the following words: *pat, sat, sit, fit, fist.*

Read Words in Context Ask children to turn to *Practice Book* page 12. Read each sentence aloud and have children echo-read. Then ask volunteers to read each sentence aloud. Ask: **Who is in a race?** (Pig and Kid) **What does Pig do?** (He wins.) **What does the winner get?** (a pin) Call on volunteers to frame and read words with short *i* and short *a* sounds. Then guide children to circle words with /i/ and underline words with /a/.

RETEACH

High-Frequency Words

Display the *High-Frequency Word Cards* for *so, hold, get, home,* and *soon.* Point to each card and read the word. Have children repeat. Have children sit with a partner and give each child a set of word cards. Children take turns reading a word for the partner to find and read. Have children match the two word cards to check.

Reading

pp. 26–33

Build Background: "So Big!"

Read the title with children. Have children suggest things they think are very big. Tell them that they will read a story about things that are so big, that they can hold other things inside.

Monitor Comprehension: "So Big!"

Have children turn to the first page of the selection. Ask a volunteer to reread the title. Guide children to look at the picture on page 26. Ask what thing they see that is so big. Encourage children to predict what the selection will be about and big things they might read about. Then guide children through the selection as they read.

pp. 26–27

Say: **This truck looks so big! Let's read to find out what this truck can hold.**

After reading the pages, ask: **What word tells the size of this truck? Frame and read the word.** (*big*) **What can the big truck hold?** (boxes) **APPLY PHONICS/NOTE DETAILS**

Ask: **What do you think is inside all these boxes on the truck?** (Possible response: lots of toys) **Where do you think the boxes are going?** (Possible response: to a store) **MAKE INFERENCES**

pp. 28–29

Say: **We know that this selection is about things that are big. Let's read to find out why a ship has to be big too.**

After reading the pages, ask: **What is so big on these pages? Frame and read the word.** (*ship*) **What can the ship hold?** (cars) **APPLY PHONICS/NOTE DETAILS**

Ask: **How do you think the cars get on the ship?** (Possible response: a big door opens and they drive the cars up a ramp.) **MAKE INFERENCES**

pp. 30–31

Say: **Look at the pictures on these pages. We see something else that is big. Let's find out what it is.**

After reading the pages, ask: **What is so big on these pages?** (a bus) **NOTE DETAILS**

Ask: **Where have you seen a bus like this before?** (Possible response: at school) **PERSONAL RESPONSE**

Ask: **What do you think the bus can hold?** (Possible response: kids) **MAKE PREDICTIONS**

Fluency

Punctuation Have children turn to "We Can Tap!" in *Heading Out*. Read the story aloud. As you read, draw attention to punctuation.

Say: **End marks show where a sentence ends. An exclamation point means read with excitement. A comma means pause a little. A question mark shows we are asking a question.**

Read the story again and have children echo-read. Have them copy your intonation and expression.

p. 32 Say: **Let's read the ending of the story to find out what a big bus can hold.**

After reading the pages, ask: **What can the big bus hold? Frame and read the word.** (*kids*) **NOTE DETAILS/APPLY PHONICS**

Ask: **Why do the truck, ship, and bus all need to be so big?** (They need to be big so that they can hold big things or lots of things.)
 CLASSIFY/CATEGORIZE

Ask: **When lots of things need to get from one place to another, what are some other big things that are used?** (Possible response: trains and planes) **DRAW CONCLUSIONS**

Ask: **Would you like the job of driving a big truck or school bus or working on a ship? Why or why not?** (Possible response: I think it would be fun to drive a big truck. It would be great sailing on a big ship in the middle of the ocean.) **PERSONAL RESPONSE**

p. 33 **Answers to *Think Critically* Questions**
Help children read and answer the *Think Critically* questions on page 33. Answers are shown below.

 1. ‹the truck› **NOTE DETAILS**
2. ‹truck, ship, bus› **SUMMARIZE**
3. ‹bulldozer› **MAKE INFERENCES**

PRETEACH
Build Robust Vocabulary

Introduce Robust Vocabulary   Read the student-friendly explanation for each word. Then discuss each word using the following examples.

Say: **A refrigerator has the capacity to hold a lot of food. What has the capacity to hold a lot of books in our classroom?**

Say: **A ship or truck can haul a lot of things. What do you use to haul a bunch of your toys from one place to another?**

Say: **I feel proud when I do something good. Name something you have done that makes you feel proud.**

RETEACH
Grammar/Writing

Photo Card

Naming Parts of Sentences   Write the following sentence frames on the board.

> The _____ is good.
> The _____ is so little.
> The _____ is big.
> The _____ ran fast.

Display *Photo Cards ant, bug, cake, hen, house, pie, octopus,* and *squirrel.* Read the first incomplete sentence aloud, saying "blank" at the beginning. Explain that the naming part is missing. Ask children to suggest a *Photo Card* to use as the naming part of the sentence. For example: *The cake is good.* Then have the child read the completed sentence. Ask for another suggestion. Continue in the same manner with the remaining sentences.

VOCABULARY
Student-Friendly Explanations

capacity   The capacity of something is the amount of space it has to hold things.

haul   If you haul something, you use a lot of effort to move it from one place to another.

proud   If you are proud, you feel very good about something you did or who you are.

DAY AT A GLANCE
Day 3

PHONEMIC AWARENESS
Phoneme Segmentation

PHONICS
Preteach Contraction *'s*

PHONICS AND SPELLING
Reteach Short Vowel /i/*i*

HIGH-FREQUENCY WORDS
Reteach *so, hold*

FLUENCY
Punctuation

COMPREHENSION
Reteach Classify/Categorize

GRAMMAR/WRITING
Reteach Sentences About Me

Materials Needed:

Write-On/
Wipe-Off
Boards with
Phonemic
Awareness
Disks

Photo
Cards

Word Builders
and Word
Builder Cards

Lesson 3
Story Strips

Heading Out
Student Edition
pp. 26–32

Spelling Words

1. in	6. did
2. pin	7. had
3. pig	8. sat
4. big	9. no
5. dig	10. too

Phonemic Awareness

Phoneme Segmentation   Have children use the three boxes on the *Write-on/Wipe-off Boards.* Tell children that the boxes stand for sounds in words. Have children repeat each step with their boards and disks. Say: *Pin.* **The first sound in *pin* is /p/.** Model placing a disk in the first box. Use this procedure for the second sound in *pin* (/i/), placing a disk in the second box, and the last sound in *pin* (/n/), placing a disk in the third box. Point to each box in sequence as children say the word *pin.* **How many sounds do you hear in *pin*? I hear three.** Repeat with *map, dog, sock, bag, win.*

PRETEACH
Phonics

Contraction *'s*   Display *Photo Card gift.* Write the following sentences on the board: *What is it? It's a gift. It is my gift!* Track the print as you read the first two sentences. Point to *it's* and say: **It's is a shorter way to say *it is.* We call this kind of word a contraction.** Point to *it is* in the last sentence. Say: **To make *it's,* the words *it* and *is* are put together. The *i* in *is* is left out and a mark called an apostrophe takes its place.** Rewrite *it is* as *it's* in the last sentence. Repeat with: *Here's a pig. What's in the sack? She's little.* Have children circle the contraction. Talk about the two words that make each contraction. *(here is, what is, she is)*

RETEACH
Phonics and Spelling

 Short Vowel /i/*i*

Build Words   Use Word Builders and Word Builder Cards to form words. Have children listen to your directions and change a letter in each word. Form *in* and have children read the word. Ask: **Which spelling word can you make by adding *p*?** *(pin)*

Follow a similar procedure with the following words: *pin* (*pig*), *pig* (*big*), *big* (*dig*), *dig* (*did*), *hat* (*had*), *had* (*sad*).

Remind children that there are some other words they have to remember how to spell. Have children say *no.* Tell them to put *Word Builder Cards n, o* in their *Word Builders,* picture the word *no* in their minds, and build the word. Write the word on the board. Follow the same procedure with *too.*

RETEACH

High-Frequency Words

Copying Masters 11–12

Duplicate and distribute *Copying Masters* 11–12 to each child. Explain that the sentences tell about "So Big!" but some have missing words.

List the words *so* and *hold* on the board. Have children read aloud each story strip sentence and name the correct word on the board that makes sense in the sentence. Have children write the missing words in the blanks and read the completed sentences aloud. Help children cut apart the strips, read the completed sentences, and arrange them in story order.

RETEACH

Comprehension

Photo Card

Focus Skill

Classify/Categorize Remind children that when they group things that are alike, they categorize these things. Display *Photo Cards* *house, library, school, berries, cake,* and *fruit.* Guide children to group the pictures in two categories and name the categories. (places we go, foods we eat) Revisit "So Big!" in *Heading Out.* Remind children that the story tells about different things that are so big. As children do a picture walk, pause to have them look for the things that are so big and respond by saying: *The _____ is so big.*

RETEACH

Grammar/Writing

Sentences About Me Display the following sentences about a boy named Josh. Read the sentences as children follow along.

> My name is Josh.
> I live on Chestnut Street.
> I like to play with my friends.
> We ride bikes and play games.
> I am on a baseball team.
> We are the Tigers.

Explain that these are sentences a boy wrote about himself. Tell children that when they write sentences about themselves, they should use words such as *I, me, my,* and *we.* The sentences should sound like they are talking to someone, and each sentence shoud begin with a capital letter and end with a period. Discuss with children how the sentences are good examples of these points. Invite volunteers to share what they learned about Josh.

High-Frequency Words

so	hold

Fluency

Punctuation Review how readers use capitalization and punctuation to understand what they read. This helps them read sentences aloud as if they were talking.

Reread "So Big!" in *Heading Out* with exaggerated expression while children follow along. Pause to model how you pay attention to capital letters, periods, question marks, and exclamation points to change the sound of your voice. Have children echo-read, imitating your intonation.

DAY AT A GLANCE

Day 4

PHONEMIC AWARENESS
Phoneme Blending

PHONICS
Reteach Contraction *'s*

PHONICS AND SPELLING
Reteach Short Vowel /i/*i*

HIGH-FREQUENCY WORDS
Reteach *so, hold, get, home, soon*

FLUENCY
Punctuation

COMPREHENSION
Reteach Classify/Categorize

GRAMMAR/WRITING
Reteach Sentences About Me

Materials Needed:

Practice
Book

Lesson 3
High-Frequency
Word Cards

Heading Out
Student Edition
pp. 26–32
pp. 16–22

Spelling Words

1. in	6. did
2. pin	7. had
3. pig	8. sat
4. big	9. no
5. dig	10. too

30+ Minutes

Phonemic Awareness

Phoneme Blending   Tell children that together you are going to play a game called "Fix It." Explain that you will say some words that are broken. They will listen to put the sounds together and say the word. Say: **Listen as I do the first one. /t/-/i/-/n/. What word does /t/-/i/-/n/ say? The word is** *tin.* **Say the word. Now you try.** Continue with the following words: /p/-/i/-/k/ (*pick*), /w/-/i/-/g/ (*wig*), /s/-/a/-/k/ (*sack*), /s/-/t/-/i/-/k/ (*stick*), /h/-/i/-/d/ (*hid*).

RETEACH

Phonics

Contraction *'s*   Remind children that two words can be put together to make a shorter word. This is called a *contraction.* Write *it is* and *it's.* Say: **The contraction *it's* comes from the words *it is.* The *i* in *is* was left out and an apostrophe takes its place. The contraction *it's* is a shorter way to say *it is.*** Guide children to form other contractions, such as *he is* (*he's*)*, there is* (*there's*)*, that is* (*that's*), and *Pat is* (*Pat's*)*.*

RETEACH

Phonics and Spelling

 Short Vowel /i/*i*
Direct children's attention to page 13 of their *Practice Books.* Complete the page together.

Assess children's progress using the following dictation sentences.

1. in   We sat **in** the park.
2. pin   I have a **pin** on my hat.
3. pig   The **pig** is very hungry.
4. big   Dinosaurs were very **big**.
5. dig   The squirrels **dig** for nuts that they buried.
6. did   I **did** my homework.

Review

7. had   I **had** grilled cheese for lunch.
8. sat   I **sat** by Mom at the game.

High-Frequency

9. no   **No**, I can't find my shoe.
10. too   Green is my favorite color, **too**!

RETEACH

High-Frequency Words

Copying Masters 9–10 Display *High-Frequency Word Cards* for this lesson's words—*so, hold, get, home,* and *soon*—and the previously learned high-frequency words. Point to words at random and ask children to read them.

RETEACH

Comprehension

Classify/Categorize Ask children the meaning of the word *categorize*. (to group together similar people, places, or things) Remind children of "Come In!" and "So Big!" in *Heading Out.* Have them look back at these stories to find things that are alike in some way and list them in a group. Start with "Come In!" Do a picture walk with children and point out things they see that are alike in some way. List the words on the board. Then repeat the procedure for "So Big!"

Animals	Fruits	Things that are Big
raccoon	apple	truck
duck	bananas	ship
owl	oranges	bus
lizard		

RETEACH

Grammar/Writing

Sentences About Me Review with children the characteristics of well-written sentences about me.

Sentences About Me

The sentences tell about me.
The sentences have words such as *I, me, my,* and *we.*
The sentences sound like I am talking to someone.
Each sentence begins with a capital letter and ends with a period.

Have children look back at Josh's sentences. Point out the characteristics of sentences about me. Have children think what they would tell about themselves. List ideas as children dictate. Lead children in writing sentences that tell about themselves. Write the sentences on chart paper as children dictate. Ask for children's help in choosing words like *I, me, my,* and *we* and using capitalization and end punctuation. Read the sentences with children.

High-Frequency Words

so	home
hold	soon
get	

Fluency

Punctuation Have children turn to "So Big!" in *Heading Out* and read the selection several times. Direct them to pay attention to capital letters that show the beginning of a new sentence, to pause when they see commas and periods, to read with excitement when they see an exclamation point, and to raise their voice when they see a question mark.

Provide encouragement and feedback for improving their fluency as they read.

DAY AT A GLANCE
Day 5

HIGH-FREQUENCY WORDS
so, hold, get, home, soon

PHONEMIC AWARENESS
Onset and Rime

PHONICS AND SPELLING
Preteach Digraph /k/*ck*

BUILD ROBUST VOCABULARY
Preteach *ambled, politely, pouted*

GRAMMAR/WRITING
Preteach Telling Parts of Sentences

Materials Needed:

Lesson 3
High-Frequency
Word Cards

Photo
Cards

Sound/
Spelling
Cards *Cc, Kk*

Word Builders
and Word
Builder Cards

Write-On/
Wipe-Off
Boards

Practice
Book

High-Frequency Words

so	home
hold	soon
get	

High-Frequency Words

Copying Masters 9–10 — Display *High-Frequency Word Cards* for *so, hold, get, home, soon,* and the other previously learned high-frequency words. Say the word *so,* ask a volunteer to point to *so,* and have children read the word aloud. Continue with the remaining high-frequency words. Repeat this activity several times to reinforce instant recognition.

Phonemic Awareness

Photo Card — **Onset and Rime** Display *Photo Cards* bug, fish, hen, king, lunch, *path,* and *sack.* Tell children that you are going to say some picture names, but you are going to say them in parts. Have children listen to see if they can figure out the picture name. Model one for children. Say: **Listen as I say this word in parts. /f/-ish—The word I said was *fish*. Now you try some: /s/-ack, /k/-ing, /h/-en, /b/-ug, /p/-ath, /l/-unch.**

PRETEACH

Phonics and Spelling

Sound/Spelling Card **Digraph /k/*ck***
Connecting Letter to Sound Say the words *sack, kick,* and *sock* and have children repeat the words. Explain that all three words end with the /k/ sound. Have children say /k/ several times. Display *Sound/Spelling Cards* Cc and Kk, and say the letter names. Tell children that the letters *c* and *k* together stand for one sound—/k/, the sound at the end of *pack.* Point out that the letters *c, k,* and *ck* together stand for the same sound. Have children say /k/ several times as you touch __*ck* on one of the cards.

Have children use *Word Builder Cards* c and k. Ask them to place the cards together to form *ck.* Say: **When I say a word that ends with /k/, hold up your cards and say /k/. When I say a word that does not end with /k/, hold your cards behind your back.** Say these words: *sick, duck, ten, back, pig, lick, tack.*

Word Blending Demonstrate each step with *Word Builder Cards* and a *Word Builder.* Have children repeat each step after you, using their *Word Builders.* Hold up s and say /s/. Hold up a and say /a/. Hold up c and k together and say /k/.

• Place the letters *s, a, c, k* in the *Word Builder.*

- Point to *s*. Say /s/. Point to *a* and say /a/. Prompt children to repeat after you.

- Slide *a* next to *s*. Run your hand under the letters as you blend the sounds, elongating them—/sa/.

- Point to *ck* and say /k/.

- Slide *ck* next to *sa*. Run your hand under *sack* as you elongate and blend the sounds—/sak/. Read *sack* naturally.

Follow the same procedure with these words: *back*, *sick*, *rack*.

Word Building Place the *Word Builder Cards* *p, i, c,* and *k* in the *Word Builder* and have children do the same. Slide your hand under the letters as you slowly read the word—*pick*. Have children build and read new words. As they build each word, write it on the board. Say:

- **Change *i* to *a*. What word did you make?** (*pack*)

Continue with the words *tack, back, sack,* and *sick*. Then have children read the words on the board. Complete *Practice Book* page 14 together.

Build Robust Vocabulary

Introduce Robust Vocabulary Read the student-friendly explanation for each word. Then discuss each word using the following examples.

Say: **Two turtles ambled down the lake shore. If you ambled, would you get somewhere quickly? Explain.**

Say: **When I speak politely, I use words like *please* and *thank you*. If you acted politely, would you frown or smile?**

Say: **If you were told to go to bed when you did not want to, you may have pouted to show you were not happy about it. Would you pout if you got a new toy? Explain.**

Grammar/Writing

Telling Parts of Sentences Write on the board: *The man sat on his hat. Dad packs the bag.* Read the sentences aloud as you track the print. Ask: **Who sat on his hat?** (the man) Remind children that the man is in the naming part of the sentence. Ask: **What did the man do?** (sat on his hat) Explain that *sat on his hat* is the telling part of the sentence—the part that tells what someone or something does. Guide children to identify the telling part of the second sentence. (*packs the bag*)

Spelling Words

1. pick	6. sick
2. pack	7. big
3. tack	8. in
4. back	9. hold
5. sack	10. so

Have children practice writing spelling words on their *Write-on/Wipe-off Boards*.

VOCABULARY

Student-Friendly Explanations

ambled If you ambled, you walked in a slow and relaxed manner.

politely If you act politely, you show that you have good manners.

pouted If you pouted, you showed you were not happy by making a face.

30+ Minutes

LESSON 4

Is Jack Late?

PHONEMIC AWARENESS
Phoneme Isolation

PHONICS AND SPELLING
Reteach Digraph /k/*ck*

COMPREHENSION
Preteach Beginning, Middle, Ending

HIGH-FREQUENCY WORDS
Preteach *late, yes, no*

FLUENCY
Punctuation

GRAMMAR/WRITING
Reteach Telling Parts of Sentences

Materials Needed:

Word Builders and Word Builder Cards

Write-On/Wipe-Off Boards

Heading Out Student Edition pp. 16–22, pp. 26–32, pp. 34–35

Photo Card
Photo Cards

Practice Book p.15
Practice Book

Spelling Words

1. pick	6. sick
2. pack	7. big
3. tack	8. in
4. back	9. hold
5. sack	10. so

Have children practice writing spelling words on their *Write-on/Wipe-off Boards.*

Phonemic Awareness

Phoneme Isolation   Say *luck* aloud, and have children repeat it. Tell children to listen to the /k/ sound at the end of *luck*. Then say the words *rock* and *moon*. Have children repeat both words. Ask: **Which word has the same /k/ sound you hear in *luck*? *Rock* does. Now you try some.** Continue with the words *clock, comb, lick; kick, fit, back; pack, duck, cave.*

RETEACH

Phonics and Spelling

Digraph /k/*ck*
Word Building   Place the *Word Builder Cards p, i, c, k* in the *Word Builder*. Ask children to say each letter name and the sound it stands for. Remind children that the letters *c* and *k* together stand for the /k/ sound. Slide your hand under the letters and read *pick* with children.

Ask children which letter you should change to make *pick* become *pack*. (Change *i* to *a*.) Have them replace the letter in their *Word Builders* and read the new word. Continue by asking them:

- **Which letter should I change to make *pack* become *tack*?** (Change *p* to *t*.)
- **Which letter should I change to make *tack* become *back*?** (Change *t* to *b*.)

Continue with the words *sack* and *sick*.

p i c k

p a c k

t a c k

Read Words in Context   Write the following sentences on chart paper. Have children read each sentence silently. Then track the print as children read the sentences aloud. Finally, point to the underlined words at random and have children read them. *Do not <u>pick</u> up the <u>sick</u> pig. Sam will come <u>back</u> home. Dad can <u>pack</u> jam in the <u>sack</u>. Dan will <u>hold</u> the <u>big</u> <u>tack</u>. My bag is <u>so</u> big!*

PRETEACH

Comprehension

Beginning, Middle, Ending   Guide children to recognize the distinguishing features of a story and understand simple story structure. Explain that a story has three parts: the beginning, the middle, and the ending. Use the story "Come In!" from *Heading Out* to illustrate.

Say: **"Come In!" begins with Dan the duck arriving at the raccoon's house. He brings apples. That is the beginning of the story. The next part of the story, when each animal arrives at the raccoon's house with food, is the middle. The last part of the story, when the animals sit down to eat, is the ending.**

Have children name the animals that arrive in the middle of the story. (Pam and Max)

PRETEACH
High-Frequency Words

pp.
34–35

Write the words *late, yes,* and *no* on the board.

- Point to and read *late*. Repeat, having children say *late* with you.
- Say: **Don't be *late* for school.**
- Repeat the word and then point to each letter as you spell it. Have children say and spell *late* with you. Have children reread the word.

Repeat for the remaining words. Use the following sentences: No, *I am not ready to go yet.* Yes, *I want a sandwich for lunch.*

Have children turn to page 34 of *Heading Out* and have them read aloud the words at the top of the page. Talk about the illustrations. Then guide children in choosing and circling the word that names each picture. (4. *sick,* 5. *pack,* 6. *tack*) Have children read aloud each word in the list on page 35. Ask volunteers to read the sentences aloud. Then have children choral-read the sentences. Guide them to choose and trace the word that completes each sentence. (1. *late,* 2. *No,* 3. *Yes*)

RETEACH
Grammar/Writing

Practice
Book
p.15

Telling Parts of Sentences Write the following poem on chart paper. Track the print as you read the sentences aloud.

> One little friend rode a bike.
> Two little friends went on a hike.
> Three little friends bake a cake.
> Four little friends swim in the lake.

Remind children that sentences have a telling part that tells what something or someone does. Read aloud the first sentence again and have children tell what one little child does. Frame the words with your hands. Guide a volunteer to underline the words in the sentence that identify the telling part. Repeat with the remaining sentences. Complete *Practice Book* page 15 together.

High-Frequency Words

late	**no**
yes	

Fluency

Punctuation Have children turn to "So Big!" in *Heading Out*. Model how readers use punctuation to comprehend. Tell children to track the print as you read aloud with exaggerated expression.

Explain how you used periods, the question mark, and the exclamation point to know how to read each sentence. Have children echo-read each line after you.

LESSON 4

DAY AT A GLANCE

Day 2

PHONEMIC AWARENESS
Phoneme Blending

PHONICS AND SPELLING
Reteach Digraph /k/*ck*

HIGH-FREQUENCY WORDS
Reteach *late, no, yes, oh*

FLUENCY
Punctuation

READING
"Is Jack Late?"

BUILD ROBUST VOCABULARY
Preteach *considerate, routine, unexpected*

GRAMMAR/WRITING
Reteach Telling Parts of Sentences

Materials Needed:

Word Builders and Word Builder Cards

Practice Book

Lesson 4 High-Frequency Word Cards

Heading Out Student Edition pp. 16–22, pp. 36–43

Photo Cards

High-Frequency Words	
late	yes
no	oh

Phonemic Awareness

Phoneme Blending   Tell children that they will need to be detectives and find out the word you are thinking about. Say: **I'm thinking of something you put on your foot before your shoe. It is a /s/ /o/ /k/. What's my word? My word is** *sock.* **Now you try some.** Continue with /l/ /o/ /k/ (*lock*), /k/ /i/ /k/ (*kick*), /s/ /a/ /k/ (*sack*), /d/ /u/ /k/ (*duck*), /n/ /e/ /k/ (*neck*).

RETEACH

Phonics and Spelling

 Digraph /k/ *ck*

Word Building   Use *Word Builders* and *Word Builder Cards* and have children repeat each step. Build the word *pack* and read it aloud with children. Remind them that the letters *ck* together stand for one sound. Lead children in building and reading new words by saying:

- **Change *ck* to *st*. Read the word.** (*past*)
- **Change *p* to *f*. Read the word.** (*fast*)

Continue with the following words: *sack, sick, silk, milk; pick, lick, last, mast.*

Practice Book p.16   **Read Words in Context**   Ask children to turn to *Practice Book* page 16. Read each sentence aloud and have children echo-read. Then ask volunteers to read each sentence aloud. Ask: **What will Jack pack?** (a big snack and milk) **Where will he pack it?** (in a sack) **Who does Jack go see?** (Rick) **What does Rick do when he sees Jack?** (picks a snack) After reading, ask them to circle all the digraph *ck* words.

RETEACH

High-Frequency Words

Copying Masters 13–14   Write the words *late, no, yes,* and *oh* on the board. Point to each word and ask a volunteer to read it. Give each child a set of *High-Frequency Word Cards,* and have children spread the cards out in front of them. Randomly call out each word, and have children hold up the matching card. Assess how well children are able to identify the words, and repeat until they can respond quickly and accurately.

Reading

pp. 36–43   **Build Background: "Is Jack Late?"**
Invite children to talk about a field trip they have been a part of or a time when they went somewhere with friends. Ask: **Where did you go? How did you decide what to do together? What did you bring?** Ask children to tell about a special day they planned with friends. Ask what they did, how they planned to meet, and if everyone was there on time.

Monitor Comprehension: "Is Jack Late?"

Ask children to look at the first page of the story and have a volunteer read the title. Then have children look at the first picture of the story and have them share their predictions about what this story will be about. Then guide children through the story as they read.

 pp. 36–37

Say: **I see some animals in the pictures. Let's read to find out who they are and what they are doing.**

After reading the pages, ask: **Who is the little bear on the first page?** (Rick) **What does Rick have?** (a red pack) NOTE DETAILS

Ask: **Who do you think the bigger bear is?** (Possible response: Rick's dad or older brother) DRAW CONCLUSIONS

Ask: **Who do you think the bears meet?** (Kim, the cat) **Why do you think Kim meets them?** (Possible response: Kim has a pack too, so they are probably going to the same place.) MAKE INFERENCES

Say: **Let's all say the sound for the letters _ck_ together.** (/k/) **What words do you see on page 36 that end with _ck_?** (Rick, pack) **Let's all point to the words _Rick_ and _pack_ and read them together.** APPLY PHONICS

 pp. 38–39

Say: **You can see that two more friends have come. Let's read to find out who they are.**

After reading the pages, ask: **Who is the first friend to come?** (Nick) **Who comes after Nick?** (Ann) SEQUENCE

Ask: **What kind of pack does Ann have?** (a black pack) NOTE DETAILS

Ask: **Is Ann's pack the same or different from Nick's pack? How?** (Possible response: It's different because Ann's is black and Nick's is yellow.) COMPARE AND CONTRAST

Ask: **What two words on the second page end the same?** (black, pack) APPLY PHONICS

Fluency

Punctuation Guide children to recognize how readers use capitalization and punctuation to comprehend. Have children turn to "Come In!" in _Heading Out._

Remind children that they can tell where a sentence begins because the first word always starts with a capital letter. Have children point to and read the first word in each sentence.

Then have them point to and name the end marks in each sentence. Remind children that the exclamation point indicates that a sentence should be said with excitement.

Model reading the story with appropriate expression and have children echo-read.

 pp. 40–41

Say: **We can see that the big bear is looking at his watch. Let's read to find out why.**

After reading the pages, ask: **Why do people look at their watches?** (Possible response: They want to see what time it is and if they are late or early.) **Why do you think the big bear is looking at his watch?** (to see if Jack is late) **CAUSE AND EFFECT/DRAW CONCLUSIONS**

Ask: **Is Jack late?** (no) **Read the sentence that tells.** (No! Jack is here.) **NOTE DETAILS**

Ask: **What word do you see on page 41 that ends with *ck*?** (*Jack*) **APPLY PHONICS**

 page 42

Say: **Now we see all the friends together. Let's read to find out what they say.**

After reading the pages, ask: **What did the animals say?** (Yes! Now we can go.) **NOTE DETAILS**

Ask: **Why do think the animals are finally ready to go?** (Possible response: Everyone has come.) **Where do you think they will go?** (Possible response: on a hike) **Do you think they will be gone long? Why or why not?** (Possible response: Yes, because they have backpacks that probably have water and snacks inside.) **DRAW CONCLUSIONS**

Ask: **If you were going to meet a group of friends, how would you make sure you would be on time?** (Possible response: I would ask my mom to get me there on time.) **PERSONAL RESPONSE**

 page 43

Answers to *Think Critically* Questions
Help children read and answer the *Think Critically* questions on page 43. Answers are shown below.

 1. ‹Rick and his dad arrive.› **BEGINNING, MIDDLE, ENDING**

2. ‹yellow backpack› **NOTE DETAILS**

 3. ‹The group heads down the trail.› **BEGINNING, MIDDLE, ENDING**

PRETEACH

Build Robust Vocabulary

 Introduce Robust Vocabulary Read the student-friendly explanation for each word. Then discuss each word using the following examples.

Say: **When I do nice things for others, I show that I can be considerate. Think of something nice someone did for you. How were they considerate?**

Say: **I follow a routine every night before I go to bed. I sit and read a book for ten minutes. What routine do you follow every night?**

Display *Photo Cards squirrel* and *octopus*. Say: **If I saw these two creatures in a tree together, it would be very unexpected.** Display *Photo Cards queen* and *lunch*. Say: **If you were in the cafeteria, which would be unexpected to see?**

RETEACH

Grammar/Writing

Telling Parts of Sentences Talk with children about things they like to do with a group of friends. Begin with a sentence about yourself, such as *I go to a movie.* Record the sentence on chart paper under a heading *Things We Do with Friends.*

Point out that *go to a movie* is the telling part of your sentence because it tells what you did. Ask volunteers to say other sentences. Record their sentences, using children's names in place of *I.* Guide children to find and underline the telling part of their sentences.

> Things We Do with Friends
>
> I go to a movie.
> We swim in the water.
> I jump rope.

VOCABULARY

Student-Friendly Explanations

considerate A considerate person thinks about the feelings of others.

routine If you follow a routine, you do the same things every time.

unexpected If something unexpected happens, it will be a surprise.

LESSON 4

30+ Minutes

DAY AT A GLANCE

Day 3

PHONEMIC AWARENESS
Phoneme Segmentation

PHONICS
Preteach Phonograms *-ick, -ink*

PHONICS AND SPELLING
Guided Practice Digraph /k/*ck*

HIGH-FREQUENCY WORDS
Review *late, no, yes*

FLUENCY
Punctuation

COMPREHENSION
Reteach Beginning, Middle, Ending

GRAMMAR/WRITING
Reteach Caption Sentences

Materials Needed:

Write-On/
Wipe-Off
Boards with
Phonemic
Awareness
Disks

Photo
Cards

Word Builders
and Word
Builder Cards

Copying
Masters
15–16

Lesson 4
Story Strips

Heading Out
Student Edition
pp. 36–42

Spelling Words

1. pick	6. sick
2. pack	7. big
3. tack	8. in
4. back	9. hold
5. sack	10. so

Phonemic Awareness

Phoneme Segmentation   Have children use the three boxes on the *Write-on/Wipe-off Boards*. Remind children that the boxes stand for sounds in words. Show *Photo Card sack* and model how to listen for sounds in words. Tell children the first sound in *sack* is /s/ as you place a disk in the first box. Identify the second sound /a/ as you place a disk in the second box. Then identify the last sound /k/ as you place a disk in the third box. Point to each box in sequence and say the word. Tell children there are three sounds in *sack*.

Have children count sounds using the same procedure. Use *Photo Cards hen, bug, moon, rose, toad*.

PRETEACH

Phonics

Phonograms *-ick, -ink*   Write on the board *sick* and *lick*. Read the words aloud. Ask how the words are the same. (They end with /ik/ and rhyme.) Write on the board and read aloud *sink* and *wink*. Ask how the words are the same. (They end with /ink/ and rhyme.) Have children read the words. Have volunteers underline *-ick* in the first pair of words and *-ink* in the second pair.

RETEACH

Phonics and Spelling

 Digraph /k/*ck*

Build Words   Use *Word Builders* and *Word Builder Cards* to form words. Have children listen to your directions and change a letter in each word to spell a spelling word. Form *kick* and have children read the word. Ask: **Which spelling words can you make by changing the first letter?** (*pick, sick*)

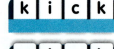

Follow a similar procedure with the following words: *pick* (*pack*), *pack* (*tack, back, sack*), *bit* (*big*), *an* (*in*).

Remind children that there are some other words they have to remember how to spell. Have children say *so*. Tell them to put *Word Builder Cards s, o* in their *Word Builders*, picture the word *so* in their minds, and build the word. Write the word on the board. Follow the same procedure with the word *hold*.

High-Frequency Words

 Copying Masters 15–16 Duplicate and distribute *Copying Masters* 15–16 to each child. Point out the boxes above the words *red, blue, yellow,* and *black*. Have children color in each box to match the word below it. Explain that the sentences tell the story "Is Jack Late?" but some have missing words.

List the words *late, yes,* and *no* on the board. Have children read aloud each story strip sentence and name the correct word on the board that makes sense in the sentence. Have children write the missing words in the blanks and read the completed sentences aloud. Help children cut apart the strips, read the completed sentences, and arrange them in story order.

Comprehension

 Beginning, Middle, Ending Remind children that every story has a beginning, middle, and ending. Have children turn to "Is Jack Late?" in *Heading Out*. Do a picture walk through the story with children. Guide them to point out what happens in the beginning, the middle, and the ending.

Grammar/Writing

Caption Sentences Display *Photo Card cake*. Model a caption for the picture by saying: **The cake is sweet**. Write the sentence on the board and read it aloud, tracking the print. Point out that the caption sentence begins with a capital letter and ends with a period. Guide children to understand that it has a naming part that tells the reader what is in the picture (*the cake*) and a telling part that gives information about the picture (*is sweet*). Remind children to keep these points in mind when they write caption sentences for pictures.

Display *Photo Card flower*. Repeat the activity, having children dictate caption sentences for the picture. Record their responses on the board without proper capitalization or punctuation. Work with children to correct the sentences.

High-Frequency Words

late	no
yes	

Fluency

Punctuation Remind children that good readers use end marks to read each sentence correctly with expression. Say:

When I read, I pay attention to capital letters so I know where a sentence begins. I also pay attention to commas and end marks.

When I see a comma, I pause.

When I see an exclamation point, I make my voice sound excited.

When I see a question mark, I sound as if I am asking a question.

I'm going to reread "Is Jack Late?" one page at a time. I'm going to pay attention to the end mark in each sentence. Read each page after me, just the way I read it.

LESSON 4

DAY AT A GLANCE
Day 4

PHONEMIC AWARENESS
Phoneme Blending

PHONICS
Reteach Phonograms *-ill, -it*

PHONICS AND SPELLING
Reteach Digraph /k/*ck*

HIGH-FREQUENCY WORDS
Reteach *late, oh, yes, no*

FLUENCY
Punctuation

COMPREHENSION
Reteach Beginning, Middle, Ending

GRAMMAR/WRITING
Reteach Caption Sentences

Materials Needed:

Practice Book

Lesson 4 High-Frequency Word Cards

Heading Out Student Edition pp. 16–22 pp. 36–42

Spelling Words

1. pick	6. sick
2. pack	7. big
3. tack	8. in
4. back	9. hold
5. sack	10. so

30+ Minutes

Phonemic Awareness

Phoneme Blending   Tell children that together you are going to play a game. Say: **See if you can put all three puzzle pieces together to make a word. Listen: /s/ /a/ /k/. What word does /s/ /a/ /k/ say? It says sack. Now you try some.** Continue with the following words: /b/ /o/ /ks/ (*box*), /r/ /o/ /k/ (*rock*), /n/ /o/ /k/ (*knock*), /p/ /a/ /th/ (*path*), /f/ /i/ /sh/ (*fish*).

PRETEACH

Phonics

Phonograms *-ill, -it*   Write on the board *bill* and *fill*. Read the words aloud. Ask how the words are the same. (They end with /il/ and rhyme.) Write on the board and read aloud *hit* and *kit*. Ask how the words are the same. (They end with /it/ and rhyme.) Have children read the words. Then have volunteers underline *-ill* in the first pair of words and *-it* in the second pair. Have children suggest other phonograms with *-ill* and *-it*. Explain that seeing a familiar word part, such as *-ill* or *-it* can help children read new words more quickly.

RETEACH

Phonics and Spelling

Practice Book p.17

Digraph /k/*ck*
Direct children's attention to page 17 of their *Practice Books*. Complete the page together.

Assess children's progress using the following sentences.

1. pick   I will **pick** a toy.
2. pack   Mom will **pack** my lunch.
3. tack   Put a **tack** in the sign.
4. back   I will stand in the **back** of the room.
5. sack   Put the bread in a **sack**.
6. sick   My cat looks **sick**.

Review

7. big   My **big** brother plays ball with me.
8. in   The pencils are **in** the desk.

High-Frequency

9. hold   I can **hold** your books.
10. so   I feel **so** cold!

RETEACH
High-Frequency Words

Copying Masters 13–14

Display *High-Frequency Word Cards* for this lesson's words—*late, oh, yes,* and *no*—and the previously learned high-frequency words. Point to words at random and ask children to read them.

RETEACH
Comprehension

Beginning, Middle, Ending   Ask children to name the three parts all stories have (beginning, middle, ending) and talk about the importance of each part.

Draw a three-column chart as shown below. Have children look at the stories "Come In!" and "Is Jack Late?" in *Heading Out*. Write these story titles as headings. Help children tell what happened in each story and record the information in the chart.

	"Come In!"	"Is Jack Late?"
Beginning	Dan gets to the raccoon's house with apples.	Rick and his dad show up for a trip.
Middle	More animals get to the raccoon's house with fruit.	More kids with packs show up.
Ending	The animals share the food.	Jack finally shows up and the kids go.

RETEACH
Grammar/Writing

Photo Card

Caption Sentences   Review with children characteristics of caption sentences.

Writing Caption Sentences
A caption sentence gives information about a picture.
A caption sentence has a naming part and a telling part.
A caption sentence begins with a capital letter and ends with a period.

Display *Photo Card hen*. Write this caption sentence on chart paper: *A hen lays eggs*. Read the sentence aloud, tracking the print. Say: **This caption sentence gives information about the picture. It tells us that a hen lays eggs.** Ask children to dictate similar sentences about the hen. Record these on chart paper. Choral-read the sentences with children.

High-Frequency Words

late	yes
oh	no

Fluency

Punctuation   Remind children that good readers use punctuation to understand a story and to read sentences correctly and with expression. Have them reread "Is Jack Late?" in *Heading Out* several times, paying close attention to end marks. Model using punctuation—periods, question marks, and exclamation points.

DAY AT A GLANCE

Day 5

HIGH-FREQUENCY WORDS
oh, late, yes

PHONEMIC AWARENESS
Onset and Rime

PHONICS AND SPELLING
Preteach Short Vowel /o/*o*

BUILD ROBUST VOCABULARY
Preteach *horrible, invigorated, presented*

GRAMMAR/WRITING
Preteach Telling Sentences

Materials Needed:

Lesson 4
High-Frequency
Word Cards

Sound/Spelling
Card *Oo*

Word Builders
and Word
Builder Cards

Write-On/
Wipe-Off
Boards

Practice
Book

High-Frequency Words

oh	yes
late	

High-Frequency Words

Copying Masters 13–14 Display *High-Frequency Word Cards* for *oh, late, yes,* and the other previously learned high-frequency words. Say the word *oh,* ask a volunteer to point to *oh,* and have children read the word aloud. Continue with the remaining high-frequency words. Repeat this activity several times to reinforce instant recognition.

Phonemic Awareness

Onset and Rime   Have children name the words as you say them in parts. Model the first one. **Listen as I say this word in parts. /l/-ot—The word I said was *lot*. Now you try some: /n/-od, /p/-op, /s/-ock, /r/-ob, /ch/-op.**

PRETEACH

Phonics and Spelling

Sound/Spelling Card   **Short Vowel /o/*o***
Connecting Letter to Sound   Say the words *on, odd,* and *ox* and have children repeat the words. Explain that all three words begin with the /o/ sound. Have children say /o/ several times. Display *Sound Spelling Card Oo,* say the letter name, and name the picture. Tell children that the letter *o* can stand for the sound /o/, the sound they hear at the beginning of *octopus*. Tell children that this is the "short *o* sound." Have children say /o/ several times as you touch the letter.

Give each child an *o* Word Builder Card. Say: **When I say a word that begins with /o/, hold up your card and say /o/. When I say a word that does not begin with /o/, hold your card behind your back.** Say these words: *on, ox, pin, October, odd, bag, octagon.* Follow the same procedure for the medial position with the following words: *hop, sock, had, stop, hit, shop.*

Word Blending   Demonstrate each step with *Word Builder Cards* and a *Word Builder.* Have children repeat each step after you. Hold up *h* and say /h/. Hold up *o* and say /o/. Hold up *p* and say /p/.

- Place the letters *h, o, p* in the *Word Builder.*
- Point to *h*. Say /h/. Point to *o*. Say /o/. Prompt children to repeat after you.
- Slide *o* next to *h*. Run your hand under the letters as you blend the sounds, elongating them—/ho/.
- Point to *p* and say /p/.

- Slide *p* next to *ho*. Run your hand under *hop* as you blend the sounds, elongating them—/hop/.
- Read *hop* naturally.

Follow the same procedure with these words: *rock, doll, dot*.

  Word Building   Place the *Word Builder Cards t, o,* and *p* in the *Word Builder* and have children do the same. Slide your hand under the letters as you read the word with children. Then read the word naturally—*top*. Have children build and read new words. As they build each word, write it on the board. Say:

- **Change *t* to *h*. What word did you make?** (*hop*)
- **Change *p* to *t*. What word did you make?** (*hot*)

Continue with the words *not, dot,* and *lot*. Then have children read the words on the board. Direct children's attention to page 18 of their *Practice Books*. Complete the page together.

Spelling Words

1. top	6. lot
2. hop	7. back
3. hot	8. pick
4. not	9. oh
5. dot	10. yes

Have children practice writing spelling words on their *Write-on/Wipe-off Boards*.

PRETEACH

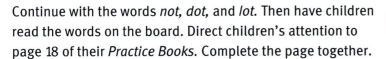

Build Robust Vocabulary

Introduce Robust Vocabulary   Read the student-friendly explanation for each word. Then discuss each word using the following examples.

Say: **A horrible storm might knock down homes. A horrible smell might make you sick. What is something that you think is horrible?**

Say: **On a hot day, drinking ice water makes me feel invigorated. What makes you feel invigorated—a good night's sleep or playing all day in the hot sun?**

Say: **If your team wins the game, you might be presented with a trophy. Tell about a time you were presented with something.**

VOCABULARY

Student-Friendly Explanations

horrible Something horrible is really bad or awful.

invigorated If you are invigorated, you feel full of energy.

presented If you presented something to a friend, you gave it to her or him.

PRETEACH

Grammar/Writing

Telling Sentences   Write these telling sentences on the board: *A dog digs. My mom runs fast.* Track the print as you read them aloud.

Explain that these are telling sentences; each one has words that tell who it is about and what happens. Tell children that the first sentence is about a dog and tells what it does—*digs*. Point out the capital letter and remind children that a sentence begins with a capital letter. Point out that telling sentences end with a period. Repeat with the second sentence.

LESSON 5

DAY AT A GLANCE

Day 1

PHONEMIC AWARENESS
Phoneme Isolation

PHONICS AND SPELLING
Reteach Short Vowel /o/*o*

COMPREHENSION
Preteach Characters

HIGH-FREQUENCY WORDS
Reteach *find, soon, much*

FLUENCY
Accuracy

GRAMMAR/WRITING
Reteach Telling Sentences

Materials Needed:

Photo Cards

Word Builders and Word Builder Cards

Write-On/Wipe-Off Boards

Heading Out Student Edition pp. 36–42 pp. 44–45

Practice Book

Spelling Words

1. top	6. lot
2. hop	7. back
3. hot	8. pick
4. not	9. oh
5. dot	10. yes

Have children practice writing spelling words on their *Write-on/Wipe-off Boards.*

Phonemic Awareness

Phoneme Isolation Display *Photo Cards box* and *ant.* Have children say the picture names after you and listen for the /o/ sound. Say: *Box, ant.* **Which picture name has the /o/ sound?** *Box* **has the /o/ sound. Now you try.** Repeat with *Photo Cards crayon* and *moon, octopus* and *ocean,* and *soccer* and *snow.*

RETEACH

Phonics and Spelling

Short Vowel /o/*o*

Word Building Place the *Word Builder Cards t, o,* and *p* in the *Word Builder.* Ask children to say each letter name and the sound it stands for. Slide your hand under the letters as you read the word with children. Ask:

- **Which letter should I change to make *top* become *hop*?** (Change *t* to *h*.)

- **Which letter should I change to make *hop* become *hot*?** (Change *p* to *t*.)

Continue with the words *not, dot,* and *lot.*

Read Words in Context Write the following sentences on chart paper. Have children read each sentence silently. Then track the print as children read the sentences aloud. Finally, point to the underlined words at random and have children read them. *Dad will be back at six. Yes, I will pick up sticks. Oh, look! My dog can hop a lot. Do not hit the hot pot. I see a dot on top of that box.*

PRETEACH

Comprehension

Characters Have children turn to "Is Jack Late?" in *Heading Out.* Say: **Some stories are about people. Some are about animals. Many stories are about both people and animals. The people and animals are called the characters. This story is about four bears—Kim, Nick, Ann, and Jack. They are the characters in the story.** Have children reread "Is Jack Late?" Point out the characters in each picture and have children name them.

RETEACH

High-Frequency Words

 Write the words *find, soon,* and *much* on the board.

- Point to and read *find.* Repeat, having children say *find* with you.
- Say: **Did you *find* your missing shoe?**
- Repeat the word and then point to each letter as you spell it. Then have children say and spell *find* with you. Have children reread the word.

Repeat for *much* and *soon.* Use the following sentence: *Sheila ate too* much *candy. If we get home* soon, *we can play outside.*

Have children turn to page 44 of *Heading Out* and have them read aloud the words at the top of the page. Talk about the illustrations. Then guide children in choosing and circling the word that names each picture. (3. *dog,* 4. *doll,* 5. *box*) Have children read aloud each word in the list on page 45. Ask volunteers to read the sentences aloud. Then have children choral-read the sentences. Guide them to read and trace the word that completes each sentence. (1. *find,* 2. *much,* 3. *soon*)

RETEACH

Grammar/Writing

Practice Book
p.19

Telling Sentences   Write the following sentences on the board: *We like to go to the beach. We swim in the water. We play in the sand.*

Read the sentences aloud as you track the print. Tell children that these are examples of telling sentences. Point out the capital letter and period in the first sentence. Then have volunteers circle the capital letters and periods in the remaining sentences.

Have children dictate telling sentences about another activity they like to do, using the sentences above as models. Write the telling sentences on the board. Track the print as you read them with children.

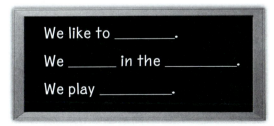

We like to _____.
We _____ in the _____.
We play _____.

Complete *Practice Book* page 19 together.

High-Frequency Words

find	**much**
soon	

Fluency

Accuracy   Tell children that good readers focus on reading the words in a story correctly. Have children turn to "Is Jack Late?" in *Heading Out.* Model reading the first two pages with expression as children track the print. Skip a word in each sentence. Then reread the sentences accurately. Ask children which reading made more sense. Remind children of the importance of reading each word in a story correctly.

PHONEMIC AWARENESS
Phoneme Blending

PHONICS AND SPELLING
Reteach Short Vowel /o/*o*

HIGH-FREQUENCY WORDS
Reteach *much, find, thank, soon*

FLUENCY
Accuracy

READING
"Where Is Tom?"

BUILD ROBUST VOCABULARY
Preteach *aid, persistent, sweltering*

GRAMMAR/WRITING
Reteach Telling Sentences

Materials Needed:

Word Builders and Word Builder Cards

Practice Book

Lesson 5 High-Frequency Word Cards

Heading Out Student Edition pp. 46–53

High-Frequency Words

much	thank
find	soon

Phonemic Awareness

Phoneme Blending   Tell children they are going to play a guessing game. Say: **Listen as I do the first one. I'm thinking of a word that means "a big stone." It is /r/ /o/ /k/. What's my word? The word is *rock*. Now you try.** Continue with clues for the following words: /l/ /o/ /t/ (*lot*), /ch/ /o/ /p/ (*chop*), /t/ /o/ /p/ (*top*), /s/ /o/ /k/ (*sock*), /b/ /l/ /o/ /k/ (*block*).

Phonics and Spelling

Short Vowel /o/*o*

Word Building   Demonstrate with a *Word Builder* and *Word Builder Cards* and have children do the same. Build the word *hop*. Run your hand under the letters as you read the word with children. Lead children in building and reading new words by saying:

* **Change *o* to *i*. Read the word.** (*hip*)
* **Change *h* to *t*. Read the word.** (*tip*)
* **Change *i* to *o*. Read the word.** (*top*)

Continue with the following words: *hot, hit, pot, pit.*

Practice Book p.20

Read Words in Context   Ask children to turn to *Practice Book* page 20. Read the sentences aloud and have children echo-read. Then ask volunteers to read each sentence aloud. Ask: **Where is Rob?** (on the dock) **Where is Bob?** (on a raft) **What does Rob have?** (a rod) **What is Tod doing?** (swimming) After reading, guide children to circle all short *o* words and underline all short *i* words.

High-Frequency Words

Copying Masters 17–18

Display the *High-Frequency Word Cards* for *much, find, thank* and *soon*. Point to each card and read the word. Have children repeat. Give each child a set of *High-Frequency Word Cards,* and have children spread the cards out in front of them. Randomly call out one of the words, and have children hold up the matching card. Assess how well children are able to identify the words, and repeat until they can respond quickly and accurately.

Reading

pp. 46–53 **Build Background: "Where Is Tom?"**
Ask children to share their experiences with pets. Ask: **What kind of silly things do your pets do? Have you read any stories about silly animals?** Invite children to discuss what they know specifically about dogs. Have volunteers tell about a pet dog and what they like best about dogs.

Monitor Comprehension: "Where Is Tom?"
Have children turn to the first page of the story. Ask a volunteer to read the title. Then have children look at the pictures of the story and share their predictions about what this story will be about. Guide children through the story as they read.

pp. 46–47 Say: **I see a girl in this picture. Let's read to find out what she is looking for.**

After reading the pages, ask: **What is the girl trying to find?** (her doll) NOTE DETAILS

Ask: **Who do you think Tom is?** (the dog) **Why do you think the girl says, "Let's find Tom?"** (She thinks Tom has her doll.) DRAW CONCLUSIONS

Say: **Let's all say the /o/ sound together. What words with the /o/ sound do you see on these pages?** (doll, Tom) APPLY PHONICS

pp. 48–49 Say: **We can see a boy in the first picture. It looks like he is looking for something, too. Let's read to see what he's missing.**

After reading the pages, ask: **What is the boy looking for?** (his ball) NOTE DETAILS

Ask: **What characters have we seen in the story so far?** (a girl, Dad, Tom, a boy) CHARACTERS

Ask: **Who does the boy think has his ball?** (Tom) **How do you know?** (He says, "Let's find Tom.") DRAW CONCLUSIONS

Fluency

Accuracy Make cards for these words: *Will, likes, to, hop.* Make a punctuation card for a period and set it aside. Display the word cards one at a time in random order. Have children reach them. Repeat, having children read the words more quickly. Then arrange the cards to form the sentence *Will likes to hop.* Have volunteers take turns reading the sentence aloud. Emphasize the importance of reading each word correctly.

Ask: **What do you think will happen next?** (Possible response: Something else will be missing.) **MAKE PREDICTIONS**

Say: **Now it looks like Mom has lost something. Let's read and see if she finds it.**

After reading the pages, ask: **What is happening now?** (Mom is missing a shoe.) **Was your prediction correct?** (Possible response: Yes, I thought something else would be missing.) **CONFIRM PREDICTIONS**

Ask: **What do you think happened to Mom's shoe?** (Possible response: Tom took it.) **How do you know?** (Possible response: They say, "Let's find Tom soon.") **Why do you think they want to find Tom soon?** (Possible response: He may have taken a lot of their things and they don't want him to take more.) **DRAW CONCLUSIONS**

Ask: **What word with the sound /o/ do you see on page 51?** (*Tom*) **APPLY PHONICS**

Say: **Now we see all the things that have gone missing. Let's read to find out who took the things.**

After reading the page, ask: **What does the family say?** ("Look! Tom got so much!) **NOTE DETAILS**

Ask: **How did all these things get outside?** (Tom took them.) **CAUSE AND EFFECT**

Ask: **Would you be surprised if you found a pile of your things in the yard? Why or why not?** (Possible response: Yes. I would be surprised because I don't keep my things outside.) **PERSONAL RESPONSE**

Answers to *Think Critically* Questions

Help children read and answer the *Think Critically* questions on page 53. Answers are shown below.

1. ‹the dog› **CHARACTERS**
2. ‹the backyard› **SETTING**
3. ‹the family finds their items› **SEQUENCE**

Build Robust Vocabulary

Introduce Robust Vocabulary   Read the student-friendly explanation for each word. Then discuss each word using the following examples.

Say: **If it is sweltering outside, I stay inside and turn on the air conditioner. If the temperature is sweltering, would you wear long pants or shorts?**

Say: **When I can't figure out a math problem, I ask someone to aid me. When might you need someone to aid you?**

Say: **I am persistent about eating breakfast every day. What are you persistent about?**

Grammar/Writing

Telling Sentences   Talk with children about a field trip they have taken. Model a telling sentence, such as *We took a field trip to the movies*. Ask volunteers to dictate other telling sentences. Record their sentences without capital letters or end marks. Read the sentences to children.

Use the sentences to reinforce the basic rules of capitalization and punctuation. Discuss the errors. Model how to make corrections by capitalizing the first letter and adding a period.

Follow a similar procedure to guide children in correcting the other sentences. Then have volunteers identify who did something in the sentences and what they did. Track the print as you read aloud the sentences.

> our class went to the movies
>
> we went into a big theater
>
> we saw a movie about bears
>
> we had fun

VOCABULARY
Student-Friendly Explanations

aid   If you aid someone, you help them.

persistent   If you are persistent, you keep trying and never give up.

sweltering   If the temperature is sweltering, it is very hot and uncomfortable.

30+ Minutes

PHONEMIC AWARENESS
Phoneme Segmentation

PHONICS
Preteach Inflections -ed, -ing

PHONICS AND SPELLING
Reteach Short Vowel /o/o

HIGH-FREQUENCY WORDS
Reteach find, soon, much

FLUENCY
Accuracy

COMPREHENSION
Reteach Characters

GRAMMAR/WRITING
Reteach Sentences About Things

Materials Needed:

Copying Masters 19–20

Write-On/ Wipe-Off Boards with Phonemic Awareness Disks

Word Builders and Word Builder Cards

Lesson 5 Story Strips

Heading Out Student Edition pp. 6–12 pp. 46–52

Spelling Words

I. top	6. lot
2. hop	7. back
3. hot	8. pick
4. not	9. oh
5. dot	IO. yes

Phonemic Awareness

 Phoneme Segmentation   Have children use the three boxes on the *Write-on/Wipe-off Boards*. Tell children that the boxes stand for sounds in words. Have children repeat each step with their boards and disks. Say: *Mop.* **The first sound in** *mop* **is /m/.** Model placing a disk in the first box. Use this procedure for the second sound in *mop* (/o/), placing a disk in the second box, and the last sound in *mop* (/p/), placing a disk in the third box. Point to each box in sequence as children say the word. **How many sounds do you hear in** *mop*? **I hear three.** Repeat with *rock, sock, pick, top,* and *hot.*

PRETEACH

Phonics

Inflections -ed, -ing   Write the following words on the board: *wanted, ripped, stayed.* As you read each word, underline the root word and point out the -ed ending. Emphasize the sounds -ed can stand for: /əd/ in *wanted*, /t/ in *ripped*, and /d/ in *stayed.* Have children repeat each word.

Write these words under the -ed words: *wanting, ripping, staying.* Read each word and underline the root word. Have children say each word. Point out that -ing stands for the same sounds in each word. Guide children to build and read words with -ed and -ing.

RETEACH

Phonics and Spelling

 Short Vowel /o/o

Build Words   Use *Word Builder Cards* and a *Word Builder* to form words. Have children listen to your directions and change a letter in each word to spell a spelling word. Form *tip* and have children read the word. Ask: **Which spelling word can you make by changing the middle letter?** (*top*)

Follow a similar procedure with the following words: *top* (*hop*), *hop* (*hot*), *hot* (*not*), *not* (*dot*), *dot* (*lot*), *pack* (*back*), *sick* (*pick*).

Remind children that there are some other words they have to remember how to spell. Have children say *oh*. Tell them to put *Word Builder Cards o, h* in their *Word Builders*, picture the word *oh* in their minds, and build the word. Write the word on the board. Follow the same procedure with *yes*.

High-Frequency Words

find	**much**
soon	

RETEACH

High-Frequency Words

 Copying Masters 19–20 Duplicate and distribute *Copying Masters* 19–20 to each child. Explain that the sentences tell about "Where Is Tom?" but some have missing words.

List the words *find, soon,* and *much* on the board. Have children read aloud each story strip sentence and name the correct word on the board that makes sense in the sentence. Have children write the missing words in the blanks and read the completed sentences aloud. Help children cut apart the strips, read the completed sentences, and arrange them in story order.

RETEACH

Comprehension

  Characters Remind children that characters are the people or animals in a story. Have children turn to "We Can Tap!" in *Heading Out*. Guide them to identify the characters. Then invite volunteers to tell about other characters they know from familiar stories.

RETEACH

Grammar/Writing

Sentences About Things Display the following sentences.

> Sid has a tan mitt.
>
> His cat is big and fast.

Read the sentences with children. Explain that the words in these sentences help to tell about things. Tell children that sentences about things should name a thing and tell about the thing. Point out that the words in the sentence should describe the thing.

Work with children to brainstorm a list of words and phrases about favorite toys. Model by saying: **My favorite toy is my old, brown teddy bear. What is yours?** Have children share their sentences.

Fluency

Accuracy Have children turn to "Where Is Tom?" in *Heading Out.* Remind children that good readers try to say each word in a story correctly. Say: **I'm going to reread "Where Is Tom?" one page at a time. I'm going to read each word and not skip any. Read each page after me, just the way I read it.**

LESSON 5

DAY AT A GLANCE

Day 4

PHONEMIC AWARENESS
Phoneme Blending

PHONICS
Reteach Inflections -ed, -ing

PHONICS AND SPELLING
Reteach Short vowel /o/o

HIGH-FREQUENCY WORDS
Reteach much, find, thank, soon

FLUENCY
Accuracy

COMPREHENSION
Reteach Characters

GRAMMAR/WRITING
Reteach Sentences About Things

Materials Needed:

Practice Book **p.21**
Practice Book

Copying Masters **17–18**
Lesson 5 High-Frequency Word Cards

Heading Out Student Edition
pp. 16–22
pp. 36–42
pp. 46–52

Spelling Words

1. top	6. lot
2. hop	7. back
3. hot	8. pick
4. not	9. oh
5. dot	10. yes

30+ Minutes

Phonemic Awareness

Phoneme Blending Tell children that together you are going to play a game called "Fix It." Explain that you will say some words that are broken. They will listen to put the sounds together and say the word. Say: **Listen as I do the first one. /t/ /o/ /p/. What word does /t/ /o/ /p/ say? The word is** *top.* **Say the word. Now you try.** Continue with the following words: /p/ /i/ /k/ (*pick*), /r/ /a/ /t/ (*rat*), /s/ /o/ /k/ (*sock*), /sh/ /o/ /k/ (*shock*), /r/ /o/ /d/ (*rod*).

RETEACH

Phonics

Inflections -ed, -ing Remind children that endings can be added to a root word to make new words. List *fill* and *filled.* Say: **The word** *filled* **is made by adding** *-ed* **to the root word** *fill.* Add *filling.* Say: **The word** *filling* **is made by adding** *-ing* **to the root word** *fill.* Have children read the words.

Guide children through the same procedure with root words *pick* and *jump.*

RETEACH

Phonics and Spelling

 Practice Book **p.21**

Short Vowel /o/o
Direct children's attention to page 21 of their *Practice Books.* Complete the page together.

Assess children's progress using the following sentences.

1. top — I am on **top** of the hill.
2. hop — Mary likes to **hop.**
3. hot — The pot is very **hot.**
4. not — Juan may **not** go to the gym.
5. dot — Make a **dot** on the board.
6. lot — I like you a **lot.**

Review

7. back — I want to go **back** to school.
8. pick — Please **pick** a good movie!

High-Frequency

9. oh — **Oh,** no! The milk spilled!
10. yes — My dad said **yes,** I can go!

High-Frequency Words

much	thank
find	soon

RETEACH

High-Frequency Words

 Display *High-Frequency Word Cards* for this lesson's words—*much, find, thank,* and *soon*—and the previously learned high-frequency words. Point to words at random and ask children to read them.

RETEACH

Comprehension

 Characters Ask children to explain the definition of characters. (people or animals in a story) Draw a three-column chart as shown below. Have children turn to "Where Is Tom?" in *Heading Out*. Point out the characters in the story and record them in the chart. Then have children look back at "Come In!" and "Is Jack Late?" Have children point out the characters in each story as you record their responses on the chart. Ask children to tell you which character they first meet in each story.

"Where Is Tom?"	"Is Jack Late?"	"Come In!"
girl, boy, Mom, Dad, Tom	Rick, Kim, Nick, Ann, Jack	Raccoon, Dan, Pam, Max

RETEACH

Grammar/Writing

Sentences About Things Review with children the characteristics of well-written sentences about things.

> ### Sentences About Things
> The sentence names the thing.
> The sentence tells about the thing.
> The words in the sentence describe the thing.

Write the following sentence on chart paper: *I had hot soup.* Explain that this sentence tells about something—it describes what you ate. Show how it has the characteristics of a sentence about a thing.

Ask children to dictate similar sentences about what they ate yesterday, using your sentence as a model. Remind children to use words that describe what they ate. Choral-read the sentences with children.

Fluency

Accuracy Have children turn to "Where Is Tom?" in *Heading Out*. Have partners reread the story three or four times. Remind them to read the words exactly as they appear on each page. Listen to partners read, giving them feedback regarding accuracy and fluency.

DAY AT A GLANCE

Day 5

HIGH-FREQUENCY WORDS
find, much, thank

PHONEMIC AWARENESS
Onset and Rime

PHONICS AND SPELLING
Preteach Variant Vowel /ô/*a*

BUILD ROBUST VOCABULARY
Preteach *commotion, muffle, overflowing*

GRAMMAR/WRITING
Preteach Questions

Materials Needed:

Lesson 5 High-Frequency Word Cards

Sound/Spelling Card *all*

Word Builders and Word Builder Cards

Write-On/ Wipe-Off Boards

Practice Book

High-Frequency Words

find	thank
much	

High-Frequency Words

Copying Masters 17–18 Display *High-Frequency Word Cards* for *find, much, thank,* and the other previously learned high-frequency words. Say the word *find,* ask a volunteer to point to *find,* and have children read the word aloud. Continue with the remaining high-frequency words. Repeat this activity several times to reinforce instant recognition.

Phonemic Awareness

Onset and Rime   Have children name the words as you say them in parts. Model the first one. **Listen as I say this word in parts. /w/-all—The word I said was *wall*. Now you try some: /h/-all, /m/-all, /k/-all, /w/-all, /sh/-awl, /t/-all, /b/-all.**

PRETEACH

Phonics and Spelling

Vowel Variant /ô/a (*all*)   Ask children to say *all* and listen for the sounds. Then say: **I can add a sound to the beginning of *all* to make a new word. I can add the sound /t/ to make *tall*.** Elongate and blend the initial sound with the sounds in *all*—/t/-/ôl/, /tôl/. Then say *tall* naturally, and have children repeat the word. Ask children to make new words by adding these sounds to the beginning of all: /k/ (call), /f/ (fall), /h/ (hall), /b/ (ball).

Sound/Spelling Card Display *Sound/Spelling Card all*. Tell children that the letter *a* can stand not only for the /a/ sound at the beginning of *apple* but also for the /ô/ sound at the beginning of *all*. Have children say *all* several times as you run your hand under the letters. Have children write *all* on an index card or a blank word card. Say: **When I say a word that ends with *all*, hold up your *all* card and repeat the word I said. When I say a word that does not end with *all*, hold your card behind your back.** Say these words: *wall, cat, mall, small, tail, stall.*

Build *all* in the *Word Builder*. Run your hand under the letters as you slowly read *all*—/ô/. Then say *all* naturally.

| a | l | l |

- Place the letter *c* in the Word Builder. Point to *c* and say /k/. Point to all and say it naturally.

| c | a | l | l |

- Slide *all* next to *c*. Run your hand under the letters as you elongate and blend the initial sound with all—/k/-*all*. Have children repeat after you.

| c | a | l | l |

- Then lead children in reading the word naturally—*call*.

Follow the same procedure with these words: *tall, ball, fall, hall, mall.*

Word Building Place the *Word Builder Cards a, l,* and *l* in the *Word Builder* and have children do the same. Slide your hand under the letters as you slowly read the word. Then read the word with children. Have children build and read new words. As they build each word, write it on the board. Say:

- **Add c to all. What word did you make?** (*call*)

- **Change c to f. What word did you make?** (*fall*)

Continue with the words *wall, ball,* and *tall.* Direct children's attention to page 22 of their *Practice Books.* Complete the page together.

Practice Book p.22

PRETEACH

Build Robust Vocabulary

Introduce Robust Vocabulary Read the student-friendly explanation for each word. Then discuss each word using the following examples.

Say: **I cause commotion when I cook because I bang pots and pans. What kinds of commotion do you hear at school?**

Say: **I might try to muffle the sound of my dog barking if my neighbors could hear. Which sound would you want to muffle—a big rig passing on the street or your favorite TV show?**

Say: **The library was overflowing with books, so the librarian had to get more shelves for them. What might happen if a sink or a tub was overflowing?**

PRETEACH

Grammar/Writing

Questions Tell children that they are going to learn about asking sentences, or questions. Write these questions:

What is your name?

What do you like to play?

Track the print as you read them aloud. Point out the capital letter and the question mark. Explain that the question mark is the signal that the sentence asks a question. Invite children to work in pairs. One child can ask each question and the partner can answer with a telling sentence. Then have the partners switch roles. Circulate as children do the activity.

Day 5

Spelling Words

1. all	6. tall
2. call	7. not
3. fall	8. top
4. wall	9. much
5. ball	10. thank

Have children practice writing spelling words on their *Write-on/Wipe-off Boards.*

VOCABULARY

Student-Friendly Explanations

commotion A commotion happens when a lot of people are running around making a lot of noise.

muffle When you muffle a sound, you cover it up so it is not so loud.

overflowing If something is overflowing, it is pouring out of its usual space.

DAY AT A GLANCE

Day 1

30+ Minutes

LESSON 6

PHONEMIC AWARENESS
Phoneme Isolation

PHONICS AND SPELLING
Reteach Variant Vowel /ô/a (all)

COMPREHENSION
Preteach Classify/Categorize

HIGH-FREQUENCY WORDS
Reteach how, get, some

FLUENCY
Punctuation

GRAMMAR/WRITING
Reteach Questions

Materials Needed:

Write-On/
Wipe-Off
Boards

Word Builders
and Word
Builder Cards

Heading Out
Student Edition
pp. 36–42
pp. 54–62

Photo
Cards

Practice
Book

Spelling Words

1. all	6. tall
2. call	7. not
3. fall	8. top
4. wall	9. much
5. ball	10. thank

 Have children practice writing spelling words on their *Write-on/Wipe-off Boards.*

Phonemic Awareness

Phoneme Isolation   Say the word *fall*. Have children repeat. Ask children to listen for other words with /ô/. Say: **Listen as I say these words: *sick, mall*. Which word has the /ô/ sound? *Mall* has the sound /ô/. Now you try.** Continue with *tall, tail; will, wall; ball, bell; came, call.*

RETEACH

Phonics and Spelling

 Variant Vowel /ô/a (all)
Word Building   Place the *Word Builder Cards a, l,* and *l* in the *Word Builder*. Slide your hand under the letters as you read the word with children. Continue building new words by asking children:

- **Which letter should I add to *all* to make *call*?**
  (Add *c*.)

- **Which letter should I change in *call* to make *fall*?**
  (Change *c* to *f*.)

Continue with a similar procedure with *wall, ball,* and *tall.*

Read Words in Context   Write the following sentences on chart paper. Have children read each sentence silently. Then track the print as children read the sentences aloud. Then point to the underlined words at random and have children read them. *I will not toss the ball at the wall. Thank you so much for the cat. I will call the tall man to help. All the bags on the top shelf will fall.*

PRETEACH

Comprehension

Classify/Categorize   Remind children that things that are alike can be grouped together. Display *Photo Cards fish* and *octopus*. Help children identify the category and name other things that belong to the same group. (sea animals; shark, whale) Repeat with *Photo Cards arm* and *head*. (parts of the body; legs, hands, feet)

Day
1

Have children turn to "The Map at Camp" in *Heading Out*. Do a picture walk and ask children to name the things they see and tell how they go together. (They all show things you see at camp.)

RETEACH

High-Frequency Words

pp. 54–55

Write the words *how, some,* and *get* on the board.

- Point to and read *how*. Repeat, having children say *how* with you.
- Say: **How will we get to the zoo?**
- Repeat the word and then point to each letter as you spell it. Then have children say and spell *how* with you. Have children read *how*.

Repeat for the remaining words. Use the following sentences: Some *children are playing games. I will* get *a puppy for my birthday.*

Have children turn to page 54 of *Heading Out* and have them read aloud the words at the top of the page. Talk about the illustrations. Then guide children in choosing and circling the word that names each picture. (4. *tall,* 5. *wall,* 6. *ball*) Have children read aloud each word in the list on page 55. Ask volunteers to read the sentences aloud. Then have children choral-read the sentences. Guide them to trace the word that completes each sentence. (1. *How,* 2. *get,* 3. *some*)

RETEACH

Grammar/Writing

Practice Book
p.23

Questions Remind children that a question is a sentence that asks something. Write the following sentence frame on the board: *Is ___ in school today?* Insert a child's name and read the sentence aloud while tracking the print. Point out the capital letter at the beginning. Then have children identify the end mark. (question mark) Ask a volunteer to answer the question with a telling sentence.

Then write the questions: *How old are you? What snack do you like?* Read each question and have children answer with a telling sentence. Then have children dictate questions they might ask a new friend at school. Write the questions on the board and read them with children, tracking the print. Complete *Practice Book* page 23 together.

High-Frequency Words

how	**get**
some	

Fluency

Punctuation Remind children how good readers use capitalization to know when a sentence begins. They use punctuation at the end of sentences to help them know when the sentence ends and how to read it.

Read aloud each page of "Is Jack Late?" Model how you contrast intonation for statements, questions, and exclamations. Then have children echo-read.

"The Map at Camp" **63**

DAY AT A GLANCE

Day 2

PHONEMIC AWARENESS
Phoneme Blending

PHONICS AND SPELLING
Reteach Variant Vowel /ô/*a* (all)

HIGH-FREQUENCY WORDS
Review *how, make, of, some, get*

FLUENCY
Punctuation

READING
"The Map at Camp"

BUILD ROBUST VOCABULARY
Preteach *locate, search, symbol*

GRAMMAR/WRITING
Reteach Questions

Materials Needed:

Word Builders and Word Builder Cards

Practice Book

Lesson 6 High-Frequency Word Cards

Heading Out Student Edition pp. 46–52 pp. 56–63

Photo Cards

High-Frequency Words

how	some
make	get
of	

Phonemic Awareness

Phoneme Blending   Tell children they are going to be word builders and put together the word you are thinking. Say: **Listen as I build a word. I'm thinking of something you do with a telephone. The word is /k/ /ô/ /l/. The word is** *call*. Continue with the following words: /b/ /ô/ /l/ (*ball*), /f/ /ô/ /l/ (*fall*), /t/ /ô/ /l/ (*tall*), /s/ /m/ /ô/ /l/ (*small*).

RETEACH

Phonics and Spelling

 Variant Vowel /ô/*a* (all)
Word Building   Use a *Word Builder* and *Word Builder Cards* and have children repeat each step with their *Word Builders* and *Word Builder Cards*. Build the word *hot*. Review that the *o* stands for the short *o* sound. Lead children in building and reading new words by saying:

- **Change *o* to *a*. Read the word.** (*hat*)
- **Change *t* to *ll*. Read the word.** (*hall*)
- **Change *a* to *i*. Read the word.** (*hill*)

Continue with the words: *fill-fall-fat, dot-doll-dill, tall-tack-tick, pack-back-ball, sack-sock-salt.*

Read Words in Context   Ask children to turn to *Practice Book* page 24. Read each sentence aloud and have children echo-read. Then ask volunteers to read each sentence aloud. Ask: **What does Dot hit?** (the ball) **Where does the ball go?** (on top of the rock wall) **What does Dot wonder about the ball?** (will it fall) **Who will get the ball down?** (tall Bob)

REVIEW

High-Frequency Words

Display the *High-Frequency Word Cards* for *how, make, of, some,* and *get.* Point to each card and read the word. Have children repeat. Distribute a set of *High-Frequency Word Cards* to each child. Play a guessing game. Provide word clues: **Who can find and read the word with two letters?** (*of*) **Who can find and read the word that rhymes with *pet*?** (*get*) Continue with clues until all the words have been identified.

Reading

pp. 56–63

Build Background: "The Map at Camp"

Invite children to tell about their experiences at a camp and tell about the things they saw and did there. For children who have not experienced camping, have them imagine being in a big forest with lots of trees, trails, and a lake. Ask them what they might see or do there. Tell children they will read a selection about children at a camp.

Monitor Comprehension: "The Map at Camp"

Have children turn to the first page of the story. Ask a volunteer to read the title. Guide children to look at the picture on page 56. Have children predict the kinds of things these children might see or do at camp and why they might need a map at camp. Then guide children through the story as they read.

pp. 56–57

Say: **The children look like they are ready to do an activity at camp. Let's read to find out where they want to go.**

After reading the pages, ask: **What are the children going to find?** (the lake) NOTE DETAILS

Ask: **What do you think the children will do at the lake? Tell why you think this.** (Possible response: The children will swim at the lake because they have towels.) DRAW CONCLUSIONS

Ask: **What do the children do first to find the lake?** (They look for the flag.) SEQUENCE

pp. 58–59

Say: **We know that the children must follow the directions to find the lake. Let's read to find out what the children look for next.**

After reading the pages, ask: **What do the children look for after the flag?** (the arrow) **Where does the arrow show them to go?** (down a path) SEQUENCE/DRAW CONCLUSIONS

Ask: **What do the children look for after the arrow?** (a rock wall) **Frame and read the word that names what is made of rock.** (wall) SEQUENCE/APPLY PHONICS

Ask: **What do you think might happen if the children do not follow the directions to the lake?** (Possible response: They would go the wrong way and not find the lake.) CAUSE AND EFFECT

Fluency

Punctuation Write a period, a question mark, and an exclamation on separate index cards. Review the use of each kind of punctuation and the different expression used when you read. Have children turn to "Where Is Tom?" in *Heading Out*. As you read each sentence aloud, hold up the corresponding punctuation card. Have children echo-read the sentence matching your intonation.

Say: **Look at the pictures on these pages. It looks like the children find the lake. Let's read to find out what they need to know next.**

After reading the pages, ask: **Where did the children find the lake?** (by the tall trees) **Frame and read the word that tells what the trees are like.** (*tall*) Note Details/Apply Phonics

Ask: **What do the children ask after they finish swimming in the lake?** (*"How will we get back?"*) Note Details

Ask: **What do you think the children will do to get back to camp safely?** (Possible response: look at a map) Make Predictions

 Say: **The children are ready to go back to camp. Let's read to see how they get there.**

After reading the pages, ask: **Do you think it is a good idea to look at a map if you are not sure of the way? Tell why.** (Possible response: Yes, because a map will show the directions for how to get from one place to another.) Express Personal Opinions

Ask: **What does the map show?** (a picture of the path the children followed) Graphic Aids

Ask: **After reading this story, do you think you would like to go to a summer camp? Tell why you think this.** (Possible responses: Yes, because it would be fun to be in the woods and go swimming and hiking with new friends. No, I might feel too homesick.) Personal Response

 Answers to *Think Critically* Questions
Help children read and answer the *Think Critically* questions on page 63. Answers are shown below.

1. ‹camp› Setting
 2. ‹lake› Classify/Categorize
3. ‹the map› Draw Conclusions

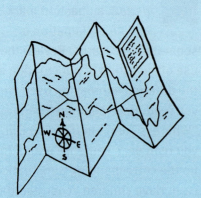

PRETEACH

Build Robust Vocabulary

Introduce Robust Vocabulary   Read the student-friendly explanation for each word. Then discuss each word using the following examples.

Say: **Have you ever gone to a mall, a zoo, or park, and looked at a map to locate a place? What place were you looking for?**

Say: **When I go to the beach, I search for seashells. What might you search for at a zoo?**

Say: **What would be a good symbol on a map for a library—a hot dog or a book?**

RETEACH

Grammar/Writing

Photo Card

Questions   Display *Photo Card ant.* Write this question on the board: *What is it?* Have children read it and answer it with a telling sentence: *It is an ant.* Then ask volunteers to dictate questions about ants. As you record their questions, omit capital letters and punctuation. Read the questions to children.

Reread the first question to children, tracking the print. Model how to rewrite it correctly by capitalizing the first letter and adding a question mark. Explain that the sentence is a question because it needs an answer and that a question ends with a question mark.

Guide children to correct the other questions. Then track the print and read aloud the questions with children. Talk about where they might find answers to their questions.

VOCABULARY

Student-Friendly Explanations

locate If you try to locate something, you try to find it.

search When you search for something, you look for it.

symbol You can use a mark or a picture called a symbol to stand for a word or an object.

DAY AT A GLANCE

Day 3

30+ Minutes

PHONEMIC AWARENESS
Phoneme Segmentation

PHONICS
Preteach Contraction *n't*

PHONICS AND SPELLING
Reteach Variant Vowel /ô/*a* (all)

HIGH-FREQUENCY WORDS
Reteach *get, how, some*

FLUENCY
Punctuation

COMPREHENSION
Reteach Classify/Categorize

GRAMMAR/WRITING
Reteach Sentences About Places

Materials Needed:

Write-On/
Wipe-Off
Boards with
Phonemic
Awareness
Disks

Word Builders
and Word
Builder Cards

Copying Masters 23–24
Lesson 6
Story Strips

Photo Card
Photo
Cards

Heading Out
Student Edition
pp. 56–62

Spelling Words

1. all	6. tall
2. call	7. not
3. fall	8. top
4. wall	9. much
5. ball	10. thank

Phonemic Awareness

Phoneme Segmentation   Have children use the three boxes on the *Write-on/Wipe-off Boards*. Remind children that the three boxes stand for sounds in words. Have children repeat each step with their *Write-on/Wipe-off Boards* as you model. Say: *Fall.* **The first sound I hear in** *fall* **is /f/.** Model placing a disk in the first box. Use this procedure with the second sound in *fall* (/ô/) placing a disk in the second box, and the last sound in *fall* (/l/) placing a disk in the third box. Point to each box in sequence as children say the word. (*fall*) **How many sounds do you hear in** *fall*? **I hear three sounds.** Repeat the procedure with: *hall, ball, tall, all.*

PRETEACH

Phonics

Contraction *n't*   Write on the board: *This is not my dog. This isn't my dog.* Read the sentences aloud and point out that they have the same meaning. Underline *is not* and *isn't.* Explain that *isn't* is a contraction—a shorter way of saying *is not.* Point to the apostrophe in *isn't* and explain that it takes the place of a letter. Ask a volunteer to name the letter that was dropped from *is not* to form the contraction *isn't.* (*o*)

Use the same procedure with the following sentences: *I did not call. I didn't call. I do not like it. I don't like it. She has not come yet. She hasn't come yet.*

RETEACH

Phonics and Spelling

 Variant Vowel /ô/*a* (all)
Build Words   Use *Word Builder Cards* and a *Word Builder* to form words. Have children listen to your directions and change one letter in each word to spell a spelling word using their *Word Builder Cards* and *Word Builders.* Form *an.* Have children read the word. Ask: **Which spelling word can you make by changing *n* to *ll*?** (*all*)

a	n

a	l	l

Follow a similar procedure by adding or changing letters to form the words: *call, wall, fall, ball, tall.*

Remind children that there are other words they have to remember how to spell. Have children say *much.* Have them put *Word Builder Cards m, u, c, h* in their *Word Builders,* picture the word *much* in their minds, and build the word. Write the word on the board. Follow the same procedure with *thank.*

RETEACH

High-Frequency Words

Copying Masters 23–24

Duplicate and distribute *Copying Masters* 23–24 to each child. Explain that the sentences tell the story "The Map at Camp" but some have missing words.

List the words *get, how,* and *some* on the board. Have children read aloud each story strip sentence and name the correct word on the board that makes sense in the sentence. Have children write the missing words in the blanks and read the completed sentences aloud. Help children cut apart the strips, read the completed sentences, and arrange them in story order.

RETEACH

Comprehension

Photo Card

Focus Skill

Classify/Categorize Remind children that things that are alike in some way can be grouped together. Distribute *Photo Cards cake, pie, squirrel, porcupine, king, queen, path, road, ice, snow.* Have children put two pictures together that are alike in some way. Then ask what they remember about "The Map at Camp." Revisit the story to do a picture walk for children to point out things found at a camp.

RETEACH

Grammar/Writing

Sentences About Places Write the following sentences on chart paper.

> I like to go to the beach on hot days.
> It's fun to jump in the waves.
> The sand feels cool on my feet.
> I feel happy when I am at the beach.

Read the sentences aloud as you track the print. Tell children that these are sentences about a place. Point out how these sentences name and tell about a place, use words to describe the place, and tell how the writer feels about the place. Guide children to dictate other sentences about places.

High-Frequency Words

get	**some**
how	

Fluency

Punctuation Remind children that good readers use punctuation and capitalization to understand what they read and to know how their voice should sound.

Reread aloud "The Map at Camp" from *Heading Out*, one page at a time. Have children echo-read. Show children how to use the punctuation to know when to use a talking voice, an excited voice, or a voice that asks a question.

LESSON 6

DAY AT A GLANCE
Day 4

30+ Minutes

PHONEMIC AWARENESS
Phoneme Blending

PHONICS
Reteach Contractions *n't*, *'s*

PHONICS AND SPELLING
Reteach Variant Vowel /ô/*a* (all)

HIGH-FREQUENCY WORDS
Reteach *how, make, of, some, get*

FLUENCY
Punctuation

COMPREHENSION
Reteach Classify/Categorize

GRAMMAR/WRITING
Reteach Sentences About Places

Materials Needed:

Practice Book p.25

Copying Masters 21–22

Practice Book

Lesson 6 High-Frequency Cards

Heading Out Student Edition pp. 16–22 pp. 56–62

Spelling Words

1. all	6. tall
2. call	7. not
3. fall	8. top
4. wall	9. much
5. ball	10. thank

High-Frequency Words

how	some
make	get
of	

Phonemic Awareness

Phoneme Blending Tell children that together you are going to play a game by putting some sounds together to make words. Say: **Listen as I do the first one. /t/ /ô/ /l/. What word does /t/ /ô/ /l/ say? The word is** *tall*. **Now you try.** Continue with /w/ /ô/ /l/ (*wall*), /h/ /o/ /t/ (*hot*), /k/ /ô/ /l/ /s/ (*calls*), /p/ /i/ /k/ (*pick*), /b/ /ô/ /l/ (*ball*), /s/ /i/ /k/ (*sick*), /b/ /a/ /k/ (*back*), /ô/ /l/ (*all*).

RETEACH
Phonics

Contractions *n't*, *'s* Remind children that a contraction is a shorter way of saying two words. Write *is not* and *isn't*. Say: **The word *isn't* comes from *is not*. The letter *o* was dropped. I put an apostrophe in its place.** Repeat using *it is* (*it's*), *what is* (*what's*), *can not* (*can't*), *here is* (*here's*).

RETEACH
Phonics and Spelling

Practice Book p.25

Variant Vowel /ô/*a* (all)
Direct children's attention to page 25 of their *Practice Books*. Complete the page together.

Assess children's progress using the following dictation sentences.

1.	all	We ate **all** the grapes.
2.	call	Did you **call** home?
3.	fall	The leaves will **fall** off the trees.
4.	wall	This **wall** needs more paint.
5.	ball	Throw the **ball** to me.
6.	tall	My dad is very **tall**.

Review

7.	not	We will **not** miss the game.
8.	top	Put icing on **top** of each cupcake.

High-Frequency

9.	much	How **much** does the book cost?
10.	thank	I will **thank** Grandpa for the bike.

REVIEW
High-Frequency Words

Copying Masters 21–22

Display *High-Frequency Word Cards* for this lesson's words—*how, make, of, some,* and *get*—and the previously learned high-frequency words. Point to words at random and ask children to read them.

RETEACH

Comprehension

Classify/Categorize Review with children that things that are alike can be grouped together in categories. Ask them what they should think about when they are categorizing things. (how the things are alike) Have children look at "The Map at Camp" and "Come In!" in *Heading Out*. Draw a two-column chart. Write the story titles in the first row. Recall with children what each story is about. Do a picture walk through "The Map at Camp." Guide children to point out things they might find at a camp. Record their findings in the chart. Repeat with "Come In!" and have children point out things to eat in the story.

"The Map at Camp" things at camp	"Come In!" things to eat
lake flag rock wall tall trees	apples bananas oranges

RETEACH

Grammar/Writing

Sentences About Places Review with children characteristics of well-written sentences about places.

> ### Writing Sentences About a Place
> You should name the place.
> You should tell about the place.
> You should use words to describe the place.
> You should tell how you feel about the place.

Lead children in looking back at the sentences about the beach that you presented on Day 3. Remind them how the sentences name the place, tell about the place, use words that describe the place and how the writer feels about being there.

Have children think of another place that is familiar to all of them, such as the classroom or playground. Ask them to tell the same information about this place. Write their ideas in a list or word web. Help children compose sentences using the ideas. Read the sentences with children.

Fluency

Punctuation Reread "The Map at Camp" from *Heading Out,* modeling fluent and expressive reading.

Point out how you looked at capital letters and punctuation to make your voice rise and fall to show expression. Remind children that good readers use punctuation to know how to read a sentence.

Have children practice rereading the story several times for fluency.

DAY AT A GLANCE
Day 5

HIGH-FREQUENCY WORDS
how, make, of, some

PHONEMIC AWARENESS
Onset and Rime

PHONICS AND SPELLING
Preteach Short Vowel /e/*e*

BUILD ROBUST VOCABULARY
Preteach *chorus, odor, shoved*

GRAMMAR/WRITING
Preteach Exclamations

Materials Needed:

Lesson 6
High-Frequency
Word Cards

Sound/
Spelling
Card *Ee*

Word Builders
and Word
Builder Cards

Write-On/
Wipe-Off
Boards

Practice
Book p.26
Practice
Book

High-Frequency Words

how	of
make	some

High-Frequency Words

Copying Masters 21–22 Display *High-Frequency Word Cards* for *how, make, of, some,* and the other previously learned high-frequency words. Say the word *how,* ask a volunteer to point to *how,* and have children read the word aloud. Continue with the remaining high-frequency words. Repeat this activity several times to reinforce instant recognition.

Phonemic Awareness

Onset and Rime   Tell children that you are going to say some words, but you are going to say them in parts. **Listen as I say this word in parts.** /m/-et—The word I said was *met*. **Now you try some:** /r/-ed, /b/-ell, /l/-et, /n/-eck, /t/-ell, /l/-eg.

PRETEACH
Phonics and Spelling

Sound/Spelling Card   **Short Vowel /e/*e***
Connecting Letter to Sound   Say the words *end, ever,* and *elephant* and have children repeat the words. Explain that all three words begin with the /e/ sound. Have children say /e/ several times. Display *Sound/Spelling Card Ee.* Say the letter name and identify the picture. Tell children that *e* can stand for the sound /e/, the sound at the beginning of *end*. Tell children that this is the "short *e* sound." Have children say /e/ several times as you touch the letter.

Give each child an *e Word Builder*. Say: **When I say a word that begins with /e/, hold up your card and say /e/. When I say a word that does not begin with /e/, hold your card behind your back.** Say these words: *elbow, land, enjoy, fry, every.* Tell children that some words have the sound /e/ in the middle. Say *net,* elongating the /e/ sound. Tell children that *net* has /e/ in the middle. Then say the following words, elongating the medial sound and having children identify those with the /e/ sound: *bed, with, fed, bell, map.*

Word Blending   Demonstrate each step with *Word Builder Cards* and a *Word Builder* and have children repeat each step after you. Hold up *p* and say /p/. Hold up *e* and say /e/. Hold up *n* and say /n/.

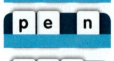

- Place the letters *p, e, n* in the *Word Builder.*
- Point to *p.* Say /p/. Point to *e* and say /e/. Prompt children to repeat after you.
- Slide *e* next to *p.* Run your hand under the letters as you blend the sounds, elongating them—/pe/.

- Point to *n* and say /n/.

- Slide *n* next to *pe*. Run your hand under *pen* as you blend the sounds, elongating them—/pen/. Read *pen* naturally.

Follow the same procedure with these words: *pet, ten, let.*

  Word Building   Place the *Word Builder Cards s, e,* and *t* in the *Word Builder.* Have children name each letter and the sound it stands for. Then read the word and have children repeat *set.* Have children build and read new words. As they build each word, write it on the board. Say:

- **Add *n* in front of *t*. What word did you make?** (*sent*)

- **Move the *t* to the front. Take off the *s*. What word did you make?** (*ten*)

Continue with the words *tell, let,* and *get.* Then have children read the words on the board. Direct children's attention to page 26 of their *Practice Books.* Complete the page together.

PRETEACH

Build Robust Vocabulary

Introduce Robust Vocabulary   Read the student-friendly explanation for each word. Then discuss each word using the following examples.

Say: **I sang in a chorus for our holiday play. Would you rather sing in a chorus or sing alone? Explain.**

Say: **When I go to the lunchroom, I get excited if I smell the odor of pizza cooking. What is an odor you like to smell at lunch?**

Say: **Sometimes, I have to shove a heavy door to close it. Would you shove dishes in a sink or pillows under your bed? Explain.**

PRETEACH

Grammar/Writing

Exclamations   Write the following simple exclamations on the board and read them aloud:

> Look out!
>
> That pot is hot!

Explain that these sentences show strong feeling. Explain that they are called **exclamations** and end with an exclamation point. Have children read the sentences silently and then read them aloud as you track the print. Point to the end mark in each sentence.

Spelling Words

1. set	6. get
2. sent	7. all
3. ten	8. call
4. tell	9. make
5. let	10. of

Have children practice writing spelling words on their *Write-on/Wipe-off Boards.*

VOCABULARY

Student-Friendly Explanations

chorus A chorus is a group singing or saying something together.

odor If something has an odor, you can tell what it is by the way it smells.

shoved If you shoved someone or something, you would push hard against that person or thing.

LESSON 7

Let's Help Cat

Let's make a pie, said Cat.

"tell" said Hen.

30+ Minutes

PHONEMIC AWARENESS
Phoneme Isolation

PHONICS AND SPELLING
Reteach Short Vowel /e/*e*

COMPREHENSION
Preteach Compare and Contrast

HIGH-FREQUENCY WORDS
Reteach *make, said, eat*

FLUENCY
Expression

GRAMMAR/WRITING
Reteach Exclamations

Materials Needed:

Photo Cards

Word Builders and Word Builder Cards

Write-On/ Wipe-Off Boards

Practice Book
p.27

Heading Out Student Edition pp. 46–52

Shooting Star Student Edition pp. 4–5

Practice Book p. 27

Phonemic Awareness

Photo Card **Phoneme Isolation**   Display *Photo Cards hen, ant,* and *berries.* Hold up *Photo Card hen.* Have children say the word *hen* aloud. Tell children to listen to the /e/ sound in the middle of the word. Have them say the name of the other two pictures. Ask: **What other picture name has the same /e/ sound you hear in *hen*?** *Berries* **has the same sound.** Continue with *Photo Cards add, ant, fish; berries, snow, toad; cake, rain, rose.*

RETEACH

Phonics and Spelling

 Short Vowel /e/*e*

Word Building   Place the *Word Builder Cards s, e, t* in the *Word Builder.* Ask children to say the name and sound of each letter. Then read the word naturally—*set.* Have children do the same. Have children build words by asking them:

- **Which letter should I add to make *set* become *sent*?** (Add *n*.)
- **Which letters should I change to make *sent* become *ten*?** (Take away the *s* and move *t* to front.)

Continue with the spelling words *tell, let,* and *get.* Have children repeat each step after you and then read the words.

Read Words in Context   Write the following sentences on chart paper. Have children read each sentence silently. Then track the print as children read the sentences aloud. Finally, point to the underlined words at random and have children read them. *Ben* <u>set</u> <u>all</u> *the bags on the bed.* <u>Let</u> *the* <u>ten</u> *cats in.* <u>Tell</u> *Tim to* <u>call</u> *his dad. Beth* <u>sent</u> *the best gift* <u>of</u> *all. Sam will* <u>get</u> *the bag. Jack can* <u>make</u> *it.*

PRETEACH

Comprehension

 Compare and Contrast   Tell children that characters in stories are alike in some ways and different in other ways. **Focus Skill** The things they do can be the same or different. Some stories have events and characters that are like other stories they have read. Explain that as they read and listen to stories, they should think about how

---

Spelling Words

1. set	6. get
2. sent	7. all
3. ten	8. call
4. tell	9. make
5. let	10. of

 Have children practice writing spelling words on their *Write-on/Wipe-off Boards.*

things are alike and different. This will help them understand the story better. Have children recall "Where Is Tom?" in *Heading Out*. Say: **When I compare characters in a story, I find the ways they are alike. In "Where is Tom?" I think about the people and Tom. They are alike because they are all in the same family. The people are different than Tom because they are people and Tom is a dog.**

High-Frequency Words

make   eat

said

RETEACH

High-Frequency Words

pp.
4–5

Write the words *make, said,* and *eat* on the board.

- Point to and read *make.* Repeat, having children say *make* with you.

- Say: **I can *make* a pie.**

- Repeat the word and then point to each letter as you spell it. Have children reread the word.

Repeat for the remaining words. Use the following sentences: *Matt* said *to sit. I want to* eat *now.*

Have children turn to page 4 of *Shooting Star* and have them read aloud the words at the top of the page. Talk about the illustrations. Then guide children in choosing and circling the word that names each picture. (4. *ten*, 5. *tell*, 6. *hen*) Have children read aloud each word in the list on page 5. Ask volunteers to read the sentences aloud. Then have children choral-read the sentences. Guide them to trace the word that completes each sentence. (1. *said*, 2. *make*, 3. *eat*)

RETEACH

Grammar/Writing

Practice Book
p.27

Exclamations   Write on the board *Look at him! That is a big dog.* Have children choral-read the sentences as you track the print. Circle the exclamation point in the first sentence. Remind children that an exclamation point means that the sentence is an exclamation, a sentence that shows strong feeling. Circle the period in the second sentence. Remind children that a period means that the sentence is a telling sentence. Talk about the differences that the end marks make in the way the sentences are read.

Have volunteers dictate exclamations, using the following sentence frame *That is a _____!* Write them on the board and read them aloud, tracking the print. Underline the exclamation mark in the first sentence. Remind children that it shows strong feeling. Rewrite the sentence with a period instead of an exclamation mark. Then read the sentence as a telling sentence and discuss the difference. Complete *Practice Book* page 27 together.

Fluency

Expression   Tell children that good readers read with expression—they read in a lively way that shows what is happening in the story and how the characters feel.

Have children open to the story "Where is Tom?" in *Heading Out*. Model by reading the first two pages to children, using appropriate expression. Then listen as children read, encouraging them to do the same.

PHONEMIC AWARENESS
Phoneme Blending

PHONICS AND SPELLING
Reteach Short Vowel /e/*e*

HIGH-FREQUENCY WORDS
Reteach *day, eat, first, said, time, was*

READING
"Let's Help Cat"

FLUENCY
Expression

BUILD ROBUST VOCABULARY
Preteach *assemble, consume, enthusiastic*

GRAMMAR/WRITING
Reteach Exclamations

Materials Needed:

Word Builders and Word Builder Cards

Practice Book p.28

Copying Masters 25–26
Lesson 7 High-Frequency Word Cards

Shooting Star Student Edition pp. 6–13

Heading Out Student Edition pp. 56–62

High-Frequency Words

day	time
eat	was
first	make
said	

Phonemic Awareness

Phoneme Blending   Tell children they are going to play a guessing game. Then say: **I'm thinking of a word that is an animal. It lays eggs. It is a /h/ /e/ /n/. What's my word? It is *hen*.** Continue with the following words: /sh/ /e/ /ll/ (*shell*), /m/ /e/ /s/ (*mess*), /r/ /e/ /d/ (*red*), /b/ /e/ /d/ (*bed*).

RETEACH

Phonics and Spelling

Short Vowel /e/*e*
Word Building   Use a *Word Builder* and *Word Builder Cards* and have children repeat each step. Build the word *let*. Blend the sounds to read the word—/let/. Then say the word naturally—*let*. Have children do the same. Lead children in building and reading new words by saying:

- **Change *e* to *o*. Read the word.** (*lot*)
- **Change *l* to *n*. Read the word.** (*not*)

Continue in a similar manner with these words: *net, pet, top, pot, plot, get, got.*

Read Words in Context   Have children turn to *Practice Book* page 28. Read each sentence aloud and have children echo-read. Then ask volunteers to read each sentence aloud. Ask: **How many eggs does Ben have?** (ten) **What does Meg have?** (a pot) **Who is helping Ben and Meg?** (Mom) Call on volunteers to frame and read short *e* and short *o* words. Then have children find and circle all the short *e* words. Finally, have them underline all the short *o* words.

RETEACH

High-Frequency Words

Write the words *day, eat, first, said, time, was,* and *make* on the board. Give each child a set of *High-Frequency Word Cards*. Point to each word on the board and read the word aloud, having children hold up the card for that word. Then have children shuffle their cards. Repeat the activity, pointing to words at random and having children hold up the card for that word.

Reading

Build Background: "Let's Help Cat"
Talk about stories in which animals are like people. Remind children of the previously read story "Is Jack Late?" in which animals talk and act like people. Explain to children that they will be reading a story in which

animals do things that people do. Then have children tell about a time they worked together with others to make something. Ask: **Did you help out? What did you do?**

Monitor Comprehension: "Let's Help Cat"

Ask children to look at the first page of the story and ask a volunteer to read the title. Then have children predict what might happen in the story. Guide children through the story as they read.

**pp.
6–7**

Say: **I see many animals in these pictures. It looks like they're excited about something. Let's read these pages to find out why.**

After reading the pages, ask: **What are the animals going to do?** (They are going to make a pie with Cat.) **Look at the picture. What kind of pie do you think Cat wants to make?** (Possible response: I see apples, so I think Cat is going to make an apple pie.) **MAKE INFERENCES**

Ask: **How many animals want to help Cat make the pie?** (five) **NOTE DETAILS**

Ask: **How are these animals alike? How are they different?** (They are alike because they are all animals, but they are different types of animals.)  **COMPARE AND CONTRAST**

Ask: **Some of the words on theses pages have the /e/ sound. Find these words and let's say them together.** (Let's, Yes, Hen) **APPLY PHONICS**

**pp.
8–9**

Say: **We can see that the animals are working. Let's read to find out more.**

After reading the pages, ask: **What are Goat and Horse doing?** (Goat is mixing and Horse is helping roll the dough.) **How do you know?** (The pictures show what they are doing and they both say what they are doing.) **NOTE DETAILS**

Ask: **How are Goat and Horse's jobs different? How are they alike?** (Goat is mixing and Horse is rolling, but they are both helping to make the pie.) **COMPARE AND CONTRAST**

Ask: **What do you think will happen next?** (Possible response: I think they will finish making the pie.) **MAKE PREDICTIONS**

Fluency

Expression Have children turn to "The Map at Camp" from *Heading Out*. Remind them that an exclamation point at the end of a sentence means that the sentence shows strong feeling, like excitement.

Model reading the last page of the story excitedly. Then remind children that a period at the end of a sentence indicates that it should be read with a calmer voice. Model with a sentence from the story.

pp. 10–11

Say: **In the first picture, I can see that Cow is busy. In the second picture, it looks like the pie is finished. It also looks like pig is up to something. Let's read to find out what happens next.**

After reading the pages, ask: **What is Cow doing?** (Cow is getting a pan to put the pie in.) **Read the sentence that tells what Cow is doing.** (*"I will get a pan," said Cow.*) Note Details

Ask: **How does Pig look on the next page?** (He looks happy.) **Why do you think he looks like this?** (Pig is happy to eat the pie.) Character's Emotions/Draw Conclusions

Ask: **Which word on these pages has the /e/ sound?** (*get*) Apply Phonics

 page 12

Say: **It looks like Pig doesn't have the pie anymore. Let's read to see what happens.**

After reading the pages, ask: **What are the animals doing?** (They are getting ready to eat the pie.) Draw Conclusions

Ask: **Why do you think Cat says "We will eat it!"?** (Possible response: Everyone helped except for Pig, so everyone should share the pie.) Make Inferences

Ask: **How do you think Pig feels about this?** (Possible response: Pig is embarrassed.) **What is Pig doing now?** (Possible response: Pig is helping with the plates so he can eat the pie, too.) Character's Traits/Draw Conclusions

 page 13

Answers to *Think Critically* Questions
Help children read and answer the *Think Critically* questions on page 13. Answers are shown below.

1. ‹apple pie› Note Details
2. ‹Goat mixes› Sequence
3. ‹Cow gets a pan› Answer Questions

PRETEACH
Build Robust Vocabulary

Introduce Robust Vocabulary Read the student-friendly explanation for each word. Then discuss each word using the following examples.

Say: **We assemble a puzzle by putting all the pieces together. What is something you would like to assemble—an apple or a model airplane?**

Say: **Elephants consume peanuts. Would you prefer to consume a chocolate sundae or a fresh salad? Explain.**

Say: **I am enthusiastic about taking a fun trip. Would you be more enthusiastic about visiting the dentist or going to the movies?**

RETEACH
Grammar/Writing

Exclamations Write the following sentences on the board:

> What is that crash?
>
> Look out! It is just my dog.
>
> He made such a mess!

Read all sentences to children as you track the print. Underline the first exclamation and reread the sentence. Say: **This is an exclamation. One of the other sentences is an exclamation, too. Which sentence is it?** Guide children to name the sentence that is an exclamation and explain how they know. Then circle the exclamation points in both exclamations.

Write the following sentence on the board: *That pot is so hot. Meg ran fast.* Have children read the sentences. Ask volunteers to come to the board and change the sentences so they are exclamations and not telling sentences. Then ask the rest of the group to read aloud the sentences and explain why they are now correct.

VOCABULARY
Student-Friendly Explanations

assemble If you assemble something, you put all of its pieces together.

consume If you consume something, you completely use it up.

enthusiastic If you are enthusiastic about something, you really like it and are excited about it.

DAY AT A GLANCE

Day 3

30+ Minutes

PHONEMIC AWARENESS
Phoneme Segmentation

PHONICS
Preteach Initial Blends with *l*

PHONICS AND SPELLING
Reteach Short Vowel /e/*e*

HIGH-FREQUENCY WORDS
Reteach *make, said, eat*

FLUENCY
Expression

COMPREHENSION
Reteach Compare and Contrast

GRAMMAR/WRITING
Reteach Sentences About Events

Materials Needed:

Write-On/Wipe-Off Boards with Phonemic Awareness Disks

Word Builders and Word Builder Cards

Lesson 7 Story Strips

Shooting Star Student Edition pp. 6–12

Photo Cards

Spelling Words

1. set	6. get
2. sent	7. all
3. ten	8. call
4. tell	9. make
5. let	10. of

Phonemic Awareness

Phoneme Segmentation   Have children use the three boxes on the *Write-on/Wipe-off Boards*. Remind children that the boxes stand for the sounds in words. Say *let* and ask: **What is the first sound you hear in** *let*? **The first sound in** *let* **is** /l/. Have children place a disk in the first box. Then have children name the second sound in *let* (/e/) and place a disk in the second box. Have them identify the last sound in *let* (/t/) and place a disk in the third box. Point to each box in sequence as children say the word. Say: **How many sounds do you hear in** *let*? **There are three.** Repeat with: *red, ten, pen, leaf, sock.*

Phonics

Initial Blends with *l*   Write the following words on the board and read them aloud: *sip, pot, back*. Then write these words on the board: *slip, plot, black*. Ask a volunteer to tell what is different between *sip* and *slip* as you point to the words. Then underline the *l* in *slip*. Pronounce the words *sip* and *slip* as you point to each word. Have children repeat. Then have them read aloud *pot-plot* and *back-black*.

Phonics and Spelling

 Short Vowel /e/*e*

Build Words   Form words and have children listen to your directions and change one letter in the word to spell a spelling word using their *Word Builder Cards* and *Word Builders*. Form *sat* and have children read the word. Ask: **Which spelling word can you make by changing the middle letter?** (*set*)

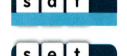

Follow a similar procedure with the following words: *set* (*sent*), *sent* (*ten*), *ten* (*tell*), *tell* (*let*), *fall* (*all, call*).

Remind children that there are some other words they have to remember how to spell. Have children say *make*. Tell them to put *Word Builder Cards* *m, a, k, e* in their *Word Builders*, picture the word *make* in their minds, and build the word. Write the word on the board. Follow the same procedure with the word *of*.

High-Frequency Words

 Duplicate and distribute *Copying Masters* 27–28 to each child. Explain that the sentences tell about the story "Let's Help Cat" but some have missing words. List the words *make, said,* and *eat* on the board. Have children read each word aloud.

Have children read aloud each story strip sentence, name the word that makes sense in the sentence, and point to the correct word on the board. Have children write the missing words in the blanks and read the completed sentences aloud. Help children cut apart the strips, read the completed sentences, and arrange them in story order.

High-Frequency Words

make   eat

said

RETEACH

Comprehension

  Compare and Contrast   Remind children how thinking about how things are alike and different can help them better understand stories and information they read.

Review the skill by comparing two things. Display *Photo Cards octopus* and *fish.* Tell children that both are similar, because they are animals and can be found living underwater, but they are different because a fish has fins and an octopus has legs or tentacles. Use these *Photo Cards* to reinforce the skill: *farm, factory; king, queen.*

RETEACH

Grammar/Writing

Sentences About Events   Write the following sentences on the board:

> I kicked a ball.
>
> I went to a big pond.

Read the sentences with children. Say: **These sentences tell about events, or things that I did.** Point out to children that sentences about events have words in them such as *I, my, me,* and *we.* Explain that each sentence begins with a capital letter and ends with an end mark. Ask children to suggest other sentences about interesting things they have done.

Fluency

Expression Say the following sentence two times, once in a monotone and once with expression: **Look at the beautiful sunshine!**

Talk with children about the differences between the two ways you said the sentence. Then have children turn to "Let's Help Cat" in *Shooting Star.*

Say: **I'm going to read "Let's Help Cat" one page at a time. I'm going to look at the marks at the ends of sentences to help me decide how to read. I'm going to use my voice to show how the characters feel. Read each page after me, just the way I read it.**

LESSON 7

30+ Minutes

DAY AT A GLANCE
Day 4

PHONEMIC AWARENESS
Phoneme Blending

PHONICS
Reteach Initial Blends with *l*

PHONICS AND SPELLING
Reteach Short Vowel /e/*e*

HIGH-FREQUENCY WORDS
Reteach *day, eat, first, said, time, was, make*

FLUENCY
Expression

COMPREHENSION
Reteach Compare and Contrast

GRAMMAR/WRITING
Reteach Sentences About Events

Materials Needed:

Practice Book

Lesson 7 High-Frequency Word Cards

Shooting Star Student Edition pp. 6–12

Heading Out Student Edition pp. 36–42

Spelling Words

1. set	6. get
2. sent	7. all
3. ten	8. call
4. tell	9. make
5. let	10. of

Phonemic Awareness

Phoneme Blending Tell children that together you are going to play a game of "Fix It." Tell them that you are going to say some words that are all broken and they should listen to see if they can put sounds together to figure out the word. Say: **/t/ /e/ /n/. What word does /t/ /e/ /n/ say? It says** *ten*. Continue with the following words: /p/ /a/ /t/ (*pat*), /s/ /i/ /k/ (*sick*), /b/ /e/ /l/ (*bell*), /f/ /i/ /t/ (*fit*), /s/ /e/ /t/ (*set*).

RETEACH
Phonics

Initial Blends with *l* Write the following words on the board: *cap, bank, fat.* Ask children to read aloud the words. Then ask what letter they would add to make *clap, blank,* and *flat.* Write *clap, blank,* and *flat* on the board under the first set of words and ask volunteers to circle the letter that is different in the second set of words.

RETEACH
Phonics and Spelling

Practice Book p.29

Short Vowel /e/*e*
Direct children's attention to page 29 of their *Practice Books.* Complete the page together.

Assess children's progress using the following dictation sentences.

1. set — **Set** that cup here.
2. sent — I **sent** her a package.
3. ten — After nine comes **ten.**
4. tell — I can **tell** the time.
5. let — Will you **let** me have a turn?
6. get — I can **get** a new book.

Review

7. all — They **all** like to play.
8. call — She will **call** me on the phone.

High-Frequency

9. make — Can you **make** me a snack?
10. of — I have a box **of** markers.

RETEACH

High-Frequency Words

Copying
Masters
25–26

Display *High-Frequency Word Cards* for this lesson's words—*day, eat, first, said, time, was* and *make*—and the previously learned high-frequency words. Point to words at random and have children read them.

RETEACH

Comprehension

Compare and Contrast Ask children to tell what it means to compare things and to contrast things. (to tell how things are alike; to tell how things are different) Have them compare and contrast two objects, such as a piece of notebook paper and a piece of construction paper.

Recall with children the story "Let's Help Cat" from *Shooting Star* and "Is Jack Late?" from *Heading Out*. On the board or on chart paper, draw a two-column chart. Discuss with children how the stories are alike and how they are different. Work together to complete the chart.

Alike	Different
• Both stories have animals as characters. • The animals talk in both stories.	• In one story, the animals are getting ready to go somewhere. In the other, they make a pie. • Different animals are in both stories.

RETEACH

Grammar/Writing

Sentences About Events Review with children sentences about events.

Sentences About Events

The sentences tell about things I have done.
They have words such as *I*, *my*, *me*, and *we*.
Each sentence begins with a capital letter and ends with an end mark.

Write the following sentence on chart paper: *I kicked the ball in the pond.* Explain that the sentence tells about something that the writer has done. Go through the list of characteristics of sentences about events and check each point with the sentence. Then ask children to dictate other sentences about things that have happened to them. Write the sentences on the paper. Read the sentences aloud and have children echo-read.

High-Frequency Words

day	time
eat	was
first	make
said	

Fluency

Expression Have children practice reading "Let's Help Cat" in *Shooting Star*. Remind them to use their voices to show the feelings they think the characters have. Listen to children read, giving them guidance to help them improve their reading with expression.

30+ Minutes

DAY AT A GLANCE

Day 5

HIGH-FREQUENCY WORDS
day, eat, first, said, time, was, make

PHONEMIC AWARENESS
Onset and Rime

PHONICS AND SPELLING
Preteach Digraph /th/*th*

BUILD ROBUST VOCABULARY
Preteach *applauded, chatty, gather*

GRAMMAR/WRITING
Preteach Nouns: People or Places

Materials Needed:

Copying Masters 25–26

Lesson 7 High-Frequency Word Cards

Sound/Spelling Card *th*

Word Builders and Word Builder Cards

Write-On/Wipe-Off Boards

Practice Book p.30

Practice Book

Photo Card

Photo Cards

High-Frequency Words

day	said	make
eat	time	
first	was	

High-Frequency Words

Copying Masters 25–26 Display *High-Frequency Word Cards* for *day, eat, first, said, time, was, make* and the other previously learned high-frequency words. Say the word *day*, ask a volunteer to point to *day*, and have children read the word aloud. Continue with the remaining high-frequency words. Repeat this activity several times to reinforce instant recognition.

Phonemic Awareness

Onset and Rime Tell children you are going to say some words, but you are going to say them in parts. Say: **Listen as I say this word in parts. /th/-en—The word I said was** *then*. **Now you try: /th/-em, /th/-at, /b/-ath, /w/-ith.**

PRETEACH

Phonics and Spelling

Sound/Spelling Card **Digraph /th/*th***
Connecting Letter to Sound Say the words *thin, thick,* and *think* and have children repeat the words. Explain that all three words begin with the /th/ sound. Have children say /th/ several times. Tell children that *th* also stands for a slightly different sound, as in the word *then*. Have children say the voiced /th/ several times. Say: **The word** *then, this, that,* **and** *the* **all begin with the /th/ sound.** Display *Sound/Spelling Card th*. Say the names of the letters and identify the picture. Tell children that the letters *t* and *h* can make the sound /th/, the sound at the beginning of *think*. Have children say /th/ several times as you touch the letters.

Give each child *t* and *h* *Word Builder* and *Word Builder Cards*. Say: **When I say a word that begins with /th/, hold up your card and say /th/. When I say a word that does not begin with /th/, hold your card behind your back.** Say these words: *think, this, the, hat, free, they*. Tell children that some words have the sound /th/ at the end. The word *math* has /th/ at the end. Follow the same procedure for the ending position with the following words: *north, moth, job, bath, jam, east, tooth*.

Word Blending Demonstrate each step with *Word Builder Cards* and a *Word Builder* and have children repeat each step after you. Hold up *th* and say /th/. Hold up *i* and say /i/. Hold up *s* and say /s/.

- Place the digraph *th* and the letters *i* and *s* in the *Word Builder*.
- Point to *th* and say /th/. Point to *i* and say /i/.

- Slide *i* next to *th*. Run your hand under the letters as you blend the sounds, elongating them—/thi/.

- Point to *s* and say /ss/.

- Slide *s* next to *thi*. Run your hand under *this* as you blend the sounds, elongating them—/this/. Read *this* naturally.

Follow the same procedure with these words: *then, path, moth*.

  Word Building Place the *Word Builder Cards t, h, e,* and *n* in the *Word Builder* and have children do the same. Ask children to say each letter name and the sound it stands for. Then read the word naturally—*then*. Have children do the same. Have children build and read new words. As they build each word, write it on the board. Say:

- **Change *n* to *m*. What word did you make?** (*them*)

- **Change *e* to *i*. Change *m* to *s*. What word did you make?** (*this*)

Continue with the words *that, path,* and *with*. Have children read the words on the board. Complete *Practice Book* page 30 together.

PRETEACH

Build Robust Vocabulary

Introduce Robust Vocabulary Read the student-friendly explanation for each word. Then discuss each word using the following examples.

Say: **I saw a great play the other night. When it was over, I applauded for the people on stage. When was a time you applauded for someone?**

Say: **My friend is very chatty when she has a lot to tell me. Who is someone you know that is very chatty? Are you very chatty? Explain.**

Say: **When we clean up the classroom, we gather books and materials to put them away. When is a time you have gathered something?**

PRETEACH

Grammar/Writing

 Nouns: People or Places Write the following sentence on the board and read it aloud: *The girl went to the park.* Ask children what place is mentioned in the sentence, and underline it. (*park*) Do the same for the person mentioned in the sentence. (*girl*) Explain that many sentences have words that name people or places and these words are called nouns. Display *Photo Cards house* and *king*. Write this sentence on the board: *The king is at his house.* Read the sentence aloud. Point out that the house is a place and a king is a person and that these words are nouns. Guide children to dictate sentences about people and places and identify the nouns.

Spelling Words

1. then	6. with
2. them	7. ten
3. this	8. get
4. that	9. said
5. path	10. was

 Have children practice writing spelling words on their *Write-on/Wipe-off Boards*.

VOCABULARY

Student-Friendly Explanations

applauded If you applauded for someone, you clapped your hands.

chatty If you are chatty, you really like to talk.

gather If you gather things, you bring them together in one place.

Day 1

30+ Minutes

LESSON 8

PHONEMIC AWARENESS
Phoneme Isolation

PHONICS AND SPELLING
Reteach Digraph /th/*th*

COMPREHENSION
Preteach Details

HIGH-FREQUENCY WORDS
Reteach *says, water, her*

FLUENCY
Expression

GRAMMAR/WRITING
Reteach Nouns: People or Places

Materials Needed:

Practice Book p.31

Word Builders
and Word
Builder Cards

Write-On/
Wipe-Off
Boards

Practice
Book

Shooting Star
Student Edition
pp. 6–12
pp. 14–15

Spelling Words

1. then	6. with
2. them	7. ten
3. this	8. get
4. that	9. said
5. path	10. was

Have children practice writing
spelling words on their
Write-on/Wipe-off Boards.

Phonemic Awareness

Phoneme Isolation   Say the word *thumb* aloud, and have children repeat
it. Tell children to listen to the /th/ sound at the beginning of *thumb.* Then
say the words *third* and *ten* and have children repeat both words. Ask: **Which
of these words has the /th/ sound you hear at the beginning of *thumb*?**
***Third* does.** Continue with: *think, too, thorn; path, bed, bath; with, pat, moth.*

RETEACH

Phonics and Spelling

Digraph /th/*th*

Word Building   Place the *Word Builder Cards t, h, e, n* in the
Word Builder. Remind children that the letters *th* stand for the sound /th/.
Ask children to say the name and sound of each letter. Then
read the word naturally—*then.* Have children do the same.
Continue building new words by asking children:

- **Which letter should I change to make *then* become
  them?** (Change *n* to *m.*)

- **Which letters should I change to make *them*
  become *this*?** (Change *em* to *is.*)

Continue with the words *that, path, with.*

Read Words in Context   Write the following sentences on chart paper.
Have children read each sentence silently. Then track the print as children
read the sentences aloud. Finally, point to the underlined words at random
and have children read them. *Can I have <u>this</u> hat or <u>that</u> hat? <u>Ten</u> hens sit on
the <u>path</u>. She <u>said</u> she will run <u>with</u> us. Can I <u>get</u> hats for <u>them</u>? I sat, <u>then</u> I
ran. Ben <u>was</u> at the pond.*

PRETEACH

Comprehension

Details   Explain that details are small bits of information
that tell more about something. Ask children to turn to the
first page of "Let's Help Cat" in *Shooting Star.* Read the
page and say: **What do we find out on this page? We find out that Cat wants
to make something. What does Cat want to make? Cat wants to make a pie.**

That is a detail. Reread the story to children and guide them to point out details in the story. Ask: **What is Goat doing?** (mixing) **What does Cow get?** (a pan) Guide children through a picture walk of the story and help them use the pictures to point out more details from the story.

RETEACH

High-Frequency Words

pp. 14–15

Write the words *says*, *water*, and *her* on the board.

- Point to and read *says*. Repeat, having children say *says* with you.
- Say: **She *says* I can go.**
- Repeat the word and then point to each letter as you spell it. Then have children say and spell *says* with you. Have children reread the word.

Repeat for the remaining words. Use the following sentences: *There is* water *in the lake.* Her *name is Latrice.*

Have children turn to page 14 of *Shooting Star* and have them read aloud the words at the top of the page. Talk about the illustrations. Then guide children in choosing and circling the word that names each picture. (4. *thick,* 5. *thin,* 6. *bath*) Have children read aloud each word in the list on page 15. Ask volunteers to read the sentences aloud. Then have children choral-read the sentences. Guide them to trace the word that completes each sentence. (1. *water,* 2. *says,* 3. *her*)

RETEACH

Grammar/Writing

Practice Book
31

Nouns: People or Places   Write these sentences on the board and read them aloud with children as you track the print.

> My mom likes to jog.
>
> My dad likes to jog, too.
>
> My mom jogs on a path.
>
> My dad jogs by the pond.
>
> My dad sees a dock.

Read each sentence aloud again, and guide children to point to and underline the nouns that name people or places. Then work with children to make two lists on the board: one with the nouns that name people and the other with nouns that name places. Discuss how the nouns that name people answer the question "Who is this sentence about?" and the nouns that name places answer "Where does the action take place?" Complete *Practice Book* page 31 together.

High-Frequency Words

says	her
water	

Fluency

Expression   Remind children that good readers read with expression—they use their voice to show how the characters in the story feel. Review with them that end marks, such as question marks, and exclamation points, are signals tthat show whether they should make their voice go up at the end of a sentence, as in a question, or read with an excited tone, as in an exclamation.

Model reading aloud "Let's Help Cat" in *Shooting Star* with expression as children follow along. Have children echo-read.

DAY AT A GLANCE
Day 2

PHONEMIC AWARENESS
Phoneme Blending

PHONICS AND SPELLING
Reteach Digraph /th/*th*

HIGH-FREQUENCY WORDS
Review *don't, her, line, Mr., new, says, water*

FLUENCY
Expression

READING
"Beth Can Help"

BUILD ROBUST VOCABULARY
Preteach *duty, envy, resent*

GRAMMAR/WRITING
Reteach Nouns: People or Places

Materials Needed:

| Word Builders and Word Builder Cards | Practice Book | Lesson 8 High-Frequency Word Cards |

Shooting Star Student Edition pp. 16–23   *Heading Out* Student Edition pp. 46–52

High-Frequency Words

don't	new
her	says
line	water
Mr.	

Phonemic Awareness

Phoneme Blending   Tell children that they are going to play a guessing game. Then say, **I'm thinking of a word that is an insect. It has wings. It is a /m/ /o/ /th/. My word is** *moth.* Have children guess the following words: /th/ /i/ /n/ (thin), /th/ /e/ /m/ (them), /b/ /a/ /th/ (bath), /m/ /a/ /th/ (math).

RETEACH

Phonics and Spelling

 **Digraph /th/*th***
Word Building   Use a *Word Builder* and *Word Builder Cards* and have children repeat each step after you. Build the word *thin.* Have children name each letter and tell whether it is a consonant or a vowel. Remind children that two consonants together, *t* and *h,* stand for the /th/ sound. Ask children to say the word naturally—*thin.* Lead children in building and reading new words. Say:

- **Change *i* to *e.* Read the word.** (then)
- **Change *e* to *a.* Read the word.** (than)
- **Add *k* to the end. Read the word.** (thank)

Continue with the following words: *thanking, thinking, think.*

 Read Words in Context   Ask children to turn to *Practice Book* page 32. Read each sentence aloud and have children echo-read. Then ask volunteers to read each sentence aloud. Ask: **Who does Seth have math with?** (Mr. Smith) **What does Seth think is fun?** (math) **When Seth thinks hard, what can he do?** (add) Guide children to circle all the words with the /th/ sound. Then have students read aloud each word with the /th/ sound.

REVIEW

High-Frequency Words

Display the *High-Frequency Word Cards* for *don't, her, line, Mr., new, says,* and *water.* Point to each card and read the word. Have children repeat. Then randomly point to the words, and ask children to read each one. Distribute one card to each child. Ask children to read their word several times silently so they know it. Tell children that you are going to play a game. Then demonstrate how the game goes by saying: **I will ask, "Who has *Mr.*?" If I have it, I will say, "I do" and show the card to everyone like this, and we will all say the word together.** Have children repeat several times, switching cards with one another each turn.

Reading

pp.
16–
23 **Build Background: "Beth Can Help"**
Read the title with children. Ask them to tell about a time that they
helped out at home. Then ask children if they have ever worked in a
garden. Invite volunteers to tell about helping in a garden. Ask: **Did you plant
something? What did you grow? Did you grow fruits? Flowers? Vegetables?**
Lead children in a brief discussion about other ways to help out.

Monitor Comprehension: "Beth Can Help"
Have children turn to the first page of the selection. Ask a volunteer to reread
the title. Have children to look at the picture on page 16. Ask children to think
about what the selection will be about and what the characters will be doing.
Then guide children through the selection as they read.

pp.
16–
17 Say: **Look at the picture. Who do you think these people might be?
What do you think they are doing? Let's read to find out.**

After reading the pages, ask: **What is the girl's name in the story?**
(Beth) **Underline the letters in her name that have the /th/ sound.**
APPLY PHONICS

Ask: **What does Mom say that Beth can do?** (dig) NOTE DETAILS

Ask: **What does Mom tell Beth to get?** (a shovel) **What will Beth do
with the shovel?** (dig) MAKE INFERENCES

pp.
18–
19 Say: **We can see that Mom and Beth are still in the garden. I also
see someone else helping. They look like they are doing something
new. Let's read on to find out what happens.**

After reading the pages, ask: **What are Mom and Beth doing in the
garden?** (They are planting.) **What is another way Mom says Beth
can help?** (Mom says that Beth can plant.) NOTE DETAILS

Ask: **What does Mom tell Beth to do to help plant?** (She tells Beth to
get some seeds.) NOTE DETAILS

Ask: **What are the ways Beth has helped so far?** (Beth has helped
dig and helped plant.) SUMMARIZE

Ask: **Who do you think the older lady is in the second picture?**
(Possible response: Beth's grandmother) DRAW CONCLUSIONS

Fluency

Expression Have children
turn to "Where is Tom?" in
Heading Out. Model how to
read with expression and have
children echo-read. Then read the
pages in a monotone, and have
children compare which way adds
more meaning to the story. Remind
children that reading with
expression is important to show
characters' feelings and to add
meaning to what is happening.

Say: **We can see that Beth and her Mom are doing other jobs. Let's read on to find out what they're doing.**

After reading the pages, ask: **What are Beth and her Mom doing?** (They are watering the garden.) **How does Beth help?** (Beth gets a bucket.) **NOTE DETAILS**

Ask: **What are the steps Beth and her Mom have gone through to make their garden?** (They dug, planted, and watered.) **SEQUENCE**

Ask: **What do you think might be the next thing that happens in the garden?** (Possible response: Plants might grow in the garden.) **MAKE PREDICTIONS**

Ask: **There are two words on page 20 with the /th/ sound. Find and read the words** (*that, Beth*) **APPLY PHONICS**

Say: **Look at the garden! Let's read on to find out what happened.**

After reading the pages, ask: **What happens in the garden?** (The plants get big.) **NOTE DETAILS**

Ask: **Why do you think the plants got so big?** (Possible response: The plants got big because they got enough water and sun and Beth and Mom took care of them.) **CAUSE AND EFFECT**

Ask: **How do you think Beth feels about the help she gave?** (Possible response: She is happy because her hard work helped grow plants.) **CHARACTERS' EMOTIONS**

Answers to *Think Critically* Questions

Help children read and answer the *Think Critically* questions on page 23. Answers are shown below.

1. ‹the garden› **SETTING**

 2. ‹elderly female from the story› **NOTE DETAILS**

3. ‹Beth next to her fully grown plants› **BEGINNING, MIDDLE, ENDING**

PRETEACH

Build Robust Vocabulary

Introduce Robust Vocabulary   Read the student-friendly explanation for each word. Then discuss each word using the following examples.

Say: **It is my duty to teach information to my class. What is a duty that you have at home?**

Say: **You might feel envy if you see someone eating pizza while you have to eat broccoli. What is something that has made you feel envy?**

Say: **You might resent someone if you see that a classmate gets to feed the class pet and you don't get to. Do you think it is good to resent someone? Why?**

RETEACH

Grammar/Writing

Nouns: People or Places   Write the following sentences on the board. Read the first one aloud.

> Six <u>boys</u> went to the (camp.)
> My <u>mom</u> ran on the (path.)
> That <u>man</u> went to the (bank.)
> His <u>dad</u> is on the (hill.)

Underline the noun that names a person in the first sentence. (*boys*) Circle the noun that names a place. (*camp*) Remind children that the words *boys* and *camp* are nouns. Then guide children to underline the nouns in the sentences that name people and circle the nouns in the sentences that name places. Have children choral-read the sentences as you track the print.

VOCABULARY

Student-Friendly Explanations

duty   A duty is a job you have to do.

envy   When you feel envy, you want something that someone else has.

resent   You might resent someone if you feel that that person is being treated better, or more fairly, than you are.

LESSON 8

30+ Minutes

PHONEMIC AWARENESS
Phoneme Segmentation

PHONICS
Preteach Initial Blends with *s*

PHONICS AND SPELLING
Reteach Digraph /th/*th*

HIGH-FREQUENCY WORDS
Reteach *says, water, her*

FLUENCY
Expression

COMPREHENSION
Reteach Details

GRAMMAR/WRITING
Reteach Questions

Materials Needed:

Copying Masters 31–32

Write-On/ Wipe-Off Boards with Phonemic Awareness Disks

Word Builders and Word Builder Cards

Lesson 8 Story Strips

Shooting Star Student Edition pp. 16–22

Spelling Words

1. then	6. with
2. them	7. ten
3. this	8. get
4. that	9. said
5. path	10. was

Phonemic Awareness

Phoneme Segmentation Have children use the three boxes on the *Write-on/Wipe-off Boards.* Remind children that the boxes stand for the sounds in words. Say the word *thumb* and ask: **What is the first sound you hear in *thumb?*** (/th/) Have children place a disk in the first box. Then have children name the second sound in *thumb* (/u/) and place a disk in the second box. Then have them identify the last sound in *thumb* (/m/) and place a disk in the third box. Point to each box in sequence as children say the word. Ask: **How many sounds do you hear in *thumb?* I hear three.** Repeat the procedure with: *thick, that, with, path.*

PRETEACH

Phonics

Initial Blends with *s* Write these words on the board: *top, nap, lick.* Read the words aloud and have children repeat the words. Then add these words: *stop, snap, slick.* Point to the word pairs, and have children read them aloud: *top-stop, nap-snap, lick-slick.* Have children tell what was added to the second word in each pair. (*s*) Then underline the *s* blend in each word. Repeat with *led-sled, lip-slip, tank-stank, mall-small, can-scan, kid-skid.* Guide children to underline the *s* blend in each word.

RETEACH

Phonics and Spelling

Digraph /th/*th*
Build Words Use *Word Builder Cards* and a *Word Builder* to form words. Have children listen to your directions and change a letter in each word to spell a spelling word. Form *the* and have children read the word. Ask: **Which two spelling words can you make by adding another letter to the end of *the?*** (*then, them*)

Follow a similar procedure with the following words: *pan* (*path*), *sat* (*that*), *win* (*with*), *thin* (*this*), *men* (*ten*), *got* (*get*).

Remind children that there are some other words they have to remember how to spell. Have children say *said.* Tell them to put *Word Builder Cards* *s, a, i, d* in their *Word Builders,* picture the word *said* in their minds, and build the word. Write the word on the board. Follow the same procedure with *was.*

RETEACH

High-Frequency Words

Copying Masters 31–32 Duplicate and distribute *Copying Masters* 31–32 to each child. Explain that the sentences tell the story "Beth Can Help" but some have missing words.

List the words *says, water,* and *her* on the board. Have children read aloud each story strip sentence and name the correct word on the board that makes sense in the sentence. Have children write the missing words in the blanks and read the completed sentences aloud. Help children cut apart the strips, read the completed sentences, and arrange them in story order.

RETEACH

Comprehension

  Details Remind children that details are bits of information that tell more about something. Have them turn to "Beth Can Help" in *Shooting Star*. Guide children to name a few details about what Beth did to help. (Beth got a shovel, bucket, and seeds.) Then do a picture walk through the story. Invite volunteers to point out other details they see in the pictures.

RETEACH

Grammar/Writing

Questions Write the following questions on the board: *When is lunch? What is your name? Who is your teacher? Where do you live?* Read the questions aloud as you track the print and have children echo-read. Explain that these sentences are called questions. Explain that questions are used to ask for information.

Read the questions to children again. Point out that questions often begin with words like *who, when, where, why,* or *how,* as you circle *When, What, Who,* and *Where* in the questions on the board. Then tell children that questions begin with a capital letter and end with a question mark. Guide children to identify the capital letter and the question mark in each sentence.

High-Frequency Words

says	**her**
water	

Fluency

Expression Have children turn to "Beth Can Help" in *Shooting Star*. Remind children that reading with expression makes what they say more interesting to the people who are listening.

Say: **I'm going to read "Beth Can Help" one page at a time. I'm going to keep in mind that quotation marks around words mean people are speaking, and I'll use my voice to sound as much like a person talking as I can. After I read each page, read the page after me, just the way I read it.**

Have children practice reading the story several times.

LESSON 8

30+ Minutes

DAY AT A GLANCE
Day 4

PHONEMIC AWARENESS
Phoneme Blending

PHONICS
Reteach Initial Blends with *s*

PHONICS AND SPELLING
Reteach Digraph /th/*th*

HIGH-FREQUENCY WORDS
Reteach *don't, her, line, Mr., new, says, water*

FLUENCY
Expression

COMPREHENSION
Reteach Details

GRAMMAR/WRITING
Reteach Questions

Materials Needed:

Practice
Book

Lesson 8
High-Frequency
Word Cards

Shooting Star
Student Edition
pp. 6–12
pp. 16–22

Photo
Cards

Spelling Words

1. then	6. with
2. them	7. ten
3. this	8. get
4. that	9. said
5. path	10. was

Phonemic Awareness

Phoneme Blending   Tell children that together you are going to play a puzzle game. Tell them you are going to say some words sound by sound, and that they should put the sounds together like the pieces of a puzzle to figure out the word. Say: **/th/ /i/ /k/. I hear those sounds and put them together to make *thick*.** Continue with the following words: /th/ /i/ /s/ (*this*), /th/ /ī/ (*thigh*), /m/ /u/ /g/ (*mug*), /th/ /e/ /n/ (*then*), /s/ /u/ /n/ (*sun*), /m/ /a/ /th/ (*math*).

RETEACH

Phonics

Initial Blends with *s*   Write the following words on the board: *tack, kill, lid*. Have children say the words aloud with you as you point to every one. Then say the words *stack, skill,* and *slid.* Ask children what letter they would add to make those words. Guide volunteers to add an *s* to make *stack, skill,* and *slid.* Then write *rip, pots, dig, tall,* and *top* on the board. Have children take turns adding *s* to the beginning of each word. Tell children that adding *s* does not always make a real word. Have children read each word and guide them to figure out if they made a real word.

RETEACH

Phonics and Spelling

Digraphs /th/*th*
Direct children's attention to page 33 of their *Practice Books*. Complete the page together.

Assess children's progress using the following sentences.

1. then — First we work and **then** we play.
2. them — Give **them** the toys.
3. this — **This** is the day we go to the park.
4. that — Eat **that** piece of fruit.
5. path — Can we take that **path** to the camp?
6. with — Did you go **with** Mikayla?

Review

7. ten — We have **ten** crayons.
8. get — Can you **get** a plate for me?

High-Frequency

9. said — She **said,** "I want to go!"
10. was — Today, he **was** early for school.

RETEACH

High-Frequency Words

Copying Masters 29–30

Display *High-Frequency Word Cards* for this lesson's words—*don't, her, line, Mr., new, says, water*—and the previously learned high-frequency words. Point to words at random and ask children to read them.

RETEACH

Comprehension

Details Review that details are small bits of information that help the reader understand a selection. Say: **In "Beth Can Help," Beth helps plant a garden. Instead of saying Beth helps, the author gives details to help us understand the story better. It says *Mom says that Beth can dig. "Get a shovel, Beth."* What kind of help did Beth give? These are details.** Guide children to point out more details from "Beth Can Help" and "Let's Help Cat" in *Shooting Star*. Record their responses on a two-column chart as shown below. Then page through the other stories and invite volunteers to point out details in the pictures they see.

"Beth Can Help"	"Let's Help Cat"
digging in the dirt	mixing the batter
planting seeds	rolling the dough
watering the seeds	

RETEACH

Grammar/Writing

Photo Card

Questions Review with children the characteristics of questions.

Questions

The sentences ask for information.
They often begin with words like *who, what, when, where, why,* or *how.*
They begin with a capital letter and end with a question mark.

Display *Photo Card moon.* Write questions about the moon on the board, such as *Where is the moon? When do you see the moon?* Read them to children. Point out the capital letters and question marks. Explain how the sentences have the characteristics of questions. Display *Photo Card sack,* and repeat the activity. Write without capitalization or end punctuation. Have children correct the sentences with capital letters and question marks.

High-Frequency Words

don't	new
her	says
line	water
Mr.	

Fluency

Expression Have children work with partners. Ask them to take turns reading pages from "Beth Can Help" in *Shooting Star.* Remind them to pause when they see commas and end marks. Remind them to notice quotation marks and remember that they show when people are speaking and to use their voices to show how the characters are feeling.

Listen to partners read, giving them feedback about their expression and improving their fluency.

DAY AT A GLANCE

Day 5

HIGH-FREQUENCY WORDS
don't, her, line, Mr., new, says, water

PHONEMIC AWARENESS
Onset and Rime

PHONICS AND SPELLING
Preteach Short Vowel /u/*u*

BUILD ROBUST VOCABULARY
Preteach *claimed, dine, groaned*

GRAMMAR/WRITING
Preteach Nouns: Animals or Things

Materials Needed:

Lesson 8 High-Frequency Word Cards

Sound/Spelling Card *Uu*

Word Builders and Word Builder Cards

Write-On/ Wipe-Off Boards

Practice Book p.34

Practice Book

Shooting Star Student Edition pp. 26–32

High-Frequency Words

don't	new
her	says
line	water
Mr.	

High-Frequency Words

Copying Masters 29–30 Display *High-Frequency Word Cards* for *don't, her, line, Mr., new, says, water,* and the other previously learned high-frequency words. Say the word *don't*, ask a volunteer to point to *don't*, and have children read the word aloud. Continue with the remaining high-frequency words. Repeat this activity several times to reinforce instant recognition.

Phonemic Awareness

Onset and Rime Tell children you are going to say some words, but you are going to say them in parts. Have children listen to see if they can figure out the word. Say: **Listen as I say this word in parts. /h/-ug—The word I said was *hug*. Now you try some: /n/-ut, /k/-up, /b/-us, /th/-umb, /f/-uzz.**

PRETEACH

Phonics and Spelling

Sound/Spelling Card **Short Vowel /u/*u***
Connecting Letter to Sound Say the words *us, upset,* and *uncle*, and have children repeat the words. Explain that all three words begin with the /u/ sound. Have children say /u/ several times. Display *Sound/Spelling Card Uu.* Say the letter name, and identify the picture. Tell children that the letter *u* can stand for the sound /u/, the sound at the beginning of *us*. Have children say /u/ several times as you touch the letter.

Give each child a *u Word Builder Card.* Say: **When I say a word that begins with /u/, like *us*, hold up your card and say /u/. When I say a word that does not begin with /u/, hold your card behind your back.** Say these words: *undo, under, when, up, bag.* Tell children that some words have the /u/ sound in the middle. Say *bus*, elongating the /u/ sound. Tell children that *bus* has /u/ in the middle. Follow the same procedure for the medial position with the following words: *bug, run, math, nut, hot, bump.*

Word Blending Demonstrate each step with *Word Builder Cards* and a *Word Builder,* and have children repeat each step after you. Hold up *s* and say /s/. Hold up *u* and say /u/. Hold up *n* and say /n/.

- Place the letters *s, u, n* in the *Word Builder.*
- Point to *s*. Say /s/. Point to *u* and say /u/. Prompt children to repeat after you.
- Slide *u* next to *s*. Run your hand under the letters as you blend the sounds, elongating them—/su/.

- Point to *n* and say /n/.
- Slide *n* next to *su*. Run your hand under *sun* as you blend the sounds, elongating them—/sun/.
- Read *sun* naturally.

Follow the same procedure with these words: *mug, up, pup.*

  Word Building Place the *Word Builder Cards u* and *s* in the *Word Builder* and have children do the same. Ask children to say each letter name and the sound it stands for. Then read the word naturally—*us*. Have children do the same. Have children build and read new words. As they build each word, write it on the board. Say:

- **Add *b* before *us*. What word did you make?** (*bus*)

- **Change *b* to *m* and add a *t* at the end. What word is it?** (*must*)

Continue with the words *cut, cub,* and *club.* Have children read the words on the board. Direct children's attention to page 34 of their *Practice Books*. Complete the page together.

PRETEACH

Build Robust Vocabulary

Introduce Robust Vocabulary Read the student-friendly explanation for each word. Then discuss each word using the following examples.

Say: **I saw my favorite book at the library, so I claimed it and checked it out. What was something you claimed this week?**

Say: **Do you like to dine outside during warm weather? Where did you dine at your last meal?**

Say: **I groaned when I saw the stormy weather outside and I couldn't go for a walk. What might make you groan—a trip to the dentist or a trip to the toy store?**

PRETEACH

Grammar/Writing

Nouns: Animals or Things Read aloud the following sentence from "Just Like Us" in *Shooting Star:* **Look at the birds.** Tell children that words that name animals, such as the word *birds*, are nouns. Read aloud another sentence from the story: **Look at the deer.** Ask children to identify the noun that tells an animal.

Then read this sentence: **Look at the trees.** Tell children that things, such as trees, are also nouns, as are cups, books, shirts, and chairs. Guide children to look around the classroom and point out other words that name things.

Spelling Words

1. us	6. club
2. bus	7. with
3. must	8. then
4. cut	9. don't
5. cub	10. says

Have children practice writing spelling words on their *Write-on/Wipe-off Boards*

VOCABULARY

Student-Friendly Explanations

claimed If you claim something, you say it is yours.

dine Saying that you dine is a fancy way of talking about eating.

groaned A person who groans makes a deep sound that shows unhappiness.

30+ Minutes

LESSON 9

Just Like Us

PHONEMIC AWARENESS
Phoneme Isolation

PHONICS AND SPELLING
Reteach Short Vowel /u/*u*

COMPREHENSION
Reteach Details

HIGH-FREQUENCY WORDS
Reteach *grow, food, live*

FLUENCY
Phrasing

GRAMMAR/WRITING
Reteach Nouns: Animals or Things

Materials Needed:

Photo Cards

Word Builders and Word Builder Cards

Write-On/ Wipe-Off Boards

Shooting Star Student Edition
pp. 6–12
pp. 16–22
pp. 24–25

Practice Book
p.35

Practice Book

Spelling Words

1. us	6. club
2. bus	7. with
3. must	8. then
4. cut	9. don't
5. cub	10. says

Have children practice writing spelling words on their *Write-on/Wipe-off Boards.*

Phonemic Awareness

Photo Card

Phoneme Isolation   Display *Photo Cards jungle, bug,* and *squirrel.* Point to *jungle,* say the word, and have children say the word after you. Have children listen to the /u/ sound in the middle of the word and then say the names of the other two photos aloud. Ask: **What other word has the /u/ sound you hear in *jungle*?** (*bug*) Continue with *Photo Cards bug, rose, lunch; fish, gift, add; add, ant, jungle.*

RETEACH

Phonics and Spelling

Short Vowel /u/*u*
Word Building   Place the *Word Builder Cards u* and *s* in the *Word Builder.* Ask children to say the name and sound of each letter. Then read the word naturally—*us.* Have children do the same. Ask:

- **Which letter should I add to *us* to make *bus*?** (Add *b.*)

- **What letters should I change or add to change *bus* to *must*?** (Change *b* to *m*; add *t* to the end.)

Continue with the words *cut, cub,* and *club.*

Read Words in Context   Write the following sentences on chart paper. Have children read each sentence silently. Then track the print as children read the sentences aloud. Finally, point to the underlined words at random and have children read them. *She <u>must</u> get off the <u>bus</u> <u>with</u> <u>us</u>. Can you <u>cut</u> the plum? The <u>cub</u> rests with its dad, and <u>then</u> gets up. He <u>says</u>, "We <u>don't</u> want that <u>club</u>."*

PRETEACH

Comprehension

Details   Remind children that details in a story are small bits of information that help explain the story. Read aloud "Let's Help Cat" in *Shooting Star.* Say: **Details tell us more about something. In "Let's Help Cat," details tell what animals are there, such as Cat, Hen, and Goat. Details give more information.** Have children name the other animals in the story. Ask children to identify details they notice in the pictures. Guide them to name details that tell how things look, sound, smell, taste, and feel.

High-Frequency Words

grow	**live**
food	

pp.
24–
25

RETEACH
High-Frequency Words

Write the words *grow, food,* and *live* on the board.

- Point to and read *grow*. Repeat, having children say *grow* with you.
- Say: **Plants *grow* from seeds.**
- Repeat the word and then point to each letter as you spell it. Then have children say and spell *grow* with you. Have children reread the word.

Repeat for the remaining words. Use the following sentences: *My favorite food is apples. I live in a little house.*

Have children turn to page 24 of *Shooting Star* and have them read aloud the words at the top of the page. Talk about the illustrations. Then guide children in choosing and circling the word that names each picture. (4. *nut,* 5. *up,* 6. *truck*) Have children read aloud each word in the list on page 25. Ask volunteers to read the sentences aloud. Then have children choral-read the sentences. Guide them to trace the word that completes each sentence. (1. *live,* 2. *grow,* 3. *food*)

RETEACH
Grammar/Writing

Practice Book
p.35

Nouns: Animals or Things   Remind children that nouns can tell about animals or things. Then read the following story, telling children to listen for nouns that name animals and things.

A duck and a goose go out to find some food. First, they see rocks, grass, and trees.

"Is this a snack?" asks Duck.

"No!" says Goose.

They go to Duck's house. They find carrots, bread, and milk.

"Now that's food!" Goose says.

They eat a snack. "Delicious!" say Duck and Goose.

Read each sentence again, and guide children to identify nouns that name animals or things. Record them on the board. Read aloud each noun as you track the print. Complete *Practice Book* page 35 together.

Fluency

Phrasing   Explain to children that good readers make their reading sound as it does when someone talks. They pause at the end of sentences, and they read words that go together in "chunks."

Model reading aloud "Beth Can Help" in *Shooting Star*. The rhythm and the rhyme of the selection can aid children in grouping the words into meaningful "chunks." Have children echo-read.

PHONEMIC AWARENESS
Phoneme Blending

PHONICS AND SPELLING
Reteach Short Vowel /u/*u*

HIGH-FREQUENCY WORDS
Reteach *be, does, food, grow, live, many*

FLUENCY
Phrasing

READING
"Just Like Us"

BUILD ROBUST VOCABULARY
Preteach *classify, function, nutritious*

GRAMMAR/WRITING
Reteach Nouns: Animals or Things

Materials Needed:

Word Builders and Word Builder Cards

Practice Book
p.36

Copying Masters 33–34

Lesson 9 High-Frequency Word Cards

Shooting Star Student Edition pp. 16–22 pp. 26–33

Photo Card

Photo Cards

High-Frequency Words

be	grow
does	live
food	many

30+ Minutes

Phonemic Awareness

Phoneme Blending   Tell children that they are going to play a guessing game. Then say, **I'm thinking of a word that is an animal. It is a kind of bird. It is a /d/ /u/ /k/. My word is duck.** Have children guess the following words: /k/ /u/ /t/ (*cut*), /b/ /u/ /n/ (*bun*), /d/ /u/ /g/ (*dug*), /b/ /u/ /d/ (*bud*).

RETEACH

Phonics and Spelling

Short Vowel /u/*u*
Word Building   Use a *Word Builder* and *Word Builder Cards* and have children repeat each step after you. Build the word *fun*. Have children name each letter and tell whether it is a consonant or a vowel. Remind children that in words with the consonant-vowel-consonant pattern, the vowel sound is often short. Ask them what vowel sound they will hear in the word. (/u/; short *u*) Then have children say the word naturally—*fun*. Lead children in building and reading new words. Say:

- **Change *f* to *r*. Read the word.** (*run*)
- **Change *n* to *st*. Read the word.** (*rust*)
- **Change *u* to *e*. Read the word.** (*rest*)

Continue with the following words: *test, best, bust, bun, sun.*

Read Words in Context   Ask children to turn to *Practice Book* page 36. Read each sentence aloud and have children echo-read. Then ask volunteers to read each sentence aloud. Ask: **What did Russ and Beth have?** (plums) **What did Russ say about the plums?** ("Yum!") **What did Beth do next?** (Beth jumped.) Guide children to circle all the words with short *u*. Then guide children to underline the short *e* words.

RETEACH

High-Frequency Words

Copying Masters 33–34

Display the *High-Frequency Word Cards* for *be, does, food, grow, live,* and *many*. Point to each card and read the word. Have children repeat. Then randomly point to the words, and ask children to read each one. Distribute cards to children and have them work with partners. Tell children to turn the cards over and shuffle them. Then have them play a memory game with the cards.

Reading

pp. 26–33

Build Background: "Just Like Us"

Read the title with children. Ask them to tell about a time they went for a walk outside in a park or a wooded area. What did they see? Have them tell how what they see at a park might be different from what they see in a building. Tell children they will be reading about a walk outside.

Monitor Comprehension: "Just Like Us"

Have children turn to the first page of the selection. Ask a volunteer to reread the title. Have children look at the picture on page 26. Ask children to think about what the selection will be about and what the characters will be doing. Then guide children through the selection as they read.

pp. 26–27

Say: **An older person and a younger person are holding hands. They look like they might be a father and a child. Let's read to find out what they are going to do.**

After reading the pages, ask: **What are the people doing?** (They are taking a walk outside.) **What things do you think they will see on their walk?** (Possible response: They might see trees, plants, and animals.) DRAW CONCLUSIONS/MAKE PREDICTIONS

Ask: **How does the man say that trees are like people?** (They grow up the way we do.) MAKE COMPARISONS

Ask: **Which words on these pages have the short *u* sound?** (up, just, us) APPLY PHONICS

pp. 28–29

Say: **We know the father and daughter are taking a walk. Let's find out what they see next on their walk.**

After reading the pages, ask: **What do they see next on their walk?** (They see a pond with birds.) SEQUENCE

Ask: **What details do you see about the place where they are?** (Possible response: I see trees, bushes, and birds.) 🌀 NOTE DETAILS

Ask: **Which words on these pages have the short *u* sound? Frame and read the short *u* words on page 29.** (must, just, us) APPLY PHONICS

Fluency

Phrasing Have children open to page 19 of "Beth Can Help" in *Shooting Star* and invite a volunteer to name the punctuation marks in the sentence. (quotation marks, comma, period)

Tell them that the comma and period helps them to know what words to "chunk" together as they read and where to pause. Point out that quotation marks tell when a character is talking.

Model reading the two pages, pausing at commas and periods. Have children echo-read, using appropriate phrasing.

Say: **Look at the pictures on these pages. What else do the people see on their walk? Let's read on to find out.**

After reading the pages, ask: **What do the people see next on their walk?** (deer) **Sequence**

Ask: **What have they seen on their walk so far?** (They have seen trees, birds, and deer.) **Summarize**

Ask: **How are the deer like the people taking the walk?** (The deer eat food like the people do.) **How are the deer different than the people?** (Possible responses: They walk on four legs, they are covered in fur. They eat grass instead of the food we eat.) **Compare and Contrast**

 Say: **Look at the picture on this page. What do you think we may find out on this page?** (The people live in the house near the animals.) **Make Predictions**

After reading the page, ask: **Was your prediction right? What did you find out?** (Possible response: Yes, I was right. The people live near the animals.) **Confirm Predictions**

Ask: **What details do you see about the place they live?** (I can see they live in a house in the woods. The animals are all around the house.) **Note Details**

Ask: **Which words have short *u* sound on this page?** (*just, us*) **Apply Phonics**

 Answers to *Think Critically* Questions
Help children read and answer the *Think Critically* questions on page 33. Answers are shown below.

1. ‹trees› **Sequence**
2. ‹water› **Note Details**
3. ‹cabin in the woods› **Beginning, Middle, Ending**

PRETEACH

Build Robust Vocabulary

Introduce Robust Vocabulary Read the student-friendly explanation for each word. Then discuss each word using the following examples.

Say: **I can classify crayons by color—putting red crayons together, blue crayons together, and so on. What is a way to classify animals?**

Say: **The function of a clock is to tell time. What is the function of a coat or jacket?**

Say: **I like to eat nutritious snacks, like carrots and apples. What is a nutritious snack? Do you think pizza or salad is more nutritious?**

RETEACH

Grammar/Writing

Nouns: Animals or Things Write the following sentences on the board, and have children read them aloud.

> Bugs can have wings.
>
> Ducks can swim.

Remind children that some nouns name animals and things. Ask volunteers to underline the nouns that name animals or things. Then read the sentences again with children, having them raise their hands when they read a noun that names an animal or thing.

Write these nouns on the board. Have children identify those that name animals and those that name things: *pack, cat, ant, belt, bus, rat, tent.*

VOCABULARY

Student-Friendly Explanations

classify When you classify something, you put it into a group with other things like it.

function Something's function is its use. The function of a hat is to cover your head.

nutritious When something is nutritious, it is healthful to eat.

LESSON 9

DAY AT A GLANCE

Day 3

PHONEMIC AWARENESS
Phoneme Segmentation

PHONICS
Preteach Initial Blends with *r*

PHONICS AND SPELLING
Reteach Short Vowel /u/*u*

HIGH-FREQUENCY WORDS
Reteach *grow, food, live*

FLUENCY
Phrasing

COMPREHENSION
Reteach Details

GRAMMAR/WRITING
Reteach Lists

Materials Needed:

Photo Cards

Write-On/ Wipe-Off Boards with Phonemic Awareness Disks

Word Builders and Word Builder Cards

Copying Masters 35–36

Lesson 9 Story Strips

Shooting Star Student Edition pp. 26–32

Spelling Words

1. us	6. club
2. bus	7. with
3. must	8. then
4. cut	9. don't
5. cub	10. says

Phonemic Awareness

Photo Card

Phoneme Segmentation Have children use the three boxes on the *Write-on/Wipe-off Boards*. Remind children that the boxes stand for the sounds in words. Show *Photo Card bug* and ask: **What is the first sound you hear in *bug*?** (/b/) Have children place a disk in the first box. Then have children name the second sound in *bug* (/u/) and place a disk in the second box. Then have them identify the last sound in bug (/g/) and place a disk in the third box. Point to each box in sequence as children say the word. **How many sounds do you hear in *bug*? I hear three.** Repeat the procedure with *Photo Cards hen, ant, hall, path, toad.*

PRETEACH

Phonics

Initial Blends with *r* Write the following words on the board and read them aloud: *tip, fog, tack.* Then write these words on the board: *trip, frog, track.*

Ask a volunteer to tell how *tip* and *trip* are different, as you point to the words. Then underline *tr* in *trip,* and tell children that many words begin with a consonant and an *r*. Read aloud *tip* and *trip* as you point to each word. Ask volunteers to read aloud *fog* and *frog* and *tack* and *track* and come to the board to underline the letters that make the *r* blend.

RETEACH

Phonics and Spelling

Short Vowel /u/*u*

Build Words Use *Word Builders* and *Word Builder Cards* to form words. Have children listen to your directions and change a letter in each word to spell a spelling word. Form *up* and have children read the word. Ask: **Which spelling word can you make by changing the second letter?** (*us*)

Follow a similar procedure with the following words: *bun* (*bus*), *mast* (*must*), *hut* (*cut*), *cab* (*cub*), *win* (*with*), *than* (*then*).

Remind children that there are some other words they have to remember how to spell. Have children say *says*. Tell them to put *Word Builder Cards s, a, y, s* in their *Word Builders,* picture the word *says* in their minds, and build the word. Write the word on the board. Follow the same procedure with *don't.*

RETEACH

High-Frequency Words

Copying Masters 35–36

Duplicate and distribute *Copying Masters* 35–36 to each child. Explain that the sentences tell the story "Just Like Us" but some have missing words.

List the words *grow, food,* and *live* on the board. Have children read aloud each story strip sentence and name the correct word on the board that makes sense in the sentence. Have children write the missing words in the blanks and read the completed sentences aloud. Help children cut apart the strips, read the completed sentences, and arrange them in story order.

RETEACH

Comprehension

page 32

Focus Skill

Details Review that details can tell how something looks, sounds, smells, tastes, feels, or acts. Have children turn to "Just Like Us" in *Shooting Star.* Guide children to do a picture walk through the selection. Ask children to identify details they see. Have children look at page 32, and guide them to identify details in the picture. Record their responses in a word web. In the center, write a title, such as *where the people and animals live.*

RETEACH

Grammar/Writing

Lists Write the following list on the board and read it aloud to children, tracking the print.

1. eggs
2. milk
3. hot dogs

Explain that this could be a list of items that you might buy at the grocery store. Explain that there are many different kinds of lists. Suggest a few, such as a list of friends or a list of things you need to do. Then ask children for other kinds of lists.

Guide children to understand that lists are usually words, not sentences. Point out that things on a list are alike in some way. Have children tell how the items on this list are alike. (they are food items) Tell them that lists are often numbered and that the most important things are often first on the list. Then make a list with children, such as "Our Favorite Foods."

High-Frequency Words

grow	**live**
food	

Fluency

Phrasing Point out that when good readers read, they read words that go together and then pause. They pause when a sentence is over and when they see a comma. Reread aloud "Just Like Us" in *Shooting Star* to show how to use appropriate phrasing.

Read aloud each sentence once with appropriate phrasing and once without, and talk about the difference.

Have children read the story aloud. Remind them to pause when they see commas and punctuation marks that signal the end of a sentence.

LESSON 9

DAY AT A GLANCE

Day 4

PHONEMIC AWARENESS
Phoneme Blending

PHONICS
Reteach Initial Blends with *r*

PHONICS AND SPELLING
Reteach Short Vowel /u/*u*

HIGH-FREQUENCY WORDS
Reteach *be, does, food, grow, live, many*

FLUENCY
Phrasing

COMPREHENSION
Reteach Details

GRAMMAR/WRITING
Reteach Lists

Materials Needed:

Practice Book

Copying Masters 33–34

Practice Book p.37

Lesson 9 High-Frequency Word Cards

Shooting Star Student Edition pp. 6–12 pp. 26–32

Spelling Words

1. us	6. club
2. bus	7. with
3. must	8. then
4. cut	9. don't
5. cub	10. says

30+ Minutes

Phonemic Awareness

Phoneme Blending Tell children they are going to be builders and that they will put some sounds together to figure out a word. **Listen: /m/ /u/ /g/. What word do the sounds /m/ /u/ /g/ say? They say *mug*.** Continue with the following words: /d/ /u/ /k/ (*duck*), /f/ /u/ /n/ (*fun*), /r/ /u/ /b/ (*rub*), /h/ /u/ /m/ (*hum*).

RETEACH

Phonics

Initial Blends with *r* Write the following words on the board: *tap, cab, dip.* Have children read the words aloud. Ask children what letter they would add to make *trap, crab,* and *drip.* Write the new words under the first set, choral-read them, and ask volunteers to underline each initial blend with *r.*

RETEACH

Phonics and Spelling

Practice Book p.37

Short Vowel /u/*u*
Direct children's attention to page 37 of their *Practice Books.* Complete the page together.

Assess children's progress using the following sentences.

1.	us	All of **us** will fit in the truck.
2.	bus	Do you ride the **bus** home?
3.	must	You **must** have a nap.
4.	cut	Can you **cut** that apple?
5.	cub	Is the bear **cub** with its mother?
6.	club	This is a fun **club**!

Review

7.	with	Play **with** me.
8.	then	First we eat, and **then** we go home.

High-Frequency

9.	don't	I **don't** want to do that.
10.	says	He **says** we can go.

RETEACH

High-Frequency Words

Copying Masters 33–34

Display *High-Frequency Word Cards* for this lesson's words—*be, does, food, grow, live,* and *many*—and the previously learned high-frequency words. Point to words at random and ask children to read them.

RETEACH

Comprehension

Details   Ask children to identify what a detail is. (a bit of information that tells more about something)

Draw a two-column chart like the one below. Have children turn to "Let's Help Cat" in *Shooting Star*. Guide children to find details in the story. Then turn to "Just Like Us" in *Shooting Star*. Ask volunteers to offer details in the story. Suggest they look at the pictures to find details that tell about the story as you record children's ideas on the chart.

"Let's Help Cat"	"Just Like Us"
apple pie five animals with Cat mixes pie with spoon Horse uses rolling pin pan is on shelf	

RETEACH

Grammar/Writing

Lists   Review with children the characteristics of lists.

> ### Lists
> Lists are usually words, not sentences.
> The things on the list are alike in some way.
> Lists are often numbered.
> The most important things are often first on the list.

Display the list you created on Day 3 and read it to children, pointing out how the list you made together is a good example of a list.

Make a sample numbered list for children, and point out the form a list takes. Then have them help you make a list of games they enjoy. Record the list and number the items.

High-Frequency Words

be	grow
does	live
food	many

Fluency

Phrasing   Have children work with partners. Ask them to take turns reading pages from "Just Like Us" in *Shooting Star*. Remind them to pause when they see commas and end marks. Listen as children read, providing feedback to help them improve their phrasing.

DAY AT A GLANCE

Day 5

30+ Minutes

HIGH-FREQUENCY WORDS
be, does, food, grow, live, many

PHONEMIC AWARENESS
Onset and Rime

PHONICS AND SPELLING
Preteach Diphthong /ng/*ng*

BUILD ROBUST VOCABULARY
Preteach *ashamed, mused, soared*

GRAMMAR/WRITING
Preteach One and More Than One

Materials Needed:

Copying Masters 33–34

Sound/Spelling Card

d o t

Lesson 9 High-Frequency Word Cards

Sound/Spelling Card *ng*

Word Builders and Word Builder Cards

Write-On/ Wipe-Off Boards

Practice Book p.38

Practice Book

High-Frequency Words

be	grow
does	live
food	many

Hi-Frequency Words

Copying Masters 33–34

Display *High-Frequency Word Cards* for *be, does, food, grow, live, many,* and the other previously learned high-frequency words. Say the word *be,* ask a volunteer to point to *be,* and have children read the word aloud. Continue with the remaining high-frequency words. Repeat this activity several times to reinforce instant recognition.

Phonemic Awareness

Onset and Rime   Tell children that you are going to say some words, but you are going to say them in parts. Have children listen to see if they can figure out the word. Demonstrate by saying: **/s/-ing–The word I said was *sing*.** Now you try some: **/r/-ing, /s/-ang, /h/-ung, /k/-ing, /w/-ing.**

PRETEACH

Phonics and Spelling

Sound/ Spelling Card

d o t

Diphthong /ng/*ng*
Connecting Letter to Sound   Say the word *sing*. Have children say the word. Repeat with *song* and str*ing*. Say: **The words *sing, song,* and *string* all end with the sound /ng/.** Have children say the /ng/ sound several times. Display *Sound/Spelling Card ng.* Say the letter names and identify the picture. Explain that the letters *ng* stand for the sound /ng/, the sound at the end of the word *sing.* Have children say /ng/ several times as you touch the letters. Give each child *n* and *g Word Builder Cards.* Say: **When I say a word that has the /ng/ sound, hold up your cards and say /ng/. When I say a word that does not have the /ng/ sound, hold your cards behind your back.** Say these words: *ring, fog, king, thin, sun, bring, long, hang, find, wrong, sand.*

d o t   **Word Blending**   Demonstrate each step with *Word Builder Cards* and a *Word Builder.* Have children repeat each step after you. Hold up *s* and say /s/. Hold up *i* and say /i/. Hold up *ng* and say /ng/.

- Place the letters *s, i, n, g* in the *Word Builder.*
- Point to *s.* Say /s/. Point to *i* and say /i/. Prompt children to repeat after you.
- Slide *i* next to *s.* Run your hand under the letters as you blend the sounds, elongating them—/si/.
- Point to *ng* and say /ng/.

- Slide *ng* next to *si*. Run your hand under *sing* as you blend the sounds, elongating them—/sing/.
- Read *sing* naturally.

Follow the same procedure with these words: *long, hang, king*.

  Word Building Place the *Word Builder Cards l, o, n,* and *g* in the *Word Builder*. Slide your hand under the letters as you slowly blend the sounds—/lloong/. Then read the word naturally—*long*. Have children build and read new words. As they build each word, write it on the board. Say:

- **Change *l* to *s*. What word did you make?** (*song*)
- **Change *o* to *i*. What word did you make?** (*sing*)

Continue with the words *ring, bring,* and *thing*. Then have children read the words on the board. Direct children's attention to page 38 of their *Practice Books*. Complete the page together.

Practice Book p.38

PRETEACH

Build Robust Vocabulary

Introduce Robust Vocabulary Read the student-friendly explanation for each word. Then discuss each word using the following examples.

Say: **Someone might feel ashamed if he called someone a name. What is another time a person might feel ashamed?**

Say: **I mused about what I would read to you today. What is something you muse about—what you will play at recess or what you will eat for dinner? Explain.**

Say: **If you have ever been in an airplane, you have soared high above the ground. Can you name some animals or things that soar?**

PRETEACH

Grammar/Writing

 One and More Than One Ask children to recall what a noun is. (a word that names a person, animal, place, or thing) Write the following sentences on the board: *Ming hopped on one leg. Ming used her legs to swim.* Read the sentences aloud, tracking the print.

Explain that in the first sentence, the noun *leg* names one thing, and in the second sentence, the noun *legs* names more than one. Underline *leg* and *legs*. Point out that *-s* was added to *leg* to name more than one. Tell children that *-s* can be added to many nouns to name more than one. Then hold up *Photo Card hen*. Say: **What is one of these?** (*hen*) **What is more than one?** (*hens*) Repeat with the *Photo Cards sack, bug, ant,* and *flower*.

Spelling Words

1. long	6. thing
2. song	7. us
3. sing	8. must
4. ring	9. does
5. bring	10. food

 Have children practice writing spelling words on their *Write-on/Wipe-off Boards*.

VOCABULARY

Student-Friendly Explanations

ashamed If you are ashamed, you feel bad about having done something wrong.

mused If you mused about something, you were thinking about it.

soared If you soared, you flew very high into the air.

LESSON 10

DAY AT A GLANCE

Day 1

PHONEMIC AWARENESS
Phoneme Isolation

PHONICS AND SPELLING
Reteach Diphthong /ng/*ng*

COMPREHENSION
Preteach Plot

HIGH-FREQUENCY WORDS
Reteach *school, your, arms*

FLUENCY
Phrasing

GRAMMAR/WRITING
Reteach One and More Than One

Materials Needed:

Word Builders and Word Builder Cards

Write-On/Wipe-Off Boards

Shooting Star Student Edition
pp. 6–12
pp. 16–22
pp. 34–35

Practice Book p.39

Practice Book

Spelling Words

1. long	6. thing
2. song	7. us
3. sing	8. must
4. ring	9. does
5. bring	10. food

 Have children practice writing spelling words on their *Write-on/Wipe-off Boards.*

Phonemic Awareness

Phoneme Isolation   Say the word *rang* aloud and have children repeat it. Tell children to listen to the /ng/ at the end of *rang*. Then say the words *wing* and *win*. Ask: **Which of these words has the /ng/ sound you hear at the end of *rang*? I hear it in *wing*.** Continue with: *sing, sang, sank; pan, long, ping; strong, stand, sting.*

RETEACH

Phonics and Spelling

Diphthong /ng/*ng*
Word Building   Place the *Word Builder Cards l, o, n, g* in the *Word Builder*. Remind children that the letters *ng* stand for the sound /ng/. Read the word *long* with children. Build new words by asking children:

| l | o | n | g |

- **Which letter should I change in *long* to make *song*?** (Change *l* to *s*.)

| s | o | n | g |

- **Which letter should I change in *song* to make *sing*?** (Change *o* to *i*.)

| s | i | n | g |

Continue using the same procedure with *ring, bring,* and *thing*.

Read Words in Context   Write the following sentences on chart paper. Have children read each sentence silently. Then track the print as children read the sentence aloud. Finally, point to the underlined words at random and have children read them. *Ben <u>does</u> <u>sing</u> a <u>long</u> <u>song</u>. See that big <u>thing</u> on the wall? We <u>must</u> see the big <u>ring</u>. Dad will <u>bring</u> the <u>food</u> to <u>us</u>.*

PRETEACH

Comprehension

 **Plot**   Tell children that the plot of a story is the events that make up the story—it's the main events that happen in the beginning, the middle, and the end. Have children turn to "Let's Help Cat" in *Shooting Star*. Say: **In the story "Let's Help Cat," the plot begins with Cat wanting to make a pie. In the middle, Cat gets help from the other animals except Pig. In the end, Pig tries to eat the pie, but Cat shares the pie with everyone for helping.**

Ask children to turn to "Beth Can Help" in *Shooting Star* and guide them to tell the plot by asking: **What happens in the beginning? In the middle? At the end?** (In the beginning, Mom says, "Beth can help." In the middle, Beth gets a shovel to dig, and plants and waters the seeds. At the end, Beth's plants get big.)

RETEACH

High-Frequency Words

pp. 34-35

Write the words *school, your,* and *arms* on the board.

- Point to and read *school*. Repeat, having children say *school* with you.
- Say: **We learn a lot in *school*.**
- Repeat the word and then point to each letter as you spell it. Then have children say and spell *school* with you. Have children reread the word.

Repeat for the remaining words. Use the following sentences: *That is* your *ball. I put up my* arms.

Have children turn to page 34 of *Shooting Star* and have them read aloud the words at the top of the page. Talk about the illustrations. Then guide children in choosing and circling the word that names each picture. (4. *swing,* 5. *strong,* 6. *ring*) Have children read aloud each word in the list on page 35. Ask volunteers to read the sentences aloud. Then have children choral-read the sentences. Guide them to trace the word that completes each sentence. (1. *your,* 2. *arms,* 3. *school*)

RETEACH

Grammar/Writing

Practice Book
p.39

One and More Than One   Review with children that some words name more than one person, place, animal, or thing. Write these examples on the board: *one ring, six balls, ten bats, two socks, one dog.* Read the examples aloud and point out the plural nouns. Remind children that *-s* can be added to nouns to name more than one. Guide volunteers to underline the *s* in each plural noun.

Direct children's attention to *Practice Book* page 39 and complete the page together.

High-Frequency Words

school	arms
your	

Fluency

Phrasing   Have children open to "Beth Can Help" in *Shooting Star* and track the print as you read aloud, using appropriate phrasing. Remind children to read "chunks" of words that go together to make their reading sound the way people do when they talk. Then have children echo-read "Beth Can Help."

DAY AT A GLANCE
Day 2

PHONEMIC AWARENESS
Phoneme Blending

PHONICS AND SPELLING
Reteach Diphthong /ng/*ng*

HIGH-FREQUENCY WORDS
Reteach *arms, every, feet, heard, school, use, way, your*

FLUENCY
Phrasing

READING
"Ben"

BUILD ROBUST VOCABULARY
Preteach *athletic, awkward, superb*

GRAMMAR/WRITING
Reteach One and More Than One

Materials Needed:

Word Builders and Word Builder Cards

Practice Book

Lesson 10 High-Frequency Word Cards

Shooting Star Student Edition pp. 6–12 pp. 36–43

Photo Cards

High-Frequency Words

arms	school
every	use
feet	way
heard	your

Phonemic Awareness

Phoneme Blending Tell children that they are going to play a guessing game. Then say: **I'm thinking of a word that means "something you sing." It is a /s/ /o/ /ng/. My word is *song*.** Continue with the following words: /k/ /i/ /ng/ (*king*), /l/ /o/ /ng/ (*long*), /s/ /t/ /i/ /ng/ (*sting*), /w/ /i/ /ng/ (*wing*).

RETEACH

Phonics and Spelling

Diphthong /ng/*ng*

Word Building Use a *Word Builder* and *Word Builder Cards*. Have children repeat each step after you. Build the word *sing*. Have children name each letter. Ask them what vowel sound they hear in the word. (short *i*) Then have them tell which two letters together stand for the /ng/ sound. Have children say the word—*sing*. Lead children in building and reading new words. Say:

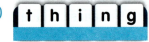

- **Add *w* after *s*. Read the word.** (*swing*)
- **Change *sw* to *r*. Read the word.** (*ring*)
- **Add *b* before *r*. Read the word.** (*bring*)
- **Change *br* to *th*. Read the word.** (*thing*)
- **Change *th* to *s* and *i* to *o*. Read the word.** (*song*)
- **Change *s* to *l*. Read the word.** (*long*)

Read Words in Context Ask children to turn to *Practice Book* page 40. Read each sentence aloud and have children echo-read. Then ask volunteers to read each sentence aloud. Ask: **What does Cal want?** (a long song) **Who sings a song?** (Ming and Tom) **What is the song about?** (a king with a ring) Call on volunteers to find and circle the words with the /ng/ sound.

RETEACH

High-Frequency Words

Write the words *arms, every, feet, heard, school, use, way,* and *your* on the board. Point to each word, and ask a volunteer to read it. Then erase or cover the words and have other volunteers spell each one. Give each child a set of *High-Frequency Word Cards* and have children spread the cards out in front of them. Randomly call out one of the words, and have children hold up and read aloud the matching card. Assess how well children are able to identify the words and repeat until they can respond quickly and accurately.

Reading

Build Background: "Ben"

pp. 36–43

Read the title with children and ask them if they or someone they know has any special talents. Have children tell about different things that they and their friends can do that make them special. Tell children that they will be reading about a boy with special talents.

Monitor Comprehension: "Ben"

Have children turn to the first page of the story. Ask a volunteer to reread the title. Have children look at the pictures on pages 36 and 37 and ask them what they think the story will be about. Then guide children through the story as they read.

pp. 36–37

Say: **I see a boy sitting alone and looking kind of shy and some boys talking to him. What do you think they want? Let's read to find out.**

After reading the pages, ask: **What do the boys want?** (The boys want Ben to play ball with them.) **MAKE INFERENCES**

Ask: **What is the setting of these pages?** (Possible response: a field outside a school) **SETTING**

Say: **This is the beginning of the story. What is happening in the beginning?** (The boys ask Ben to bring his ball.) **PLOT**

Ask: **What word on these pages has the /ng/ sound?** (*bring*) **APPLY PHONICS**

pp. 38–39

Say: **It looks like Ben is playing ball. Let's read to find out what happens next.**

After reading the pages, ask: **What happens next with Ben and the boys?** (They play ball and Ben kicks the ball far.) **PLOT**

Ask: **Why do the boys say that Ben's legs are strong?** (Ben kicks the ball far.) **CAUSE AND EFFECT**

Ask: **What word on these pages has the /ng/ sound?** (*strong*) **APPLY PHONICS**

Fluency

Phrasing Have children open to "Let's Help Cat" in *Shooting Star*. Remind children that good readers read groups of words that go together in "chunks" to make their reading sound the way it does when someone is speaking.

Read aloud this sentence from "Let's Help Cat," once with appropriate phrasing and once without:

"Let's make a pie," / said Cat.

"Let's make / a pie," said / Cat.

Discuss the difference, and point out how the first example demonstrates appropriate phrasing. Echo-read pages of the story with children, modeling appropriate phrasing.

Say: **Ben seems to be doing well playing ball. Let's see if he keeps it up.**

pp. 40–41

After reading the pages, ask: **What are the boys doing now?** (The boys are still playing with the ball.) **NOTE DETAILS**

Ask: **What do the boys think of how Ben plays?** (They think he plays well.) **How can you tell?** (Possible response: It looks like they are cheering for him and they say he is strong.) **MAKE INFERENCES**

Say: **Ben is really helping the boys out. What do you think will happen next?** (Possible response: Ben will help the team win the game.) **MAKE PREDICTIONS**

Ask: **What word on these two pages has the /ng/ sound?** (*long*) **APPLY PHONICS**

page 42

Say: **It looks like Ben is the star of the game. Everyone is cheering. Let's read to find out what's happening.**

After reading the page, ask: **How do the children feel about Ben now?** (They like him.) **How can you tell?** (The children are cheering for Ben.) **MAKE INFERENCES**

Ask: **How is Ben different from the other children?** (Possible response: Ben is very tall with long arms and legs.) **COMPARE AND CONTRAST**

Ask: **Why do the children think Ben will help them win?** (Possible response: Ben is a very good player and he is special.) **DRAW CONCLUSIONS**

page 43

Answers to *Think Critically* Questions

Help children read and answer the *Think Critically* questions on page 43. Answers are shown below.

1. ‹playground› **SETTING**

2. ‹kickball› **NOTE DETAILS**

 3. ‹Ben's team wins.› **PLOT**

VOCABULARY

PRETEACH
Build Robust Vocabulary

Photo Card

Introduce Robust Vocabulary   Read the student-friendly explanation for each word. Then discuss each word using the following examples.

Say: **An athletic person might play a lot of sports.** Display *Photo Cards house, soccer,* and *library.* **Which of these has to do with being athletic? Explain.**

Say: **A big box might be awkward to move or carry because you can't get your hands around it.** Display *Photo Cards rose, sack,* and *octopus.* **Which of these might be awkward to carry? Explain.**

Say: **I had a superb meal for my birthday. It was delicious!** Show *Photo Cards berries, ant,* and *toad.* **Which of these would make a superb snack?**

RETEACH
Grammar/Writing

Photo Card

One and More Than One   Display *Photo Card crayon.* Say: **Damien used a crayon to draw a picture. We used many crayons to make holiday cards.** Have children tell which sentence talks about more than one. Then ask children what they would add to the word *crayon* to make it mean more than one crayon. (*-s*) Write the following words on the board:

> ring, song, flag, bug

Have children read the words. Then say: **I have two ring. That doesn't sound right. I have more than one ring, so I should add *s* to the end and say that I have two rings.** Guide children to add *-s* to the words on the board.

VOCABULARY
Student-Friendly Explanations

athletic   An athletic person is active, strong, and able to play sports well.

awkward   If you are awkward, you move in a clumsy, rough way.

superb   If something is superb, it is the best it can be, or excellent.

LESSON 10

DAY AT A GLANCE

Day 3

30+ Minutes

PHONEMIC AWARENESS
Phoneme Segmentation

PHONICS
Preteach Contraction *'ll*

PHONICS AND SPELLING
Reteach Diphthong /ng/*ng*

HIGH-FREQUENCY WORDS
Reteach *school, your, arms*

FLUENCY
Phrasing

COMPREHENSION
Reteach Plot

GRAMMAR/WRITING
Reteach Dialogue

Materials Needed:

Write-On/
Wipe-Off
Boards with
Phonemic
Awareness
Disks

Word Builders
and Word
Builder Cards

Copying Masters 39–40
Lesson 10
Story Strips

Shooting Star
Student Edition
pp. 6–12
pp. 36–42

Spelling Words

1. long	6. thing
2. song	7. us
3. sing	8. must
4. ring	9. does
5. bring	10. food

Phonemic Awareness

Phoneme Segmentation Have children use the three boxes on the *Write-on/Wipe-off Boards.* Remind children that the boxes stand for the sounds in words. Say the word *ring* and ask: **What is the first sound you hear in *ring*?** (/r/) Have children place a disk in the first box. Then have children name the second sound in *ring* (/i/) and place a disk in the second box. Then have them identify the last sound in *ring* (/ng/) and place a disk in the third box. Point to each box in sequence as children say the word. **How many sounds do you hear in *ring*? I hear three.** Repeat this procedure with the following words: *bang, hang, wing, king.*

PRETEACH

Phonics

Contraction *'ll* Remind children that a contraction is a shorter way to say or write two words. Review that an apostrophe can be used to show that a letter or letters are missing. Next, write these sentences on the board. Have children read them silently and then aloud. *I will run up the hill. I'll run up the hill.* Underline *I will* and *I'll.*

Say: **I will can be shortened to I'll. The contraction for I will is I'll.** Have children read aloud the sentences. Point out the letters that are missing. (*wi*)

Ask a volunteer to say a sentence using *she will.* Record it on the board. Guide children to rewrite the sentence using a contraction for *she will.* Rewrite the sentence and read it with children, tracking the print. Repeat with *he will, you will,* and *it will.*

RETEACH

Phonics and Spelling

Diphthong /ng/*ng*
Build Words Use *Word Builders* and *Word Builder Cards* to form words. Have children listen to your directions and change a letter in each word to spell a spelling word. Form *sung* and have children read the word. Ask: **Which spelling words can you make by changing the letter that stands for /u/?** (*song, sing*)

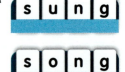

Form *song* and have children read the word. Ask: **Which spelling word can you make by changing the first letter?** (*long*)

Follow a similar process with the following words: *rang* (*ring*), *brink* (*bring*), *thin* (*thing*), *up* (*us*), *mist* (*must*).

Remind children that there are some other words they have to remember how to spell. Have children say *does.* Tell them to put *Word Builder Cards d, o, e, s* in their *Word Builders,* picture the word *does* in their minds, and build the word. Write the word on the board. Follow this procedure with the word *food.*

RETEACH

High-Frequency Words

Copying Masters 39–40

Duplicate and distribute *Copying Masters 39–40* to each child. Explain that the sentences tell the story "Ben" in *Shooting Star* but some have missing words.

List the words *school, your,* and *arms* on the board. Have children read aloud each story strip sentence and name the correct word on the board that makes sense in the sentence. Have children write the missing words in the blanks and read the completed sentences aloud. Help children cut apart the strips, read the completed sentences, and arrange them in story order.

RETEACH

Comprehension

Plot Review with children that a story's plot is made up of the important events that happen in the beginning, middle, and ending of a story. Have children turn to "Ben" in *Shooting Star* and briefly review what happens in the story.

Ask: **Which sentence best tells about the plot? The story is about some boys playing ball. The story is about a boy with long legs. The story is about a boy who joins a game and helps his team win because he has strong arms and legs.** Guide children to understand that the most important part of the story is how Ben joins the team and helps the team win.

RETEACH

Grammar/Writing

p. 37 **Dialogue** Have children turn to "Ben" in *Shooting Star.* Direct their attention to page 37. Explain that when characters in a story talk to each other, the words they say are known as *dialogue.* Use the story to review how dialogue appears in a story.

Point out that the sentences of dialogue have exact words people say to each other. Show children how quotation marks are used around the words. Tell children that a comma is often used after the exact words and that the sentences have words like *said* and *asked.* Guide children to recognize the characteristics of dialogue using "Let's Help Cat" in *Shooting Star.*

High-Frequency Words

school	arms
your	

Fluency

Phrasing Remind children that when good readers read, it sounds like talking. Point out that good readers pause, or stop a little, at the end of dialogue, at the end of sentences, and wherever else it sounds right.

Have partners reread "Ben" in *Shooting Star* aloud several times. Remind them to read the words in "chunks" that belong together to make their reading sound like people do when they speak.

LESSON 10

DAY AT A GLANCE

Day 4

30+ Minutes

PHONEMIC AWARENESS
Phoneme Blending

PHONICS
Reteach Contraction *'ll*

PHONICS AND SPELLING
Reteach Diphthong /ng/*ng*

HIGH-FREQUENCY WORDS
Reteach *arms, every, feet, heard, school, use, way, your*

FLUENCY
Phrasing

COMPREHENSION
Reteach Plot

GRAMMAR/WRITING
Reteach Dialogue

Materials Needed:

Practice Book

Lesson 10 High-Frequency Word Cards

Shooting Star Student Edition pp. 16–22 pp. 36–42

Spelling Words

1. long	6. thing
2. song	7. us
3. sing	8. must
4. ring	9. does
5. bring	10. food

Phonemic Awareness

Phoneme Blending Tell children that together you are going to play a game of "Fix It." Tell them that you are going to say some words that are all broken up and they should listen to see if they can put them back together to figure out the word. Say: **Listen: /s/ /i/ /ng/. What word does /s/ /i/ /ng/ say? It says *sing*. Now you try with these sounds: /r/ /i/ /ng/** (ring), **/h/ /a/ /ng/** (hang), **/k/ /i/ /ng/** (king), **/b/ /a/ /ng/** (bang), **/d/ /i/ /ng/** (ding).

RETEACH

Phonics

Contraction *'ll* Remind children that a contraction is made by joining two words. An apostrophe shows where letters are missing. Write *we* and *will*. Say the words. Write *we'll* underneath.

Say: **The word *we'll* is made by writing *we,* an apostrophe, and the letters *l-l*. The letters *w-i* are missing. The apostrophe is the punctuation mark that shows the missing letters.** Ask children to write the words that make up *I'll* and *she'll*. (*I* and *will* and *she* and *will*)

RETEACH

Phonics and Spelling

Diphthong /ng/*ng*
Direct children's attention to page 41 of their *Practice Book*s. Complete the page together.

Assess children's progress using the following dictation sentences.

1. long   See that dog's **long** tail?
2. song   Can you hear the **song** on the stereo?
3. sing   We like to **sing** when we play.
4. ring   Her **ring** is on her hand.
5. bring   Please **bring** the pencil to me.
6. thing   A crayon is a colorful **thing**.

Review
7. us   She gave **us** the ball.
8. must   We all **must** take a walk.

High-Frequency
9. does   **Does** Ray like milk?
10. food   That is the best **food** for lunch.

High-Frequency Words

arms	school
every	use
feet	way
heard	your

RETEACH

High-Frequency Words

Copying Masters 37–38

Display *High-Frequency Word Cards* for this lesson's words—*arms, every, feet, heard, school, use, way, your*—and the previously learned high-frequency words. Point to words at random and ask children to read them.

RETEACH

Comprehension

Plot Ask children to explain what plot is. (the events that take place in a story) Make a chart on the board like the one below. Work with children to recall the plot of "Ben" and "Beth Can Help" in *Shooting Star*. Record their responses on the chart.

	"Ben"	**"Beth Can Help"**
Beginning	The children ask Ben to play ball.	
Middle	Ben plays with the children and they tell him what a good player he is.	
Ending	The children say Ben will help them win.	

RETEACH

Grammar/Writing

Dialogue Review with children characteristics of well-written dialogue.

Dialogue

The sentences have exact words people say to each other.
Quotation marks (" ") are used around the words.
A comma (,) is often used after the exact words.
The sentences have words like *said* and *asked*.

Write these sentences on the board: *Thanks said Jack. Bring me that map said Kim.* Explain that these sentences have dialogue in them, but they are missing some very important things. Correct the first sentence as you point out what is missing. (*"Thanks," said Jack.*) Then guide children to correct the second sentence. (*"Bring me that map," said Kim.*) Read the sentences aloud and have children echo-read.

Fluency

Phrasing Remind children that when good readers read, it sounds like talking. Their reading has the same rhythm as speech.

Have children turn to "Ben" in *Shooting Star* and practice rereading the story several times as you listen to them read.

Give them feedback about improving their phrasing and guidance for improving fluency.

DAY AT A GLANCE
Day 5

HIGH-FREQUENCY WORDS
arms, every, feet, heard, school, use, way, your

PHONEMIC AWARENESS
Onset and Rime

PHONICS AND SPELLING
Preteach *r*-Controlled Vowel /ôr/*or, ore*

BUILD ROBUST VOCABULARY
Preteach *nuzzled, pranced, raging*

GRAMMAR/WRITING
Preteach Special Names and Titles for People

Materials Needed:

Lesson 10 High-Frequency Word Cards

Sound/Spelling Card *or*

Word Builders and Word Builder Cards

Write-On/ Wipe-Off Boards

Practice Book **p.42**
Practice Book

High-Frequency Words

arms	school
every	use
feet	way
heard	your

High-Frequency Words

Copying Masters 37–38 Display *High-Frequency Word Cards* for *arms, every, feet, heard, school, use, way, your,* and the other previously learned high-frequency words. Say the word *arms,* ask a volunteer to point to *arms,* and have children read the word aloud. Continue with the remaining high-frequency words. Repeat this activity several times to reinforce instant recognition.

Phonemic Awareness

Onset and Rime Tell children you are going to say some words, but you are going to say them in parts. Have children listen to see if they can figure out the word. Say: **/f/-ort—The word I said was *fort*. Now you try some:** **/k/-orn, /th/-orn, /f/-ork, /b/-orn, /f/-orth.**

> PRETEACH

Phonics and Spelling

dot ***r*-Controlled Vowel /ôr/*or, ore***
Connecting Letter to Sound Say the words *order* and *orange,* and have children repeat the words. Explain that both words begin with the /ôr/ sound. Have children say /ôr/ several times. Display *Sound/Spelling Card or,* and say the letter names. Tell children that the letters *or* and *ore* can stand for the sound /ôr/, the sound they hear at the beginning of *order.* Have children say /ôr/ several times as you touch each set of letters.

Give each child *o* and *r* Word Builder Cards. Say: **When I say a word that has the /ôr/ sound, you hold up your cards together and say /ôr/. When I say a word that does not have the /ôr/ sound, hold your cards behind your back.** Say these words: *order, orbit, brain, organize, live, orchestra.* Tell children that some words have the /ôr/ sound in the middle. Follow the same procedure with these words: *tore, dish, storm, fork, ball, fort.*

dot Word Blending Demonstrate each step with *Word Builder Cards* and a *Word Builder* and have children repeat each step after you. Hold up *f* and say /f/. Hold up *or* and say /ôr/. Hold up *t* and say /t/.

- Place the letters *f, o, r, t* in the *Word Builder.*

- Point to *f.* Say /f/. Point to *o* and *r* together and say /ôr/. Prompt children to repeat after you.

- Slide *or* next to *f.* Run your hand under the letters as you blend the sounds, elongating them—/fôr/.

- Point to *t* and say /t/.
- Slide *t* next to *for*. Run your hand under the letters as you blend the sounds, elongating them—/fôrt/.
- Read *fort* naturally.

Follow the same procedure with these words: *for, store, form.*

  Word Building Place the *Word Builder Cards o* and *r* in the *Word Builder* and have children do the same. Ask children to say each letter name and the sound it stands for. Then read the word naturally—*or*. Have children do the same. Have children build and read new words. As they build each word, write it on the board. Say:

- **Add *f* in front of *or*. What word did you make?** (*for*)
- **Add *m* after *or*. What word did you make?** (*form*)

Continue with the words *more, store, sort.* Have children read the words on the board. Direct children's attention to page 42 of their *Practice Books.* Complete the page together.

PRETEACH

Build Robust Vocabulary

Introduce Robust Vocabulary Read the student-friendly explanation for each word. Then discuss each word using the following examples.

Say: **My dog nuzzled me to wake me up because he was hungry. Has your pet ever nuzzled you? Explain.**

Say: **My little sister pranced around the stage during a school performance. Where else might you see someone or something prance?**

Say: **A hurricane has strong, raging winds that can be dangerous. Have you ever seen weather raging? Did it scare you? Explain.**

PRETEACH

Grammar/Writing

Special Names and Titles for People Write these sentences on the board: *Mrs. Dell is here. Dr. Lin has a pet.* Have children read the sentences aloud as you track the print. Explain that each of these sentences is about a certain person.

Point to the capital letters in both *Dell* and *Lin.* Then point to the titles and explain that some people have a special title such as *Mr., Mrs., Ms., Miss,* or *Dr.* Explain that these titles are abbreviations, such as *doctor/Dr.,* and that most begin with a capital letter and end with a period.

Spelling Words

1.	or	6.	sort
2.	for	7.	long
3.	form	8.	bring
4.	more	9.	your
5.	store	10.	head

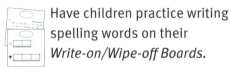 Have children practice writing spelling words on their *Write-on/Wipe-off Boards.*

VOCABULARY
Student-Friendly Explanations

nuzzled If an animal nuzzled against you, it would be rubbing you with its face or nose.

pranced If you pranced around, you would be walking in a bouncy, springy way, like a horse.

raging When something is raging, it is happening in a strong or out-of-control way.

Some Animals

PHONEMIC AWARENESS
Phoneme Isolation

PHONICS AND SPELLING
Reteach r-Controlled Vowel /ôr/or, ore

COMPREHENSION
Preteach Compare and Contrast

HIGH-FREQUENCY WORDS
Reteach animals, from, cold

FLUENCY
Phrasing

GRAMMAR/WRITING
Reteach Special Names and Titles for People

Materials Needed:

Word Builders and Word Builder Cards

Photo Cards

Write-On/Wipe-Off Boards

Shooting Star Student Edition pp. 36–42 pp. 44–45

Practice Book p.43

Spelling Words

1.	or	6.	sort
2.	for	7.	long
3.	form	8.	bring
4.	more	9.	your
5.	store	10.	head

Have children practice writing spelling words on their *Write-on/Wipe-off Boards.*

LESSON 11

⏱ 30+ Minutes

Phonemic Awareness

Phoneme Isolation   Say the word *born* aloud and have children repeat it. Tell children to listen to the /ôr/ in the middle of *born*. Then say the words *corn* and *sing* and have children repeat both words. Say: **Which of these words has the /ôr/ sound your hear in *born*? I hear it in *corn*. Now you try some: *store, fan, sob; play, more, friend; horn, cow, hat.***

RETEACH

Phonics and Spelling

dot   *r*-Controlled Vowel /ôr/or, ore
Word Building   Place the *Word Builder Cards o* and *r* in the *Word Builder*. Ask children to say each letter name and the sound that both letters together stand for. Then read the word naturally—*or*. Have children do the same. Say:

- **Which letter should I add to *or* to make *for*?** (Add *f*.)

o r

- **What letter should I add to make *for* become *form*?** (Add *m*.)

f o r

Continue with the words *more, store, sort.*

f o r m

Read Words in Context   Write the following sentences on chart paper. Have children read each sentence silently. Then track the print as children read the sentences aloud. Finally, point to the underlined words at random and have children read them. *Pat will get more milk at the store. Will you bring your hat or cap with you? Come and put your head here. The yarn is too long. This sort of hen can form a nest for its chicks.*

PRETEACH

Comprehension

Compare and Contrast   Tell children that to compare things is to tell how they are alike and to contrast things is to tell how they are different. Display *Photo Cards rose* and *berries*. Say: **Berries and roses are alike in some ways. They both grow from seeds and on plants. They are also different in some ways. Berries are round and juicy. A rose has petals and smells sweet. You can eat many berries, but you probably shouldn't eat a rose.** Repeat with *Photo Cards snow, rain; porcupine, squirrel; box, sack.*

RETEACH

High-Frequency Words

pp.
44–
45

Write the words *animals, from,* and *cold* on the board.

- Point to and read *animals.* Repeat, having children say *animals* with you.

- Say: **We fed the *animals.***

- Repeat the word and then point to each letter as you spell it. Then have children say and spell *animals* with you. Have children reread the word.

Repeat for the remaining words. Use the following sentences: *I came* from *home. It is* cold *in the winter.*

Have children turn to page 44 of *Shooting Star* and have them read aloud the words at the top of the page. Talk about the illustrations. Then guide children in choosing and circling the word that names each picture. (4. *fork,* 5. *corn,* 6. *store*) Have children read aloud each word in the list on page 45. Ask volunteers to read the sentences aloud. Then have children choral-read the sentences. Guide them to choose and trace the word that completes each sentence. (1. *animals,* 2. *from,* 3. *cold*)

RETEACH

Grammar/Writing

Practice
Book

p.43

Special Names and Titles for People   Remind children that people have names that begin with capital letters and that some have special titles such as *Mr., Mrs., Ms., Miss,* and *Dr.* that begin with a capital letter and often end with a period.

Write the following sentence on the board: *Mrs. Fort is my teacher.* Read the sentence aloud and then with children. Ask: **What is the name of the person? Which word is the special name?** (*Fort*) **What is the title?** (*Mrs.*) **What does each word begin with?** (a capital letter) **How does the title end?** (a period)

Have children dictate other special names of people they know. Record the names on the board without capitalization or punctuation. Work with children to correct the names. Complete *Practice Book* page 43 together.

High-Frequency Words

animals	cold
from	

Fluency

Phrasing   Remind children that good readers pay attention to groups of words that go together, reading one meaningful "chunk" at a time. Have children turn to "Ben" in *Shooting Star.* Read aloud the story, one page at a time, modeling appropriate phrasing. Have children echo-read.

PHONEMIC AWARENESS
Phoneme Blending

PHONICS AND SPELLING
Reteach *r*-Controlled Vowel /ôr/*or, ore*

HIGH-FREQUENCY WORDS
Reteach *animals, cold, fish, from, their, under, very*

FLUENCY
Phrasing

READING
"Some Animals"

BUILD ROBUST VOCABULARY
Preteach *adapt, intriguing, inhabit*

GRAMMAR/WRITING
Reteach Special Names and Titles for People

Materials Needed:

Word Builders and Word Builder Cards

Practice Book
p.44

Practice Book

Copying Masters 41–42

Lesson 11 High-Frequency Word Cards

Shooting Star
Student Edition
pp. 26–32
pp. 46–53

High-Frequency Words

animals	their
cold	under
fish	very
from	

30+ Minutes

Phonemic Awareness

Phoneme Blending   Tell children that they are going to play a guessing game. Then say: **I'm thinking of a word that is a vegetable. It is yellow. It is /k/ /ôr/ /n/. My word is *corn*.** Continue with the following words: /f/ /ôr/ /k/ (*fork*), /sh/ /ôr/ (*shore*), /c/ /ôr/ (*core*), /h/ /ôr/ /s/ (*horse*).

RETEACH

Phonics and Spelling

 *r*-**Controlled Vowel /ôr/*or, ore***
Word Building   Use a *Word Builder* and *Word Builder Cards* and have children repeat each step after you. Build the word *for*. Have children name each letter. Ask them what vowel sound they hear in the word. Have them tell which two letters together stand for the /ôr/ sound. Then have them say the word naturally—*for*. Lead children in building and reading new words by saying:

- **Add *t* after *r*. Read the word.** (*fort*)
- **Change *f* to *s*. Read the word.** (*sort*)
- **Add *p* after *s*. Read the word.** (*sport*)

f o r

f o r t

Continue with the following words: *spot, pot, port.*

 Practice Book p.44   **Read Words in Context**   Ask children to turn to *Practice Book* page 44. Read each sentence aloud and have children echo-read. Then ask volunteers to read each sentence aloud. Ask: **What are the children doing?** (playing at the shore) **Why do they go to the store?** (to get new balls) **Why are they happy with the new balls?** (They score more with the new balls.) Call on volunteers to frame and read words with /ôr/. Then guide children to circle words with the /ôr/ sound.

RETEACH

High-Frequency Words

 Copying Masters 41–42   Display the *High-Frequency Word Cards* for *animals, cold, fish, from, their, under,* and *very*. Point to each card and read the word. Have children repeat. Give each child a set of cards. Then say: **I'm thinking of a word that rhymes with *old*. It means "not warm." Which word am I thinking of?** Have children hold up the card for *cold*. Repeat with remaining words.

Reading

pp. 46–53 **Build Background: "Some Animals"**
Read the title with children and ask them what animal they see on the page. Ask children if they have ever seen a penguin. Explain that zoos often have penguins, and ask children what other animals are in zoos. Tell them that they will be reading about animals that live in different kinds of places, but that many of them are also in zoos.

Monitor Comprehension: "Some Animals"
Have children turn to the first page of the selection. Ask a volunteer to reread the title. Guide children to look at the picture on page 46 and ask children what they think the selection will be about. Then guide children through the selection as they read.

pp. 46–47 Say: **Those penguins seem to live in a very cold place. Let's read to find out what the penguins will do.**

After reading the pages, ask: **So far, what are the penguins doing?** (They are walking, swimming, and looking for food.) **MAIN IDEA AND DETAILS**

Ask: **What is the setting of these pages?** (a cold place where penguins live) **SETTING**

Ask: **What word on these pages has the /ôr/ sound?** (more) **APPLY PHONICS**

pp. 48–49 Say: **We found out more about penguins. Now let's read to find out about some other animals.**

After reading the pages, ask: **What animals did you find out about on these pages?** (camels) **Where do they live?** (in a hot land) **MAIN IDEA AND DETAILS**

Ask: **How is the place the camels live different from where the penguins live?** (The penguins live in a cold place and the camels live in a hot place.) **How are the camels different from the penguins?** (Possible response: Penguins swim and camels walk on four legs.) **COMPARE AND CONTRAST**

Ask: **What word on these two pages has the /ôr/ sound?** (stores) **APPLY PHONICS**

Fluency

Phrasing Read aloud the first several pages of "Just Like Us" in *Shooting Star* modeling correct phrasing. Have children echo-read, making their voices rise and fall just as yours does and pausing at the end of each sentence. Then have partners finish reading aloud together from this familiar text with fluency, demonstrating appropriate phrasing as they read.

Circulate and listen to partners read, giving them feedback about their phrasing and guidance for improving their fluency.

pp. 50–51

Say: **Let's read on to find out about a different kind of animal.**

After reading the pages, ask: **What kind of animals are these?** (seals) **Are these animals more like penguins or camels? Explain.** (Possible response: They are more like penguins because they both swim.)

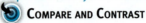 **COMPARE AND CONTRAST**

Ask: **What is the setting of these pages?** (near water and in water) **SETTING**

Say: **Look at page 51. What do you think the seal's snack might be?** (a fish) **DRAW CONCLUSIONS**

Say: **What word on these two pages has the /ôr/ sound?** (*for*) **APPLY PHONICS**

 p. 52

Say: **We've seen animals in hot places, cold places, and wet places. How do you think the animals on this page will be the same and different from those? Let's read to find out.**

After reading the page, ask: **How are these animals the same and different from the others you have read about?** (Possible response: They are the same because they are all animals and they all like to eat. They are different because they are different kinds of animals and live in a different places.) **COMPARE AND CONTRAST**

Ask: **Which of these animals would you most like to visit? Why?** (Possible response: I would like to see the zebras, because I like the way they look.) **PERSONAL RESPONSE**

 p. 53

Answers to *Think Critically* Questions

Help children read and answer the *Think Critically* questions on page 53. Answers are shown below.

 1. ‹ the penguin › **COMPARE AND CONTRAST**

2. ‹ the fish › **MAKE INFERENCES**

3. ‹ the desert scene › **SETTING**

PRETEACH

Build Robust Vocabulary

Introduce Robust Vocabulary Read the student-friendly explanation for each word. Then discuss each word using the following examples.

Say: **A camel's hump helps it adapt to dry, hot weather. The hump stores water for long periods of time. What might you need to adapt if you suddenly had to live in the jungle?**

Say: **I think that China is intriguing. I've always wanted to go, and I love reading about it. What place do you find intriguing?**

Say: **I'm glad that I inhabit a place with lots of things to see and do. Where in the world would you like to inhabit?**

RETEACH

Grammar/Writing

Special Names and Titles for People Invite children to write a note to the principal telling him or her about an interesting story they have read. Explain that they need to include special names and titles in the note. Work with children to write a note similar to this one without correct punctuation.

> Dear dr cho,
>
> We read "Some Animals." It is by mr clark edward. We learned about camels.
>
> Sincerely,
>
> miss free's class

Read the letter aloud and circle a special name when it is read. Work with children to correct the special names in the letter. Then read the corrected note with children.

VOCABULARY

Student-Friendly Explanations

adapt If an animal adapts to a place, it has body parts or ways of acting that help it live there.

intriguing If you think that something is intriguing, you are curious about it and very interested in it.

inhabit If you inhabit a place, you live there.

LESSON 11

DAY AT A GLANCE
Day 3

30+ Minutes

PHONEMIC AWARENESS
Phoneme Segmentation

PHONICS
Preteach Compound Words

PHONICS AND SPELLING
Reteach *r*-Controlled Vowel /ôr/*or, ore*

HIGH-FREQUENCY WORDS
Reteach *animals, from, cold*

FLUENCY
Phrasing

COMPREHENSION
Reteach Compare and Contrast

GRAMMAR/WRITING
Reteach Interview Questions

Materials Needed:

Write-On/
Wipe-Off
Boards with
Phonemic
Awareness
Disks

Word Builders
and Word
Builder Cards

Copying
Masters
43–44

Lesson 11
Story Strips

Shooting Star
Student Edition
pp. 36–42
pp. 46–52

Spelling Words

1. or	6. sort
2. for	7. long
3. form	8. bring
4. more	9. your
5. store	10. head

Phonemic Awareness

Phoneme Segmentation Have children use the three boxes on the *Write-on/Wipe-off Boards.* Remind children that the boxes stand for the sounds in words. Say the word *horn* and ask: **What is the first sound you hear in *horn*?** (/h/) Have children place a disk in the first box. Then have children name the second sound in *horn* (/ôr/) and place a disk in the second box. Then have them identify the last sound in *horn* (/n/) and place a disk in the third box. Point to each box in sequence as children say the word. **How many sounds do you hear in *horn*? I hear three.** Repeat this procedure with the following words: *thorn, fork, sort, born.*

PRETEACH

Phonics

Compound Words Explain that some words, called *compound words*, are made by joining two smaller words. Write *popcorn* on the board, and explain that two words make up *popcorn—pop* and *corn.* Tell children that they can look for and read each small word in a longer word like *popcorn* to figure it out. Guide children to find the words that make up *inside* and *forklift.*

RETEACH

Phonics and Spelling

d o t ***r*-Controlled Vowel /ôr/*or, ore***
Build Words Use *Word Builders and Word Builder Cards* to form words. Have children listen to your directions and change a letter in each word to spell a spelling word. Form *or* and have children read the word. Ask: **Which spelling word can you make by adding a letter to the beginning?** (*for*)

o r

f o r

Follow a similar procedure with the following words: *fort* (form), *core* (more), *stork* (store), *lung* (long), *brang* (bring).

Remind children that there are some other words they have to remember how to spell. Have children say *your.* Tell them to put *Word Builder Cards y, o, u, r* in their *Word Builders,* picture the word *your* in their minds, and build the word. Write the word on the board. Follow the same procedure with *head.*

RETEACH

High-Frequency Words

 Copying Masters 43–44

Duplicate and distribute *Copying Masters* 43–44 to each child. Explain that the sentences tell the selection "Some Animals" but some have missing words.

List the words *animals, from,* and *cold* on the board. Have children read aloud each story strip sentence and name the correct word on the board that makes sense in the sentence. Have children write the missing words in the blanks and read the completed sentences aloud. Help children cut apart the strips, read the completed sentences, and arrange them in story order.

RETEACH

Comprehension

Compare and Contrast Remind children that people compare things to show how they are alike and contrast things to show how they are different. Have children turn to "Ben" in *Shooting Star.* Guide children through a picture walk to compare and contrast Ben and the other children in the story. Say: **Ben is like the other students in some ways and he is different as well. He has some special gifts that make him different, like his long legs. What are some other ways he is different? How is he the same?**

RETEACH

Grammar/Writing

Interview Questions Explain that a person interviews someone to find out more about that person. He or she asks questions to find out more. Remind children that questions begin with a capital letter and end with a question mark.

Explain that interview questions often begin with words such as *Who, What, When, Where, Why,* and *How.* Have children suggest someone they would like to know more about, such as a school worker or a celebrity. Choose one person. Then have children dictate questions they would ask if they could interview that person. Explain to children that it is important to ask interview questions in an order that makes sense. First, ask questions to get to know a person and then ask questions about his or her job or other important things.

High-Frequency Words

animals   cold

from

Fluency

Phrasing Tell children that reading should sound the way people do when they talk. The words should have the same kind of rhythm. To do this, good readers read "chunks" of words that go together. Remind children to notice capital letters and end marks to know where sentences begin and end, and to read groups of words that belong together.

Have children turn to "Some Animals" in *Shooting Star.* Read aloud the first few pages, once word by word and once with appropriate phrasing. Discuss the difference with children. Then model reading with appropriate phrasing and have them echo-read.

LESSON 11

DAY AT A GLANCE

Day 4

30+ Minutes

PHONEMIC AWARENESS
Phoneme Blending

PHONICS
Reteach Compound Words

PHONICS AND SPELLING
Reteach *r*-Controlled Vowel /ôr/*or, ore*

HIGH-FREQUENCY WORDS
Reteach *animals, cold, fish, from, their, under, very*

FLUENCY
Phrasing

COMPREHENSION
Reteach Compare and Contrast

GRAMMAR/WRITING
Reteach Interview Questions

Materials Needed:

Practice Book

Lesson 11 High-Frequency Word Cards

Sweet Success Student Edition pp. 26–32 pp. 46–52

Spelling Words

1. or	6. sort
2. for	7. long
3. form	8. bring
4. more	9. your
5. store	10. head

Phonemic Awareness

Phoneme Blending   Tell children that together you are going to play a game and say some sounds that they should put together to figure out a whole word. Say: **Listen: /f/ /ôr/ /t/. The word is** *fort.* **Now you try some.** Continue with: /sh/ /ôr/ /t/ (*short*), /h/ /ôr/ /n/ (*horn*), /f/ /ôr/ /m/ (*form*), /k/ /ôr/ /n/ (*corn*), /t/ /ôr/ /n/ (*torn*), /w/ /ôr/ /n/ (*worn*).

RETEACH

Phonics

Compound Words   Remind children that compound words are made by joining two smaller words. Write *sun* and *set.* Point to each word and have children read it. Write *sunset* underneath and have children read it. Say: ***Sunset* is made by putting together** *sun* **and** *set.* **This is a compound word. It means when the sun goes down.** Repeat with *eggshell, kickball,* and *something.*

RETEACH

Phonics and Spelling

Practice Book p.45   ***r*-Controlled Vowel /ôr/*or, ore***
Direct children's attention to page 45 of their *Practice Books.* Complete the page together.

Assess children's progress using the following sentences.

1. or   We can eat eggs **or** ham.
2. for   I had plums **for** a snack.
3. form   Can you **form** a tent with sticks?
4. more   Beth would like **more** juice.
5. store   We went to the **store** to get crayons.
6. sort   Will you **sort** the blocks with me?

Review

7. long   That bug is very **long.**
8. bring   Can you **bring** me the glasses?

High-Frequency

9. your   Is that **your** dog?
10. head   I got a bump on my **head.**

High-Frequency Words

animals	their
cold	under
fish	very
from	

RETEACH

High-Frequency Words

Copying Masters 41–42

Display *High-Frequency Word Cards* for this lesson's words—*animals, cold, fish, from, their, under,* and *very*—and the previously learned high-frequency words. Point to words at random and ask children to read them.

RETEACH

Comprehension

Compare and Contrast   Ask children what it means to compare things and contrast things. (to tell how things are alike; to tell how things are different) Have them compare two classroom objects. Then recall with children "Some Animals" and "Just Like Us" in *Shooting Star.* On the board or on chart paper, draw a two-column chart. Ask children how the selections are alike and how they are different. Record their responses on the chart.

Alike	Different
Both stories have animals. Both stories are nonfiction.	One story has trees, deer, and birds. The other story has camels, zebras, penguins, and seals.

RETEACH

Grammar/Writing

Interview Questions   Review with children characteristics of well-written interview questions.

> ### Interview Questions
>
> The questions help you find out about a person.
> Sentences begin with words such as *Who, What, When, Where, Why,* and *How.*
> Questions end with a question mark.

Invite a volunteer to roleplay an interview with you. Ask the volunteer questions about things he or she likes to do in school. Then have children dictate some of the questions you asked and write them on the board. Point out the characteristics in the questions you wrote. Have partners practice interviewing one another and share one question each with the group.

Fluency

Phrasing   Have children turn to "Some Animals" in *Shooting Star* and have partners reread the selection three or four times, demonstrating appropriate phrasing. Listen to partners read, giving feedback and guidance for improving fluency.

DAY AT A GLANCE

Day 5

30+ Minutes

HIGH-FREQUENCY WORDS
animals, cold, fish, from, their, under, very

PHONEMIC AWARENESS
Onset and Rime

PHONICS AND SPELLING
Preteach Digraph /sh/*sh*

BUILD ROBUST VOCABULARY
Preteach *reward, handsomely, cruel*

GRAMMAR/WRITING
Preteach Special Names of Places

Materials Needed:

Lesson 11
High-Frequency
Word Cards

Sound/
Spelling
Card *sh*

Word Builders
and Word
Builder Cards

Write-On/
Wipe-Off
Boards

Practice Book p.46
Practice
Book

Photo Card
Photo
Cards

High-Frequency Words

animals	**their**
cold	**under**
fish	**very**
from	

High-Frequency Words

Copying Masters 41–42

Display *High-Frequency Word Cards* for *animals, cold, fish, from, their, under, very,* and the other previously learned high-frequency words. Say the word *animals,* ask a volunteer to point to *animals,* and have children read the word aloud. Continue with the remaining high-frequency words. Repeat this activity several times to reinforce instant recognition.

Phonemic Awareness

Onset and Rime   Tell children that you are going to say some words, but you are going to say them in parts. Have children listen to see if they can figure out the word. Demonstrate by saying: **/sh/-ut—The word I said was *shut*. Now you try some: /sh/-ore, /sh/-irt, /h/-ush, /f/-ish, /k/-ash.**

PRETEACH

Phonics and Spelling

Sound/ Spelling Card   **d o t**   **Digraph /sh/*sh***
Connecting Letter to Sound   Say the words *ship, shop,* and *shot,* and have children repeat the words. Explain that all three words begin with the /sh/ sound. Have children say /sh/ several times. Display *Sound/Spelling Card sh,* say the sound name, and identify the picture. Tell children that the letters *sh* together can stand for the sound /sh/, the sound at the beginning of *ship.* Have children say /sh/ several times as you touch the letters.

Give each child *s* and *h Word Builder Cards.* Say: **When I say a word that has the /sh/ sound, put the cards on your shoe and say /sh/. When I say a word that does not have the /sh/ sound, hold your cards behind your back.** Say these words: *shell, dog, shin, shirt, port, ship.* Tell children that some words have the sound /sh/ at the end. Say *dish,* elongating the /sh/ sound. Tell children that the word *dish* has /sh/ at the end. Repeat the process for words that end in /sh/ with: *rush, trap, fish, hug, mush, wash, wish.*

d o t   **Word Blending**   Demonstrate each step with *Word Builder Cards* and a *Word Builder.* Have children repeat each step after you. Hold up *s* and *h* and say /sh/. Hold up *i* and say /i/. Hold up *p* and say /p/.

- Place the letters *s, h, i, p* in the *Word Builder.*

- Point to *sh.* Say /sh/. Point to *i* and say /i/. Prompt children to repeat after you.

- Slide *i* next to *sh.* Run your hand under the letters as you blend the sounds, elongating them—/shi/.

- Point to *p* and say /p/.
- Slide *p* next to *shi*. Run your hand under *ship* as you blend the sounds, elongating them—/ship/. Read *ship* naturally.

Follow the same procedure with these words: *shut, crash, shell.*

  Word Building Place the *Word Builder Cards s, h, o,* and *p* in the *Word Builder.* Have children repeat with their *Word Builders.* Slide your hand under the letters and read the word—*shop.* Repeat, and have children read it. Have children build and read new words. As they build each word, write it on the board. Say:

- **Change the *p* to *t*. What word did you make?** (*shot*)
- **Change the *o* to *u*. What word did you make?** (*shut*)

Continue with the words *rush, wish,* and *fish.* Then have children read the words on the board. Direct children's attention to page 46 of their *Practice Books.* Complete the page together.

PRETEACH

Build Robust Vocabulary

Introduce Robust Vocabulary Read the student-friendly explanation for each word. Then discuss each word using the following examples.

Say: **If I lost my dog and someone found and returned him, I would reward the person with a gift. When would you reward someone?**

Say: **I was rewarded handsomely when my students gave me a birthday card. What do you think would be a handsome reward?**

Say: **To call someone names or to be mean is cruel. Tell about a cruel character from a movie that you have seen.**

PRETEACH

Grammar/Writing

 Special Names of Places Display a map of North America. Point to the United States and your state. Write each name on the board and discuss that each place is special, so each has a special name. Point out the capital letter at the beginning. Remind children that special names for people begin with a capital letter.

Display *Photo Card school.* Write *school* and the name of your school on the board. Point out the capital letters in the name of your school. Explain that while *school* could mean any school, your school's name is special and there is only one like it, so it begins with capital letters.

Spelling Words

1. shop	6. fish
2. shot	7. for
3. shut	8. more
4. rush	9. from
5. wish	10. very

 Have children practice writing spelling words on their *Write-on/Wipe-off Boards*

VOCABULARY
Student-Friendly Explanations

reward If you reward someone, you give something special or nice to that person for something he or she has done.

handsomely To do something handsomely means to do it in a way that is great or more than you expected.

cruel Something is cruel when it brings pain or makes you feel bad.

30+ Minutes

LESSON 12

The Water Dish

PHONEMIC AWARENESS
Phoneme Isolation

PHONICS AND SPELLING
Reteach Digraph /sh/*sh*

COMPREHENSION
Preteach Setting

HIGH-FREQUENCY WORDS
Reteach *saw, could, was*

FLUENCY
Expression

GRAMMAR/WRITING
Reteach Special Names of Places

Materials Needed:

Word Builders and Word Builder Cards

Write-On/ Wipe-Off Boards

Shooting Star Student Edition pp. 16–22 pp. 54–55

Practice Book
p.47

Practice Book

Spelling Words

1. shop	6. fish
2. shot	7. for
3. shut	8. more
4. rush	9. from
5. wish	10. very

Have children practice writing spelling words on their *Write-on/Wipe-off Boards*

Phonemic Awareness

Phoneme Isolation Say the word *shut* aloud and have children repeat it. Tell children to listen to the /sh/ at the beginning of *shut*. Then say the words *shine* and *time*. Ask: **Which of these words has the /sh/ sound you hear in shut? I hear it in shine.** Continue with: *fish, wash, at; lash, wish, make; ship, shape, said; shut, shoe, has.*

RETEACH

Phonics and Spelling

Digraph/sh/*sh*
Word Building Place the *Word Builder Cards s, h, o,* and *p* in the *Word Builder.* Ask children to say each letter name and sound it stands for. Review that the letters *sh* together stand for one sound—/sh/. Read the word naturally—*shop.* Have children do the same. Ask:

- **Which letter should I change to make shop become shot?** (Change *p* to *t.*)

- **What letter should I change in shot to make shut?** (Change *o* to *u.*)

Continue with the words *rush, wish,* and *fish.*

Read Words in Context Write the following sentences on chart paper. Have children read each sentence silently. Then track the print as children read the sentences aloud. Finally, point to the underlined words at random and have children read them. *She will make a wish. Do you have to get a shot? You can shop for more fish. Pat likes to rush home from school. Please shut the door. My cat can run very fast.*

PRETEACH

Comprehension

Setting Tell children that the setting of the story is where and when it takes place. Have children turn to "Beth Can Help" in *Shooting Star*. Say: **Look at the pictures in "Beth Can Help." Beth is working in a garden outside. There are plants around her. The people are wearing hats to shade them from the sun. These pictures tell me that the setting is a garden outside on a sunny day.** Do a picture walk through other stories and guide children to identify the setting of each.

High-Frequency Words

saw	was
could	

RETEACH

High-Frequency Words

 Write the words *saw*, *could*, and *was* on the board.

- Point to and read *saw*. Repeat, having children say *saw* with you.
- Say: **I looked in the tree and *saw* a bird.**
- Repeat the word and then point to each letter as you spell it. Then have children say and spell *saw* with you. Have children reread the word.

Repeat for the remaining words. Use the following sentences: *We* could *go to the zoo. Yesterday's lunch* was *good.*

Have children turn to page 54 of *Shooting Star* and have them read aloud the words at the top of the page. Talk about the illustrations. Then guide children in choosing and circling the word that names each picture. (4. *shell,* 5. *dish,* 6. *brush*) Have children read aloud each word in the list on page 55. Ask volunteers to read the sentences aloud. Then have children choral-read the sentences. Guide them to trace the word that completes each sentence. (1. *saw,* 2. *was,* 3. *could*)

RETEACH

Grammar/Writing

Practice Book p.47 **Special Names of Places** Write common place-names on separate sheets of chart paper, such as *school, lake, park, street,* and *store.* Display the sheets with place-names. Invite children to make up special names for each, such as *Aspen School, Grand Lake,* and so on. Write the names on the board. Ask children what they notice about the words. (They begin with a capital letter.) Remind children that each word in the name of a special place begins with a capital letter. Then complete *Practice Book* page 47 together.

Fluency

Expression Tell children that good readers use their voices to show characters' feelings. Review that an exclamation point is a signal to read the sentence with excitement. Have children open to "Beth Can Help" in *Shooting Star*. Model reading with appropriate expression and have children echo-read.

LESSON 12

DAY AT A GLANCE

Day 2

30+ Minutes

PHONEMIC AWARENESS
Phoneme Blending

PHONICS AND SPELLING
Reteach Digraph /sh/*sh*

HIGH-FREQUENCY WORDS
Reteach *came, could, gold, happy, made, night, saw, were, was*

FLUENCY
Punctuation

READING
"The Water Dish"

BUILD ROBUST VOCABULARY
Preteach *greedy, consequences, regret*

GRAMMAR/WRITING
Reteach Special Names of Places

Materials Needed:

Practice Book p.48

Copying Masters 45–46

Word Builders and Word Builder Cards

Practice Book

Lesson 12 High-Frequency Word Cards

Photo Card

Shooting Star Student Edition pp. 46–52 pp. 56–63

Photo Cards

High-Frequency Words

came	night
could	saw
gold	were
happy	was
made	

Phonemic Awareness

Phoneme Blending   Tell children that they are going to play a guessing game. Then say: **I'm thinking of a word that is something you put on your foot. It is a /sh/ /ū/. My word is *shoe*.** Continue with the following words: /sh/ /i/ /p/ (*ship*), /sh/ /ôr/ (*shore*), /d/ /i/ /sh/ (*dish*), /sh/ /a/ /k/ (*shack*).

RETEACH

Phonics and Spelling

Digraph /sh/*sh*

Word Building   Use a *Word Builder* and *Word Builder Cards* and have children repeat each step with their *Word Builders* and *Word Builder Cards*. Build the word *shin*. Then have children read the word naturally. Lead children in building and reading new words. Help them discriminate between the /sh/ and /th/ sounds as they say the words. Say:

s	h	i	n

t	h	i	n

- **Change *sh* to *th*. Read the word.** (*thin*)
- **Change *n* to *ck*. Read the word.** (*thick*)

Practice Book p.48

Read Words in Context   Ask children to turn to *Practice Book* page 48. Read each sentence aloud and have children echo-read. Then ask volunteers to read each sentence aloud. Ask: **What are the children doing?** (fishing) **Which kids got fish?** (All the kids got fish.) **What will they do with the fish?** (They will eat the fish.) Guide children to circle the words that have the /sh/ sound and underline words that have the /th/ sound.

RETEACH

High-Frequency Words

Copying Masters 45–46

Display the *High-Frequency Word Cards* for *came, could, gold, happy, made, night, saw, were,* and *was*. Point to and read each card, having children repeat. Give each child a set of *High-Frequency Word Cards*. Have children spread out the cards. Tell children that when you say a word, they should hold up the matching card and read it aloud. Repeat the activity until children respond quickly and accurately.

Reading

pp. 56–63

Build Background: "The Water Dish"

Read the title with children and ask them what animal they see. Ask children if they have ever seen a seagull, which is the bird on this page. Invite volunteers to tell of any experiences they have had at the shore, including seagull sightings. Tell them that they will be reading about a seagull's adventure near the shore.

Monitor Comprehension: "The Water Dish"

Have children turn to the first page of the story. Ask a volunteer to reread the title. Guide children to look at the pictures on pages 56 and 57 and ask children what they think the story will be about. Then guide children through the story as they read.

 Say: **This bird seems to be looking for something. Let's read to find out what is going on.**

After reading the pages, ask: **What does Bird want?** (She wants a drink of water.) **NOTE DETAILS**

Ask: **What is the setting of these pages?** (a seashore during the day) **SETTING**

Ask: **What words on these pages have the /sh/ sound?** (*she, dish*) **APPLY PHONICS**

 Say: **We found out what Bird wants. Now let's read to find out if she will be able to get a drink.**

After reading the pages, ask: **Can the bird get a drink?** (no) **Why not?** (The glass is too deep.) **MAKE INFERENCES**

Ask: **What do you think Bird will do to get a drink?** (Possible response: Bird could knock over the glass.) **MAKE PREDICTIONS**

Ask: **What word on these two pages has the /sh/ sound?** (*she*) **APPLY PHONICS**

 Say: **Let's read on to find out what happens next.**

After reading the pages, ask: **How does the bird get a drink?** (She drops shells in the dish.) **PROBLEM/SOLUTION**

Ask: **How is the glass of water different at the end than at the beginning of the story?** (The glass of water has seashells in it at the end and the water is higher.) **COMPARE AND CONTRAST**

Fluency

Punctuation Have children open to pages 51 and 52 of "Some Animals" in *Shooting Star* and ask a volunteer to name the end punctuation of each of the sentences.

Remind them that the exclamation point at the end of the second sentence indicates that the sentence should be said with strong feeling. Model reading "All animals like to eat!" excitedly.

Have children take turns reading the sentences aloud with appropriate expression.

Say: **What can you tell about the bird from what she does in this story?** (Possible response: You can tell the bird is smart because she solved her problem.) **DRAW CONCLUSIONS**

Ask: **What words on these two pages have the /sh/ sound?** (*Splash, she, shells, she*) **APPLY PHONICS**

 page 62

Say: **Bird is able to get a drink of water. How do you think she feels now? Let's read to find out.**

After reading the page, ask: **How does Bird feel now?** (happy) **How can you tell?** (Possible response: She thinks the water was good and looks happy in the picture.) **DRAW CONCLUSIONS**

Ask: **How is the bird different now from how she was at the beginning of the story?** (Possible response: At the beginning, she is thirsty and wants a drink of water and at the end she has had a drink and is happy.) **COMPARE AND CONTRAST**

 page 63

Answers to *Think Critically* Questions

Help children read and answer the *Think Critically* questions on page 63. Answers are shown below.

1. ‹sand dune scene› 🔄 **SETTING**
2. ‹seashells› **NOTE DETAILS**
3. ‹Bird dropping shells into the dish› **PLOT**

PRETEACH
Build Robust Vocabulary

Introduce Robust Vocabulary Read the student-friendly explanation for each word. Then discuss each word using the following examples.

Say: **A greedy dog wants all the bones. Would it be greedy to eat all the jelly beans in a bag or to share them with others?**

Say: **If you don't wear a coat when it is snowing, the consequences might be that you get cold. What might a consequence be if you forget to tie your shoes?**

Say: **I felt regret when I was mean to my friend. What might make you feel regret—if you forget to study for a test or if you learn something new?**

VOCABULARY

Student-Friendly Explanations

greedy A greedy person wants a lot of something and does not want to share it.

consequences Consequences happen as the result of another action. If I walk on thin ice, the consequences might be that I fall through the ice.

regret A person who has a regret feels sorry for something he or she did.

RETEACH

Grammar/Writing

Special Names of Places Tell children they will make up special names of places in a make-believe town. Write *town* on the board. Tell children that a town has a special name. Make up a name that uses your last name, such as *Jackson Springs* or *Jacksonville*. Write the name on the board without proper capitalization.

jacksonville

grant park

dog river

don's books

Point out that the town's name is special because it is the only place with that name. Point out that each word in the name should begin with a capital letter. Correct the name.

Guide children to brainstorm other places a town needs, such as a library, a police station, a park, a lake or river, and a store. Write the common nouns on chart paper and invite children to suggest special names. Write the special names beside the common nouns without proper capitalization. Guide children to correct the names and read them aloud. Have children echo-read.

LESSON 12

DAY AT A GLANCE
Day 3

30+ Minutes

PHONEMIC AWARENESS
Phoneme Segmentation

PHONICS
Preteach Initial Blends with *l, s, r*

PHONICS AND SPELLING
Reteach Digraph /sh/*sh*

HIGH-FREQUENCY WORDS
Reteach *saw, could, was*

FLUENCY
Expression

COMPREHENSION
Reteach Setting

GRAMMAR/WRITING
Reteach Riddles

Materials Needed:

Write-On/
Wipe-Off
Boards with
Phonemic
Awareness
Disks

Photo
Cards

Word Builders
and Word
Builder Cards

Copying
Masters
47–48

Lesson 12
Story Strips

Shooting Star
Student Edition
pp. 56–62

Spelling Words

1. shop	6. fish
2. shot	7. for
3. shut	8. more
4. rush	9. from
5. wish	10. very

Phonemic Awareness

Phoneme Segmentation   Have children use the three boxes on the *Write-on/Wipe-off Boards*. Remind children that the boxes stand for the sounds in words. Display *Photo Card fish* and ask: **What is the first sound you hear in *fish*?** (/f/) Have children place a disk in the first box. Then have children name the second sound in *fish* (/i/) and place a disk in the second box. Then have them identify the last sound in *fish* (/sh/) and place a disk in the third box. Point to each box in sequence as children say the word. **How many sounds do you hear in *fish*? I hear three.** Repeat this procedure with *Photo Cards hall, shoe, sack.*

PRETEACH

Phonics

Initial Blends with *l, s, r*   Write *pretty* on the board. Point out that *pretty* has the consonant blend *pr*. Review that a consonant blend is made up of two or three consonants next to each other, but each letter stands for its own sound. On chart paper, write *s* blends as column headings: *sc, sk, sl, sm, sn, sp, st, sw, scr, str.* Guide children to name words with those blends. Ask children to use some of the words in sentences. Repeat with *l* blends (*bl, cl, fl, gl, pl*) and *r* blends. (*br, cr, dr, fr, gr, pr, tr*)

RETEACH

Phonics and Spelling

Digraph /sh/*sh*

Build Words   Use *Word Builders* and *Word Builder Cards* to form words. Have children listen to your directions and change a letter in each word to spell a spelling word. Form *mop* and have children read the word. Ask: **Which spelling word can you make by changing the first letter?** (*shop*)

Follow a similar procedure with the following words: *short* (*shot*), *blush* (*rush*), *cut* (*shut*), *fish* (*wish*), *form* (*for*), *bore* (*more*).

Remind children that there are other words they have to remember how to spell. Have children say *from*. Tell them to put *Word Builder Cards f, r, o, m* in their *Word Builders*, picture the word *from* in their minds, and build the word. Write the word on the board. Follow the same procedure with the word *very*.

High-Frequency Words

saw	was
could	

RETEACH

High-Frequency Words

Copying Masters 47–48

Duplicate and distribute *Copying Masters* 47–48 to each child. Explain that the sentences tell the story "The Water Dish" but some have missing words.

List the words *saw, could,* and *was* on the board. Have children read aloud each story strip sentence and name the correct word on the board that makes sense in the sentence. Have children write the missing words in the blanks and read the completed sentences aloud. Help children cut apart the strips, read the completed sentences, and arrange them in story order.

RETEACH

Comprehension

Setting Remind children that the setting is when and where a story takes place. Have children turn to "The Water Dish" in *Shooting Star* and point out the setting. Then lead children in a discussion about why the setting is important to the story's meaning. (The setting is outside near the ocean during the day. The story is about a bird trying to get water from a dish. The setting is important because most birds live outside and this bird probably lives near the ocean.) Ask children how the story might be different if the setting was inside a house.

RETEACH

Grammar/Writing

Photo Card

Riddles Hold *Photo Card rain* behind your back. Tell children you will say some clues about something and they are going to guess what it is. Say: **I am wet. I fall from the sky. My cloud is where I come from. You might use an umbrella to keep me away. What am I?** Allow children to guess the thing and explain their reasoning. Then display *Photo Card rain* to show them the answer.

Tell children that the sentences you told them make up a riddle. Write the sentences on the board and read them aloud, tracking the print. Point out the following:

- The sentences give clues about something and that the clues use *I, me,* and *my.*
- The clues begin with a capital letter and end with a period.
- A question ends the riddle.

Remind children that questions begin with a capital letter and end with a question mark. Have volunteers circle the capital letters, end punctuation, and the words *I, me, my* in the riddle.

Fluency

Expression Reread "The Water Dish" in *Shooting Star*, modeling expressive reading. Ask: **Did I read with expression? Did I read with excitement when there was an exclamation point?** Remind children to notice end marks and to use their voices to show different feelings. Have children practice rereading the story for fluency.

LESSON 12

30+ Minutes

DAY AT A GLANCE

Day 4

PHONEMIC AWARENESS
Phoneme Blending

PHONICS
Reteach Initial Blends with *l, s, r*

PHONICS AND SPELLING
Reteach Digraph /sh/*sh*

HIGH-FREQUENCY WORDS
Reteach *came, could, gold, happy, made, night, saw, were, was*

FLUENCY
Expression

COMPREHENSION
Reteach Setting

GRAMMAR/WRITING
Reteach Riddles

Materials Needed:

Practice Book

Lesson 12 High-Frequency Word Cards

Shooting Star Student Edition
pp. 16–22
pp. 36–42
pp. 56–62

Spelling Words

1. shop	6. fish
2. shot	7. for
3. shut	8. more
4. rush	9. from
5. wish	10. very

Phonemic Awareness

Phoneme Blending   Tell children that together you are going to play a puzzle game. Tell them that you are going to say some words in pieces, like a puzzle, and they should listen to see if they can put the puzzle pieces together to figure out the word. Say: **Listen: /sh/ /i/ /p/. The word is** *ship.* **Now you try with these sounds: /sh/ /ôr/** (*shore*), **/h/ /u/ /sh/** (*hush*), **/ch/ /i/ /p/** (*chip*), **/k/ /a/ /sh/** (*cash*), **/d/ /i/ /sh/** (*dish*).

RETEACH

Phonics

Initial Blends with *l, s, r*   Review that a consonant blend is made up of two or three consonants next to each other, but each letter stands for its own sound. Remind children that the consonants *l, s,* and *r* can be used beside other consonants to make blends. Write *black* on the board and circle *bl*. Say: **The word** *black* **has the consonant blend** *bl* **at the beginning. You can hear the /b/ and the /l/ sounds.** Say *black* slowly and listen for each sound. Write *spot* and *trap* and have children circle the blends.

RETEACH

Phonics and Spelling

 Digraph /sh/*sh*

Direct children's attention to page 49 of their *Practice Books.* Complete the page together.

Assess children's progress using the following sentences.

1. shop   Can you **shop** for a new hat?
2. shot   The nurse will give Hal a **shot.**
3. shut   I will **shut** the window.
4. rush   You will catch the bus if you **rush.**
5. wish   I will make a **wish** on a star.
6. fish   That **fish** jumped from the pond.

Review

7. for   We will get that gift **for** Mom.
8. more   Will the cat drink **more** milk?

High-Frequency

9. from   That cake is **from** Mrs. Block.
10. very   That trip was **very** short.

Day 4

RETEACH

High-Frequency Words

 Copying Masters 45–46

Display *High-Frequency Word Cards* for this lesson's words—*came, could, gold, happy, made, night, saw, were,* and *was*—and the previously learned high-frequency words. Point to words at random and ask children to read them.

RETEACH

Comprehension

  Setting   Ask children to tell what the setting of a story is. (where and when a story takes place) Draw a chart on the board like the one below. Remind children that these are stories that they have read. Briefly review "The Water Dish," "Beth Can Help," and "Ben" in *Shooting Star*. Point out the setting of "The Water Dish" and record it on the chart. Then guide children to describe the setting of "Beth Can Help" and "Ben." Discuss with children how the settings of the three stories are alike and how they are different.

Setting	"The Water Dish"	"Beth Can Help"	"Ben"
Where	outside, by the water on a dock		
When	sunny day		

RETEACH

Grammar/Writing

 Photo Card

Riddles   Review characteristics of riddles.

Riddles

Sentences give clues about something.
The clues use *I, me,* and *my.*
Clues begin with a capital letter and end with a period.
A question ends the riddle.
The question begins with a capital letter and ends with a question mark.

Display *Photo Card sandcastle.* Tell children that you will work together to make a riddle about a sandcastle. Guide children to dictate clues about a sandcastle as you write the sentences on the board. Guide them to dictate a question to end the riddle. Record their riddle with incorrect capitalization and spelling. Have children correct the sentences with you.

High-Frequency Words

came	night
could	saw
gold	were
happy	was
made	

Fluency

Expression   Remind children that good readers use expression when they read to show different feelings. Have partners read "The Water Dish" in *Shooting Star* aloud three or four times, demonstrating appropriate expression as they read. Listen to partners read, giving them feedback about their expression and guidance for improving their fluency. Remind children to pay attention to end marks and to use their voices to show different feelings.

"The Water Dish"   143

DAY AT A GLANCE

Day 5

HIGH-FREQUENCY WORDS
came, could, gold, happy, made, night, saw, were

PHONEMIC AWARENESS
Onset and Rime

PHONICS AND SPELLING
Preteach Digraphs /ch/*ch, tch*

BUILD ROBUST VOCABULARY
Preteach *astonishing, continue, doubt*

GRAMMAR/WRITING
Preteach Names of Days and Months

Materials Needed:

Lesson 12 High-Frequency Word Cards

Sound/Spelling Card *ch*

Word Builders and Word Builder Cards

Write-On/ Wipe-Off Boards

Practice Book

High-Frequency Words

came	made
could	night
gold	saw
happy	were

High-Frequency Words

Copying Masters 45–46
Display *High-Frequency Word Cards* for *came, could, gold, happy, made, night, saw, were* and the other previously learned high-frequency words. Say the word *came*, ask a volunteer to point to *came*, and have children read the word aloud. Continue with the remaining high-frequency words. Repeat this activity several times to reinforce instant recognition.

Phonemic Awareness

Onset and Rime   Tell children that you are going to say some words, but you are going to say them in parts. Have children listen to see if they can figure out the word. **Listen as I say this word in parts. /ch/-in—The word I said was *chin*. Now you try some /m/-uch, /h/-atch, /ch/-ild, /b/-atch.**

PRETEACH

Phonics and Spelling

 Digraphs /ch/ *ch, tch*
Connecting Letter to Sound   Say the word *chin*. Explain that *chin* begins with the /ch/ sound. Have children say /ch/ several times. Display *Sound/Spelling Card ch,* and say the letter names. Explain that the letters *c* and *h* together stand for the sound /ch/, the sound at the beginning of *cherry*. Have children say /ch/ several times as you touch the letters. Then explain that the letters *tch* at the end of a word also stand for the /ch/ sound, as in the word *patch*.

Say: **When I say a word that begins with /ch/, raise your hand and say /ch/. When I say a word that does not begin with /ch/, put your hand behind your back.** Say these words: *chess, cat, champ, tree, chore.* Tell children that some words, like *such,* have the sound /ch/ at the end. Follow the same procedure for the final position with the following words: *hutch, jump, which, much, pinch, lip.*

Word Blending   Demonstrate each step with *Word Builder Cards* and a *Word Builder.* Have children repeat each step after you. Hold up *c* and *h* together and say /ch/. Hold up *u* and say /u/. Hold up *g* and say /g/.

- Place the letters *c, h, u, g* in the *Word Builder.*
- Point to *c* and *h* together. Say /ch/. Point to *u* and say /u/. Prompt children to repeat after you.
- Slide *u* next to *ch*. Run your hand under the letters as you blend the sounds, elongating them— /chu/.

- Point to *g* and say /g/.
- Slide *g* next to *chu*. Run your hand under *chug* as you blend the sounds, elongating them—/chug/. Read *chug* naturally.

Follow the same procedure with these words: *chin, lunch, chum, latch, ditch.*

  Word Building Model how to blend *chip*. Place the *Word Builder Cards c, h, i,* and *p* in the *Word Builder* and have children do the same.

Slide your hand under the letters as you slowly read *chip*. Have children build and read new words. As they build each word, write it on the board. Say:

- **Change *p* to *n*. What word did you make?** (chin)
- **Move *ch* after *in*. What word did you make?** (inch)

Continue with the words *such, catch,* and *match.* Then have children read the words on the board. Direct children's attention to page 50 of their *Practice Books.* Complete the page together.

Spelling Words

1. chip	6. match
2. chin	7. wish
3. inch	8. shop
4. such	9. saw
5. catch	10. were

Have children practice writing spelling words on their *Write-on/Wipe-off Boards.*

PRETEACH
Build Robust Vocabulary

Introduce Robust Vocabulary Read the student-friendly explanation for each word. Then discuss each word using the following examples.

Say: **I think it is astonishing when a caterpillar turns into a butterfly. What is something that you think is astonishing?**

Say: **We continue our work until we learn something. Would you rather continue reading a book or continue cleaning your room? Explain.**

Say: **If you have a lot of work to do, you may doubt that you will ever finish. Would you doubt that a pig could fly or that a chicken could lay eggs? Explain.**

VOCABULARY
Student-Friendly Explanations

astonishing If something is astonishing, it amazes and surprises you.

continue If you continue to do something, you keep doing it.

doubt If you doubt something, you do not believe that it is true.

PRETEACH
Grammar/Writing

Names of Days and Months Write the following sentences on the board. Track the print as you read them aloud and have children listen for the names of days and months. *We go to grandma's every Saturday; My birthday is in June.*

Display a calendar. Point out the names of the days and the months. Tell children that these names always begin with a capital letter. Have children point to each day of the week as you read aloud the names of the days. Then point to each month and read the names of the months aloud. Repeat, and ask children to echo-read each word. Ask children to tell what letter begins the name of each day and month. Make sure they respond with "capital *J*," for example.

LESSON 13

DAY AT A GLANCE

Day 1

PHONEMIC AWARENESS
Phoneme Isolation

PHONICS AND SPELLING
Reteach Digraph /ch/*ch, tch*

COMPREHENSION
Preteach Sequence

HIGH-FREQUENCY WORDS
Reteach *many, watch, fly, their*

FLUENCY BUILDER
Intonation

GRAMMAR/WRITING
Reteach Names of Days and Months

Materials Needed:

Word Builders and Word Builder Cards

Write-On/ Wipe-Off Boards

Practice Book p.51
Practice Book

Shooting Star Student Edition pp. 6–12 pp. 56–62

What a Thrill! Student Edition pp. 4–5

Practice Book

Spelling Words

1. chip	6. match
2. chin	7. wish
3. inch	8. shop
4. such	9. saw
5. catch	10. were

 Have children practice writing spelling words on their *Write-on/Wipe-off Boards.*

Phonemic Awareness

Phoneme Isolation   Say the word *chip* and have children repeat it. Have children listen for other words with the /ch/ sound. Say the words *chin* and *corn.* Say: **Which of these words has the /ch/ sound? *Chin* has this sound. Now you try some.** Continue with: *clock, patch, beach; much, peach, pack; save, champ, choose.*

RETEACH

Phonics and Spelling

Digraph /ch/*ch, tch*

Word Building   Place the *Word Builder Cards c, h, i,* and *p* in the *Word Builder.* Ask children to say each letter name and the sound it stands for. Then read the word *chip* with children. Build new words by asking children:

- **Which letter should I change in *chip* to make *chin?*** (Change *p* to *n.*)
- **Which should I change to make *chin* become *inch?*** (Move the *ch* to the end of the word.)

Continue with the words *such, catch,* and *match.*

Read Words in Context   Write the following sentences on chart paper. Have children read each sentence silently. Then track the print as children read the sentences aloud. Finally, point to the underlined words at random and have children read them. *The dish has a <u>chip</u> on it. Ben hit his <u>chin</u> on the shelf. That is <u>such</u> a big cat. That shell is one <u>inch</u> long. They <u>wish</u> they could <u>catch</u> a fish. Hal <u>saw</u> that the dogs <u>were</u> here. He will <u>shop</u> for a cap to <u>match</u> his vest.*

PRETEACH

Comprehension

Sequence   Tell children that the sequence is the order in which things happen in a story. Have children turn to "The Water Dish" in *Shooting Star.* Say: **This story is about a bird that wants water. First, the bird could not get a drink. Then, she dropped shells in the dish. At the end, she was able to get a drink of water.** Point out that words such as *first, next, then, last,* and *after* can help them understand the sequence of events in a story.

RETEACH

High-Frequency Words

p. 4–5

Write the words *many, watch, fly,* and *their* on the board.

- Point to and read *many.* Repeat, having children say *many* with you.
- Say: **There are *many* children in our class.**
- Repeat the word and then point to each letter as you spell it. Have children reread the word.

Repeat for the remaining words. Use the following sentences: *We will* watch *the play. Birds use their wings to* fly. *Sara and Tom have* their *own bikes.*

Have children turn to page 4 of *What a Thrill!* and have them read aloud the words at the top of the page. Talk about the illustrations. Then guide children in choosing and writing the word that names each picture. (4. *catch,* 5. *hatch,* 6. *chick*) Have children read aloud each word in the list on page 5. Ask volunteers to read the sentences aloud. Then have children choral-read the sentences. Guide them to choose and circle the word that completes each sentence. (1. *many,* 2. *watch,* 3. *their,* 4. *fly*)

RETEACH

Grammar/Writing

Practice Book
p.51

Names of Days and Months   Tell children that they will sing a song that names the days of the week. Sing the following song to children then have them sing along with you.

(Sung to the tune of "Clementine.")

Sunday, Monday, Tuesday, Wednesday, Thursday, Friday, Saturday.

There are seven days, there are seven days, there are seven days in a week.

Write the names of the days of the week on chart paper. Track the print and read the words with children. Ask what kind of letter is found at the beginning of each word. (capital letter) Display the names for the months of the year.

Have volunteers dictate sentences about what they do on certain days or during certain months. Write the sentences without capitalizing the days or months. Track the print as you read each sentence. Ask children to point out the names of the days or months. Guide children to correct the sentences by adding capital letters. Complete *Practice Book* page 51 together.

High-Frequency Words

many	fly
watch	their

Fluency

Intonation   Have children open to "Let's Help Cat" in *Shooting Star.* Tell children that good readers make their reading sound like someone is talking. Explain that their voices usually go up at the end of questions and that some words in a sentence are spoken more strongly than others.

Have children track the print as you model reading the first three pages, first without intonation and then with appropriate intonation.

Then read aloud the rest of the selection and have children echo-read.

LESSON 13

DAY AT A GLANCE

Day 2

30+ Minutes

PHONEMIC AWARENESS
Phoneme Blending

PHONICS AND SPELLING
Reteach Digraphs /ch/*ch, tch*

HIGH-FREQUENCY WORDS
Reteach *air, fly, friends, grew, need, play, rain, watch, many, their*

FLUENCY
Review Intonation

READING
"How Many?"

BUILD ROBUST VOCABULARY
Preteach *transform, examine, devour*

GRAMMAR/WRITING
Reteach Names of Days and Months

Materials Needed:

Word Builders and Word Builder Cards

Practice Book p.52
Practice Book

Copying Masters 49–50
Lesson 13 High-Frequency Word Cards

Shooting Star Student Edition p. 47

What a Thrill! Student Edition pp. 6–13

High-Frequency Words

air	play
fly	rain
friends	watch
grew	many
need	their

Phonemic Awareness

Phoneme Blending Tell children that they are going to play a guessing game. Then say: **I'm thinking of a word that means the same as friend. It is /ch/ /u/ /m/. What's my word?** (*chum*) Continue with the following words: /ch/ /i/ /k/ (*chick*), /l/ /a/ /ch/ (*latch*), /ch/ /a/ /p/ (*chap*), and /p/ /a/ /ch/ (*patch*).

RETEACH

Phonics and Spelling

Digraphs /ch/*ch, tch*
Word Building Use a *Word Builder* and *Word Builder Cards* and have children repeat each step. Build the word *such*. Blend the sounds to read the word—/ssuuch/. Then say the word naturally—*such*. Have children do the same. Lead children in building and reading new words by saying:

- **Change *s* to *h* and change *ch* to *sh*. Read the word.** (*hush*)

- **Change *sh* to *nch*. Read the word.** (*hunch*)

Continue in a similar manner to have children change consonant digraphs to build and read these words: *chart, chant, chat, chap, chip, ship.*

Practice Book p.52
Read Words in Context Ask children to turn to *Practice Book* page 52. Read each sentence aloud and have children echo-read. Then ask volunteers to read each sentence aloud. Ask: **What is Chad sitting on?** (a bench) **Where is the bench?** (on the porch) **What did he eat for lunch?** (a ham sandwich and chips) Call on volunteers to frame and read words with the /ch/ sound. Then ask children to find and circle all the words with the /ch/ sound at the beginning of the word. Finally, have them underline all the words with the /ch/ sound at the ending of the word.

RETEACH

High-Frequency Words

Copying Masters 49–50
Display the *High-Frequency Word Cards* for *air, fly, friends, grew, need, play, rain, watch, many,* and *their*. Point to each card and read the word. Have children repeat. Give each child a set of *High-Frequency Word Cards*, and have children spread the cards out in front of them. Randomly call out one of the words, and have children hold up and read the matching card. Assess how well children are able to identify the words, and repeat until they can respond quickly and accurately.

Reading

pp. 6–13

Build Background: "How Many?"

Ask children to share their experiences with baby chicks by asking: **Have you ever seen a baby chick? Have you ever seen one hatch from an egg? Have you read about chicks?** Ask children to discuss what they know about chicks. Have volunteers tell about a time they have seen a real baby chick and what happened.

Monitor Comprehension: "How Many?"

Have children turn to the first page of the selection. Ask a volunteer to reread the title. Then have children look at the first picture in the selection and have them share their predictions about what this selection will be about. Guide children through the selection as they read.

pp. 6–7

Say: **We can see eggs in this picture. Let's read and see what happens to the eggs.**

After reading the pages, ask: **How many eggs do you see in the first picture?** (two) **Look at the second picture. What happened to the eggs?** (They cracked open.) NOTE DETAILS

Ask: **What is coming out of the eggs? Frame and read the word that tells.** (chicks) **Where are the eggs?** (in a nest) APPLY PHONICS/ NOTE DETAILS

Say: **Let's all say the sound /ch/. This sound can be spelled *ch* and *tch*. Look at the words on page 7. Which words on this page have the /ch/ sound?** (chicks, watch, hatch) APPLY PHONICS

pp. 8–9

Say: **It looks like there are three chicks. Let's read on to find out what the chicks do.**

After reading the pages, ask: **What do the chicks do?** (they dig) **What happens when they dig?** (they find bugs) CAUSE AND EFFECT

Ask: **What do you think the chicks will do with the bugs?** (Possible response: They will eat the bugs.) **Why?** (Possible response: They look like they are eating them in the picture and I know that birds eat bugs.) DRAW CONCLUSIONS/USE PRIOR KNOWLEDGE

pp. 10–11

Say: **Now we can see four chicks in the picture. Let's read to find out what they do.**

After reading the pages, ask: **What are the chicks doing in the second picture?** (They are flapping their wings.) **Why do they flap their wings?** (They are trying to fly.) MAKE INFERENCES

Fluency

Intonation Remind children that we say some words more strongly than others when we speak and read aloud.

Words that name people, places, things, and actions are usually more important and so are said a little louder. "Little words" like *of, the, to,* and *for,* are said more softly.

Have children turn to page 47 in *Shooting Star* and identify the word you stress as you read the sentence two different ways.

Say: **This *penguin* wants more food.**

***This* penguin wants more food.**

Have children repeat. Talk about how reading the sentence in different ways makes it mean different things.

Ask: **What words with the /ch/ sound do you see on page 11?** (*watch, chicks*) Say: **Let's all point to the word *watch* and read it aloud. Ask: Where is the /ch/ sound in *watch*? At the beginning or the ending?** (ending) **APPLY PHONICS**

Ask: **What do you think the chicks will do next?** (Possible response: They will fly.) **Why do you think that?** (Possible response: The story says "soon the chicks can fly.") **MAKE PREDICTIONS**

 Say: **Now we see six big chickens. Let's read to find out what happened to the chicks.**

After reading the pages, ask: **What happened to the chicks?** (They got big.) **NOTE DETAILS**

Ask: **What do the chicks turn into when they get big?** (hens) **CONTEXT CLUES**

 Answers to *Think Critically* Questions
Help children read and answer the *Think Critically* questions on page 13. Answers are shown below.
 1. ‹*hatch*› **SEQUENCE**
2. ‹*bugs*› **CAUSE AND EFFECT**
3. ‹*chicks get big*› **MAIN IDEA**

PRETEACH

Build Robust Vocabulary

Introduce Robust Vocabulary Read the student-friendly explanation for each word. Then discuss each word using the following examples.

Say: **Sometimes, eggs transform into chicks, like the story we just read. What are some other things that transform?**

Say: **Scientists examine things to learn more about them. What is something you would like to examine to learn more about? Would you rather examine an anthill or a box of crayons?**

Say: **When I see my favorite food, I want to devour it. What are some foods you like to devour?**

RETEACH

Grammar/Writing

Names of Days and Months Model sentences about school using the name of a day or a month, such as **We go to the school library every Tuesday.** Ask children to dictate other sentences that include the name of a day or a month. Record their sentences without capitalizing these proper nouns. Read the sentences to children.

> We go to the school library every tuesday.
> There are many books about fall displayed in october.
> In april, we will be able to check out two books.

Reread the first sentence to children, tracking the print. Model how to rewrite it correctly by capitalizing the name of the day of the week. Explain: **The word** *Tuesday* **is the name of the day of the week. We always capitalize the first letter of the names of days and months.**

Follow a similar procedure to guide children to correct the other sentences. Have a volunteer identify the word that names a day or a month. Then track the print and read the corrected sentences, asking children if the capital letters are correct.

VOCABULARY

Student-Friendly Explanations

transform If you transform something, you totally change it.

examine If you examine something, you look at it closely.

devour If you devour something, you eat it all up very quickly.

LESSON 13

DAY AT A GLANCE

Day 3

PHONEMIC AWARENESS
Phoneme Segmentation

PHONICS
Preteach Inflection -es

PHONICS AND SPELLING
Reteach Digraphs /ch/ch, tch

HIGH-FREQUENCY WORDS
Reteach many, watch, fly, their

FLUENCY
Intonation

COMPREHENSION
Reteach Sequence

GRAMMAR/WRITING
Reteach Sequence Story

Materials Needed:

Write-On/
Wipe-Off
Boards with
Phonemic
Awareness
Disks

Photo
Cards

Word Builders
and Word
Builder Cards

Copying Masters 51–52
Lesson 13
Story Strips

What a Thrill!
Student Edition
pp. 6-12

Spelling Words

1. chip	6. match
2. chin	7. wish
3. inch	8. shop
4. such	9. saw
5. catch	10. were

30+ Minutes

Phonemic Awareness

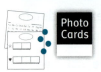 **Photo Cards**

Phoneme Segmentation   Have children use the three boxes on the *Write-on/Wipe-off Boards*. Remind children that the boxes stand for the sounds in words. Show *Photo Card fish* and tell children that the first sound they hear in *fish* is (/f/). Place a disk in the first box. Point out the second sound in *fish* (/i/) and place a disk in the second box. Then identify the last sound in *fish* (/sh/) and place a disk in the third box. Point to each box in sequence as children say the word. Ask: **How many sounds do you hear in *fish*? I hear three.** Repeat the procedure with *bug, hen, lunch, path,* and *sack.*

PRETEACH

Phonics

Inflection -es   Write the following words on the board: *buses, dishes, lunches, matches, patches, glasses, fizzes, boxes.* As you read each word, underline the root word and point out the *-es* ending. Have children repeat each word. Ask: **How are all these words alike?** (They all have the ending *-es.*) Explain that *-es* rather than *-s* is added when a word ends in *x, s, ss, ch, tch, sh* or *zz.* Adding *-es* makes it possible to pronounce the word.

RETEACH

Phonics and Spelling

Digraph /ch/ch, tch
Build Words   Use *Word Builder Cards* and a *Word Builder* to form words. Have children listen to your directions and change a letter in each word to spell a spelling word using their *Word Builder Cards* and *Word Builders.* Form *chap* and have children read the word. Ask: **Which spelling word can you make by changing *a*?** (*chip*)

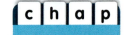

Follow a similar procedure with the following words: *chip* (*chin*), *chin* (*inch*), *much* (*such*), *patch* (*match*), *match* (*catch*).

Remind children that there are some other words they have to remember how to spell. Have children say *saw.* Tell them to put *Word Builder Cards s, a, w* in their *Word Builders,* picture the word *saw* in their minds, and build the word. Write the word on the board. Follow the same procedure with the word *were.*

RETEACH

High-Frequency Words

Copying Masters 51–52

Duplicate and distribute *Copying Masters* 51–52 to each child. Explain that the sentences tell the story "How Many?" but some have missing words.

List the words *many, watch, fly,* and *their* on the board. Have children read aloud each story strip sentence and name the correct word on the board that makes sense in the sentence. Have children write the missing words in the blanks and read the completed sentences aloud. Help children cut apart the strips, read the completed sentences, and arrange them in story order.

RETEACH

Comprehension

Focus Skill

Sequence Review what the sequence of a story or non-fiction selection is. (The sequence is the order of the events.) Have children turn to "How Many?" in *What a Thrill!* Point out that in the story the chicks do things in a certain order. At first, the eggs crack. Then the chicks hatch. Guide children through the sequence of events in "How Many?"

RETEACH

Grammar/Writing

Sequence Story Write the following sentences on chart paper:

> The circus show was great!
> First, the clowns made us laugh.
> Next, the elephants performed.
> Last, the acrobats flew in the air.

Point out that these sentences make up a sequence story that tells about a trip to a circus. Read the sentences to children, and discuss what they learned about the experience. Point out that the story tells the events in order. Then tell children that a sequence story uses words such as *first, next,* and *last.* Underline *first, next,* and *last* in the sentences. Then guide the children to understand that sequence stories have a beginning, middle, and an ending.

High-Frequency Words

many	**fly**
watch	**their**

Fluency

Intonation Remind children that when good readers read, they make it sound the way it does when someone is talking. Model using correct intonation for children.

Reread aloud "How Many?" in *What a Thrill!,* and have children echo-read. Point out that you will make sure your voice goes up and down and that you say some words more strongly than others.

LESSON 13

30+ Minutes

DAY AT A GLANCE
Day 4

PHONEMIC AWARENESS
Phoneme Blending

PHONICS
Reteach Inflection -es

PHONICS AND SPELLING
Reteach Digraphs /ch/ch, tch

HIGH-FREQUENCY WORDS
Reteach air, fly, friends, grew, need, play, rain, watch, many, their

FLUENCY
Intonation

COMPREHENSION
Reteach Sequence

GRAMMAR/WRITING
Reteach Sequence Story

Materials Needed:

Practice Book

Lesson 13 High-Frequency Word Cards

What a Thrill! Student Edition pp. 6–12

Shooting Star Student Edition pp. 36–42

Photo Cards

Spelling Words

1. chip	6. match
2. chin	7. wish
3. inch	8. shop
4. such	9. saw
5. catch	10. were

Phonemic Awareness

Phoneme Blending Tell children that together you are going to play a game called "Fix It." Tell them that you are going to say some words that are broken and they should listen to see if they can put the sounds together to figure out the word. Say: **Listen as I do the first one: /ch/ /i/ /p/. The word is chip.** Continue with the following words: /i/ /ch/ (*itch*), /k/ /a/ /ch/ (*catch*), /f/ /e/ /ch/ (*fetch*), /kw/ /ē/ /n/ (*queen*), /sh/ /ĭr/ /t/ (*shirt*).

RETEACH
Phonics

Inflection -es Remind children that when a word ends in *ch, tch, sh, x, s, ss,* or *zz,* the ending *-es* is added to make the word plural. Write *batch.* Say: **The word *batches* is made by adding *-es* to the root word *batch*.** Write *batches.* Say: **I baked one *batch* of cookies. I baked four *batches* of cookies last night.** Repeat with *lunch* and *lunches,* and have children use both words in sentences. Point out that *lunches* is plural.

RETEACH
Phonics and Spelling

 Digraphs /ch/ch, tch
Direct children's attention to page 53 of their *Practice Books.* Complete the page together.

Assess children's progress using the following sentences.

1. chip — There is a **chip** on this broken dish.
2. chin — Your **chin** is above your neck.
3. inch — The bug is about one **inch** long.
4. such — That is **such** a big dog!
5. catch — Will you play **catch** with me?
6. match — Can you **match** the animals to their homes?

Review

7. wish — I **wish** I could go camping.
8. shop — That **shop** sells backpacks.

High-Frequency

9. saw — I **saw** my dad at home.
10. were — There **were** muffins in the bag.

RETEACH

High-Frequency Words

Copying Masters 49–50 Display *High-Frequency Word Cards* for this lesson's words—*air, fly, friends, grew, need, play, rain, watch, many,* and *their*—and the previously learned high-frequency words. Point to words at random and ask children to read them.

High-Frequency Words

air	play
fly	rain
friends	watch
grew	many
need	their

RETEACH

Comprehension

Sequence   Remind children that sequence is the order of events in a story. Draw a two-column chart on the board, and add the titles "How Many?" and "Ben." Guide children to recall the sequence of events from "How Many?" in *What a Thrill!,* and record their responses. Walk children through "Ben" in *Shooting Star* and have volunteers tell the sequence. Record their responses.

"How Many?"	"Ben"
First, chicks hatch out of eggs. Next, the chicks eat and flap their wings. Last, the chicks get big and become hens.	

RETEACH

Grammar/Writing

Photo Card **Sequence Story**   Review with children characteristics of well-written sequence stories.

Sequence Story

It tells events in order.
It uses words such as *first, next,* and *last.*
It has a beginning, a middle, and an ending.

 Show *Photo Card farm.* Discuss with children what they might see on a farm. Write the following sentences on chart paper and read them aloud to children: *We went on a field trip to a farm. First, we rode on a bus.*

Point out that the second sentence uses the word *first* and tells what happened in the beginning of the story. Ask children to dictate similar sentences about the field trip. Record the sentences on chart paper. Point to and read aloud the sentences to children.

Fluency

Intonation Remind children that good readers make their voices rise and fall in pitch and say some words more strongly to convey meaning. Have children practice rereading "How Many" in *What a Thrill!* for fluency.

30+ Minutes

DAY AT A GLANCE
Day 5

HIGH-FREQUENCY WORDS
air, fly, friends, grew, need, play, rain, watch

PHONEMIC AWARENESS
Onset and Rime

PHONICS AND SPELLING
Preteach *r*-Controlled Vowel /är/*ar*

BUILD ROBUST VOCABULARY
Preteach *approached, energetic, pace*

GRAMMAR/WRITING
Preteach Names of Holidays

Materials Needed:

Lesson 13
High-Frequency
Word Cards

Sound/
Spelling
Card *ar*

Word Builder
and Word
Builder Cards

Write-On/
Wipe-Off
Boards

Practice Book
p.54
Practice
Book

High-Frequency Words

air	need
fly	play
friends	rain
grew	watch

High-Frequency Words

Copying Masters 49–50 Display the *High-Frequency Word Cards* for *air, fly, friends, grew, need, play, rain, watch,* and the other previously learned high-frequency words. Say *air,* ask a volunteer to point to *air,* and have children read the word aloud. Continue with the remaining high-frequency words. Repeat this activity several times to reinforce instant recognition.

Phonemic Awareness

Onset and Rime Have children name words as you say them in parts. Model the first one. **Listen as I say this word in parts: /d/-ark. The word I said was *dark*. Now you try some: /h/-arm, /k/-ard, /st/-art, /p/-art, /y/-ard, /är/-cade.**

PRETEACH

Phonics and Spelling

Sound/Spelling Card ***r*-Controlled Vowel /är/*ar***
Connecting Letter to Sound Say the word *art.* Have children say the word. Repeat for the words *arm* and *arch.* Say: **The words *art, arm,* and *arch* begin with the /är/ sound.** Have children say /är/ several times. Display *Sound/Spelling Card ar* and say the letter names. Explain that the letters *a* and *r* together stand for the sound /är/, the sound at the beginning of *art.* Have children say /är/ several times as you touch the letters.

Give each child an *a* and an *r Word Builder Card.* Say: **When I say a word that begins with /är/, hold up your cards and say /är/. When I say a word that does not begin with /är/, hold the cards behind your back.** Say these words: *artist, army, wrong, ark, arrest, day.* Tell children that some words have the sound /är/ in the middle. Tell children that *dark* has /är/ in the middle. Say *dark,* elongating the vowel sound—/däärrk/. Then say it naturally—*dark.* Say the following words, elongating the medial sound, and have children identify the words that have the /är/ sound: *mark, snack, chart, ramp, start.*

Word Blending Demonstrate each step with *Word Builder Cards* and a *Word Builder,* and have children repeat each step after you. Hold up *j* and say /j/. Hold up *a* and *r* together and say /är/.

- Place the letters *j, a, r* in the *Word Builder.* Make sure the letters *a* and *r* touch.

- Point to *j.* Say /j/. Point to *a* and *r* together and say /är/. Prompt children to repeat after you.

- Slide the *a* and *r* next to *j*. Run your hand under the letters as you blend the sound by elongating them—/jär/. Read *jar* naturally.

Follow the same procedure with these words: *far, dart, scarf.*

  Word Building Place the *Word Builder Cards f, a, r* in the *Word Builder* and have children do the same. Have children say the name and sound for the letter *f* and for *a* and *r* together. Then read *far* naturally. Have children build and read new words. As they build each word, write it on the board. Say:

- **Add *m* to the end of *far*. What word did you make?** (*farm*)

- **Take away the *f*. What word did you make?** (*arm*)

Continue with the words *art, part,* and *park.* Have children read the words on the board. Complete *Practice Book* page 54 together.

PRETEACH

Build Robust Vocabulary

Introduce Robust Vocabulary Read the student-friendly explanation for each word. Then discuss each word using the following examples.

Say: **If I was approached by a pack of big dogs, I would be very scared! What are you scared of being approached by? Why?**

Say: **I feel energetic when I sleep well and eat a good breakfast—then I feel like I can do anything. What makes you feel energetic?**

Say: **I eat at a slow pace, but I ride my bike at a fast pace. What do you do at a slow pace? What do you do at a fast pace?**

PRETEACH

Grammar/Writing

Names of Holidays Display an annual calendar. Explain that many calendars show important holidays. Turn to the month of May and point out the last Monday of the month. Point to and track the words *Memorial Day* as you read them aloud.

Write the following sentences on the board and track the print as you read the sentences: *We celebrate Thanksgiving in November. We celebrate Father's Day in June.* Underline the holidays in each sentence. Point out that each holiday name begins with a capital letter, and when the holiday has two or more words, such as *Father's Day,* both words are usually capitalized. Point out other holidays on the calendar, write them on the board, and have volunteers circle the capital letters.

Spelling Words

1. far	6. park
2. farm	7. chin
3. arm	8. such
4. art	9. fly
5. part	10. watch

Have children practice writing spelling words on their *Write-on/Wipe-off Boards.*

VOCABULARY

Student-Friendly Explanations

aproached If you approached something, you moved toward it.

energetic If you are energetic, you are filled with energy.

pace Your pace is how fast you are going.

LESSON 14

Star

DAY AT A GLANCE

Day 1

PHONEMIC AWARENESS
Phoneme Isolation

PHONICS AND SPELLING
Reteach *r*-Controlled Vowel /är/*ar*

COMPREHENSION
Preteach Author's Purpose/Point of View

HIGH-FREQUENCY WORDS
Reteach *very, Mrs., happy, your*

FLUENCY
Intonation

GRAMMAR/WRITING
Reteach Names of Holidays

Materials Needed:

Word Builders and Word Builder Cards

Write-On/Wipe-Off Boards

What a Thrill!
Student Edition
pp. 6–12
pp. 14–15

Shooting Star
Student Edition
pp. 56–62

Practice Book
p.55

Practice Book

Spelling Words

1. far	6. park
2. farm	7. chin
3. arm	8. such
4. art	9. fly
5. part	10. watch

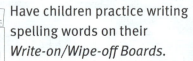
Have children practice writing spelling words on their *Write-on/Wipe-off Boards.*

Phonemic Awareness

Phoneme Isolation   Say the word *farm* and have children repeat it. Have children listen for other words with the /är/ sound. Say the words *chin* and *card.* Say: **Which of these words has the /är/ sound?** *Card* **has this sound. Now you try some.** Continue with: *chart, card, cane; park, barn, bat; art, arm, ant.*

RETEACH

Phonics and Spelling

 r-**Controlled Vowel /är/*ar***
   Word Building   Place the *Word Builder Cards f, a,* and *r* in the *Word Builder.* Arrange the cards so that *a* and *r* are touching. Remind children that the letters *ar* together stand for one sound—/är/. Ask children to say the name and sound of each letter. Then read the word naturally—*far.* Have children do the same. Ask:

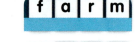

- **Which letter should I add to make *far* become *farm*?** (add *m*)
- **Which letters should I take away to make *farm* become *arm*?** (take away *f*)

Continue with the words *art, part,* and *park.*

Read Words in Context   Write the following sentences on chart paper. Have children read each sentence silently. Then track the print as children read the sentences aloud. Finally, point to the underlined words at random and have children read them. *We went far to get to the farm. I banged my arm on the shelf. Art class is the fun part of the day. Tran said he could go to the park with me. Keshon had a small scar on his chin. Beth has such a lot to say. We will watch the jet fly!*

PRETEACH

Comprehension

 Author's Purpose/Point of View   Tell children that an author has a reason for writing a story. Explain that sometimes the author writes a story to entertain the reader and sometimes the author writes a story to give the reader information. Have children turn to "How Many?" in *What a Thrill!* Read the selection aloud. Say: **In "How Many?" we learn about chicks that hatch and turn into hens. The author tells us a lot of things about chicks. We learn how they hatch, look for food, and grow up. I think the author's purpose is to give us information about chickens.**

High-Frequency Words

very	happy
Mrs.	your

RETEACH
High-Frequency Words

 Write the words *very, Mrs., happy,* and *your* on the board.

- Point to and read *very*. Repeat with children.

- Say: **I am *very* glad that it's sunny out.**

- Repeat the word and then point to each letter as you spell it. Have children say and spell *very* with you. Have children reread *very*.

Repeat for the remaining words. Use the following sentences: *Mrs. Sanchez is my teacher. Hector was* happy *to make the team. Here is* your *book.*

Have children turn to page 14 of *What a Thrill!* and read aloud the words at the top of the page. Talk about the illustrations. Then guide children in choosing and writing the word that names each picture. (4. *march,* 5. *star,* 6. *park*) Have children read aloud each word in the list on page 15. Ask volunteers to read the sentences aloud. Then have children choral-read the sentences. Guide them to choose and circle the word that completes each sentence. (1. *happy,* 2. *Mrs.,* 3. *your,* 4. *very*)

RETEACH
Grammar/Writing

Practice Book p.55 **Names of Holidays** Tell children that today they will listen to a rhyme that tells about a holiday.

> Flags on Parade
>
> Today the flags are on parade.
> They dance about the sky.
> Red, white, and blue, with stars so bright,
> Hooray for the Fourth of July!

Write the last two lines of the rhyme on the board. Track the print and read the sentence to children. Guide children to name the holiday and tell what kind of letter is used to begin each important word (Fourth of July; a capital letter) Have volunteers name different holidays that they are familiar with. Write the names of the holidays on the board without capitalizing the first letter. Guide students to correct the names and complete *Practice Book* page 55 together.

Fluency

Intonation Have children turn to "The Water Dish" in *Shooting Star*. Remind children that good readers emphasize some words more than others—usually the most important words. Explain that changing your intonation can change the meaning of a sentence.

Read from the story: ***Now** she could get a drink,* and then *Now **she** could get a drink.* Point out that while both readings make sense, the first reading fits better with the story in which the bird has been trying hard to get a drink.

LESSON 14

DAY AT A GLANCE
Day 2

PHONEMIC AWARENESS
Phoneme Blending

PHONICS AND SPELLING
Reteach *r*-Controlled Vowel /är/*ar*

HIGH-FREQUENCY WORDS
Reteach *again, feel, house, know, loud, Mrs., put, say, happy, very, your*

FLUENCY
Intonation

READING
"Star"

BUILD ROBUST VOCABULARY
Preteach *blunder, reassure, excel*

GRAMMAR/WRITING
Reteach Names of Holidays

Materials Needed:

  Word Builders and Word Builder Cards

Practice Book p.56 Practice Book

Copying Masters 53–54 Lesson 14 High-Frequency Word Cards

Shooting Star Student Edition pp. 6–12

What a Thrill! Student Edition pp. 16–23

High-Frequency Words

again	put
feel	say
house	happy
know	very
loud	your
Mrs.	

Phonemic Awareness

Phoneme Blending Tell children that they are going to be detectives and find the word you are thinking about. Say: **I'm thinking of a word that means "not easy." The word is /h/ /är/ /d/. The word is** *hard.* **Now you try some.** Continue with: /m/ /är/ /k/ (mark), /p/ /är/ /t/ (part), and /l/ /är/ /k/ (lark).

RETEACH

Phonics and Spelling

  r-Controlled Vowel /är/*ar*
Word Building Use a *Word Builder* and *Word Builder Cards* and have children repeat each step after you. Build the word *far.* Then say the word naturally—*far.* Lead children in building and reading words that contain the *r*-controlled vowels *ar* and *or.* Say:

- **Change the *a* to *o*. Read the word.** (*for*)
- **Add an *m* after *r*. Read the word.** (*form*)
- **Change the *o* to *a*. Read the word.** (*farm*)

Continue in a similar manner to have children build and read these words: *art, cart, part, port; core, cord, card, cart.*

Practice Book p.56 **Read Words in Context** Ask children to turn to *Practice Book* page 56. Read each sentence aloud and have children echo-read. Then ask volunteers to read each sentence aloud. Ask: **Where are Mark and Doris?** (at the farm) **What did Doris see?** (animals) **What did Mark see?** (a cart) **What was the cart filled with?** (corn) Guide children to find and circle words that have the sound /är/ or /ôr/.

RETEACH

High-Frequency Words

Copying Masters 53–54 Display the *High-Frequency Word Cards* for *again, feel, house, know, loud, Mrs., put, say, happy, very,* and *your.* Point to each card and read the word. Have children repeat. Give each child a set of word cards and have children spread the cards out in front of them. Randomly call out one of the words, and have children hold up the matching card, repeating the word aloud. Continue until they can respond quickly and accurately.

Reading

pp. 16–23 ### Build Background: "Star"

Read the title with children. Then have children look at the first picture and share their predictions about the story. Ask children to think of a time they had to do something they did not want to do. Have them tell how it turned out.

Monitor Comprehension: "Star"

Have children turn to the first page of the story. Ask a volunteer to reread the title. Have children look at the picture on page 16. Ask children to think about where the story takes place and what the characters will be doing. Then guide children through the selection as they read.

pp. 16–17 Say: **In the first picture, I see an elephant asleep in her bed. Let's read to find out who she is.**

After reading the pages, ask: **Who is the elephant?** (Star) **What is she doing?** (sleeping) NOTE DETAILS

Ask: **Why do you think Star does not want to get up?** (Possible response: She is tired.) **Do you think that Star will wake up for school?** (Possible response: Yes, because her mom is waking her up.) DRAW CONCLUSIONS/MAKE PREDICTIONS

Say: **Which word on these pages has the /är/ sound? Find and frame the word on both pages.** (Star) APPLY PHONICS

pp. 18–19 Say: **I see many other animals on these pages. It looks like they are playing instruments. Let's read to find out more.**

After reading the pages, ask: **Where are the animals?** (school) **Who are the other animals?** (Star's classmates and teacher) SETTING/ CHARACTERS

Ask: **What are the animals doing?** (marching) **Why do you think that Star doesn't want to march?** (Possible response: Star doesn't think she will like it.) NOTE DETAILS/MAKE INFERENCES

Ask: **Who is Star's teacher?** (Mrs. Park) **Find and read the words that tell.** MAKE INFERENCES/APPLY PHONICS

Fluency

Intonation Remind children that punctuation in sentences gives them clues about how loudly or softly to read words. Have children turn to "Let's Help Cat" in *Shooting Star*.

Explain that the exclamation points on pages 11 and 12 often signal for readers to read strongly and a little louder. Model reading these two pages and have children repeat.

Then remind them that a sentence ending with a period is read in a calmer, softer voice, while an exclamation point means to read words in a stronger way.

Ask: **Is "Star" real or make-believe?** (make-believe) **How can you tell?** (Possible response: The animals are playing instruments and talking like people. Animals can't do those things in real life.) **Genre**

Say: **In the first picture, it looks like Star still doesn't want to march. Let's read to see what happens next.**

After reading the pages, ask: **How do you think Star feels at first?** (Possible response: She is nervous and shy because she might not know how to march.) **Characters' Emotions**

Ask: **Do you think Star will march with her friends? Explain your answer.** (Possible response: Yes, because she looks like she has a smile on her face and all her friends asked her to march with them.) **Make Predictions**

Ask: **Which words on these pages have the /är/ sound?** (*Star, march*) **Apply Phonics**

Say: **Look! It looks like Star is marching with her friends. Let's read to see how the story ends.**

After reading the pages, ask: **How do you think Star feels about marching with her friends?** (Possible response: She is very happy.) **Why?** (Possible response: She says that it is fun, and she looks happy.) **Characters' Emotion**

Ask: **Why do you think Star changed her mind about marching?** (Possible response: She decided to give it a try since all her friends asked her to.) **Draw Conclusions**

Ask: **What do you think is the author's purpose for writing this story?** (Possible response: To show that sometimes you just have to try something new and you might like it.) **Author's Purpose**

Answers to *Think Critically* Questions

Help children read and answer the *Think Critically* questions on page 22. Answers are shown below.

1. ‹*school*› **Setting**

2. ‹*march*› **Note Details**

 3. ‹*friends help us*› **Author's Purpose**

PRETEACH

Build Robust Vocabulary

Introduce Robust Vocabulary   Read the student-friendly explanation for each word. Then discuss each word using the following examples.

Say: **I made a blunder when I dropped a cup of milk on the floor. Which would be a blunder—forgetting your lunch on the bus or playing in the park?**

Say: **My friend reassures me when she says "I believe in you." What would you say to reassure a friend?**

Say: **I excel at basketball because I practice every day. My dad excels at math. Name something that you excel at.**

RETEACH

Grammar/Writing

Names of Holidays   Talk with children about class celebrations of various holidays. Model a sentence about one of these holidays, such as: **On Valentine's Day, we make cards to give one another.**

Ask children to dictate other sentences that include the name of a holiday. Record their sentences without capitalizing these proper nouns. Then read the sentences to children.

> On mother's day, I do nice things for Mom.
>
> For thanksgiving, we eat.
>
> halloween is when we dress up.

Guide children to identify the names of the holidays. Reread the first sentence to children, tracking the print. Model how to correct it by capitalizing the first letter in each important word in the name of the holiday. Then guide children to point out and correct the important words in the other holiday names.

VOCABULARY

Student-Friendly Explanations

blunder   If you make a blunder, you make a bad or silly mistake.

reassure   If you reassure someone, you tell him or her that everything will be all right.

excel   If you excel at something, you are very good at it.

LESSON 14

30+ Minutes

DAY AT A GLANCE
Day 3

PHONEMIC AWARENESS
Phoneme Segmentation

PHONICS
Preteach Inflections -s, -ed, -ing

PHONICS AND SPELLING
Reteach r-Controlled Vowel /är/ar

HIGH-FREQUENCY WORDS
Reteach very, Mrs., happy, your

FLUENCY
Intonation

COMPREHENSION
Reteach Author's Purpose/Point of View

GRAMMAR/WRITING
Reteach E-mail

Materials Needed:

Write-On/
Wipe-Off
Boards with
Phonemic
Awareness
Disks

Photo
Cards

Word Builders
and Word
Builder Cards

Copying
Masters
55–56

Lesson 14
Story Strips

What a Thrill!
Student Edition
pp. 16–22

Spelling Words

1. far	6. park
2. farm	7. chin
3. arm	8. such
4. art	9. fly
5. part	10. watch

Phonemic Awareness

Phoneme Segmentation   Have children use the three boxes on the *Write-on/Wipe-off Boards.* Tell children that the boxes stand for the sounds in words. Have children repeat each step with their *Write-on/Wipe-Off Boards.* Show *Photo Card arm.* Say: **The first sound I hear in *arm* is /är/.** Model placing a disk in the first box. Use this procedure for the second sound in *arm* (/m/), placing a disk in the second box. Point to each box in sequence as children say the word. Ask: **How many sounds do you hear in *arm?* I hear two.** Repeat this procedure with *Photo Cards bug, fish, path,* and *rain.*

PRETEACH

Phonics

Inflections -s, -ed, -ing   Write the following words on the board and have children read them: *pick, picks, picked, picking.* Review with children how the words are alike and different. (They all have the same root word; the last three words have different endings.) Guide children to underline the root words and circle the endings. Then write the word *snack* on the board four times. Guide children to add -s, -ed, and -ing to make the different words.

RETEACH

Phonics and Spelling

 r-Controlled Vowel /är/ar

Build Words   Use *Word Builders* and *Word Builder Cards* to form words. Have children listen to your directions and change a letter in each word to spell a spelling word. Form *far* and have children read the word. Ask: **Which spelling word can you make by adding a letter?** (*farm*)

Follow a similar procedure with the following words: *farm* (*arm*), *arm* (*art*), *art* (*part*), *part* (*park*), *chip* (*chin*), and *much* (*such*).

Remind children that there are some other words they have to remember how to spell. Tell them that *fly* is one such word. Have children say *fly.* Tell them to put *Word Builder Cards f, l, y* in their *Word Builders,* picture the word *fly* in their minds, and build the word. Write the word on the board. Follow the same procedure with *watch.*

RETEACH

High-Frequency Words

Copying Masters 55–56 Duplicate and distribute *Copying Masters* 55–56 to each child. Explain that the sentences tell the story "Star," but some have missing words.

List *very, Mrs., happy,* and *your* on the board. Have children read aloud each story strip sentence and name the word on the board that makes sense in the sentence. Have children write the missing words in the blanks and read the completed sentences aloud. Help children cut apart the strips, read the completed sentences, and arrange them in story order.

RETEACH

Comprehension

  Author's Purpose/Point of View Ask children to identify purposes that authors have when writing a story. (to inform, to give directions, to entertain, to teach a lesson) Explain that authors or characters may tell the story. Have children turn to "Star" in *What a Thrill!* Remind children of the author's purpose. Then invite children to think who is telling the story as you read. Point out that the author tells the story. Explain that if Star was telling the story, the first sentence might say: *I did not want to get up.* Discuss with children the difference.

RETEACH

Grammar/Writing

E-mail Display and read aloud the following e-mail:

> From: kat@net.com
>
> To: lenfox@net.com
>
> Subject: Ted's Surprise Party
>
> Dear Len,
>
> I will throw a party for Ted this Saturday at 3. I hope that you can come!
>
> Your friend,
>
> Kat

Point out the e-mail's different parts. Say: **You use a computer to get and send e-mail.** *From* **shows your e-mail address.** *To* **shows the e-mail address of the person the message is going to.** *Subject* **tells what the e-mail is about.** Point out that the message begins with a greeting and ends with your name.

High-Frequency Words

very	happy
Mrs.	your

Fluency

Intonation Remind children that when good readers read, they say some words louder than others. Show children how to stress a word in a sentence to show that it is important and how to change the meaning of a sentence by stressing a different word.

Have children turn to "Star" in *What a Thrill!* and model reading with appropriate intonation. Have children echo-read each page with you.

PHONEMIC AWARENESS
Phoneme Blending

PHONICS
Reteach Inflections -s, -ed, -ing

PHONICS AND SPELLING
Reteach r-Controlled Vowel /är/ar

HIGH-FREQUENCY WORDS
Reteach again, feel, house, know, loud, Mrs., put, say, happy, very, your

FLUENCY
Intonation

COMPREHENSION
Reteach Author's Purpose/Point of View

GRAMMAR/WRITING
Reteach E-mail

Materials Needed:

Practice Book
p.57

Practice Book

Copying Masters **53–54**

Lesson 14 High-Frequency Word Cards

Shooting Star Student Edition pp. 26–32

What a Thrill! Student Edition pp. 16–22

Spelling Words

1. far	6. park
2. farm	7. chin
3. arm	8. such
4. art	9. fly
5. part	10. watch

30+ Minutes

Phonemic Awareness

Phoneme Blending Tell children that together you are going to play a puzzle game. Tell them that you are going to say some words in pieces and they should listen to see if they can put the puzzle pieces together to figure out the word. Say: /k/ /är/ /d/. **What word does /k/ /är/ /d/ say? It says** *card*. Continue with the following words: /f/ /är/ /m/ (*farm*), /ch/ /är/ /t/ (*chart*), /s/ /m/ /är/ /t/ (*smart*), /s/ /t/ /är/ /t/ (*start*).

RETEACH

Phonics

Inflections -s, -ed, -ing Remind children that endings can be added to root words to make new words. Write *bang*. Say: **The word** *bangs* **is made by adding -s to the root word** *bang*. Write *bangs*. Follow the same procedure to review the formation of the words *banged* and *banging*. Then guide children in forming new words from the root words *kick, sort, cook,* and *pick*.

RETEACH

Phonics and Spelling

 Practice Book **p.57**

r-Controlled Vowel /är/*ar*
Direct children's attention to page 57 of their *Practice Books*. Complete the page together.

Assess children's progress using the following sentences.

1. far — The North Pole is **far** away.
2. farm — Chickens live on a **farm**.
3. arm — I have a cut on my right **arm**.
4. art — Frank drew animals in **art** class.
5. part — Tran ate **part** of the cake.
6. park — We played catch at the **park**.

Review

7. chin — The man had food on his **chin**.
8. such — There is **such** a mess in the closet!

High-Frequency

9. fly — A cat made the birds **fly** away.
10. watch — Mom will **watch** Mitch and Seth.

RETEACH

High-Frequency Words

Copying Masters 53–54

Display the *High-Frequency Word Cards* for this lesson—*again, feel, house, know, loud, Mrs., put, say, happy, very,* and *your*—and the previously learned high-frequency words. Point to words at random and ask children to read them.

RETEACH

Comprehension

Author's Purpose/Point of View Discuss the different reasons why authors write stories and articles. (to entertain, to inform, to give instructions) Then remind children that authors may tell the story themselves or have a character tell it. Draw a chart like the one below. Have children look at "Just Like Us" in *Shooting Star* and "Star" in *What a Thrill!* Help children remember and discuss why the author wrote "Star" and identify who is telling the story. Then help them repeat the process for "Just Like Us." Record their responses on the chart.

	"Star"	"Just Like Us"
Author's Purpose	to teach a lesson	to inform
Point of View	the author	the man

RETEACH

Grammar/Writing

E-mail Review with children the characteristics of an e-mail message.

E-mail Message

Use a computer to get and send e-mail.

From shows your e-mail address.

To shows the e-mail address of the person the message is going to.

Subject tells what the e-mail is about.

The message begins with a greeting and ends with your name.

Have children think of a fun class event, such as a field trip or a party. Tell them they are going to send an e-mail to a friend about the event. Have children dictate each part of the e-mail. Work with children to write the message together. Then echo-read the e-mail message and have volunteers point out its different parts.

High-Frequency Words

again	put
feel	say
house	happy
know	very
loud	your
Mrs.	

Fluency

Intonation Have children practice reading aloud "Star" in *What a Thrill!* Remind children that good readers emphasize some words more than others when they read. Have them reread their stories several times to practice reading with appropriate intonation.

Model reading with intonation as necessary and having children echo-read sentences. Give children feedback for improving their fluency.

30+ Minutes

DAY AT A GLANCE
Day 5

HIGH-FREQUENCY WORDS
again, feel, house, know, loud, Mrs., put, say, friends, school, your

PHONEMIC AWARENESS
Onset and Rime

PHONICS AND SPELLING
Preteach Digraphs /kw/*qu,* /hw/*wh*

BUILD ROBUST VOCABULARY
Preteach *cozily, interrupted, triumphantly*

GRAMMAR/WRITING
Preteach Using *I* and *Me*

Materials Needed:

Lesson 14
High-Frequency
Word Cards

Sound/Spelling
Cards *Qq*
and *wh*

Word Builders
and Word
Builder Cards

Write-On/
Wipe-Off
Boards

Practice
Book

High-Frequency Words

again	put
feel	say
house	friends
know	school
loud	your
Mrs.	

High-Frequency Words

Copying Masters 53–54 Display the *High-Frequency Word Cards* for *again, feel, house, know, loud, Mrs., put, say, friends, school, your,* and the other previously learned high-frequency words. Say the word *again,* ask a volunteer to point to *again,* and have children read the word aloud. Continue with the remaining high-frequency words. Repeat this activity several times to reinforce instant recognition.

Phonemic Awareness

Onset and Rime Have children name the words as you say them in parts. Model the first one. **Listen as I say this word in parts: /kw/-iet. The word I said was *quiet.* Now you try some: /hw/-ere, /hw/-en, /kw/-estion, /hw/-ite, /kw/-ick, /kw/-ail.**

> PRETEACH

Phonics and Spelling

Sound/Spelling Card **d o t** **Digraphs /kw/*qu,* /hw/*wh***
Connecting Letter to Sound Say the words *quiet, quail,* and *queen,* and have children repeat the words. Explain that all three words begin with the /kw/ sound. Have children say /kw/ several times. Display *Sound/Spelling Card Qq,* and say the letter name. Point out the *qu* and explain that the letters *q* and *u* together stand for the sound /kw/. Then hold up *Sound/Spelling Card wh,* and say the letter names. Explain that these letters together stand for the /hw/ sound, the sound at the beginning of *white.* Have children say /hw/ as you point to the letters.

Give each child a *q* and a *u Word Builder Card.* Say: **When I say a word that begins with /kw/, hold up your cards and say /kw/. When I say a word that does not begin with /kw/, keep the cards in your lap.** Say these words: *quiz, key, quack, quill, cat.* Then distribute *Word Builder Cards w* and *h.* Follow the same procedure with: *whip, whiz, horse, when, hat, while.*

d o t **Word Blending** Demonstrate each step with *Word Builders* and *Word Builder Cards,* and have children repeat each step after you. Hold up *q* and *u* together and say /kw/. Hold up *i* and say /ĭ/. Hold up *z* and say /z/.

- Place the letters *q, u, i, z* in the *Word Builder.*

- Point to *qu.* Say /kw/. Point to *i* and say /ĭ/. Prompt children to repeat after you.

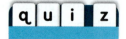

- Slide *i* next to *qu.* Run your hand under the letters as you blend the sounds, elongating them— /kwĭ/.

- Point to *z* and say /zz/.
- Slide *z* next to *qui*. Run your hand under *quiz* as you blend the sounds, elongating them—/kwiz/. Read *quiz* naturally.

Follow the same procedure with *quick, quill,* and *quack.* Then lead children in blending words with /hw/*wh,* like *when, which,* and *whip.*

  Word Building Place the *Word Builder Cards q, u, i,* and *t* in the *Word Builder* and have children do the same. Read *quit* with children. Have children build and read new words.

As they build each word, write it on the board. Say:

- **Change *t* to *ck*. What word did you make?** (*quick*)
- **Change *ck* to *z*. What word did you make?** (*quiz*)

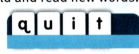

Continue with the words *whiz, which,* and *when.* Then have children read the words on the board. Direct children's attention to page 58 in the *Practice Book.* Complete the page together.

PRETEACH

Build Robust Vocabulary

Introduce Robust Vocabulary Read the student-friendly explanation for each word. Then discuss each word using the following examples.

Say: **I was so comfortable lying cozily on my couch by a fire that I did not want to get up. When do you feel cozy in your home?**

Say: **Once I interrupted someone when they were talking. How do you feel when someone interrupts you?**

Say: **I was so happy when I triumphantly won the spelling contest. Tell about a time when you did something triumphantly.**

PRETEACH

Grammar/Writing

Using *I* and *Me* Write these sentences on the board: *I like cookies. My grandma makes me cookies.* Underline *I* and *me* as you read the sentences. Explain that *I* is used in the naming part of the sentence, and *me* is used in the telling—or action—part of the sentence. Guide children to identify the naming part of the first sentence. (*I*) Remind children that *I* is always written with a capital letter. Then guide them to identify the telling part of this sentence. (*like cookies*) Repeat with the second sentence.

Spelling Words

1. quit	6. when
2. quick	7. arm
3. quiz	8. part
4. whiz	9. house
5. which	10. put

Have children practice writing spelling words on their *Write-on/Wipe-off Boards.*

VOCABULARY

Student-Friendly Explanations

cozily If you lay cozily in bed, you are warm, comfortable, and relaxed.

interrupted If you interrupted something, you stopped it in the middle.

triumphantly If you say something triumphantly, you say it in an excited way that shows you are proud of what you have done.

LESSON 15

Tom's Books

Day at a Glance

PHONEMIC AWARENESS
Phoneme Isolation

PHONICS AND SPELLING
Reteach Digraphs /kw/*qu*, /hw/*wh*

COMPREHENSION
Reteach Sequence

HIGH-FREQUENCY WORDS
Reteach *read, books, writing, does*

FLUENCY
Reading Rate

GRAMMAR/WRITING
Reteach Using *I* and *Me*

Materials Needed:

Photo
Cards

Word Builders
and Word
Builder Cards

Write-On/
Wipe-Off
Boards

What a Thrill!
Student Edition
pp. 6–12
pp. 24–25

Shooting Star
Student Edition
pp. 46–52

Practice Book
p.59

Practice
Book

Spelling Words

1. quit	6. when
2. quick	7. arm
3. quiz	8. part
4. whiz	9. house
5. which	10. put

 Have children practice writing spelling words on their *Write-on/Wipe-off Boards*.

Phonemic Awareness

 Photo Card **Phoneme Isolation** Say *whale* and have children repeat it. Have children listen for other words with the /hw/ sound. Say *whiz* and *farm*. Say: **Which word has the /hw/ sound?** *Whiz* **has this sound. Now you try some.** Continue with: *when, what, wish; what, where, now.*

Show *Photo Card queen* and say *queen* aloud. Ask children what sound they hear at the beginning of *queen*. (/kw/) Have children listen for other words with the /kw/ sound. Say *quiz* and *itch*. Say: **Which of these words has the /kw/ sound?** *Quiz* **has this sound. Now you try some.** Continue with: *quick, quit, cart; quack, crack, quest.*

RETEACH

Phonics and Spelling

 Digraphs /kw/*qu*, /hw/*wh*

Word Building Place the *Word Builder Cards q, u, i,* and *t* in the *Word Builder*. Arrange the cards so that *q* and *u* are touching. Ask children to say the name and sound of each letter, reminding them that the letters *qu* stand for one sound—/kw/. Then read the word naturally—*quit*. Have children do the same. Ask: **Which letter should I change to make *quit* become *quick*?** (change *t* to *ck*.)

q u i t

q u i c k

Continue with the words *quiz, whiz, which,* and *when.*

Read Words in Context Write the following sentences on chart paper. Have children read each sentence silently. Then track the print as children read the sentences aloud. Finally, point to the underlined words at random and have children read them. *Mrs. Todd gave us a quick quiz in class. Which part is missing? When is the math quiz? Greg is a whiz at adding. Quit punching his arm! Put the bags in the house.*

PRETEACH

Comprehension

 Sequence Remind children that the sequence of a piece of writing is the order in which the events happen. Read aloud "How Many?" in *What a Thrill!* Say: **I know the order of the story is important because this story shows how chicks hatch and become hens. After the chicks hatch, they look for bugs to eat. If the**

sequence of the story is changed so that the chicks look for bugs before they even hatch, the story would not make sense. Reread the story with children. Ask children to think about the sequence of the story and tell what happens first, next, and last.

RETEACH

High-Frequency Words

 pp. 24–25

Write the words *read, books, writing,* and *does* on the board.

- Point to and read *read*. Repeat, having children say *read* with you.
- Say: **I like to *read* books.**
- Repeat the word and then point to each letter as you spell it. Then have children say and spell *read* with you. Have children reread the word.

Repeat for the remaining words. Use the following sentences: *There are* books *in the library. I am* writing *a letter. What time* does *school start?*

Have children turn to page 24 of *What a Thrill!* and have them read aloud the words at the top of the page. Talk about the illustrations. Then guide children in choosing and writing the word that names each picture. (4. *quiz,* 5. *quick,* 6. *when*) Have children read aloud each word in the list on page 25. Ask volunteers to read the sentences aloud. Then have children choral-read the sentences. Guide them to choose and circle the word that completes each sentence. (1. *books,* 2. *read,* 3. *does,* 4. *writing*)

RETEACH

Grammar/Writing

 Practice Book p.59

Using *I* and *Me*   Read the following sentences, emphasizing the words *I* and *me.*

> I eat muffins.
> My mom gets them for me.
> I like to drink milk.
> My mom gets me a glass.

Write the first two sentences on the board and read them aloud as you track the print. Have children echo-read the lines. Ask them which sentence has *I* and which has *me.* Say: **I is used in the naming part. In which part of the sentence is *me* used?** (the telling part) Substitute *me* for *I* in the first sentence so that children can hear an incorrect example. Then say the sentence correctly. Repeat for the second sentence. Complete *Practice Book* page 59 together.

High-Frequency Words

read	writing
books	does

Fluency

Reading Rate   Tell children that good readers read at a speed that helps them understand a story. Explain that they should slow down when they read important facts to be sure they understand the information. Model for children how to adjust reading rate as you read pages from "Some Animals" from *Shooting Star.* Have children follow along and echo-read.

30+ Minutes

PHONEMIC AWARENESS
Phoneme Blending

PHONICS AND SPELLING
Reteach Digraphs /kw/*qu*, /hw/*wh*

HIGH-FREQUENCY WORDS
Reteach *about, books, family, name, read, work, writing, people, does*

FLUENCY
Reading Rate

READING
"Tom's Books"

BUILD ROBUST VOCABULARY
Preteach *accomplishment, admire, ambition*

GRAMMAR/WRITING
Reteach Using *I* and *Me*

Materials Needed:

Word Builders and Word Builder Cards

Practice Book p.60
Practice Book

Copying Masters 57–58
Lesson 15 High-Frequency Word Cards

What a Thrill!
Student Edition
pp. 16–22
pp. 26–33

High-Frequency Words

about	work
books	writing
family	people
name	does
read	

Phonemic Awareness

Phoneme Blending Tell children that they are going to be detectives and find the word you are thinking about. Say: **I'm thinking of a word that is something a duck says. The word is /kw/ /a/ /k/. The word is *quack*. Now you try some.** Continue with: /hw/ /e/ /n/ (*when*), /hw/ /i/ /z/ (*whiz*), and /kw/ /ā/ /k/ (*quake*).

RETEACH

Phonics and Spelling

 Digraphs /kw/*qu*, /hw/*wh*
Word Building Use *Word Builders* and *Word Builder Cards,* and have children repeat each step. Build the word *whack*. Then say the word naturally—*whack*. Lead children in building and reading new words. Say:

w	h	a	c	k

- **Change *wh* to *qu*. Read the word.** (*quack*)

q	u	a	c	k

- **Change *a* to *i*. Read the word.** (*quick*)

q	u	i	c	k

- **Change *qu* to *th*. Read the word.** (*thick*)

t	h	i	c	k

Continue in a similar manner to have children change initial consonant digraphs to build the following words: *then-when, whip-quip*.

Practice Book p.60 **Read Words in Context** Ask children to turn to *Practice Book* page 60. Read each sentence aloud and have children echo-read. Then ask volunteers to read each sentence aloud. Ask: **What is the name of the duck?** (Quinn) **How does she talk?** (She quacks.) **What is Quinn's quest?** (to catch ten fish) Guide children to find and circle words that have /kw/*qu* and underline words that have /hw/*wh*.

RETEACH

High-Frequency Words

Copying Masters 57–58 Display the *High-Frequency Word Cards* for *about, books, family, name, read, work, writing, people,* and *does*. Point to each card and read the word. Have children repeat. Give each child a set of word cards and have children spread the cards out in front of them. Randomly call out one of the words, and have children hold up the matching card, repeating the word aloud. Continue until they can respond quickly and accurately.

Reading

Build Background: "Tom's Books"
pp. 26–33

Read the title with children. Ask them if they like books. Invite children to name some of their favorite books or stories. Have children tell where they can find books. Tell children they will be reading about a boy who likes to read.

Monitor Comprehension: "Tom's Books"
Have children turn to the first page of the story. Ask a volunteer to reread the title. Have children look at the picture on page 26. Ask children to think about where the story takes place and what the characters will be doing. Then guide children through the story as they read.

pp. 26–27
Say: **A person is standing near a chalkboard, and others are sitting at desks. It looks like they are in a classroom. Let's read to find out who the story is about and what is happening.**

After reading the pages, ask: **Who do you think is the main character of this story?** (Tom) **Who is the lady?** (Mrs. March, his teacher) CHARACTERS/DRAW CONCLUSIONS

Ask: **Where does Tom go to get books to read?** (his class bookshelf or class library) MAKE INFERENCES

Ask: **What sound do q and u make when said together?** (/kw/) **Which word on page 26 has the /kw/ sound?** (quit) APPLY PHONICS

pp. 28–29
Say: **Tom is reading, but now he is in his bedroom. There is an older man there too. Let's read to find out what happens.**

After reading the pages, ask: **Who is the man in the picture?** (Tom's dad) **Where does the man take Tom?** (to the library) MAKE INFERENCES/NOTE DETAILS

Ask: **Do you like books as much as Tom does? Explain.** (Possible response: Yes, I love reading all kinds of books too. My favorite place is the library.) MAKE CONNECTIONS

Ask: **Which word on page 29 begins with the /hw/ sound?** (when) APPLY PHONICS

Fluency

Reading Rate Have children open to pages 17 and 19 of "Star" in *What a Thrill!* and invite a pair of volunteers to read the parts of Star's mom and Mrs. Park. Guide children to read the dialogue so that it sounds as if the characters are really speaking.

Then have another volunteer read page 18. Tell children to read this part more slowly to help everyone understand the important information. Read aloud pages 20–22, adjusting the reading rate as needed. Have children echo-read each page.

pp. 30–31

Say: **Now Tom is sitting near a tree. He looks a little older in this picture. He is holding a pencil, so he probably isn't reading a book. Let's read to find out what he is doing.**

After reading the pages, ask: **What is Tom doing?** (He is writing a book that he will read to his friends). **NOTE DETAILS**

Ask: **Why do his friends ask him *When*?** (Possible response: They are asking him when his book will be finished.) **MAKE INFERENCES**

Ask: **Which digraph *wh* word is used to ask a question on page 31?** (*when*) **APPLY PHONICS**

 page 32

Say: **There is an older man sitting at a table. Let's read to find out who he is and what he is doing.**

After reading the pages, ask: **Who is the man at the table?** (Tom as an adult) **What is Tom doing?** (signing books) **CHARACTERS/NOTE DETAILS**

Ask: **Why is Tom signing books?** (Possible response: Because he is a famous author now, and those are his books) **MAKE INFERENCES**

Ask: **What happens at the beginning of the story?** (Possible response: Tom read a lot.) **What happens at the end of the story?** (Possible response: Tom wrote books and is signing them.)
 SEQUENCE

 page 33

Answers to *Think Critically* Questions

Help children read and answer the *Think Critically* questions on page 33. Answers are shown below.

 1. ‹*read*› **SEQUENCE**

2. ‹*quit*› **CHARACTER**

3. ‹*writes books*› **COMPARE/CONTRAST**

PRETEACH

Build Robust Vocabulary

Introduce Robust Vocabulary Read the student-friendly explanation for each word. Then discuss each word using the following examples.

Say: **Graduating from college was a big accomplishment for me. What do you think is a big accomplishment—waking up from a nap or hitting a home run?**

Say: **I admire my mom because she does so much for me. Name someone that you admire, and tell why.**

Say: **My ambition is to learn how to snowboard. What is one of your ambitions? Why?**

RETEACH

Grammar/Writing

Using *I* and *Me* Remind children that *I* is used in the naming part of a sentence and *me* is used in the telling part. Then have children dictate sentences about something that they did or saw recently with a family member. Record their sentences, and read them with children. Ask volunteers to underline *I* and *me*. Write the following sentence frames on the board.

> Beth and ___ went to school.
>
> Grant went with Beth and _____.

Have children read the sentences. Guide children to choose which sentence uses *I* and which sentence uses *me*. Reread each sentence to make sure it sounds correct.

VOCABULARY

Student-Friendly Explanations

accomplishment If you have had an accomplishment, you have worked hard to get something done.

admire If you admire someone, you think that person is special in some way.

ambition If you have an ambition, you very much want to do something.

DAY AT A GLANCE

Day 3

PHONEMIC AWARENESS
Phoneme Segmentation

PHONICS
Preteach Inflections *-ed, -ing*

PHONICS AND SPELLING
Reteach Digraphs /kw/*qu*, /hw/*wh*

HIGH-FREQUENCY WORDS
Reteach *read, books, writing, does*

FLUENCY
Reading Rate

COMPREHENSION
Reteach Sequence

GRAMMAR/WRITING
Reteach Personal Narrative

Materials Needed:

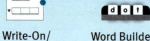

Write-On/ Wipe-Off Boards with Phonemic Awareness Disks

Word Builders and Word Builder Cards

Photo Cards

Copying Masters 59–60

Lesson 15 Story Strips

What a Thrill! Student Edition pp. 26–32

Spelling Words

1. quit	6. when
2. quick	7. arm
3. quiz	8. part
4. whiz	9. house
5. which	10. put

30+ Minutes

Phonemic Awareness

Phoneme Segmentation Have children use the three boxes on the *Write-on/Wipe-off Boards*. Tell children that the boxes stand for the sounds in words. Have children repeat each step with their *Write-on/Wipe-off Boards*. Say: **Nut. The first sound I hear in *nut* is /n/.** Model placing a disk in the first box. Use this procedure for the second sound in *nut* (/u/), placing a disk in the second box, and the last sound in *nut* (/t/), placing a disk in the third box. Point to each box in sequence as children say the word. Ask: **How many sounds do you hear in *nut*? I hear three.** Repeat this procedure with: *six, sock, sun, ten*.

PRETEACH

Phonics

Inflections *-ed, -ing* Write the words *drop, dropped,* and *dropping* on the board. Read the words and guide children to identify the root word and the endings added to it. (*drop, -ed, -ing*) Point out how the root word changed when each ending was added. (The *p* was doubled.) Explain that when the root word has a short vowel followed by one consonant, the final consonant is doubled before the ending is added. Guide children to add the endings *-ed* and *-ing* to the following words: *chat, rip, beg, flop*.

RETEACH

Phonics and Spelling

 Digraphs /kw/*qu*, /hw/*wh*

Build Words Use *Word Builder Cards* and a *Word Builder* to form words. Have children listen to your directions and change a letter in each word to spell a spelling word. Form *quilt* and have children read the word. Ask: **Which spelling word can you make by taking out *l*?** (*quit*)

Follow a similar procedure with the following words: *whip* (*whiz*), *whiz* (*quiz*), *quiz* (*quick*), *then* (*when*), *art* (*part*), *farm* (*arm*), *and rich* (*which*).

Remind children that there are some other words they have to remember how to spell. Display *Photo Card house*. Have children say *house*. Tell them to put *Word Builder Cards h, o, u, s, e* in their *Word Builders,* picture the word *house* in their minds, and build the word. Write the word on the board. Then have children build the word *put* using the *Word Builder Cards p, u, t*. Write the word on the board.

RETEACH
High-Frequency Words

Copying Masters 59–60

Duplicate and distribute *Copying Masters* 59–60 to each child. Explain that the sentences tell about the story "Tom's Books" but some have missing words.

List the words *read, books, writing,* and *does* on the board. Have children read aloud each story strip sentence and name the correct word on the board that makes sense in the sentence. Have children write the missing words in the blanks and read the completed sentences aloud. Help children cut apart the strips, read the completed sentences, and arrange them in story order.

RETEACH
Comprehension

Sequence Remind children that events in a story happen in a sequence that makes sense. Review how to recognize the sequence of events in a selection. Ask children to think about "Tom's Books" in *What a Thrill!* Ask: **Could Tom sign the books that he wrote before he learned how to read?** Lead children to conclude that the sequence in the story matches the order in which things happen in real life.

RETEACH
Grammar/Writing

Personal Narrative Write the following story on the board.

> I started the first day at my new school. I just moved here. I missed my friends, but I hoped to make new ones. The bell rang. I walked to my line. There was a girl. She asked me my name. She said she would show me around the school. I met a new friend.

Explain that this is a story written by a girl about an event in her life. Read the story aloud to children as you track the print. Explain to children that this kind of story is called a personal narrative, and that a personal narrative tells about something that has happened in a person's life. Point out that personal narratives have a beginning, a middle, and an end. Point out that they have words like *I* and *me* as you circle the words. Discuss with children what you learned about the girl in the story.

High-Frequency Words

read	**writing**
books	**does**

Fluency

Reading Rate Remind children that when good readers read, they are careful to read at the right speed so that they can understand the words. If they read too quickly, they might miss some words. If they read too slowly, they may forget what the story is about.

Model reading "Tom's Books" in *What a Thrill!* at an appropriate rate. Tell children that you may read a little faster if the characters are speaking or a little slower if there is a lot of important information. Have partners read the story several times to practice adjusting their reading rate and improve their fluency.

LESSON 15

DAY AT A GLANCE
Day 4

30+ Minutes

PHONEMIC AWARENESS
Phoneme Blending

PHONICS
Reteach Inflections -ed, -ing

PHONICS AND SPELLING
Reteach Digraphs /kw/qu, /hw/wh

HIGH-FREQUENCY WORDS
Reteach about, books, family, name, read, work, writing, people, does

FLUENCY
Reading Rate

COMPREHENSION
Guided Practice Sequence

GRAMMAR/WRITING
Reteach Personal Narrative

Materials Needed:

Practice
Book p.61

Practice
Book

Copying
Masters
57–58

Lesson 15
High-Frequency
Word Cards

What a Thrill!
Student Edition
pp. 6–12
pp. 26–32

Spelling Words

1. quit	6. when
2. quick	7. arm
3. quiz	8. part
4. whiz	9. house
5. which	10. put

Phonemic Awareness

Phoneme Blending   Tell children that together you are going to play a puzzle game. Tell them that you are going to say some words in pieces and they should listen to see if they can put the puzzle pieces together to figure out the word. Say: **/b/ /l/ /a/ /k/. What word does /b/ /l/ /a/ /k/ say? It says *black*.** Continue with the following words: /c/ /l/ /a/ /s/ (*class*), /f/ /l/ /u/ /sh/ (*flush*), /g/ /l/ /ā/ /z/ (*glaze*), /p/ /l/ /u/ /m/ (*plum*), /b/ /l/ /ā/ /z/ (*blaze*).

RETEACH

Phonics

Inflections -ed, -ing   Remind children that if the root word has a short vowel followed by one consonant, the final consonant is doubled before adding an ending. Write *sip*. Say: **The word *sipping* is made by doubling the final consonant of *sip* and adding *-ing*: s-i-p-p-i-n-g.** Repeat for *sipped*. Write the following root words on the board: *whip, stop, hop*. Read them aloud with children. Then guide children to double the consonant and add endings to form new words. Write the new words on the board. (*whipping, stopping, hopping; whipped, stopped, hopped*)

RETEACH

Phonics and Spelling

Practice
Book p.61

Digraphs /kw/qu, /hw/wh
Direct children's attention to page 61 of their *Practice Books*. Complete the page together.

Assess children's progress using the following sentences.
1. quit   Don't **quit** until you are done.
2. quick   Jeff was **quick** and won the race.
3. quiz   I got a good grade on the **quiz**.
4. whiz   Tyrone is a **whiz** at math.
5. which   Kate chose **which** hat to put on.
6. when   Please let me know **when** you are ready.

Review
7. arm   Rick hurt his **arm**.
8. part   Dad's truck needs a new **part**.

High-Frequency
9. house   My **house** is north of the park.
10. put   Carla **put** a note on the door.

RETEACH

High-Frequency Words

Copying Masters 57–58

Display the *High-Frequency Word Cards* for this lesson's words—*about, books, family, name, read, work, writing, people,* and *does*—and the previously-learned high-frequency words. Point to words at random and ask children to read them.

RETEACH

Comprehension

Sequence   Explain that the sequence of a story is the order in which events happen in a story. Draw a two-column chart labeled "How Many?" and "Tom's Books." Have children turn to "How Many?" in *What a Thrill!* Guide children to name its sequence of events. Have children repeat for "Tom's Books" in *What a Thrill!* Write their responses in the chart.

"How Many?"	"Tom's Books"
First, the chicks hatch from the eggs.	First,
Next, they find bugs to eat and flap their wings.	Next,
Last, they become hens.	Last,

RETEACH

Grammar/Writing

Personal Narrative   Review with children characteristics of a personal narrative.

Personal Narrative

A personal narrative tells about something that has happened in a person's life.
It has a beginning, a middle, and an end.
It has words like *I* and *me*.

Write the following sentences on the board and read them aloud: *I met a new girl at school. I helped her get her lunch. She sat with me on the playground. I like my new friend.* Guide children through the characteristics of this personal narrative. Then invite children to think about an event that has happened to them at school. Have them take turns telling about the event. Invite volunteers to dictate sentences as you write a personal narrative together.

High-Frequency Words

about	work
books	writing
family	people
name	does
read	

Fluency

Reading Rate   Remind children that good readers are careful to read at the right speed so that they can understand the words. Say: **I'm going to read "Tom's Books" in *What a Thrill!* one page at a time. I'm going to make sure that I am reading at the right speed so that I can understand all the words and ideas. At times, I may read a little faster if the characters are speaking or a little slower if there is a lot of important information. Read each page after me, just the way I read it.**

DAY AT A GLANCE
Day 5

HIGH-FREQUENCY WORDS
about, books, family, name, read, work, writing, people

PHONEMIC AWARENESS
Onset and Rime

PHONICS AND SPELLING
Preteach *r*-Controlled Vowels /ûr/*er, ir, ur*

BUILD ROBUST VOCABULARY
Preteach *captured, mercy, struggling*

GRAMMAR/WRITING
Preteach Using *He, She, It, They*

Materials Needed:

Lesson 15
High-Frequency
Word Cards

Sound/
Spelling
Card *ir, er, ur*

Word Builders
and Word
Builder Cards

Write-On/
Wipe-Off
Boards

Practice
Book

High-Frequency Words

about	read
books	work
family	writing
name	people

High-Frequency Words

Copying Masters 57–58 Display *High-Frequency Word Cards* for *about, books, family, name, read, work, writing, people,* and the other previously learned high-frequency words. Say the word *about,* ask a volunteer to point to *about,* and have children read the word aloud. Continue with the remaining high-frequency words. Repeat this activity several times to reinforce instant recognition.

Phonemic Awareness

Onset and Rime Have children name the following words as you say them in parts. Model the first one. **Listen as I say this word in parts: /p/-urse. The word I said was *purse*. Now you try some: /th/-ird, /j/-erm, /st/-ern, /p/-erch, /b/-urst.**

PRETEACH

Phonics and Spelling

Sound/Spelling Card ***r*-Controlled Vowels /ûr/*er, ir, ur***
Connecting Letter to Sound Say the words *dirt, herd,* and *burn.* Have children repeat the words. Say: **The words *dirt, herd,* and *burn* have the /ûr/ sound.** Have children say /ûr/ several times. Display *Sound/Spelling Card ir, er, ur.*

Say the letter names. Explain that each pair of letters can stand for the /ûr/ sound, as in *dirt.* Say: **When I say a word that ends with /ûr/, clap your hands. When I say a word that does not end with /ûr/, put your hands on your lap.** Say these words: *blur, stir, ball, her, heart.* Tell children that some words have the /ûr/ sound in the middle. Say *twirl,* elongating the /ûr/ sound. Tell children that *twirl* has the /ûr/ sound in the middle. Then follow the same procedure for the medial position with the following words: *skirt, short, fern, hurt, hard.*

Word Blending Demonstrate each step with *Word Builder Cards* and a *Word Builder.* Have children repeat each step after you. Hold up *t* and say /t/. Hold up *u* and *r* together and say /ûr/. Hold up *n* and say /n/.

- Place the letters *t, u, r, n* in the *Word Builder.*

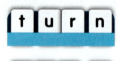

- Point to *t.* Say /t/. Point to *u* and *r* together and say /ûr/. Prompt children to repeat after you.

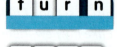

- Slide *ur* next to *t.* Run your hand under the letters as you blend the sounds, elongating them—/tûr/.

- Point to *n* and say /n/.
- Slide *n* next to *tur*. Run your hand under *turn* as you blend the sounds, elongating them—/tûrn/.
- Read *turn* naturally.

Follow the same procedure with these words: *bird, her, hurt*.

  Word Building   Place the *Word Builder Cards h, e,* and *r* in the *Word Builder*, and have children do the same. Slide your hand under the letters as you slowly read the word /hhûrr/. Then read the word naturally—*her*. Have children build and read new words. As they build each word, write it on the board. Say:

- **Change *h* to *f*. Change *e* to *u*. What word did you make?** (*fur*)

- **Change *f* to *t* and add *n* at the end. What word did you make?** (*turn*)

Continue with the words *bird, girl,* and *first*. Then have children read the words on the board. Direct children's attention to page 62 of their *Practice Books*. Complete the page together.

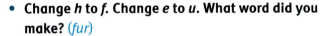
PRETEACH
Build Robust Vocabulary

Introduce Robust Vocabulary   Read the student-friendly explanation for each word. Then discuss each word using the following examples.

Say: **Once I captured a ladybug in my hand. Have you ever captured something? Explain.**

Say: **I showed mercy to my brother when he broke my toy. Would you show mercy to someone who broke something of yours? Explain.**

Say: **I was struggling to learn how to ride a bike. Do you think it would be more of a struggle to run a race or play an instrument? Explain.**

PRETEACH
Grammar/Writing

Using *He, She, It, They*   Write the following sentences on the board. *Dennis has a black cat. Meg is at her desk. The desk is black. The kids went to lunch.* Read the first sentence aloud and then say: **He has a black cat.** Explain that both sentences tell about Dennis, but the second sentence begins with *He* instead of *Dennis*. Say: **He can take the place of the name of an animal, a boy, or a man.** Read the sentences aloud. Elicit that *She* can replace *Meg, It* can replace *The desk,* and *They* can replace *The kids.*

Spelling Words

1. her	6. first
2. fur	7. quit
3. turn	8. when
4. bird	9. name
5. girl	10. work

Have children practice writing spelling words on their *Write-on/Wipe-off Boards.*

VOCABULARY

Student-Friendly Explanations

captured If you have captured something, you have caught it and are not letting go.

mercy If you show kindness or forgiveness to someone who has done something wrong, you show mercy.

struggling If you are struggling, you are making a great effort with your body or mind to do something.

30+ Minutes

LESSON 16

PHONEMIC AWARENESS
Phoneme Isolation

PHONICS AND SPELLING
Reteach *r*-Controlled Vowels /ûr/*er, ir, ur*

COMPREHENSION
Preteach Main Idea

HIGH-FREQUENCY WORDS
Reteach *join, please, room, need*

FLUENCY
Reading Rate

GRAMMAR/WRITING
Reteach Using *He, She, It, They*

Materials Needed:

Word Builders
and Word
Builder Cards

Write-On/
Wipe-Off
Boards

What a Thrill!
Student Edition
pp. 6–12
pp. 34–35

**Practice
Book**
p.63

Practice
Book

Spelling Words

1. her	6. first
2. fur	7. quit
3. turn	8. when
4. bird	9. name
5. girl	10. work

Have children practice writing
spelling words on their
Write-on/Wipe-off Boards.

Phonemic Awareness

Phoneme Isolation   Say the word *bird* and have children repeat it. Have children listen for other words with the /ûr/ sound. Say the words *fur* and *fun.* Say: **Which of these words has the /ûr/ sound? *Fur* has this sound. Now you try some.** Continue with: *curl, card, her; burst, pan, skirt; stir, surf, city.*

RETEACH

Phonics and Spelling

 r*-Controlled Vowels /ûr/*er, ir, ur
Word Building   Place the *Word Builder Cards h, e,* and *r* in the *Word Builder.* Ask children to say each letter name and the sound it stands for. Say the word naturally—*her.* Have children do the same. Ask:

- **Which letters should I change to make *her* become *fur*?** (Change *h* to *f* and *e* to *u*.)

- **Which letters should I change or add to make *fur* become *turn*?** (Change *f* to *t* and add *n* at the end.)

- **Which letters should I change to make *turn* become *bird*?** (Change *t* to *b, u* to *i,* and *n* to *d*.)

Continue with the words *girl* and *first.*

Read Words in Context   Write the following sentences on chart paper. Have children read each sentence silently. Then track the print as children read the sentences aloud. Finally, point to the underlined words at random and have children read them. *The girl wanted a turn after me. A bird does not have fur. Her first name is Corey. Did you quit work when it got dark?*

PRETEACH

Comprehension

 Main Idea   Tell children that the main idea is the most important idea in a story or a part of a story. The main idea is what that part of the selection is mostly about. Have children turn to "How Many?" in *What a Thrill!* Have children tell what the story is about. Then say: **We learned many things about chicks in this story. We learned about how they hatch, eat, and learn to fly. All these things tell us how chicks grow. That is the main idea of the story—that chicks grow into hens.**

High-Frequency Words

join	room
please	need

RETEACH

High-Frequency Words

pp. 34–35

Write the words *join, please, room,* and *need* on the board.

- Point to and read *join*. Repeat with children.

- Say: **Please** *join* **us.**

- Repeat the word *join* and then point to each letter as you spell it. Have children say and spell *join* with you. Have children reread *join*.

Repeat for the remaining words. Use the following sentences: Please *hand me a crayon. There is* room *for all of us.* I need *some help.*

Have children turn to page 34 of *What a Thrill!* and read aloud the words at the top of the page. Talk about the illustrations. Then guide children in choosing and writing the word that names each picture. (4. *curl,* 5. *fern,* 6. *bird*) Have children read aloud each word in the list on page 35. Ask volunteers to read the sentences aloud. Then have children choral-read the sentences. Guide them to choose and circle the word that completes each sentence. (1. *room,* 2. *join,* 3. *Please,* 4. *need*)

RETEACH

Grammar/Writing

Practice Book p.63

Using *He, She, It, They* Remind children that *he, she, it,* and *they* can replace the names of people, animals, or things. Write the following sentences on the board.

> Pam and Brad go to school.
>
> School is fun.
>
> Pam reads at school.
>
> Brad does math at school.

Read the sentences aloud with children. Guide children to help you rewrite the sentences using *he, she, it,* or *they* in place of the underlined words. Complete *Practice Book* page 63 together.

Fluency

Reading Rate Have children turn to "How Many?" in *What a Thrill!* Remind them to read silently at a rate that allows them to understand what they read and to read aloud at a rate that allows listeners to understand and stay interested in what is being read. Have children track the print as you model reading aloud at an appropriate rate.

LESSON 16

DAY AT A GLANCE

Day 2

PHONEMIC AWARENESS
Phoneme Blending

PHONICS AND SPELLING
Reteach *r*-Controlled Vowels /ûr/*er, ir, ur*

HIGH-FREQUENCY WORDS
Reteach *always, by, cow's, join, nice, please, room, need*

FLUENCY
Reading Rate

READING
"Please Get In!"

BUILD ROBUST VOCABULARY
Preteach *compatible, amiable, relax*

GRAMMAR/WRITING
Reteach Using *He, She, It, They*

Materials Needed:

Word Builders and Word Builder Cards | Practice Book | Lesson 16 High-Frequency Word Cards

What a Thrill! Student Edition pp. 26–32 pp. 36–43 | Photo Cards

High-Frequency Words

always	nice
by	please
Cow's	room
join	need

30+ Minutes

Phonemic Awareness

Phoneme Blending Tell children that they are going to be detectives and find the word you are thinking about. Say: **I'm thinking of an animal with feathers that flies. I'm thinking of a /b/ /ûr/ /d/. The word is bird. Now you try some.** Continue with: /d/ /ûr/ /t/ (*dirt*), /b/ /ûr/ /n/ (*burn*), and /s/ /ûr/ (*sir*).

RETEACH

Phonics and Spelling

dot *r*-Controlled Vowels /ûr/*er, ir, ur*
Word Building Use a *Word Builder* and *Word Builder Cards* and have children repeat each step after you. Build the word *hut*. Blend the sounds to read the word—/hhuut/. Then say the word naturally—*hut*. Have children do the same. Lead children in building and reading new words. Say:

- **Add *r* after *u*. Read the word.** (*hurt*)

Continue with the following words: *chip/chirp, skit/skirt, bet/Bert,* and *bust/burst.*

Practice Book p.64 **Read Words in Context** Ask children to turn to *Practice Book* page 64. Read each sentence aloud and have children echo-read. Then ask volunteers to read each sentence aloud. Ask: **What do Kirk and Bert like to do?** (surf) **Where are they?** (in the water) **Who surfs first?** (Bert) **What does Bert do when he was surfing?** (a perfect turn) After reading, have children find and circle words with the /ûr/ sound.

RETEACH

High-Frequency Words

Copying Masters 61–62 Display the *High-Frequency Word Cards* for *always, by, Cow's, join, nice, please, room,* and *need*. Point to each card and read the word. Have children repeat. Give each child a set of word cards and have children spread the cards out in front of them. Randomly call out one of the words, and have children hold up the matching card, repeating the word aloud. Continue until they can respond quickly and accurately.

Reading

Build Background: "Please Get In!"

pp. 36–43 Read the title with children. Ask them what they think the animals will be getting into. Have them pretend to be getting into a boat. Ask them to tell of any experiences they have had riding a boat. Tell them that they will read a story about animals in a boat.

Monitor Comprehension: "Please Get In!"

Have children turn to the first page of the story. Ask a volunteer to reread the title. Guide children to look at the picture on page 36. Encourage children to predict what the story will be about. Then guide children through the story as they read.

pp. 36–37 Say: **There are two birds and two ducks. Let's read to find out what they are doing.**

After reading the pages, ask: **What are the ducks doing?** (asking to get in the boat) **Why do you think they want to go in the boat?** (Possible response: They want to go for a boat ride.) **NOTE DETAILS/ DRAW CONCLUSIONS**

Ask: **Who were the first ones in the boat?** (the birds) **How are the birds different than the ducks? How are they the same?** (Possible response: The ducks are different colors than the birds and the ducks have different beaks, but they all have feathers.) **SEQUENCE/ COMPARE AND CONTRAST**

Ask: **Which words have the /ûr/ sound on page 37?** (birds, chirp) **APPLY PHONICS**

pp. 38–39 Say: **Two hens are flying near the boat. Let's read to find out if they get in the boat.**

After reading the pages, ask: **Do the birds let the hens in?** (yes) **What words tell you this?** (You can! Please get in.) **NOTE DETAILS**

Ask: **Is this story real or make-believe? Explain.** (Make-believe because hens, ducks, and birds can't talk like people.) **GENRE**

Ask: **Which /ûr/ word on page 39 tells how the birds talk?** (chirp) **APPLY PHONICS**

Fluency

Reading Rate Have children open "Tom's Books" in *What a Thrill!* Invite a volunteer to name the punctuation in each sentence, including quotation marks, commas, and end punctuation. Discuss the importance of punctuation and how it affects reading rate. For example, remind children to pause briefly at each end punctuation mark before continuing to read.

Have children follow along as you model reading spoken words in a way that sounds natural and as you add meaning by changing the rate of your reading. Have children echo-read after you.

pp.
40–
41

Say: **Two swans are coming toward the boat. Let's read to find out if they get in the boat too.**

After reading the pages, ask: **Was there room for the swans to get in?** (yes) **Do you think there will be room for more animals in the boat?** (Possible response: no, because the boat looks full) NOTE DETAILS/MAKE INFERENCES

Say: **What /ûr/ words do you see on page 41?** (*turn, birds, chirp*) APPLY PHONICS

Say: **The swans ask to join the birds. Have you ever asked a friend if you could join them in doing something? Explain.** (Possible response: Yes, once I asked my friend if I could play soccer with him.) MAKE CONNECTIONS

page
42

Say: **The animals look puzzled. Let's read to find out what the problem is.**

After reading the pages, ask: **What is the problem?** (The boat is not in the water.) NOTE DETAILS

Ask: **What do you think the animals should do now?** (Possible response: I think they should find a lake or ocean to put the boat in.) EXPRESS PERSONAL OPINIONS

Ask: **How do you think the characters are feeling right now?** (Possible response: sad that there is no water, but happy that they are all together) CHARACTERS' EMOTIONS

page
43

Answers to *Think Critically* Questions
Help children read and answer the *Think Critically* questions on page 43. Answers are shown below.

1. ‹water› PLOT

 2. ‹friends› MAIN IDEA

3. ‹8 birds› DRAW CONCLUSIONS

Build Robust Vocabulary

Introduce Robust Vocabulary Read the student-friendly explanation for each word. Then discuss each word using the following examples.

Say: **I have two dogs that are compatible. They get along and never fight.** Display *Photo Card queen,* then display *Photo Cards king* and *porcupine.* Say: **Which do you think is more compatible with a queen. Why?**

Say: **My friend is amiable. She is so friendly. Name someone you know who is amiable. Explain why you think he or she is amiable.**

Say: **I like to lie on my sofa and read a book to relax. What do you do to relax?** Display *Photo Cards school, island,* and *factory.* Say: **Which place would you want to go to relax?**

Grammar/Writing

Using *He, She, It, They* Model and write a sentence on the board about a child, such as *Stan wore a black shirt.* Ask volunteers to dictate more sentences with the name or names of other children and things. Underline the name or names of children and things. Ask children what words they can use to take the place of the underlined words. (*he, she, it,* or *they*)

Rewrite each sentence below the original sentence, using an incorrect pronoun such as *She wore a black shirt.* Read aloud the first pair of sentences and model how to rewrite the second sentence correctly. (*He wore a black shirt.*) Have children help you correct the remaining sentences.

Student-Friendly Explanations

compatible When people or animals are compatible, they are able to be together or get along with each other.

amiable Someone who is amiable is good-natured and friendly.

relax When you relax, you are not uneasy or upset about anything; you spend time resting or doing things for fun.

DAY AT A GLANCE

Day 3

30+ Minutes

PHONEMIC AWARENESS
Phoneme Segmentation

PHONICS
Preteach Inflections *-er, -est*

PHONICS AND SPELLING
Reteach *r*-Controlled Vowels /ûr/*er, ir, ur*

HIGH-FREQUENCY WORDS
Reteach *join, please, room, need*

FLUENCY
Reading Rate

COMPREHENSION
Reteach Main Idea

GRAMMAR/WRITING
Reteach Invitation

Materials Needed:

Write-On/
Wipe-Off
Boards with
Phonemic
Awareness
Disks

Word Builders
and Word
Builder Cards

Copying Masters 63–64

Lesson 16
Story Strips

What a Thrill!
Student Edition
pp. 16–22

Spelling Words

1. her	6. first
2. fur	7. quit
3. turn	8. when
4. bird	9. name
5. girl	10. work

Phonemic Awareness

Phoneme Segmentation Have children use the three boxes on the *Write-on/Wipe-off Boards.* Tell children that the boxes stand for the sounds in words. Have children repeat each step with their *Write-on/Wipe-Off Boards.* Say: **Kite. The first sound I hear in *kite* is /k/.** Model placing a disk in the first box. Use this procedure for the second sound in *kite* (/ī/) placing a disk in the second box, and the third sound in *kite* (t) placing a disk in the third box. Point to each box in sequence as children say the word. **How many sounds do you hear in *kite*? I hear three.** Repeat this procedure with: *nine, thumb, pin,* and *red.*

PRETEACH

Phonics

Inflections *-er, -est* Cut three strips of paper, each one longer and wider than the next. Write the following words as column headings on the board: *long, longer, longest.* Display the strips of paper and describe them as follows: **This strip is long. This strip is longer. This strip is longest.** Repeat the words *long, longer,* and *longest,* pointing to each one on the board and the strip it describes. Read each word and underline the inflection. Use the same process with the following sentences: *This strip is wide. This strip is wider. This strip is widest.*

RETEACH

Phonics and Spelling

r-Controlled Vowel /ûr/*er, ir, ur*
Build Words Use *Word Builders* and *Word Builder Cards* to form words. Have children listen to your directions and change a letter in each word to spell a spelling word. Form *hen* and have children read the word. Ask: **Which spelling word can you make by changing the last letter?** (*her*)

h e n

h e r

f u r

Follow a similar procedure with the following words: *her* (*fur*), *fur* (*turn*), *third* (*bird*), *twirl* (*girl*), *sit* (*quit*), *hen* (*when*).

Remind children that there are some other words they have to remember how to spell. Tell them that *name* is one such word. Have children say *name.* Tell them to put *Word Builder Cards n, a, m, e* in their *Word Builders,* picture the word *name* in their minds, and build the word. Write the word on the board. Follow the same procedure with *work.*

High-Frequency Words

join	room
please	need

RETEACH

High-Frequency Words

 Copying Masters 63–64

Duplicate and distribute *Copying Masters* 63–64 to each child. Explain that the sentences tell the story "Please Get In!" but some have missing words.

List the words *join, please, room,* and *need* on the board. Have children read aloud each story strip sentence and name the correct word on the board that makes sense in the sentence. Have children write the missing words in the blanks and read the completed sentences aloud. Help children cut apart the strips, read the completed sentences, and arrange them in story order.

RETEACH

Comprehension

 Main Idea Remind children that the main idea of a story or a selection is what it is mostly about. Have children recall "Star" in *What a Thrill!* and guide them to determine the main idea. Read these sentences and have children choose the one that best tells the main idea. *Star is very tired. Trying new things can be fun. Star's classmates like to march.*

RETEACH

Grammar/Writing

Invitation Ask children to tell about a time they were invited to do something. Have them tell about how they were invited—in person, by written invitation, or by phone. Then write the following on the board:

> To: Juana Sanchez
> From: Kina
> You are invited to my birthday party!
> When: Saturday, April 18, 11:30 to 2:30
> Where: The Pizza Place

Say: **This is an invitation. An invitation tells *who* is invited, *what* the event is, *when* the event is, *where* the event is, and *who* is sending the invitation.** Read the invitation and point out the parts. Have children tell the main idea of the invitation. Point out how the rest of the invitation gives important information about the event to help the person being invited understand. Guide children to restate the important and/or interesting ideas in the model.

Fluency

Reading Rate Have children turn to "Star" in *What a Thrill!* Discuss with children a reading rate that might be a typical way one of the characters in a story might speak, for example, slowly for Star, the tired elephant or more quickly for the parts of Mrs. Park and the quickly moving students. Then have children choose a sentence that a character says and read the chosen sentence with a reading rate that helps portray the character. After children read, provide encouragement and feedback.

PHONEMIC AWARENESS
Phoneme Blending

PHONICS
Reteach Inflections -er, -est

PHONICS AND SPELLING
Reteach r-Controlled Vowels /ûr/er, ir, ur

HIGH-FREQUENCY WORDS
Reteach always, by, Cow's, join, nice, please, room, need

FLUENCY
Reading Rate

COMPREHENSION
Guided Practice Main Idea

GRAMMAR/WRITING
Reteach Invitation

Materials Needed:

Practice Book

Lesson 16 High-Frequency Word Cards

What a Thrill! Student Edition pp. 26–32 pp. 36–42

Spelling Words

1.	her	6.	first
2.	fur	7.	quit
3.	turn	8.	when
4.	bird	9.	name
5.	girl	10.	work

Phonemic Awareness

Phoneme Blending   Tell children that together you are going to play a puzzle game. Explain that you are going to say some words in pieces and they should listen to see if they can put the puzzle pieces together to figure out the word. Say: **/b/ /ûr/ /d/. What word does /b/ /ûr/ /d/ say? It says** *bird.* Continue with the following words: **/b/ /ûr/ /th/** (*birth*), **/s/ /ûr/ /f/** (*surf*), **/s/ /t/ /ûr/** (*stir*), **/k/ /ûr/ /b/** (*curb*).

RETEACH

Phonics

Inflections *-er, -est*   Tell children that *-er* and *-est* can be added to describing words to describe two or more people, animals, places, or things. Explain that *-er* can also be added to words to make a naming word. Write *work + er* on the board. Say: **By adding *-er* to *work,* we made a naming *word*.** Have children read the word *worker*. Use the same procedure with *fight + -er, speak + -er, climb + -er,* and *walk + -er*.

RETEACH

Phonics and Spelling

 r*-Controlled Vowels /ûr/*er, ir, ur
Direct children's attention to page 65 of their *Practice Books*. Complete the page together.

Assess children's progress using the following sentences.

1.	her	Where did Maria put **her** backpack?
2.	fur	Our dog has soft **fur** on its head.
3.	turn	It's your **turn** to hit the ball.
4.	bird	A big **bird** flew to its home.
5.	girl	Gwen is the new **girl** at our school.
6.	first	Sal was the **first** one to get there.

Review

7.	quit	The workers have **quit** for lunch.
8.	when	Please stop **when** you see a car.

High-Frequency

9.	name	My **name** is Janet.
10.	work	Does your mom **work** hard at her job?

RETEACH

High-Frequency Words

Copying Masters 61–62

Display *High-Frequency Word Cards* for this lesson's words—*always, by, Cow's, join, nice, please, room,* and *need*—and the previously learned high-frequency words. Point to words at random and ask children to read them.

RETEACH

Comprehension

Main Idea   Ask children to explain the main idea. (what a story is mostly about) Draw a chart on the board like the one below. Have children turn to "Please Get In!" in *What a Thrill!* Review the main idea and write it in the chart. Then guide children in figuring out the main idea of "Tom's Books." Record their responses in the chart.

"Please Get In!"	"Tom's Books"
Different friends start filling up a boat, but there is room for everyone.	A boy works hard to learn new things and reach his goals.

RETEACH

Grammar/Writing

Invitation   Review with children the characteristics of an invitation.

An Invitation Tells

who is invited   when the event is

what the event is   where the event is

who is sending the invitation

Model an invitation, such as: **You are invited to a class party. We'll celebrate reaching our reading goals with a pizza party. Date: Friday, March 3. Time: 11:30–12:30. Where: In Room 24. From: Your teacher.** Point out that you told who is invited, what the event is, when and where to come, and who sent the invitation.

Ask children to think of a special occasion or event for which they would want to send an invitation. Then work together to write an invitation to the event.

High-Frequency Words

always	nice
by	please
Cow's	room
join	need

Fluency

Reading Rate   Have partners practice reading aloud "Please Get In!" in *What a Thrill!* Remind children to read at a steady pace so that they and their listeners will understand and stay interested in the story. Listen to partners read, giving them feedback about their reading rate and guidance for improving their fluency.

30+ Minutes

DAY AT A GLANCE
Day 5

HIGH-FREQUENCY WORDS
always, by, Cow's, join, nice, please, room

PHONEMIC AWARENESS
Onset and Rime

PHONICS AND SPELLING
Preteach Syllable /əl/-*le*

BUILD ROBUST VOCABULARY
Preteach *agreement, unnoticed, unthinkable*

GRAMMAR/WRITING
Preteach Possessives

Materials Needed:

Lesson 16
High-Frequency
Word Cards

Sound/
Spelling
Card *le*

Word Builders
and Word
Builder Cards

Write-On/
Wipe-Off
Boards

Practice
Book

Photo
Cards

High-Frequency Words

always	nice
by	please
Cow's	room
join	

High-Frequency Words

Copying Masters 61–62

Display *High-Frequency Word Cards* for *always, by, Cow's, join, nice, please, room,* and the other previously learned high-frequency words. Say the word *always,* ask a volunteer to point to *always,* and have children read the word aloud. Continue with the remaining high-frequency words. Repeat this activity several times to reinforce instant recognition.

Phonemic Awareness

Onset and Rime Have children name the following words as you say them in parts. Model the first one. **Listen as I say this word in parts: /n/-oodle. The word I said was** *noodle.* **Now you try some: /s/-imple, /m/-eddle, /br/-ittle, /dr/-izzle, /k/-obbler.**

PRETEACH

Phonics and Spelling

Sound/ Spelling Card

Syllable /əl/-*le*
Connecting Letter to Sound Say the words *pick* and *pickle.* Lead children in clapping each syllable as they say the words. Repeat with *start* and *startle.* Point out that *pickle* and *startle* have two syllables, and they end with the same sound. Repeat each word, slightly elongating these sounds in the last syllable: /əəll/.

Then say the following words and have children add /əl/. Say these words: *hand* (*handle*), *tick* (*tickle*). Display *Sound/Spelling Card -le.* Say the picture name and explain that the letters *-le* can stand for the sound at the end of *table*—/əl/. Have children say /əl/ several times as you touch the letters.

Say: **When I say a word that ends with /əl/, raise your hand. When I say a word that does not end with /əl/, hold your hand behind your back.** Say these words: *jingle, riddle, harden, little, open, turtle.*

 Word Blending Demonstrate each step with *Word Builder Cards* and a *Word Builder,* and have children repeat each step after you. Hold up *t* and say /t/. Hold up *i* and say /i/. Hold up *ck* and say /k/. Hold up *le* and say /əl/.

- Place the letters *t, i, c, k, l, e* in the *Word Builder.*

- Slide the letters *ick* next to *t.* Run your hand under the letters as you read the word—*tick.* Have children repeat.

- Slide *le* next to *tick.* Slide your hand under *tickle* as you blend the sounds in the second syllable—tick-/əl/. Have children repeat.

t	i	c	k	l	e

t	i	c	k	l e

t	i	c	k	l e

- Read *tickle* naturally. Repeat, having children read the word with you.

Follow the same procedure with these words: *handle, giggle, middle.*

  Word Building   Build *hand.* Have children do the same with their *Word Builders* and *Word Builder Cards.* Run your hand under the letters as you read the word—*hand.* Have children build and read new words. As they build each word, write it on the board. Say:

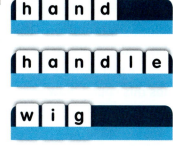

- **Add *le* to *hand.* What word did you make?** (*handle*)

Build *wig* and read it with children. Say:

- **Add *gle* to *wig.* What word did you make?** (*wiggle*)

Continue with *sing-single, lit-little.* Then have children read the words on the board. Direct children's attention to page 66 of their *Practice Books.* Complete the page together.

Spelling Words

1. hand	6. little
2. handle	7. turn
3. wig	8. girl
4. wiggle	9. by
5. single	10. room

Have children practice writing spelling words on their *Write-on/Wipe-off Boards.*

PRETEACH

Build Robust Vocabulary

 Introduce Robust Vocabulary   Read the student-friendly explanation for each word. Then discuss each word using the following examples.

Say: **My mom and I are in agreement that if I do my homework, I can play outside after. What agreements do you have at home?**

Say: **There were so many people in the room that I was unnoticed. Would you be unnoticed in a class full of children or with only three children?**

Say: **A day without breakfast is unthinkable to me.** Show *Photo Cards toad* and *fruit.* **Which would be unthinkable for you to eat?**

VOCABULARY

Student-Friendly Explanations

agreement When you are in agreement with others, you all think the same thing.

unnoticed If you go unnoticed, no one sees you.

unthinkable An unthinkable event is something you never thought could or would happen.

PRETEACH

Grammar/Writing

Possessives   Write on the board: *Jan's dog is black. Fred's ankle is hurt.* Have children read the sentences aloud. Explain that the words *Jan's* and *Fred's* show ownership. They show that the dog belongs to Jan and the ankle belongs to Fred. Underline the names, and then circle the apostrophe and identify it for children. Explain that adding the *'s* to *Jan* and *Fred* shows that the dog is Jan's and the ankle is Fred's.

Have a child hold up a crayon. Write on the board the child's name and *crayon.* Underline the child's name. Guide children to add *'s* to the name. Repeat with different students and classroom objects.

DAY AT A GLANCE

Day 1

30+ Minutes

LESSON 17

PHONEMIC AWARENESS
Phoneme Isolation

PHONICS AND SPELLING
Reteach Syllable /əl/-*le*

COMPREHENSION
Reteach Main Idea

HIGH-FREQUENCY WORDS
Preteach *paint, paper, always*

FLUENCY
Intonation

GRAMMAR/WRITING
Reteach Possessives

Materials Needed:

Word Builders and Word Builder Cards

Write-On/Wipe-Off Boards

Shooting Star Student Edition pp. 46–52

What a Thrill! Student Edition pp. 16–22 pp. 44–45

Practice Book p.67
Practice Book

Spelling Words

1. hand	6. little
2. handle	7. turn
3. wig	8. girl
4. wiggle	9. by
5. single	10. room

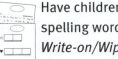
Have children practice writing spelling words on their *Write-on/Wipe-off Boards.*

Phonemic Awareness

Phoneme Isolation   Say the word *struggle* and have children repeat it. Have children listen for other words with the /əl/ sound. Say the words *trouble* and *stirring.* Say: **Which of these words has the /əl/ sound?** *Trouble* **has this sound. Now you try some.** Continue with: *cycle, sick, gentle; noble, follow, people; able, beagle, books.*

RETEACH

Phonics and Spelling

 Syllable /əl/-*le*
Word Building   Place the *Word Builder Cards h, a, n, d* in the Word Builder. Read the word with children. Ask:

Which letters should I add to *hand* to make *handle*? (add *le*)

After children read *handle,* replace the cards with *w, i, g,* and read the word with children. Lead children in building *wiggle.* Use a similar procedure to build *single* and *little.*

Read Words in Context   Write the following sentences on chart paper. Have children read each sentence silently. Then track the print as children read the sentences aloud. Finally, point to the underlined words at random and have children read them. *Please <u>turn</u> the <u>handle</u> to the left. The <u>little</u> <u>girl</u> had a long <u>wig</u> on. I am so full that I cannot eat a <u>single</u> thing. There is <u>room</u> on the bench for Don to sit <u>by</u> me. Ross has to <u>wiggle</u> and can't stand still. Please raise your <u>hand</u> before you get out of your seat.*

RETEACH

Comprehension

 Main Idea   Review main idea with children. Guide them to determine the main idea of a selection and identify supporting details. Have children turn to "Some Animals" in *Shooting Star.* Read aloud the following sentences: **Some animals are from a cold land. This camel stores water in his hump. All animals like to eat!** Then model how to identify the main idea. Say: **The main idea is the most important idea. The first sentence tells me about animals from a cold land, but this is only one part of the selection. It is a detail, not the main idea. The next sentence tells me about a camel, but this is also only a detail, not the main idea. The last sentence tells me what _all_ animals like to do. This is the main idea or most important idea of the story.**

High-Frequency Words

paint   always

paper

PRETEACH

High-Frequency Words

 pp. 44–45

Write the words _paint, paper,_ and _always_ on the board.

- Point to and read _paint._ Repeat with children.

- Say: **Let's _paint_ a picture.**

- Repeat the word and then point to each letter as you spell it. Have children say and spell _paint_ with you. Have children reread _paint._

Repeat for the remaining words. Use the following sentences: _Write your name on the_ paper. _I_ always _have cereal for breakfast._

Have children turn to page 44 of _What a Thrill!_ and read aloud the words at the top of the page. Talk about the illustrations. Then guide children in choosing and writing the word that names each picture. (4. _handle,_ 5. _cuddle,_ 6. _little_) Have children read aloud each word in the list on page 45. Ask volunteers to read the sentences aloud. Then have children choral-read the sentences. Guide them to choose and circle the word that completes each sentence. (1. _always,_ 2. _paint,_ 3. _paper_)

RETEACH

Grammar/Writing

Practice Book

p.67

Possessives   Write the following sentences on the board: _The boy has a marker. The boy's marker is red._ Read the sentences with children. Circle _boy's_ and point out that the word shows ownership. Point to the apostrophe, and have children recall the name of this mark. Explain that _'s_ can be added to many naming words, such as _boy,_ to show ownership. Ask children to tell what the boy owns. (a marker)

Write on the board _Gavin has a car. The girl has a bike. A bird has a nest._ Read the sentences aloud. Then write _Gavin's car._ Repeat for the other sentences, guiding children to write the possessive naming word on the board. Complete _Practice Book_ page 67 together.

Fluency

Intonation   Remind children that good readers make their voices rise and fall so that their reading sounds like natural speech. They also let their voice get louder and softer, just like someone talking. Have children open to "Star" in _What a Thrill!_ and track the print as you read aloud with expressive intonation. Have children echo-read.

DAY AT A GLANCE

Day 2

PHONEMIC AWARENESS
Phoneme Blending

PHONICS AND SPELLING
Reteach Syllable /əl/-*le*

HIGH-FREQUENCY WORDS
Reteach *buy, carry, money, other, paint, paper, would, always*

FLUENCY
Punctuation

READING
"Paint Your Dog!"

BUILD ROBUST VOCABULARY
Preteach *rejoice, predicament, extraordinary*

GRAMMAR/WRITING
Reteach Possessives

Materials Needed:

Word Builders and Word Builder Cards

Practice Book p.68
Practice Book

Copying Masters 65–66
Lesson 17 High-Frequency Word Cards

What a Thrill!
Student Edition
pp. 16–22
pp. 46–53

High-Frequency Words

buy	paint
carry	paper
money	would
other	always

Phonemic Awareness

Phoneme Blending   Tell children that they are going to be detectives and find the word you are thinking about. Say: **I'm thinking of a word that is something a king lives in. It is /k/ /a/ /s/ /əl/. The word is *castle*. Now you try some.** Continue with: /p/ /ûr/ /p/ /əl/ (*purple*), /t/ /a/ /k/ /əl/ (*tackle*), and /hw/ /i/ /s/ /əl/ (*whistle*).

RETEACH

Phonics and Spelling

Syllable /əl/-*le*
Word Building   Use *Word Builders* and *Word Builder Cards* and have children repeat each step. Build the word *pad*. Blend the sounds to read the word—/paad/. Then say the word naturally—*pad*. Have children do the same. Lead children in building and reading new words. Say:

- **Double the final consonant. Then add the syllable /əl/ at the end. Read the word.** (*paddle*)

Continue with the following one-syllable words: *trip, start, pick, cat, jug.*

After each word is built, have children add /əl/ to form these two-syllable words: *triple, startle, pickle, cattle, juggle.*

Read Words in Context   Ask children to turn to *Practice Book* page 68. Read each sentence aloud and have children echo-read. Then ask volunteers to read each sentence aloud. Ask: **What does Chad's little sister play with?** (a rattle) **When does she giggle?** (when Chad tickles her) **What makes Chad chuckle?** (when she babbles) Guide children to find and circle words that end with /əl/.

RETEACH

High-Frequency Words

Copying Masters 65–66   Display the *High-Frequency Word Cards* for *buy, carry, money, other, paint, paper, would,* and *always*. Point to each card and read the word. Have children repeat. Give each child a set of word cards and have children spread the cards out in front of them. Randomly call out one of the words, and have children hold up the matching card, repeating the word aloud. Continue until they can respond quickly and accurately.

Reading

Build Background: "Paint Your Dog!"

pp. 46–53

Read the title with children. Ask them if they have a dog. If so, ask them to tell about their dog. If not, ask them to discuss what they know about dogs. Tell them that they will read a story about a girl and her dog.

Monitor Comprehension: "Paint Your Dog!"

Have children turn to the first page of the story. Ask a volunteer to reread the title. Guide children to look at the picture on page 46. Encourage children to predict what the story will be about and what the characters might do. Then guide children through the story as they read.

pp. 46–47

Say: **It looks like the girl is going to pick up the dog. Let's read to find out what happens.**

After reading the pages, ask: **Why does the girl want to pick up the dog?** (to cuddle it) **Was she able to pick it up? Explain.** (Possible response: No, because the dog moves around a lot.) NOTE DETAILS/ CAUSE AND EFFECT

Ask: **Which words on page 46 end with /əl/?** (cuddle, little) APPLY PHONICS

Ask: **Do you think holding the painting of a dog is the same as holding a real dog? Explain.** (Possible response: No, because a real dog is soft and cuddly, a piece of paper is not.) PERSONAL RESPONSE

pp. 48–49

Say: **Now the dog looks like she is hiding from the kids. Let's read to find out what is happening.**

After reading the pages, ask: **Why do you think the dog is hiding from the kids?** (Possible response: Because the dog is afraid of the kids.) **Do you think it's easier for a little dog to hide or a big dog? Explain.** (a little dog because they can get into smaller places) DRAW CONCLUSIONS/GENERALIZE

Ask: **How is looking at the painting different from seeing the real dog?** (Possible response: You can't pet the painting. The painting doesn't bark or wag its tail.) COMPARE AND CONTRAST

Say: **Which word on page 48 ends with /əl/?** (little) APPLY PHONICS

Fluency

Punctuation Have children turn to "Star" in *What a Thrill!* and guide children to name the end punctuation used for each sentence. Remind children that the exclamation point indicates that the sentence should be read with excitement. Model reading *March with us!* excitedly.

Then remind children to pause briefly when they see a comma and to make a slightly longer pause when they see a period. Model reading other sentences in the story with intonation, then have children echo-read.

Say: **The girl is drawing a picture. Let's read to find out what she is drawing.**

After reading the pages, ask: **What is the girl doing?** (making a simple sketch) **What is her drawing going to be of?** (her dog) NOTE DETAILS/MAKE INFERENCES

Ask: **What is the first thing the girl did?** (get paper) SEQUENCE

Ask: **What word on page 50 ends with /əl/?** (*simple*) **Let's all point to the word *simple* and read it aloud.** APPLY PHONICS

 Say: **The girl is holding her painting. Let's read to find out if it is finished.**

After reading the pages, ask: **Did the girl finish the painting? How do you know?** (Possible response: Yes, because she is holding it up to show people and because the picture looks complete) **What do you think she is going to do with the painting?** (Possible response: She's going to show it to people or look at it when she cannot find or hold her dog.) CONTEXT CLUES/DRAW CONCLUSIONS

Ask: **Do you think the girl is a good artist?** (Possible response: Yes, because her painting looks just like her dog) PERSONAL OPINION

 Answers to *Think Critically* Questions

Help children read and answer the *Think Critically* questions on page 53. Answers are shown below.

1. ‹*dog*› CHARACTERS

2. ‹*paper*› SEQUENCE

 3. ‹*always be with you*› MAIN IDEA

PRETEACH

Build Robust Vocabulary

Introduce Robust Vocabulary   Read the student-friendly explanation for each word. Then discuss each word using the following examples.

Say: **I rejoice when I see my students learning. What makes you rejoice?**

Say: **I would be in a predicament if my car broke down or if I locked myself out of my classroom. Describe a predicament that you've been in. Explain how you got out of it.**

Say: **I think any animal that can do tricks is extraordinary. Tell about an extraordinary talent that you or someone you know has.**

RETEACH

Grammar/Writing

Possessives   Write the following sentences on chart paper: *Ron's cat is big. The girl's dog runs fast.* Have children read them aloud. Point out the possessive naming words and the apostrophes. Tell children that some words like *his, her,* and *hers* can take the place of naming words, and that they also show ownership. Write these sentences under the corresponding ones above: *His cat is big. Her dog runs fast. The dog is hers.* Underline *his, her,* and *hers.* Track the print and have children read the sentences. Guide them to tell who *his, her,* and *hers* refer to.

VOCABULARY

Student-Friendly Explanations

rejoice   If you rejoice, you show that you are very happy.

predicament   If you have a predicament, you have a serious or difficult problem.

extraordinary   Something extraordinary is something that is very unusual or remarkable.

LESSON 17

30+ Minutes

DAY AT A GLANCE

Day 3

PHONEMIC AWARENESS
Phoneme Segmentation

PHONICS
Preteach Inflections -ed, -ing

PHONICS AND SPELLING
Reteach Syllable /əl/-le

HIGH-FREQUENCY WORDS
Reteach paint, paper, always

FLUENCY
Intonation

COMPREHENSION
Reteach Main Idea

GRAMMAR/WRITING
Reteach Friendly Letter

Materials Needed:

Write-On/
Wipe-Off
Boards with
Phonemic
Awareness
Disks

Word Builders
and Word
Builder Cards

Copying Masters 67–68

Lesson 17
Story Strips

What a Thrill!
Student Edition
pp. 46–52

Spelling Words

I. hand	6. little
2. handle	7. turn
3. wig	8. girl
4. wiggle	9. by
5. single	10. room

Phonemic Awareness

 Phoneme Segmentation Distribute the four-box papers to children. Tell them that the boxes stand for sounds in words. Have children repeat each step with their four-box paper. Say: **Puddle. The first sound I hear in *puddle* is /p/.** Model placing a disk in the first box. Use this procedure for the second sound in *puddle* (/u/) placing a disk in the second box, the third sound in *puddle* (/d/) and the last sound (əl) placing a disk in the third and fourth boxes. Point to each box in sequence as children say the word. **How many sounds do you hear in *puddle*? I hear four.** Repeat this procedure with: *juggle, giggle, settle.*

PRETEACH

Phonics

Inflections -ed, -ing Write on the board: *drip, dripped, dripping.* After you read the words guide children to identify the root word and the endings added to it. Point out to children how the root word changed when each ending was added. (The *p* was doubled.) Remind children that when the root word has a short vowel followed by one consonant, the final consonant is doubled before the ending is added. Frame the ending *ed* in *dripped* and have children identify the final sound in the word. Tell children that the ending *ed* can stand for the sound /t/ in *dripped*, /d/ in *planned*, and /əd/ in *trotted*.

RETEACH

Phonics and Spelling

Syllable /əl/-le
Build Words Use *Word Builders* and *Word Builder Cards* to form words. Have children listen to your directions and change letters in each word to spell a spelling word. Form *wig* and have children read the word. Ask: **Which spelling word can you make by adding *gle*?** (*wiggle*)

Follow a similar procedure with the following words: wiggle (*single*), single (*little*), hand (*handle*), burn (*turn*), and whirl (*girl*).

w	i	g

w	i	g	g	l	e

s	i	n	g	l	e

Remind children that there are some other words they have to remember how to spell. Tell them that *by* is one such word. Have children say *by*. Tell them to put *Word Builder Cards b, y* in their *Word Builders,* picture the word *by* in their minds, and build the word. Write the word on the board. Follow the same procedure with *room.*

RETEACH

High-Frequency Words

Copying Masters 67–68

Duplicate and distribute *Copying Masters* 67–68 to each child. Explain that the sentences tell the story "Paint Your Dog!" but some have missing words.

List the words *paint, paper,* and *always* on the board. Have children read aloud each story strip sentence and name the correct word on the board that makes sense in the sentence. Have children write the missing words in the blanks and read the completed sentences aloud. Help children cut apart the strips, read the completed sentences, and arrange them in story order.

RETEACH

Comprehension

Main Idea   Discuss with children that the main idea of a story is what the story is mostly about. Then guide children to recognize the main idea in "Paint Your Dog!" Say: **Little dogs get up and go. Is that the main idea of this story or just a detail?** Guide children to point out that the sentence you said is a detail. Repeat with other details from the story and elicit from children the main idea of the story.

RETEACH

Grammar/Writing

Friendly Letter   Write the following letter on the board.

> January 16, 20–
>
> Dear Gavin,
>
> How is your new school? Have you met new friends? I have a new little sister. Her name is Devin. Please send me a letter.
>
> Your friend,
>
> Beth

Explain that a girl wrote this letter to a friend who lives far away. Read the letter and talk about its parts. Explain to children that in a friendly letter, the heading gives the date. Point out the greeting, the body, and the closing. Explain that the greeting tells who gets the message, the body is the message, and the closing says good-bye. Finally, point out the signature and tell children that is the writer's name.

High-Frequency Words

paint	**always**
paper	

Fluency

Intonation   Remind children that when good readers read, they make sure their voices rise and fall so their reading sounds like natural speech. Explain that they can make their voice fall at the end of a sentence when a character is concerned or upset and make their voice rise at the end of a question or when a character is feeling happy or enthusiastic.

Reread aloud "Paint Your Dog!" from *What a Thrill!* and have children echo-read. Show children how to use their voice to show enthusiasm as they read the story.

LESSON 17

30+ Minutes

DAY AT A GLANCE
Day 4

PHONEMIC AWARENESS
Phoneme Blending

PHONICS
Reteach Inflections *-ed, -ing*

PHONICS AND SPELLING
Reteach Syllable /əl/*-le*

HIGH-FREQUENCY WORDS
Reteach *buy, carry, money, other, paint, paper, would, always*

FLUENCY
Intonation

COMPREHENSION
Reteach Main Idea

GRAMMAR/WRITING
Reteach Friendly Letter

Materials Needed:

Practice Book
p.69

Practice Book

Lesson 17 High-Frequency Word Cards

What a Thrill! Student Edition pp. 46–52

Shooting Star Student Edition pp. 36–42

Spelling Words

1. hand	6. little
2. handle	7. turn
3. wig	8. girl
4. wiggle	9. by
5. single	10. room

Phonemic Awareness

Phoneme Blending   Tell children that together you are going to play a puzzle game. Tell them that you are going to say some words in pieces and they should listen to see if they can put the puzzle pieces together to figure out the word. Say: **/p/ /e/ /b/ /əl/. What word do the sounds /p/ /e/ /b/ /əl/ say? They say *pebble.*** Continue with the following words: **/s/ /a/ /d/ /əl/** (*saddle*); **/s/ /ō/ /p/** (*soap*); **/r/ /i/ /d/ /əl/** (*riddle*); **/b/ /ō/** (*bow*); **/m/ /ā/ /p/ /əl/** (*maple*); **/r/ /ō/** (*row*).

RETEACH

Phonics

Inflections *-ed, -ing*   Remind children that endings can be added to a base word to make new words. Write *chat.* Say: **The word *chatted* is made by doubling the final consonant and adding *-ed* to the base word.** Write *chatted.* Repeat this procedure to form *chatting.*

RETEACH

Phonics and Spelling

Practice Book
p.69

Syllable /əl/*-le*
Direct children's attention to page 69 of their *Practice Books.* Complete the page together.

Assess children's progress using the following sentences.

1.	hand	Raise your **hand** if you want to go.
2.	handle	Hold the pot by the **handle.**
3.	wig	The girl wore a red **wig** on her head.
4.	wiggle	We saw the fish **wiggle.**
5.	single	There isn't a **single** can on the shelf.
6.	little	My baby sister is very **little.**

Review

7.	turn	Please **turn** on the lights when you come in.
8.	girl	Is that **girl** your friend?

High-Frequency

9.	by	Please sit **by** your mom.
10.	room	Jill cleaned her messy **room.**

RETEACH

High-Frequency Words

Copying Masters
65–66

Display *High-Frequency Word Cards* for this lesson's words—*buy, carry, money, other, paint, paper, would,* and *always*—and the previously learned high-frequency words. Point to words at random and ask children to read them.

RETEACH

Comprehension

 Main Idea Ask children what a story's main idea is. (what the story is mostly about) Draw a three-column chart on the board like the one below. Review "Paint Your Dog!" in *What a Thrill!* and the main idea of the story. Fill in the chart. Then do a picture walk through "Ben" in *Shooting Star.* Guide children to determine the main idea and record their responses in the chart.

	"Paint Your Dog!"	"Ben"
Main Idea	If you paint your dog, you will always have your dog with you.	Ben joins a game and helps his team win.
Detail	Little dogs can be hard to find.	Ben has strong legs.

RETEACH

Grammar/Writing

Friendly Letter Review with children characteristics of a friendly letter.

Friendly Letter

The *heading* gives the date.
The *greeting* tells who gets the letter.
The *body* is the message.
The *closing* says good-bye.
The *signature* is the writer's name.

Lead children in looking at the letter you presented on Day 3. Review friendly letter characteristics using the Day 3 letter. Remind children that the body of a letter is the message. Share several sentences children might write to a friend, such as **My class is going on a field trip to the zoo,** or **We have a new student in our class.** Talk about the news each example gives. Have children share news that they might put in a letter to a friend. Work with children to arrange the news into a friendly letter. Read the letter with children and point out its characteristics.

High-Frequency Words

buy	paint
carry	paper
money	would
other	always

Fluency

Intonation Have children practice reading aloud "Paint Your Dog!" in *What a Thrill!* Remind children that good readers make sure that their voices rise and fall so their reading sounds like natural speech.

Have them reread the story several times to practice reading with appropriate intonation. Model reading with intonation as necessary and having children echo-read sentences. Give children feedback for improving their fluency.

30+ Minutes

HIGH-FREQUENCY WORDS
buy, carry, money, other, paint, paper, would

PHONEMIC AWARENESS
Onset and Rime

PHONICS AND SPELLING
Preteach Long Vowel /ō/*ow, oa*

BUILD ROBUST VOCABULARY
Preteach *bulged, jostled, argue*

GRAMMAR/WRITING
Preteach Troublesome Words: Homophones

Materials Needed:

Copying Masters 65–66

Lesson 17 High-Frequency Word Cards

Sound/ Spelling Card

Sound/ Spelling Card *Oo*

Word Builders and Word Builder Cards

Write-On/ Wipe-Off Boards

Practice Book 70

Practice Book

High-Frequency Words

buy	paint
carry	paper
money	would
other	

High-Frequency Words

Copying Masters 65–66 Display *High-Frequency Word Cards* for *buy, carry, money, other, paint, paper, would,* and the other previously learned high-frequency words. Say the word *buy,* ask a volunteer to point to *buy,* and have children read the word aloud. Continue with the remaining high-frequency words. Repeat this activity several times to reinforce instant recognition.

Phonemic Awareness

Onset and Rime Have children name the following words as you say them in parts. Model the first one. Say: **Listen as I say this word in parts: /thr/-ow—The word I said was** *throw.* **Now you try some: /r/-ow, /b/-oat, /l/-ow, /fl/-oat, /t/-oad.**

PRETEACH

Phonics and Spelling

Sound/Spelling Card **Long Vowel /ō/*ow, oa***
Connecting Letter to Sound Say the words *coat, crow,* and *show,* and have children repeat the words. Explain that all three words have the /ō/ sound, the long *o* sound. Have children say /ō/ several times. Display *Sound/Spelling Card Oo.* Say the letter name and identify the picture. Explain that two letters can work together to stand for one sound. In the word *coat,* the letters *o* and *a* stand for /ō/. In *crow* and *show,* the letters *o* and *w* stand for the long *o* sound.

Say: **When I say a word that begins with /ō/, form an** *o* **with your thumb and index finger. When I say a word that does not begin with /ō/, keep your hands on your desk.** Say these words: *oats, octopus, owe, otter, own.* Tell children that some words have the sound /ō/ in the middle. Say *float,* elongating the /ō/ sound. Tell children that *float* has the /ō/ sound in the middle. Then say the following words, elongating the medial sound and having children name that sound: *showing, coast, block, goat, lint, road.*

Word Blending Demonstrate each step with *Word Builder Cards* and a *Word Builder,* and have children repeat each step after you. Hold up *r* and say /r/. Hold up *o* and *a* together and say /ō/. Hold up *d* and say /d/.

- Place the letters *r, o, a, d* in the *Word Builder.*
- Point to *r.* Say /r/. Point to *o* and *a* together and say /ō/. Prompt children to repeat after you.

- Slide *oa* next to *r.* Run your hand under the letters as you blend the sounds, elongating them—/rō/.

- Point to *d* and say /d/.
- Slide *d* next to *roa*. Run your hand under *road* as you blend the sounds, elongating them—/rōd/.
- Read *road* naturally.

Follow the same procedure with these words: *load, soap, show,* and *tow.*

  Word Building   Place the *Word Builder Cards l, o,* and *w* in the *Word Builder* and have children do the same. Slide your hand under the letters as you slowly blend the sounds to read the word /llōō/. Then read the word naturally—*low.* Have children build and read new words. As they build each word, write it on the board. Say:

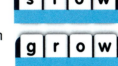

- **Add *s* before *l*. What word did you make?** (*slow*)
- **Change *sl* to *gr*. What word did you make?** (*grow*)

Continue with the words *road, soap,* and *boat.* Then have children read the words on the board. Direct children's attention to page 70 of their *Practice Books.* Complete the page together.

PRETEACH

Build Robust Vocabulary

Introduce Robust Vocabulary   Read the student-friendly explanation for each word. Then discuss each word using the following examples.

Say: **I put too much stuff in my bag, so it bulged. Has your backpack or pocket ever bulged? Why? What did you have in there?**

Say: **Sometimes I get jostled when I'm in a crowd because there's not enough room for everyone. If you were jostled, what would you do?**

Say: **I might argue with someone who said something that was not true. Tell about a time that you argued with someone.**

PRETEACH

Grammar/Writing

Troublesome Words: Homophones   Write these sentences on the board: *The wind blew the blue kite. They went to two stores.* Read them aloud and then with children. Ask children which words sound alike in the first sentence. Underline *blew* and *blue* and explain that these words are called homophones because they sound alike but have different spellings and meanings. Follow the same procedure with the second sentence.

Spelling Words

1. low	6. boat
2. slow	7. little
3. grow	8. handle
4. road	9. carry
5. soap	10. would

 Have children practice writing spelling words on their *Write-on/Wipe-off Boards.*

VOCABULARY

Student-Friendly Explanations

bulged If a container bulged, its sides stuck out like it is going to burst.

jostled When you jostle people, you bump them or poke them to make them move.

argue When you argue with someone, you disagree loudly.

LESSON 18

First Snow

DAY AT A GLANCE

Day 1

PHONEMIC AWARENESS
Phoneme Isolation

PHONICS AND SPELLING
Reteach Long Vowel /ō/ow, oa

COMPREHENSION
Preteach Author's Purpose/Point of View

HIGH-FREQUENCY WORDS
Reteach *time, put, feel, know*

FLUENCY
Reading Rate

GRAMMAR/WRITING
Reteach Troublesome Words: Homophones

Materials Needed:

Word Builders and Word Builder Cards

Write-On/ Wipe-Off Boards

Shooting Star Student Edition pp. 46–52

What a Thrill! Student Edition pp. 6–12 pp. 54–55

Photo Card

Photo Cards

Practice Book p. 71

Practice Book

Spelling Words

1. low	6. boat
2. slow	7. little
3. grow	8. handle
4. road	9. carry
5. soap	10. would

Have children practice writing spelling words on their *Write-on/Wipe-off Boards.*

Phonemic Awareness

Phoneme Isolation Say the word *boat* and have children repeat it. Have children listen for other words with the /ō/ sound. Say the words *goat* and *mop*. Say: **Which of these words has the /ō/ sound? *Goat* has this sound. Now you try some.** Continue with: *rose, lock, goat; goat, fox, rose; boat, rose, box.*

RETEACH

Phonics and Spelling

Long Vowel /ō/ow, oa
Word Building Place the *Word Builder Cards l, o,* and *w* in the *Word Builder.* Ask children to say the name and sound of each letter. Then read the word naturally—*low.* Have children do the same. Ask:

- **Which letter should I add to make *low* become *slow*?** (Add *s* before *l.*)

- **Which letters should I change to make *slow* become *grow*?** (Change *sl* to *gr.*)

Continue with the words *road, soap,* and *boat.*

Read Words in Context Write the following sentences on chart paper. Have children read each sentence silently. Then track the print as children read the sentences aloud. Finally, point to the underlined words at random and have children read them. *Low plants grow next to the road. Meg can carry the little pot by its handle. Would Nick lend me a bar of soap? The old boat is very slow.*

PRETEACH

Comprehension

Author's Purpose/Point of View Tell children that authors write for a reason, or purpose. They may want to entertain or teach. Read aloud "Some Animals" in *Shooting Star.* Say: **In this story the author tells about animals and where they are from. I can learn where penguins live and what they eat. The author's purpose here is to teach.** Then read pages 48–49. Guide children to use the illustrations and the text to determine that the author's purpose is to teach.

High-Frequency Words

pp. 54–55

Write the words *time, put, feel,* and *know* on the board.

- Point to and read *time.* Repeat, having children say *time* with you.
- Say: **It is *time* to go home.**
- Repeat the word *time* and then point to each letter as you spell it. Then have children say and spell *time* with you. Have children reread the word.

Repeat for the remaining words. Use the following sentences: *Please* put *your things away. I* feel *cold when I am in the snow. Do you* know *my mom?*

Have children turn to page 54 of *What a Thrill!* and have them read aloud the words at the top of the page. Talk about the illustrations. Then guide children in choosing and writing the word that names each picture. (4. *coat,* 5. *bowl,* 6. *snow*) Have children read aloud each word in the list on page 55. Ask volunteers to read the sentences aloud. Then have children choral-read the sentences. Guide them to choose and circle the word that completes each sentence. (1. *put,* 2. *time,* 3. *feel,* 4. *know*)

Grammar/Writing

 Photo Card

 Practice Book p.71

Troublesome Words: Homophones   Show *Photo Card road.* Ask children to identify the photo, and then write the word *road* on the board. Say: **The car drove on the *road*.** Then say: **I *rode* my bike.** Write *rode* on the board. Remind children that *road* and *rode* are homophones because they are two words that sound the same but are spelled differently and have different meanings. Then write the following sentences on the board without the underlining. Read them with children, and have volunteers find the homophones.

> We read a <u>tale</u> about a dog with a short <u>tail</u>.
>
> Joan <u>sent</u> a one <u>cent</u> stamp to her pal.
>
> Mick <u>read</u> a book about a <u>red</u> bird.

Underline the homophones children identify. Reread the words with children, and discuss the meaning of each one. Complete *Practice Book* page 71 together.

High-Frequency Words

time	feel
put	know

Fluency

Reading Rate Have children turn to "How Many?" in *What a Thrill!* and track the print as you read aloud at a consistent rate. Remind children that their goal is to read as naturally as they talk, without stopping to correct mistakes or to sound out words.

LESSON 18

DAY AT A GLANCE

Day 2

PHONEMIC AWARENESS
Phoneme Blending

PHONICS AND SPELLING
Reteach Long Vowel /ō/ *ow, oa*

HIGH-FREQUENCY WORDS
Reteach *mouse, our, over, pretty, surprise, three, time, put, feel, know*

FLUENCY
Reading Rate

READING
"First Snow"

BUILD ROBUST VOCABULARY
Preteach *command, labored, wary*

GRAMMAR/WRITING
Reteach Troublesome Words: Homophones

Materials Needed:

Practice Book
p.72

Copying Masters
69–70

Word Builders and Word Builder Cards

Practice Book

Lesson 18 High-Frequency Word Cards

What a Thrill! Student Edition pp. 36–42 pp. 56–63

Photo Cards

High-Frequency Words

mouse	three
our	time
over	put
pretty	feel
surprise	know

30+ Minutes

Phonemic Awareness

Phoneme Blending   Tell children that they are going to be detectives and find the word you are thinking about. Say: **I'm thinking of a word that is someone who leads a team. The word is /k/ō/ch/. The word is *coach*.** Continue with: /m/ō/n/ (*moan*), /th/r/ō/ (*throw*), and /b/l/ō/ (*blow*).

RETEACH

Phonics and Spelling

 Long Vowel /ō/ *ow, oa*

Word Building   Use a *Word Builder* and *Word Builder Cards* and have children repeat each step after you. Build the word *lot*. Then say the word naturally—*lot*. Lead children in building and reading new words. Say:

- **Change *t* to *w*. Read the word.** (*low*)
- **Add *s* before *l*. Read the word.** (*slow*)
- **Change *l* to *h*. Read the word.** (*show*)
- **Change *w* to *t*. Read the word.** (*shot*)

Continue with the following words: *got, goat, coat, cot*.

Practice Book p.72 **Read Words in Context**   Ask children to turn to *Practice Book* page 72. Read each sentence aloud and have children echo-read. Then ask volunteers to read each sentence aloud. Ask: **What are Dot and Greg in?** (a boat) **Where is the boat?** (in a pond) **What does Greg tell Dot?** (to row the boat) Call on volunteers to frame and read the long *o* words. Guide children to underline words that have the long *o* sound and circle words with the short *o* sound.

 l o t

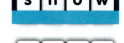 l o w

 s l o w

s h o w

s h o t

RETEACH

High-Frequency Words

Copying Masters 69–70 Display the *High-Frequency Word Cards* for *mouse, our, over, pretty, surprise, three, time, put, feel,* and *know*. Point to each card and read the word. Have children repeat. Give each child a set of word cards and have children spread the cards out in front of them. Randomly call out one of the words, and have children hold up the matching card. Assess how well children are able to identify the words and repeat until they can respond quickly and accurately.

Reading

 pp. 56–63

Build Background: "First Snow"

Read the title with children. Ask them if they have ever seen snow. If so, ask them to tell how snow feels and how they dress when they go out in the snow. Tell children that they will be reading about snow.

Monitor Comprehension: "First Snow"

Have children turn to the first page of the story. Ask a volunteer to reread the title. Invite children to look at the picture on page 56. Ask them to think about what the selection will be about and what the characters will be doing. Then guide children through the selection as they read.

 pp. 56–57

Say: **An older person is talking to a younger person. They look like they could be a father and a child. Let's read to find out what they are saying.**

After reading the pages, ask: **What are the people talking about?** (The snow) **Who are the people?** (Meg and her dad) Note Details/ Characters

Ask: **Who do you think the boy is on page 57?** (Meg's brother) Draw Conclusions

Ask: **Which word on pages 56 and 57 has the long *o* sound?** (*snow*) Apply Phonics

 pp. 58–59

Say: **A woman is with the two children. They are putting on coats and mittens. Let's read to find out what they are going to do.**

After reading the pages, ask: **Who is the woman?** (the children's mom*)* **Why is she telling the children to put on a coat and a scarf?** (Possible response: Because it is cold outside) Characters/Cause and Effect

Ask: **How do you think the children are feeling? Explain.** (Possible response: Excited because they are playing in the snow for the first time) Characters' Emotions/Make Inferences

Ask: **Which words on these pages have the long *o* sound?** (*coat, snow*) Apply Phonics

Fluency

Reading Rate Have children open to page 40 of "Please Get In!" in *What a Thrill!* and invite children to name the punctuation marks they see on that page. Remind children that they should pause briefly at commas, and pause a slight bit longer when there is end punctuation.

Remind children that they should read like they would talk, at an appropriate rate, so they can be understood. Have each child select a page from the story and practice reading it aloud until they are reading at an appropriate rate.

Say: **The children are still outside in the snow. Let's read to find out what they are going to do next.**

After reading the pages, ask: **What are Tim and Meg doing?** (making snowballs and watching the snow float) **What did they make?** (a snowman) NOTE DETAILS

Ask: **How do Tim and Meg feel about the snow?** (They like it.) CHARACTERS' EMOTIONS

Ask: **Which long *o* word tells how the snow is moving?** (*float*) APPLY PHONICS

 Say: **The family is inside now. Let's read to find out what they are doing.**

After reading the pages, ask: **What do you think the children are eating?** (Possible response: hot soup) **Why do you think they are eating that?** (Possible response: They are cold from being in the snow.) CONTEXT CLUES/DRAW CONCLUSIONS

Ask: **What do the children know about snow now?** (that it is cold) NOTE DETAILS

Ask: **Why do you think the author wrote this story? Explain.** (Possible response: to inform because it tells facts about snow) AUTHOR'S PURPOSE/POINT OF VIEW

Answers to *Think Critically* Questions

Help children read and answer the *Think Critically* questions on page 63. Answers are shown below.

1. ‹winter› SETTING

2. ‹cold› COMPARE AND CONTRAST

 3. ‹likes snow› AUTHOR'S PURPOSE/POINT OF VIEW

PRETEACH

Build Robust Vocabulary

 Introduce Robust Vocabulary Read the student-friendly explanation for each word. Then discuss each word using the following examples.

Say: **An example of a command is when I say "Write your name on your paper." Tell what you might say when you command someone to do something.**

Say: **I labored all day to clean up my backyard. Tell about a time that you labored and explain what you did.**

Say: **I am wary of spiders because I am afraid they will bite me.** Show *Photo Cards ant* and *arm*. Ask: **Which would you be more wary of? Why?**

RETEACH

Grammar/Writing

Troublesome Words: Homophones Explain that homophones are words that sound alike but have different spellings and meanings. Write on the board some homophone pairs such as *by/buy, to/two, tale/tail,* and *red/read*. Review the meaning of each word and invite children to dictate sentences that include these words. Write their sentences using the incorrect homophone. Reread the first sentence to children, tracking the print. Model how to use context clues to identify and replace the incorrect homophone. Follow a similar procedure for the remaining sentences.

VOCABULARY

Student-Friendly Explanations

command When you command someone, you tell him or her what to do.

labored If you labored, you worked very hard.

wary When you are cautious and unsure about something that might be dangerous, you are wary.

Day 3

30+ Minutes

PHONEMIC AWARENESS
Phoneme Segmentation

PHONICS
Preteach Phonograms *-ow, -oat*

PHONICS AND SPELLING
Reteach Long Vowel /ō/*ow, oa*

HIGH-FREQUENCY WORDS
Reteach *time, put, feel, know*

FLUENCY
Reading Rate

COMPREHENSION
Reteach Author's Purpose/Point of View

GRAMMAR/WRITING
Reteach Thank-You Letter

Materials Needed:

Write-On/
Wipe-Off
Boards with
Phonemic
Awareness
Disks

Word Builders
and Word
Builder Cards

Copying
Masters
71–72

Lesson 18
Story Strips

What a Thrill!
Student Edition
pp. 46–52
pp. 56–62

Spelling Words

1. low	6. boat
2. slow	7. little
3. grow	8. handle
4. road	9. carry
5. soap	10. would

Phonemic Awareness

Phoneme Segmentation Have children use the three boxes on the *Write-on/Wipe-off Boards.* Tell children that the boxes stand for the sounds in words. Have children repeat each step with their *Write-on/Wipe-off Boards.* Say: *Goat.* **The first sound I hear in *goat* is /g/.** Model placing a disk in the first box. Use this procedure for the second sound in *goat* (/ō/), placing a disk in the second box, and the last sound in *goat* (/t/) placing a disk in the third box. Point to each box in sequence as children say the word. Ask: **How many sounds do you hear in *goat*? I hear three.** Repeat this procedure with: *cup, fan, boat, fish.*

PRETEACH

Phonics

Phonograms *-ow, -oat* Say the words *show* and *low.* Ask children how the words are the same. (They both end with /ō/. They rhyme.) Using the words *bow, boat, tow, day, crow,* and *know,* have children show "thumbs up" when they hear a word that rhymes with *show.* Then say the words *goat* and *boat.* Ask how these words are the same. (They both end with /ō/. They rhyme.) Have children show "thumbs up" when they hear a word that rhymes with *goat.* Say *float, moat,* and *mut.*

RETEACH

Phonics and Spelling

 Long Vowel /ō/*ow, oa*
Build Words Use *Word Builders* and *Word Builder Cards* to form words. Have children listen to your directions and change a letter in each word to spell a spelling word. Form *lot* and have children read the word. Ask: **Which spelling word can you make by changing the last letter?** (*low*)

Follow a similar procedure with the following words: *slot* (*slow*), *row* (*grow*), *toad* (*road*), *sap* (*soap*).

Remind children that there are some other words they have to remember how to spell. Have children say *carry.* Tell them to put *Word Builder Cards c, a, r, r, y* in their *Word Builders,* picture the word *carry* in their minds, and build the word. Write the word on the board. Follow the same procedure with *would.*

RETEACH

High-Frequency Words

Copying Masters 71–72 Duplicate and distribute *Copying Masters* 71–72 to each child. Explain that the sentences tell the story "First Snow" in *What a Thrill!* but some have missing words.

List the words *time, put, feel,* and *know* on the board. Have children read aloud each story strip sentence and name the correct word on the board that makes sense in the sentence. Have children write the missing words in the blanks and read the completed sentences aloud. Help children cut apart the strips, read the completed sentences, and arrange them in story order.

RETEACH

Comprehension

 Author's Purpose/Point of View Tell children that authors write for a reason, or purpose—(to inform, to entertain, to teach a lesson.) Have children turn to "Paint Your Dog!" in *What a Thrill!* Guide children to find the author's purpose. Confirm that the author's purpose is to inform. Lead children in a discussion of how the selection might be different if the author's purpose was to entertain or to teach a lesson. Then point out that the story is told from the author's point of view. Discuss how the selection might be different if it was written with a different point of view.

RETEACH

Grammar/Writing

Thank-You Letter Tell children that they have learned how to write a friendly letter. Explain that a thank-you letter is a special kind of friendly letter and has the same parts. Write the following model on chart paper.

November 27, 20--

Dear Jill,

Thank you for the game you gave me. It is the perfect gift. I will play it with my brother. It looks like a fun game. It was nice of you to think of me.

Your friend,
Glenn

Read the letter to children, and talk about its parts. Guide children to understand that a thank-you letter is written to thank someone, that the heading is the date, the greeting tells who gets the letter, the body is the message, the closing says good-bye, and the signature is your name.

High-Frequency Words

time	feel
put	know

Fluency

Reading Rate Remind children that when good readers read, it sounds like talking. They do not speak too fast or too slowly. They speak at a rate that can be understood by the listener.

Have children turn to "First Snow" in *What a Thrill!* Have partners reread the story aloud three or four times. Remind them to use the punctuation to signal them when to pause. Encourage them to increase their reading rate with each reading. Remind them that their reading should be understandable. Listen to partners read, giving them feedback about their reading rate.

LESSON 18

DAY AT A GLANCE

Day 4

PHONEMIC AWARENESS
Phoneme Blending

PHONICS
Reteach Phonograms -own, -oast

PHONICS AND SPELLING
Reteach Long Vowel /ō/ow, oa

HIGH-FREQUENCY WORDS
Reteach *mouse, our, over, pretty, surprise, three, time, put, feel, know*

FLUENCY
Reading Rate

COMPREHENSION
Reteach Author's Purpose/
Point of View

GRAMMAR/WRITING
Reteach Thank-You Letter

Materials Needed:

Practice
Book

Lesson 18
High-Frequency
Word Cards

What a Thrill!
Student Edition
pp. 26–32
pp. 56–62

Spelling Words

1. low	6. boat
2. slow	7. little
3. grow	8. handle
4. road	9. carry
5. soap	10. would

30+ Minutes

Phonemic Awareness

Phoneme Blending   Tell children that together you are going to play a puzzle game. Tell them that you are going to say some words in pieces and they should listen to see if they can put the puzzle pieces together to figure out the word. Say: /k/-/l/-/ō/-/k/. **What word does /k/ /l/ /ō/ /k/ say? It says cloak.** Continue with the following words: /g/ /l// ō/ /t/ (*gloat*), /f/ /l/ /ō/ (*flow*), /t/ /ō/ /d/ (*toad*), /l/ /ē/ /f/ (*leaf*).

RETEACH

Phonics

Phonograms -own, -oast   Tell children that words that rhyme often have the same ending letters. Write *flown* on the board. Say: **A word that rhymes with flown and ends with the same letters is shown.** Write *shown*.

Write *roast*. Say: **A word that rhymes with roast and ends with the same letters is boast.** Write *boast*. Draw a two-column chart with the heads -own and -oast. Have children suggest words that end with either -own or -oast and say what letter or letters are needed to start the words. Have children read each word as it is added to the chart.

RETEACH

Phonics and Spelling

Practice
Book
p.73

Long Vowel /ō/ow, oa
Direct children's attention to page 73 of their *Practice Books*. Complete the page together.

Assess children's progress using the following sentences.

1.	low	The dog easily jumped over the **low** fence.
2.	slow	To win the race, Jill could not be **slow**.
3.	grow	We **grow** vegetables on our farm.
4.	road	The turtle slowly crossed the **road**.
5.	soap	Use **soap** and water to wash your hands.
6.	boat	My family sailed around the lake in a **boat**.

Review

7.	little	A newborn baby is very **little**.
8.	handle	Always hold a hot pot by its **handle**.

High-Frequency

9.	carry	Janet will **carry** her book in her backpack.
10.	would	What **would** you like to eat for lunch?

High-Frequency Words

mouse	three
our	time
over	put
pretty	feel
surprise	know

RETEACH

High-Frequency Words

Copying Masters 69–70

Display *High-Frequency Word Cards* for this lesson's words—*mouse, our, over, pretty, surprise, three, time, put, feel,* and *know*—and the previously learned high-frequency words. Point to words at random and ask children to read them.

RETEACH

Comprehension

Author's Purpose/Point of View   Ask children to explain why authors write stories and articles. (to entertain, to inform, to teach a lesson) Remind them that authors may tell the story themselves or have a character do it. Draw a two-column chart labeled "Tom's Books" and "First Snow." Draw rows for "Author's Purpose" and "Point of View." Reread "Tom's Books" in *What a Thrill!* as children follow along. Guide children to tell why the author wrote the story and identify who is telling the story. Then reread "First Snow" in *What a Thrill!* Have children tell the author's purpose and the story's point of view. (Purpose: to entertain; Point of view: the author) Write their responses in the chart.

	Tom's Books	First Snow
Author's Purpose	to entertain	
Point of View	the author	

RETEACH

Grammar/Writing

Thank-You Letter   Review with children characteristics of a thank-you letter.

Thank-You Letter

It is written to thank someone.
The *heading* is the date.
The *greeting* tells who gets the letter.
The *body* is the message. It tells why you are thankful.
The *closing* says good-bye.
The *signature* is your name.

Display the letter created on Day 3 and read it to children. Point out and discuss its characteristics. Invite children to draw a picture of a person giving them a gift or helping them. Ask partners to share their pictures and tell what they would like to say to thank the person. Then guide them to write a thank-you letter to the person.

Fluency

Reading Rate   Have children work with partners. Ask them to take turns reading pages from "First Snow" in *What a Thrill!* Remind them to read at an appropriate rate so that the listener is able to understand what is being read. Listen as children read, providing feedback and support. Have children practice rereading the story for fluency.

DAY AT A GLANCE

Day 5

30+ Minutes

HIGH-FREQUENCY WORDS
mouse, our, over, pretty, surprise, three

PHONEMIC AWARENESS
Onset and Rime

PHONICS AND SPELLING
Preteach Long Vowel /ē/*e, ee, ea*

BUILD ROBUST VOCABULARY
Preteach *rapidly, devious, courteous*

GRAMMAR/WRITING
Preteach Describing Words: Color, Size, and Shape

Materials Needed:

Copying Masters 69–70

Lesson 18 High-Frequency Word Cards

Sound/ Spelling Card *Ee*

Word Builders and Word Builder Cards

Write-On/ Wipe-Off Boards

Practice Book p.74

Practice Book

Photo Card

Photo Cards

High-Frequency Words

mouse	pretty
our	surprise
over	three

High-Frequency Words

Copying Masters 69–70

Display *High-Frequency Word Cards* for *mouse, our, over, pretty, surprise, three,* and the other previously learned high-frequency words. Say the word *mouse,* ask a volunteer to point to *mouse,* and have children read the word aloud. Continue with the remaining high-frequency words. Repeat this activity several times to reinforce instant recognition.

Phonemic Awareness

Onset and Rime   Tell children you are going to say some words in parts. They can listen and then say the word. Say: **Listen as I say this word in parts. /s/-eat—The word I said was *seat*. Now you try some: /m/-ean, /sp/-eed, /t/-eam, /s/-ee, /w/-e, /tr/-eat, /b/-ean**

PRETEACH

Phonics and Spelling

Sound/ Spelling Card

Long Vowel /ē/*e, ee, ea*
Connecting Letter to Sound   Say the words *eat, eel,* and *east* and have children repeat the words. Explain that all three words begin with the /ē/ sound. Have children say /ē/ several times. Display *Sound Spelling Card Ee,* say the letter name and point to *ea, ee, e.* Tell children that the letters *ea, ee,* and *e* can stand for /ē/, the sound at the beginning of *eat.* Tell children that this is the "long e sound." Have children say /ē/ several times as you point to the letters.

Say: **When I say a word that begins with /ē/, raise your hand and say /ē/. When I say a word that does not begin with /ē/, put your hand behind your back.** Say these words: *each, eel, igloo, eagle, ant, equal,* and *east.* Tell children that some words, like *clean,* have the sound /ē/ in the middle. Follow the same procedure with the words: *meat, queen, sit, beat, cake, seen, feel.*

Word Blending   Demonstrate each step with *Word Builder Cards* and a *Word Builder* and have children repeat each step after you. Hold up *m* and say /mm/. Hold up *e* and *a* together and say /ēē/. Hold up *l* and say /ll/.

- Place the letters *m, e, a, l* in the *Word Builder.*
- Point to *m.* Say /m/. Point to *ea* and say /ē/. Prompt children to repeat after you.
- Slide *ea* next to *m.* Run your hand under the letters as you blend the sounds, elongating them—/mē/.

- Point to *l* and say /l/.
- Slide *l* next to *mea*. Run your hand under *meal* as you blend the sounds, elongating them—/mēl/.
- Read *meal* naturally.

Follow the same procedure with these words: *keep, eat, be,* and *me.*

  Word Building Place the *Word Builder Cards m* and *e* in the *Word Builder* and have children do the same. Slide your hand under the letters as you slowly blend the sounds to read the word /mmēē/. Then read the word naturally—*me.* Have children build and read new words. As they build each word, write it on the board. Say:

- **Add an *e* on the end and change *m* to *s*. What word did you make?** (*see*)

- **Change *s* to *f* and add a *t* on the end. What word did you make?** (*feet*)

Continue with the words *seat, mean,* and *team.* Then have children read the words on the board. Direct children's attention to page 74 of their *Practice Books.* Complete the page together.

PRETEACH

Build Robust Vocabulary

Introduce Robust Vocabulary Read the student-friendly explanation for each word. Then discuss each word using the following examples.

Say: **I walk rapidly if I am going somewhere and I'm late. When do you walk or move rapidly?**

Say: **A devious person might try to trick you into doing something you don't want to do. Which do you consider to be devious—tricking someone to do your work or going to a party? Explain.**

Say: **I say please to be courteous. What are some other courteous words you might use?**

PRETEACH

Grammar/Writing

 Describing Words: Color, Size, and Shape Describe something in your classroom. For example, say: **What is red, white, and blue; is not too large; and is a rectangle?** After children guess *flag,* say: **The words *red, white,* and *blue* describe color. *Not too large* describes size. *Rectangle* describes shape.** Explain that we use describing words like these to give others a clear picture of what we are talking about. Show a variety of *Photo Cards.* Have children use describing words to tell about one for the others to guess.

Spelling Words

1. me	6. team
2. see	7. slow
3. feet	8. road
4. seat	9. our
5. mean	10. over

 Have children practice writing spelling words on their *Write-on/Wipe-off Boards*

VOCABULARY

Student-Friendly Explanations

rapidly If you are walking rapidly, you are walking very fast.

devious A devious person is not being truthful and might try to trick you.

courteous Someone who is courteous is very polite.

DAY AT A GLANCE
Day 1

PHONEMIC AWARENESS
Phoneme Isolation

PHONICS AND SPELLING
Reteach Long Vowel /ē/e, ee, ea

COMPREHENSION
Preteach Cause and Effect

HIGH-FREQUENCY WORDS
Reteach hurry, by, dear

FLUENCY
Phrasing

GRAMMAR/WRITING
Reteach Describing Words: Color, Size, and Shape

Materials Needed:

Photo Cards

Word Builders and Word Builder Cards

Write-On/Wipe-Off Boards

Practice Book p.75
Practice Book

What a Thrill! Student Edition pp. 26–32

Happy Landings Student Edition pp. 4–5

Spelling Words

1. me	6. team
2. see	7. slow
3. feet	8. road
4. seat	9. our
5. mean	10. over

Have children practice writing spelling words on their *Write-on/Wipe-off Boards*

Phonemic Awareness

 Phoneme Isolation Display *Photo Cards leaves* and *snow*. Have children say the picture names after you and listen for the /ē/ sound. Say: *Leaves, snow.* **Which picture name has the /ē/ sound?** *Leaves* **has the /ē/ sound. Now you try.** Repeat with the *Photo Cards road* and *queen*. Have children categorize the pictures into two groups with /ē/ and /ē/ names.

RETEACH

Phonics and Spelling

Long Vowel /ē/ e, ee, ea
Word Building Place the *Word Builder Cards m* and *e* in the *Word Builder*. Ask children to say each letter name and the sound it stands for. Then read the word naturally—*me.* Ask children which letters you should change to make *me* become *see.* (Change *m* to *s* and add another *e* at the end.) Have them replace the letters in their *Word Builders* and read the new word. Ask:

- **Which letters should I change to make *see* become *feet*?** (Change *s* to *f* and add *t* to the end.)

- **Which letters should I change to make *feet* become *seat*?** (Change *f* to *s* and change *ee* to *ea*.)

Continue with the words *mean* and *team*.

Read Words in Context Write the following sentences on chart paper. Have children read each sentence silently. Then track the print as children read the sentences aloud. Finally, point to the underlined words at random and have children read them. *Bill is on my team. Dad will see me play. Did you put your feet on the seat? Did you mean to do that? A slow truck was on the road. Our family came over to the park.*

PRETEACH

Comprehension

  Cause and Effect Tell children that things that happen in a story, happen for a reason. What happens is called the effect. What makes it happen is called the cause. Give examples: **I put on a coat, because it's cold outside. Putting on a coat is the effect and the cold weather is the cause or why I did it. Another example is: I slipped and fell, because I walked on the ice.** Guide children to give examples using the following sentence frames: *I _____ because _____.*

High-Frequency Words

**pp.
4–5**

Write the words *hurry, by,* and *dear* on the board.

- Point to and read *hurry*. Repeat, having children say *hurry* with you.

- Say: Hurry *or we will be late for the bus.*

- Repeat the word and point to each letter as you spell it. Then have children say and spell *hurry* with you. Have children reread the word.

Repeat for *by* and *dear*. Use the following sentences: *Put the plant* by *the window. My* dear *friend is Pete.*

Have children turn to page 4 of *Happy Landings* and have them read aloud the words at the top of the page. Talk about the illustrations. Then guide children in choosing and writing the word that names each picture. (4. *me,* 5. *sleep,* 6. *leap*) Have children read aloud each word in the list on page 5. Ask volunteers to read the sentences aloud. Then have children choral-read the sentences. Guide them to read and circle the word that completes each sentence. (1. *by,* 2. *dear,* 3. *hurry*)

Grammar/Writing

**Practice Book
p.75**

Describing Words: Color, Size, and Shape   Review that using words that tell the color, size, and shape of things helps others know what you are describing.

- Write the sentences: *I have a red apple. It is round. My apple has a small stem on top.*

- Read aloud the sentences while you track the print. Have children echo-read.

- Ask children to name color, size, and shape words you used to describe the apple.

- Invite children to describe their favorite foods.

Complete *Practice Book* page 75 together.

High-Frequency Words

hurry	dear
by	

Fluency

Phrasing Remind children that a phrase is a group of two or more words that can be read together in a sentence. Reading in phrases rather than one word at a time will help them become better readers.

Have children turn to "Tom's Books" in *What a Thrill!* Model reading the sentences on a few pages, emphasizing phrasing. Reread the sentences one word at a time. Ask children which way sounds better. Then read again with correct phrasing while children echo-read.

PHONEMIC AWARENESS
Phoneme Blending

PHONICS AND SPELLING
Reteach Long Vowel /ē/e, ee, ea

HIGH-FREQUENCY WORDS
Reteach *hurry, mother, should, sky, told, door, dear, by*

FLUENCY
Phrasing

READING
"Frog and Rabbit"

BUILD ROBUST VOCABULARY
Preteach *gullible, hastily, unreasonable*

GRAMMAR/WRITING
Reteach Describing Words: Color, Size, and Shape

Materials Needed:

Word Builders and Word Builder Cards

Practice Book
p.76

Copying Masters 73–74
Lesson 19 High-Frequency Word Cards

What a Thrill! Student Edition pp. 46–52

Happy Landings Student Edition pp. 6–12

Photo Card
Photo Cards

High-Frequency Words

hurry	told
mother	door
should	dear
sky	by

30+ Minutes

Phonemic Awareness

Phoneme Blending   Tell children they are going to play a guessing game. Say: **Listen as I do the first one. I'm thinking of a word that names something you do every night. It is /s/ /l/ /ē/ /p/. The word is *sleep.*** Continue with clues for the words: /s/ /ē/ /l/ (*seal*), /m/ /ē/ /t/ (*meat*), /w/ /ē/ (*we*), /t/ /ē/ /m/ (*team*), /w/ /ē/ /k/ (*week*).

RETEACH

Phonics and Spelling

Long Vowel /ē/e, ee, ea
Word Building   Use a *Word Builder* and *Word Builder Cards* and have children repeat each step after you. Build the word *eat*. Blend the sounds to read the word—/ēt/. Then say the word naturally—*eat*. Have children do the same. Lead children in building and reading new words.

- **Change *ea* to *oa*. Read the word.** (*oat*)
- **Add *b* to *oat*. Read the word.** (*boat*)
- **Change *oa* to *ea*. Read the word.** (*beat*)

Continue with the following words: *be-bow-low-loaf-leaf.*

Read Words in Context   Ask children to turn to *Practice Book* page 76. Read each sentence aloud and have children echo-read. Ask volunteers to read each sentence aloud. Ask: **Where do Joan and Dean go?** (to the beach) **How long will they be there?** (a week) **What will they row?** (a little green boat) **How will Joan and Dean learn to swim and fish?** (Dad will teach them.) Guide children to circle all words with long vowel *e* and underline all words with long vowel *o*.

RETEACH

High-Frequency Words

Display the *High-Frequency Word Cards* for *hurry, mother, should, sky, told, door, dear,* and *by*. Point to each card and read the word. Play a guessing game. Say, for example: **I'm thinking of two words that rhyme. Who can find and read the words?** (*sky, by*) **Which word begins with the same sound as *muffin*?** (*mother*) Repeat with clues for all the words.

Reading

pp. 6–13

Build Background: "Frog and Rabbit"

Read the title with children. Have children tell what they know about each animal. Explain that they will read a story about a frog and rabbit that are in a race. Ask children if they were going to run in a race, what they would do to win.

Monitor Comprehension: "Frog and Rabbit"

Have children turn to the first page of the story. Ask a volunteer to reread the title. Guide children to look at the picture on page 6. Ask children to describe what they see. Encourage children to predict what the story will be about and which animal—the frog or the rabbit—will win. Then guide children through the story as they read.

pp. 6–7

Say: **I see Rabbit and Frog ready to start a race. Let's read to find out what Rabbit is saying to Frog.**

After reading the pages, ask: **What does Rabbit say he will do?** (He will beat Frog.) **Frame and read the word that tells.** (beat) **NOTE DETAILS/APPLY PHONICS**

Ask: **Who says, "Slow can win, too?"** (Frog) **CHARACTER**

Ask: **Is this story about real or imaginary animals? How do you know?** (Possible response: Imaginary; the animals are in a race, talking, and wearing clothes like people.) **REALITY/FANTASY**

pp. 8–9

Say: **Look at the pictures. I see Rabbit running ahead of Frog. Let's read on to find out what happens once the race begins.**

After reading the pages, ask: **What happens first once the race begins?** (Rabbit runs fast and passes Frog.) **SEQUENCE**

Ask: **What word tells how Frog moves? Frame and read the word.** (leaping) **NOTE DETAILS/APPLY PHONICS**

Ask: **Why do you think Frog keeps saying "Slow can win, too?"** (Possible response: Frog is trying hard and believes that he can win.) **DRAW CONCLUSIONS**

Fluency

Phrasing Remind children that good readers read words in phrases and not one word at a time. Have children turn to "Paint Your Dog" in *What a Thrill!*

Say: **I'm going to read the first page of "Paint Your Dog" one word at a time. Then I'll read it in phrases. Listen to the difference and tell me which sounds better.** Then have children take turns reading one page to a partner.

Say: **Look at the pictures on these pages. Something has changed during the race. Let's find out what it is.**

After reading the pages, ask: **What causes Rabbit to stop and sleep during the race?** (Possible response: He thinks Frog can't beat him, even if he does hurry. So Rabbit decides to rest.) **CAUSE AND EFFECT**

Say: **There are four long _e_ words on page 10 and one on page 11. Frame each word as we read them together.** (he, me, beat, sleep, he) **APPLY PHONICS**

Ask: **Do you think going to sleep is a good or a bad idea? Tell why.** (Possible response: I think it's a bad idea, because he might not wake up.) **PERSONAL RESPONSE**

Ask: **Who do you think will win the race? Tell why you think so.** (Possible response: I think Frog might win now because Rabbit is sleeping.) **MAKE PREDICTIONS**

page 12 Say: **Let's read the ending of the story to find out who wins the race.**

After reading the pages, ask: **How do you think Rabbit feels? Why does he feel this way?** (Possible response: I think he feels mad at himself because he took a nap and lost the race. He looks mad in the picture.) **How do you think Frog feels? How can you tell?** (I think Frog feels proud. He is smiling and showing his medal.) **CHARACTERS EMOTIONS/MAKE INFERENCES**

Do you think slow is best? Tell why or why not? (Possible response: Sometimes slow is best if you take your time to do something carefully.) **MAKE JUDGEMENTS**

Ask: **What lesson do you think Rabbit learned?** (Possible response: He should not brag and think he will be the best if he doesn't do his best.) **MAIN IDEA**

Ask: **Would you change the end of the story? Why or why not?** (Possible response: No, because I think Frog should win because he tried the hardest.) **PERSONAL RESPONSE**

Answers to *Think Critically* Questions

Help children read and answer the *Think Critically* questions on page 13. Answers are shown below.

1. *‹race›* LITERAL

2. *‹Frog›* PLOT

 3. *‹fell asleep›* CAUSE AND EFFECT

PRETEACH

Build Robust Vocabulary

Introduce Robust Vocabulary Read the student-friendly explanation for each word. Then discuss each word using the following examples.

Say: **When would you be gullible—if you believed you could have a birthday once a month or that your birthday is once a year?**

Say: **If I am late for school, I move hastily to get to class. Would you walk hastily if your friends were outside waiting for you? Why?**

Say: **I think it is unreasonable to try and flap your arms to fly. Which is unreasonable: to ask for help with your homework or to think your parents should do your homework for you?**

RETEACH

Grammar/Writing

Photo Card **Describing Words: Color, Size, and Shape** Display *Photo Card squirrel.* Write the following sentence on the board without describing words:

> This is a squirrel.

Read the sentence and have children echo-read as they look at the picture. Ask volunteers to dictate color, size, and shape words to tell more about the squirrel. As you write the new, expanded sentence, include errors for children to correct, such as capital letters and end marks. Guide children in correcting the sentence. Then read the expanded sentence aloud, for example: *This is a little brown squirrel.* Repeat with other *Photo Cards* that you select.

VOCABULARY

Student-Friendly Explanations

gullible If you believe everything you hear, even very silly things, you are gullible.

hastily If you do things hastily, you are doing them in a big hurry.

unreasonable If you are unreasonable, you would do things that don't make sense.

30+ Minutes

DAY AT A GLANCE

Day 3

PHONEMIC AWARENESS
Phoneme Segmentation

PHONICS
Preteach Contractions 've, 're

PHONICS AND SPELLING
Reteach Long Vowel /ē/e, ee, ea

HIGH-FREQUENCY WORDS
hurry, by, dear

FLUENCY
Phrasing

COMPREHENSION
Reteach Cause and Effect

GRAMMAR/WRITING
Reteach Description of a Thing

Materials Needed:

Write-On/
Wipe-Off
Boards with
Phonemic
Awareness
Disks

Word Builders
and Word
Builder Cards

Lesson 19
Story Strips

Copying Masters 75–76

Happy Landings
Student Edition
pp. 6–12

Spelling Words

1. me	6. team
2. see	7. slow
3. feet	8. road
4. seat	9. our
5. mean	10. over

Phonemic Awareness

Phoneme Segmentation   Have children use the three boxes on the *Write-on/Wipe-off Boards*. Remind children that the boxes stand for sounds in words. Have children repeat each step with their boards and disks. Say: *leaf.* **The first sound in *leaf* is /l/.** Model placing a disk in the first box. Use this procedure for the second sound in *leaf* (/ē/), placing a disk in the second box, and the last sound in *leaf* (/f/), placing a disk in the third box. Point to each box in sequence as children say the word: *leaf.* **How many sounds do you hear in *leaf*? I hear three.** Repeat with *heat, tree, eat, feel, need, each.*

PRETEACH

Phonics

Contractions 've, 're   Write on the board: *We've seen the cat. We're in our seats.* Track the print as you read the sentences. Point to *We've* and say: **We've is a shorter way to say *we have*.** Write *we have* and ask children to name the letters the apostrophe replaced. (*ha*) Repeat with *we're.* (*we are*) Continue with the sentences: *I've missed the bus. You've come too! They've run a race. You're the new girl. They're going to the park.*

RETEACH

Phonics and Spelling

Long Vowel /ē/e, ee, ea

Build Words   Use *Word Builders* and *Word Builder Cards* to form words. Have children listen to your directions and change letters in each word to spell a spelling word. Form *be* and have children read the word. Ask: **Which spelling word can you make by changing the first letter?** (*me*)

Form *bee* in the pocket chart and have children read it. Ask: **Which spelling word can you make by changing the first letter?** (*see*)

Follow a similar procedure with the following words: *fat* (*feet*), *seal* (*seat*), *man* (*mean*), *beam* (*team*), *read* (*road*), *slot* (*slow*).

Remind children that there are some words they have to remember how to spell. Have children say *our.* Tell them to put *Word Builder Cards o, u, r* in their *Word Builders,* picture the word *our* in their minds, and build the word. Write the word on the board. Follow the same procedure with the word *over.*

RETEACH

High-Frequency Words

Copying Masters 75–76

Duplicate and distribute *Copying Masters* 75–76 to each child. Explain that the sentences tell about the story "Frog and Rabbit" but some have missing words.

List the words *hurry, by,* and *dear* on the board. Have children read aloud each story strip sentence and name the correct word on the board that makes sense in the sentence. Have children write the missing words in the blanks and read the completed sentences aloud. Help children cut apart the strips, read the completed sentences, and arrange them in story order.

RETEACH

Comprehension

Cause and Effect   Remind children that what makes something happen in a story is called the cause. What happens is called the effect. Revisit "Frog and Rabbit" in *Happy Landings.* Guide children to find examples of cause and effect in the story. Say: **Rabbit said he was going to win the race. That is an effect. What was the cause of Rabbit saying this? Rabbit thought he could win the race because he knew he could run fast and he knew Frog was slow. Rabbit lost the race, though. What caused Rabbit to lose?** (Rabbit took a nap and Frog passed him by.)

RETEACH

Grammar/Writing

Description of a Thing   Remind children that they have talked about writing descriptions. They use words that tell the color, size, and shape of things. Write the following sentences about a spider. Read the sentences as children follow along. Ask children if they can picture what the girl saw.

> I saw a big spider this morning. It had a small, round head and a larger, round body. It was brown. It had eight long, black legs and two short pinchers.

- Guide children to understand that the sentences help you see something in your mind.
- Remind children that a description tells about how something looks— that the sentences have describing words for color, size, and shape.
- Explain to children that a description should also be interesting.
- Ask children to draw what they think this spider looks like from the description. Ask children to share their drawings.

High-Frequency Words

hurry	dear
by	

Fluency

Phrasing   Review how good readers read words in phrases and not one word at a time. This helps them understand what they read.

Reread a few pages of "Frog and Rabbit" in *Happy Landings*, one word at a time and again with correct phrasing while children follow along. Discuss which way sounds better and why.

Invite children to read with a partner, imitating your phrasing. Listen as children read and offer feedback.

PHONEMIC AWARENESS
Phoneme Blending

PHONICS
Reteach Contractions 've, 're

PHONICS AND SPELLING
Reteach Long Vowel /ē/e, ee, ea

HIGH-FREQUENCY WORDS
Reteach hurry, mother, should, sky, told, door, dear, by

FLUENCY
Phrasing

COMPREHENSION
Reteach Cause and Effect

GRAMMAR/WRITING
Reteach Description of a Thing

Materials Needed:

Photo Cards

Practice Book

Lesson 19 High-Frequency Word Cards

What a Thrill! Student Edition pp. 56–62

Happy Landings Student Edition pp. 6–12

Spelling Words

1. me	6. team
2. see	7. slow
3. feet	8. road
4. seat	9. our
5. mean	10. over

Phonemic Awareness

Photo Card

Phoneme Blending   Tell children that together you are going to play a puzzle game. Explain that you will say the picture names in pieces like a puzzle. They will listen to put the pieces together and say the picture name. Display *Photo Cards leaves, road, farm, queen, snow,* and *toad.* Say: **Listen as I do the first one. /l/ /ē/ /v/ /s/. What word does /l/ /ē/ /v/ /s/ say? The word is *leaves*. Now you try.** Continue with the following words: /r/ /ō/ /d/ (*road*), /f/ /är/ /m/ (*farm*), /kw/ /ē/ /n/ (*queen*), /s/ /n/ /ō/ (*snow*), /t/ /ō/ /d/ (*toad*).

RETEACH

Phonics and Spelling

Contractions 've, 're   Remind children that two words can be put together to make a shorter word. This is called a *contraction*. Write *you are* and *you're.* Say: **The contraction *you're* comes from the words *you are*. The *a* was left out and an apostrophe takes its place. The contraction *you're* is a shorter way to say *you are*.** Use the same procedure and guide children to make contractions from *they are* (*they're*), *we are* (*we're*), *I have* (*I've*), *you have* (*you've*), *they have* (*they've*), and *we have* (*we've*).

RETEACH

Phonics and Spelling

Practice Book p.77

Long Vowel /ē/e, ee, ea   Direct children's attention to page 77 of their *Practice Books*. Complete the page together.

Assess children's progress using the following sentences.

1.	me	Help **me**!
2.	see	Can you **see** my brother?
3.	feet	My **feet** are bigger than yours.
4.	seat	Sit in this **seat**.
5.	mean	I don't know what you **mean**.
6.	team	Our **team** is the Tigers.

Review

7.	slow	A snail is **slow**.
8.	road	Let's take this **road**.

High-Frequency

9.	our	Can you come to **our** school?
10.	over	The park is **over** there.

RETEACH

High-Frequency Words

Copying Masters 73–74

Display *High-Frequency Word Cards* for this lesson's words—*hurry, mother, should, sky, told, door, dear,* and *by*—and the previously learned high-frequency words. Point to words at random and ask children to read them.

RETEACH

Comprehension

Cause and Effect   Ask children to explain what cause and effect is. (The effect is what happened; the cause is why it happened.) Draw a three-column chart on the board like the one below. Have children turn to "First Snow" in *What a Thrill!* Read the story together and guide children to point out a cause and effect for the story. Repeat with "Frog and Rabbit" in *Happy Landings*. Guide children to find causes and effects. Record children's responses on the chart.

Title	Effect What happened?	Cause Why it happened?
"First Snow"	Meg and Tim find out how cold snow is.	Meg and Tim go out to play in the snow for the first time.
"Frog and Rabbit"		

RETEACH

Grammar/Writing

Photo Card

Description of a Thing   Review with children the characteristics of a description of a thing.

Description of a Thing

The sentences help you see the thing in your mind.
The sentences have describing words for color, size, and shape.
The description is interesting.

Display *Photo Card porcupine.* Discuss the way the porcupine looks. Have children dictate a description of the porcupine. Guide them to use describing words for color, size, and shape. Then read aloud the description and have children echo-read. Point out the characteristics you discussed earlier.

High-Frequency Words

hurry	told
mother	door
should	dear
sky	by

Fluency

Phrasing Remind children that reading in phrases instead of word-by-word helps both readers and listeners to understand the story. Reread "Frog and Rabbit" from *Happy Landings.* Model fluency and phrasing as children follow along. Have children track the print.

Then have each child select a page to read. Comment on children's ability to read with correct phrasing.

DAY AT A GLANCE
Day 5

HIGH-FREQUENCY WORDS
hurry, mother, should, sky, told, door, dear

PHONEMIC AWARENESS
Onset and Rime

PHONICS AND SPELLING
Preteach Long Vowel /ā/*ai, ay*

BUILD ROBUST VOCABULARY
Preteach *grumbling, chided, realized*

GRAMMAR/WRITING
Preteach Describing Words: Taste, Smell, Sound, and Feel

Materials Needed:

Lesson 19 High-Frequency Word Cards

Sound/Spelling Card *Aa*

Word Builders and Word Builder Cards

Write-On/ Wipe-Off Boards

Practice Book

Photo Cards

High-Frequency Words

hurry	told
mother	door
should	dear
sky	

High-Frequency Words

Copying Masters 73–74 Display *High-Frequency Word Cards* for *hurry, mother, should, sky, told, door, dear,* and the other previously learned high-frequency words. Say the word *hurry,* ask a volunteer to point to *hurry,* and have children read the word aloud. Continue with the remaining high-frequency words. Repeat this activity several times to reinforce instant recognition.

Phonemic Awareness

Onset and Rime Tell children you are going to say some words, but you will say them in parts. Have children listen to see if they can figure out the word. Say: **Listen as I say this word in parts: /s/-ay. The word I said was *say*. Now you try some: /p/-ail, /r/-oad, /d/-ay, /w/-ait, /f/-eet.**

PRETEACH

Phonics and Spelling

Sound/Spelling Card **Long Vowel /ā/*ai, ay***
Connecting Letter to Sound Say the words *aid, ail,* and *aim* and have children repeat the words. Explain that all three words begin with the /ā/ sound. Have children say /ā/ several times. Display *Sound Spelling Card Aa.* Say the letter name and identify the picture. Tell children that the letters *ai* and *ay* can stand for /ā/, the sound in the middle of *rain.* Tell children that this is the "long *a* sound." Point to the letter several times as children say /ā/.

Say: **When I say a word with /ā/ in the beginning, raise your hand and say /ā/. When I say a word that does not begin with /ā/, put your hand behind your back.** Say these words: *add, aim, ail, each, aid.* Tell children that some words, like *rain,* have the /ā/ sound in the middle. Follow the same procedure for the medial position with the words: *train, wait, coat, nail, snail, feet,* and for the final sound /ā/ with: *day, play, fly, clay, row, stay.*

  Word Blending Demonstrate each step with *Word Builder Cards* and a *Word Builder,* and have children repeat each step after you. Hold up *s* and say /s/. Hold up *ai* and say /ā/. Hold up *l* and say /l/.

- Place the letters *s, a, i, l* in the *Word Builder.*
- Point to *s.* Say /ss/. Point to *ai* and say /ā/. Prompt children to repeat after you.
- Slide *ai* next to *s.* Run your hand under the letters as you blend the sounds, elongating them—/sā/.

- Point to *l* and say /l/.
- Slide *l* next to *sai*. Run your hand under *sail* as you blend the sounds, elongating them—/sāl/.
- Read *sail* naturally.

Follow the same procedure with the words *pail* and *pain*. Then do the same for *Word Builder Cards s* and *ay* for *say*.

Word Building Place the *Word Builder Cards d, a,* and *y* in the *Word Builder* and have children do the same. Slide your hand under the letters as you slowly read the word—/dā/. Then read the word naturally—*day*. Have children build and read new words. As they build each word, write it on the board. Say:

- **Change *d* to *s*. What word did you make?** (*say*)
- **Change *s* to *pl*. What word did you make?** (*play*)

Continue with the words *plain, rain,* and *wait*. Then have children read the words on the board. Direct children's attention to page 78 of their *Practice Books*. Complete the page together.

PRETEACH

Build Robust Vocabulary

Introduce Robust Vocabulary Read the student-friendly explanation for each word. Then discuss each word using the following examples.

Say: **I start grumbling when it rains. When do you start grumbling?**

Say: **I chided my dad when he got lost on the way to the zoo. Would you be chided for misspelling a friend's name or for getting an *A* on a test?**

Say: **When I looked at my feet, I realized I had on two different socks. If you realized you left your homework on the bus, what would you do?**

PRETEACH

Grammar/Writing

Describing Words: Taste, Smell, Sound, and Feel Tell children that a describing word tells about something. Words that tell about color, size, and shape are describing words. Explain that they will learn some new describing words for taste, smell, sound, and feel.

Display *Photo Cards ice, rose, berries,* and *rain*. Identify the pictures with children. Say: **I love sweet berries. *Sweet* is a describing word that tells how something tastes. Name something else that is sweet.** Repeat using the sentences: *The ice is cold. The rose smells good. The rain is loud.*

Spelling Words

1.	day	6.	wait
2.	say	7.	feet
3.	play	8.	me
4.	plain	9.	door
5.	rain	10.	told

 Have children practice writing spelling words on their *Write-on/Wipe-off Boards*.

VOCABULARY

Student-Friendly Explanations

grumbling If you are grumbling, you are complaining or letting others know you are unhappy about something.

chided If I chided you, I corrected you.

realized If you realized something, you suddenly understood or knew it.

30+ Minutes

LESSON 20

PHONEMIC AWARENESS
Phoneme Isolation

PHONICS AND SPELLING
Reteach Long Vowel /ā/*ai, ay*

COMPREHENSION
Reteach Cause and Effect

HIGH-FREQUENCY WORDS
Reteach *place, dry, warm, cool*

FLUENCY
Phrasing

GRAMMAR/WRITING
Reteach Describing Words: Taste, Smell, Sound, and Feel

Materials Needed:

Photo
Cards

Word Builders
and Word
Builder Cards

Write-On/
Wipe-Off
Boards

Happy Landings
Student Edition
pp. 14–15

What a Thrill!
Student Edition
pp. 56–62

Practice Book
p.79
Practice
Book

Spelling Words

1.	day	6.	wait
2.	say	7.	feet
3.	play	8.	me
4.	plain	9.	door
5.	rain	10.	told

Have children practice writing spelling words on their *Write-on/Wipe-off Boards.*

Phonemic Awareness

Photo
Card

Phoneme Isolation Display *Photo Cards stage* and *leaves.* Have children say the picture names after you and listen for the /ā/ sound. Say: *Stage, leaves.* **Which picture name has the /ā/ sound?** *Stage* has the /ā/ sound. **Now you try.** Repeat with *Photo Cards rain* and *snow; queen* and *cake; crayon* and *head.*

RETEACH

Phonics and Spelling

Long Vowel /ā/*ai, ay*

Word Building Place the *Word Builder Cards d, a,* and *y* in the *Word Builder.* Ask children what sound the letters *ay* stand for. (long *a,* /ā/) Slide your hand under the letters as you blend the sounds—/dāāā/. Then read the word naturally—*day.* Have children repeat the process. Continue building new words. Ask:

- **Which letter should I change to turn *day* into *say*?** (Change *d* to *s.*)
- **Which letter should I change to turn *say* into *play*?** (Change *s* to *pl.*)

Continue with the words *plain, rain,* and *wait.*

Read Words in Context Write the following sentences on chart paper. Have children read each sentence silently, then aloud as you track the print. Finally, point to the underlined words at random and have children read them. *If we wait to go, the rain will stop. Let's play here all day. What did Sam say? He told me to use that door. I like plain socks on my feet.*

RETEACH

Comprehension

Cause and Effect Explain to children that the things that happen in a story, happen for a reason. What happens is called the effect. What makes something happen is the cause. Give examples: **I sat down to have a cup of cocoa because I felt tired and chilly. I went to the store after work because I needed milk and bread.** Ask children to give examples of something they did today and the reason why they did it. Prompt them by asking: **What happened? Why did it happen?**

RETEACH

High-Frequency Words

pp. 14–15

Write the words *place, dry, warm,* and *cool* on the board.

- Point to and read *place*. Repeat, having children say *place* with you.

- Say: **I live in a *place* that gets very hot.**

- Repeat the word *place* and point to each letter as you spell it. Then have children say and spell *place* with you. Have children reread the word.

Repeat for *dry, warm,* and *cool*. Use the following sentences: *The desert is very* dry. *It feels* warm *outside today. Can you feel the* cool *breeze?*

Have children turn to page 14 in *Happy Landings* and have them read aloud the words at the top of the page. Talk about the illustrations. Then guide children in choosing and writing the word that names each picture. (4. *play,* 5. *rain,* 6. *train*) Have children read aloud each word in the list on page 15. Ask volunteers to read the sentences aloud. Then have children choral-read the sentences. Guide them to read and circle the word that completes each sentence. (1. *place,* 2. *warm,* 3. *cool,* 4. *dry*)

RETEACH

Grammar/Writing

Practice Book
p.79

Describing Words: Taste, Smell, Sound, and Feel   Read the following poem aloud as children listen:

> I like hot summer days, salty pretzels;
> quiet mornings, petting my soft cat;
> the smell of fresh baked bread, and nice things like that.
> I don't like sour lemon drops, loud scary noises;
> cold feet, bitter turnip greens, and stinky shoes.
> I can do without these things, what about you?

Read the poem again, line-by-line and have children repeat after you while listening for words that describe what you taste, feel, smell, or hear. (*salty, sour, bitter; hot, soft, cold; fresh-baked, stinky; quiet, loud*) Record the words on the board in groups and read them aloud. Invite children to name things they like or dislike using these or other describing words. Complete *Practice Book* page 79 together.

High-Frequency Words

place	warm
dry	cool

Fluency

Phrasing   Remind children that a phrase is a group of two or more words that can be read together in a sentence. Have children turn to "First Snow" in *What a Thrill!* Model reading aloud a few pages of "First Snow" one word at a time. Reread the same sentences using appropriate phrasing. Ask children which way sounds better. Then read the entire story again with appropriate phrasing while children echo-read.

LESSON 20

DAY AT A GLANCE
Day 2

PHONEMIC AWARENESS
Phoneme Blending

PHONICS AND SPELLING
Reteach Long Vowel /ā/*ai, ay*

HIGH-FREQUENCY WORDS
Reteach *cool, dry, four, holes, move, place, warm*

FLUENCY
Phrasing

READING
"In Each Place"

BUILD ROBUST VOCABULARY
Preteach *bitterly, dwelling, amusement*

GRAMMAR/WRITING
Reteach Describing Words: Taste, Smell, Sound, and Feel

Materials Needed:

Word Builders and Word Builder Cards

Practice Book p.80
Practice Book

Copying Masters 77–78
Lesson 20 High-Frequency Word Cards

Happy Landings Student Edition pp. 8–11 pp. 16–23

High-Frequency Words

cool	move
dry	place
four	warm
holes	

Phonemic Awareness

Phoneme Blending Tell children they are going to be detectives and figure out the word you are thinking about. Say: **Listen as I do the first one. I'm thinking of a word that names something that falls from the sky. It is /r/ /ā/ /n/. What's my word? The word is *rain*. Now you try.** Continue with clues for the words: /t/ /ā/ /l/ (*tail*), /d/ /ā/ (*day*), /m/ /ā/ /l/ (*mail*), /p/ /l/ /ā/ (*play*), /c/ /l/ /ā/ (*clay*).

RETEACH

Phonics and Spelling

Long Vowel /ā/*ai, ay*
Word Building Use *Word Builders* and *Word Builder Cards* and have children repeat each step after you. Build the word *pay*. Blend the sounds to read the word—/pā/. Then say the word naturally—*pay*. Have children do the same. Lead children in building and reading new words. Say:

- **Change *ay* to *ail*. Read the word.** (*pail*)
- **Change *p* to *s*. Read the word.** (*sail*)
- **Change *ail* to *ay*. Read the word.** (*say*)

Continue with the following words: *hail-hay-way-wait*. Remind children that the vowel sound /ā/ can be spelled *ai* and *ay*.

Read Words in Context Ask children to turn to **Practice Book p.80** *Practice Book* page 80. Read the sentences and have children echo-read. Then ask volunteers to read each sentence aloud. Ask: **What will Fay use?** (gray clay) **How does Fay's pot look?** (plain) **What will Fay do with the plain pot?** (paint it) **What will Fay paint on her pot?** (a snail) Call on volunteers to frame and read words with the long *a* sound. Then guide children to circle the words with the spelling *ai* and underline the words with the spelling *ay*.

RETEACH

High-Frequency Words

Copying Masters 77–78 Display the *High-Frequency Word Cards* for *cool, dry, four, holes, move, place* and *warm*. Point to each card and read the word. Distribute cards to children and have them work in pairs. Have children take turns reading a word on one of the cards for the partner to find and read.

Reading

 ### Build Background: "In Each Place"

pp. 16–23

Read the title with children. Have children tell what the place where they live is like. Explain that they will read about places all over the world that are very special in different ways. Have children think about which place they would like to visit.

Monitor Comprehension: "In Each Place"

Have children turn to the first page of the story. Ask a volunteer to reread the title. Guide children to look at the pictures on page 16 and think about what the selection will be about. Encourage children to predict what different kinds of places they will read about. Then guide children through the selection as they read.

pp. 16–17

Say: **I see people living in a lot of different places. They all look different. Let's read to find out what one place is like.**

After reading the pages, ask: **What can you find in the places on the first page?** (Possible response: I see people in each place. They are all wearing different clothes. Two places have snow.) **NOTE DETAILS**

Ask: **How do some places look alike? How do they look different?** (Possible response: Some places look cold with people wearing coats. Other places look hot.) **COMPARE AND CONTRAST**

Ask: **Look at the desert on page 17. What do you see?** (a lot of sand, sunshine) **What words describe what it feels like there?** (hot, dry) **Frame and read the word that tells what the desert does not get much of.** (rain) **NOTE DETAILS/APPLY PHONICS**

 pp. 18–19

Say: **The next two places are a rain forest and the Arctic. Let's read to find out what they are like.**

After reading the pages, ask: **What is the weather like in the rain forest?** (warm and wet with lots of rain) **What can you see in this place?** (a stream and lots of green trees, grass, and plants) **NOTE DETAILS**

Fluency

Phrasing Remind children that good readers read words in phrases and not one word at a time. Have children turn to pages 8–9 of "Frog and Rabbit" in *Happy Landings*. Say: **I'm going to read these pages one word at a time. Then I'll read them in phrases. Listen to the difference and tell me which sounds better.**

Then have children turn to pages 10–11. Ask them to tell what words they think should be read together. Have partners practice reading the pages aloud as you provide encouragement and feedback for improving children's phrasing.

Ask: **Why is it warm and wet in the rainforest?** (because it rains a lot) **What causes all the green plants to grow there?** (the rain and the weather) **CAUSE AND EFFECT/DRAW CONCLUSIONS**

Ask: **How is the Arctic different from the rain forest?** (It's white with snow and ice and looks very cold. Polar bears live there.) **COMPARE AND CONTRAST**

Ask: **Which words on these pages have the long *a* sound?** (*place, may, rain, days*) **APPLY PHONICS**

pp. 20–21

Say: **Look at the pictures of the next two places. What do you think these places will be like?** (Possible responses: One place is by the water. It looks sunny and warm. The other place is in the hills.) **Let's read to find out if you are right. MAKE PREDICTIONS**

After reading the pages, ask: **What did you find out about these places? Were your predictions right?** (Possible response: Yes, I was right. The place by the water is warm.) **MAKE PREDICTIONS**

Ask: **Why do you think the place by the water is warm and dry?** (Possible response: because there are lots of rocks) **MAKE INFERENCES**

Ask: **What is the place by the big hills like?** (It has cool summers and cold winters.) **NOTE DETAILS**

page 22

Say: **Look at the places on this page. Does any picture look like the place where you live?** (Possible response: The place with the trees and colored leaves looks like my neighborhood in fall.) **PERSONAL RESPONSE**

Let's read this last page. After reading the page, ask: **What can you see in each place on this page?** (Possible response: I see lots of snow in one place, colored leaves falling off trees in another, and two places are by the water.) **NOTE DETAILS**

Ask: **What is the place where you live like?** (Possible response: The place where I live is different all year long. Winter is cold with snow. Summer can be hot with lots of sun.) **Which place in this story would you like to visit. Tell why.** (Possible response: I would like to go to the desert and ride a camel.) **PERSONAL RESPONSE**

page
23

Answers to *Think Critically* Questions

Help children read and answer the *Think Critically* questions on page 23. Answers are shown below.

1. ‹*coat*› MAKE INFERENCES
2. ‹*warm and dry*› COMPARE AND CONTRAST
 3. ‹*rain*› CAUSE AND EFFECT

PRETEACH

Build Robust Vocabulary

Introduce Robust Vocabulary   Read the student-friendly explanation for each word. Then discuss each word using the following examples.

Say: **It is bitterly cold in Alaska in winter. If your family felt bitterly cold, would they put the heat on or open the windows?**

Say: **The dwelling I live in is in the country. In your dwelling, would you find your classroom or your bedroom?**

Say: **I like to paint pictures for amusement. Would you play a game or dry the dishes for amusement? Tell about something else you might do for amusement.**

RETEACH

Grammar/Writing

Describing Words: Taste, Smell, Sound, and Feel   Engage children in an imaginary trip to the beach. Start by saying: **Let's grab our swimming gear, our lotion, and sunglasses, and our picnic lunch and blankets. We're off to the beach!** Ask children to dictate sentences that tell about their experience. Say: **The air smells fresh and clean.** As children dictate, guide them to include describing words by asking questions, such as: **I don't know if the sand feels hot or cold, crunchy or soft. Which words can we use? Can you think of a word that tells how that watermelon tastes?** Add describing words children suggest.

VOCABULARY

Student-Friendly Explanations

bitterly A place that is bitterly cold is very, very cold.

dwelling A dwelling is a place where people live.

amusement If you do something for amusement, you do it for fun.

LESSON 20

DAY AT A GLANCE

Day 3

PHONEMIC AWARENESS
Phoneme Segmentation

PHONICS
Preteach Phonograms -ay, -ain

PHONICS AND SPELLING
Reteach Long Vowel /ā/ai, ay

HIGH-FREQUENCY WORDS
Reteach place, dry, warm, cool

FLUENCY
Phrasing

COMPREHENSION
Reteach Cause and Effect

GRAMMAR/WRITING
Reteach Description of a Place

Materials Needed:

Write-On/
Wipe-Off
Boards with
Phonemic
Awareness
Disks

Photo
Cards

Word Builders
and Word
Builder Cards

Copying
Masters
79–80

Lesson 20
Story Strips

Heading Out
Student Edition
pp. 46–52

Happy Landings
Student Edition
pp. 16–22

Spelling Words

1.	day	6.	wait
2.	say	7.	feet
3.	play	8.	me
4.	plain	9.	door
5.	rain	10.	told

30+ Minutes

Phonemic Awareness

Phoneme Segmentation Have children use the three boxes on the *Write-on/Wipe-off Boards.* Remind children that the boxes stand for sounds in words. Show *Photo Card rain* and ask: **What is the first sound in rain?** (/r/) Have children place a disk in the first box along with you. Have them name the second sound in *rain* (/ā/) and place a disk in the second box. Then have them identify the last sound in *rain* (/n/) and place a disk in the third box. Point to each box in sequence as children say the word. **How many sounds do you hear in rain? I hear three.** Repeat with *Photo Cards queen, toad, cake, road, farm,* and *fish.*

PRETEACH

Phonics

Phonograms -ay, -ain Write the words *may, stay,* and *play* on the board. Read *may* and underline *ay.* Explain that the phonogram -ay stands for /ā/. Read the remaining words, emphasizing /ā/ and underlining *ay.* Lead children in reading all three words. Follow the same procedure to teach the phonogram -ain, using *train, pain,* and *brain.* Write *gr* on the board. Then guide children to use the phonograms to write and read *gray* and *grain.* Repeat the process with *st* and *m.*

RETEACH

Phonics and Spelling

Long Vowel /ā/ay, ai
Build Words Use *Word Builders* and *Word Builder Cards* to form words. Have children listen to your directions and change letters in each word to spell a spelling word. Form *day* and have children read the word. Ask: **Which spelling word can you make by changing d to s?** (say)

Follow a similar procedure with the following words: *say* (play), *play* (plain), *plain* (rain), *rain* (wait), *meet* (feet), *met* (me).

Remind children that there are some other words they have to spell. Have children say *door.* Have them put *Word Builder Cards d, o, o, r* in their *Word Builders,* picture the word *door* in their minds, and build the word. Write the word on the board. Follow the same procedure with *told.*

RETEACH

High-Frequency Words

Copying Masters 79–80 Duplicate and distribute *Copying Masters* 79–80 to each child. Explain that the sentences tell the selection "In Each Place" but some have missing words.

List the words *place, dry, warm,* and *cool* on the board. Have children read aloud each story strip sentence and name the correct word on the board that makes sense in the sentence. Have children write the missing words in the blanks and read the completed sentences aloud. Help children cut apart the strips, read the completed sentences, and arrange them in story order.

RETEACH

Comprehension

Cause and Effect Tell children that story events happen for a reason. Remind them to ask themselves *What happened?* and *Why did it happen?* Revisit "Where Is Tom?" in *Heading Out.* Read the story together and look for examples of cause and effect. For example: A doll, a ball, and a shoe are missing. (effect) Tom, the dog has taken them. (cause) Record children's ideas in a chart. Create two columns labeled: *What happened?* and *Why did it happen?*

RETEACH

Grammar/Writing

Description of a Place Write the following description on the board. Explain to children that these sentences describe a place. Read the sentences as children follow along.

> I like Mom's garden. There are lots of flowers. They smell nice. Buzzing bees fly around. There are rows of fruits and vegetables. The tomatoes are too green to pick. But the red strawberries are sweet, juicy, and ready to eat.

Tell children that a description of a place names the place and tells what you can see, taste, smell, hear, and feel. Ask children what they can taste, smell, hear, or feel in Mom's garden. (sweet, juicy strawberries; fresh flowers; buzzing bees; green tomatoes) Point out how the description helps readers feel as if they are in the place. Guide children to use describing words to share other things that they might find in a garden like this.

High-Frequency Words

place	warm
dry	cool

Fluency

Phrasing Remind children that when good readers read, they read words that go together and then pause. They also pause when they see a comma or come to the end of a sentence.

Have children turn to "In Each Place" in *Happy Landings.* Reread the selection, modeling appropriate phrasing. Read each sentence, first word by word, and then in phrases. Discuss the difference. Have children read the story aloud, pausing at appropriate places.

DAY AT A GLANCE

Day 4

PHONEMIC AWARENESS
Phoneme Blending

PHONICS
Preteach Phonograms -ail, -aid

PHONICS AND SPELLING
Reteach Long Vowel /ā/ai, ay

HIGH-FREQUENCY WORDS
Reteach cool, dry, four, holes, move, place, warm

FLUENCY
Phrasing

COMPREHENSION
Reteach Cause and Effect

GRAMMAR/WRITING
Reteach Description of a Place

Materials Needed:

Practice Book

Lesson 20 High-Frequency Word Cards

What a Thrill! Student Edition pp. 26–32

Happy Landings Student Edition pp. 6–12 pp. 16–22

Photo Cards

Spelling Words

1.	day	6.	wait
2.	say	7.	feet
3.	play	8.	me
4.	plain	9.	door
5.	rain	10.	told

30+ Minutes

Phonemic Awareness

Phoneme Blending   Tell children that they will be builders and that they will put together sounds to figure out a word. Say: **Listen as I do the first one. /p/ /ā/ /n/. What word does /p/ /ā/ /n/ say? It says** *pain.* **Now you try.** Continue with: /r/ /ā/ /n/ (*rain*), /s/ /ā/ (*say*), /l/ /ā/ /m/ (*lame*), /m/ /ā/ /l/ (*mail*), /s/ /t/ /ā/ /n/ (*stain*).

PRETEACH

Phonics

Phonograms -ail, -aid   Write the words *mail* and *pail* on the board. Read *mail* and underline *ail.* Explain that the phonogram *-ail* stands for /āl/. Read *pail,* emphasizing /āl/ and underlining *ail.* Lead children in reading *pail.* Guide children in writing and reading other words with phonogram *-ail,* such as *sail, trail, nail,* and *fail.* Follow the same procedure to teach phonogram *-aid,* using *maid* and *paid.*

RETEACH

Phonics and Spelling

Practice Book p.81

Long Vowel /ā/*ai, ay*
Direct children's attention to page 81 of their *Practice Books.* Complete the page together.

Assess children's progress using the following sentences.

1. day — This will be a sunny **day.**
2. say — What did Dad **say**?
3. play — He can **play** with us.
4. plain — I like to eat **plain** cheese pizza.
5. rain — Do you think it will **rain** today?
6. wait — **Wait** for the bus!

Review

7. feet — Your **feet** will stay dry in boots.
8. me — My sister looks like **me.**

High-Frequency

9. door — Please open the **door.**
10. told — Mom **told** us about lunch.

RETEACH

High-Frequency Words

Copying Masters 77–78

Display *High-Frequency Word Cards* for this lesson's words—*cool, dry, four, holes, move, place,* and *warm*—and the previously learned high-frequency words. Point to words at random and ask children to read them.

RETEACH

Comprehension

Cause and Effect Review that an effect is an event and a cause is the reason the event happened. Draw a chart on the board like the one below. Have children turn to "Tom's Books" in *What a Thrill!* Point out examples of cause and effect. Then guide children through a picture walk of "Frog and Rabbit" in *Happy Landings*. Help them find examples of cause and effect. Record children's responses.

	What Happens	Why It Happens?
"Tom's Books"	Tom begins to read. Many children read Tom's books.	Tom learns his letters and sounds. Tom writes his own books.
"Frog and Rabbit"		

RETEACH

Grammar/Writing

Photo Card

Description of a Place Review with children the characteristics of a description of a place.

Description of a Place

It starts with the name of the place.
It tells more about the place.
It tells what you can taste, smell, hear, and feel.
It helps readers feel as if they are in the place.

Display *Photo Card jungle*. Invite children to imagine they are walking through the jungle. Have them tell what they hear, smell, taste, or feel. Record their ideas and work together to write a description of a jungle. Read the description together, pointing out its characteristics.

High-Frequency Words

cool	move
dry	place
four	warm
holes	

Fluency

Phrasing Have children work with partners. Ask them to take turns reading pages from "In Each Place" in *Happy Landings*. Remind children to pause after groups of words that go together, commas, and end marks. Listen as children read to one another. Provide feedback to help them improve their phrasing.

DAY AT A GLANCE
Day 5

30+ Minutes

HIGH-FREQUENCY WORDS
cool, dry, four, holes, move, place, warm

PHONEMIC AWARENESS
Onset and Rime

PHONICS AND SPELLING
Preteach Long Vowel /ā/*a-e*

BUILD ROBUST VOCABULARY
Preteach *sympathy, sensitive, devoted*

GRAMMAR/WRITING
Preteach Describing Words: How Many

Materials Needed:

Lesson 20 High-Frequency Word Cards

Sound/ Spelling Card *Aa*

Word Builders and Word Builder Cards

Practice Book p.82

Practice Book

Write-On/ Wipe-Off Boards

Photo Cards

High-Frequency Words

cool	move
dry	place
four	warm
holes	

High-Frequency Words

Copying Masters 77–78 Display *High-Frequency Word Cards* for *cool, dry, four, holes, move, place, warm,* and the other previously learned high-frequency words. Say the word *cool,* ask a volunteer to point to *cool,* and have children read the word aloud. Continue with the remaining high-frequency words. Repeat this activity several times to reinforce instant recognition.

Phonemic Awareness

Onset and Rime Tell children you are going to say some words, but you will say them in parts. Have children listen to see if they can figure out the word. Say: **Listen as I say this word in parts: /n/-ame. The word I said was** *name.* **Now you try some: /g/-ave, /l/-ake, /p/-ane, /sh/-ape, /m/-ade.**

PRETEACH

Phonics and Spelling

Sound/ Spelling Card **Long Vowel /ā/*a-e***
Connecting Letter to Sound Say the words *age, ape,* and *ache* and have children repeat the words. Explain that all three words begin with the /ā/ sound. Have children say /ā/ several times. Display *Sound/ Spelling Card Aa.* Say the letter name and identify the picture. Tell children that *a* can stand for the sound /ā/, the sound they hear at the beginning of *ape.* Remind children that this is the "long *a* sound." Point to the letter several times as children say /ā/.

Say: **When I say a word with /ā/ in the beginning, raise your hand and say /ā/. When I say a word that does not begin with /ā/, put your hands behind your back.** Say these words: *ate, ace, eel, ape, oat, age.* Tell children that some words, like *name,* have the sound /ā/ in the middle. Follow the same procedure with: *tape, gate, boat, cage, feet, wave.*

Word Blending Demonstrate each step with *Word Builder Cards* and a *Word Builder* and have children repeat each step after you. Hold up *t* and say /t/. Hold up *a* and say /ā/. Hold up *p* and say /p/. Hold up *e* and remind children that the silent *e* means that *a* stands for the long *a* sound.

- Place the letters *t, a, p, e* in the *Word Builder.*
- Point to *t.* Say /t/. Point to *a* and say /ā/. Prompt children to repeat after you.
- Slide *a* next to *t.* Run your hand under the letters as you blend the sounds, elongating them—/tā/.

- Point to *pe* and say /p/.
- Slide *pe* next to *ta*. Run your hand under *tape* as you blend the sounds, elongating them—/tāp/.
- Read *tape* naturally.

Follow the same procedure with the words *tale* and *make*.

  Word Building   Place the *Word Builder Cards c, a, m,* and *e* in the *Word Builder* and have children do the same. Slide your hand under the letters as you slowly blend the sounds to read the word—/kāāmm/. Then read the word naturally—*came.* Have children build and read new words. As they build each word, write it on the board. Say:

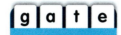

- **Change *c* to *g*. What word did you make?** (*game*)
- **Change *m* to *t*. What word did you make?** (*gate*)

Continue with the words *late, lake,* and *take.* Then have children read the words on the board. Direct children's attention to page 82 of their *Practice Books.* Complete the page together.

PRETEACH

Build Robust Vocabulary

Introduce Robust Vocabulary   Read the student-friendly explanation for each word. Then discuss each word using the following examples.

Say: **I show sympathy for a sad friend by trying to cheer up my friend. How would you show sympathy for a sick friend?**

Say: **Would you be sensitive to a hurt friend if you walked away or if you offered help?**

Say: **If you love to play soccer, are you devoted to your team or the team you are playing against?**

PRETEACH

Grammar/Writing

 Describing Words: How Many   Remind children that a describing word, or adjective, tells more about something. Today they will learn about describing words that tell how many. Display *Photo Cards* such as *squirrel, octopus, ant,* and *jungle.* Say: **A squirrel has four legs, two ears, and one bushy tail.** Guide children to name the describing words that tell how many. (*four, two, one*) Continue with: **An octopus has eight tentacles.** (*eight*) **An ant has three body parts, six legs, and two antennae.** (*three, six, two*) **A jungle has many trees and plants.** (*many*) Invite children to choose a *Photo Card* to describe.

Spelling Words

1. came	6. take
2. game	7. day
3. gate	8. play
4. late	9. four
5. lake	10. place

 Have children practice writing spelling words on their *Write-on/Wipe-off Boards.*

VOCABULARY

Student-Friendly Explanations

sympathy When you let others know you are sorry they feel bad, you are showing sympathy.

sensitive If you are sensitive, you care about other people's feelings.

devoted If you are devoted to someone, you love and want to take care of that person.

PHONEMIC AWARENESS
Phoneme Isolation

PHONICS AND SPELLING
Reteach Long Vowel /ā/a-e

COMPREHENSION
Reteach Problem/Solution

HIGH-FREQUENCY WORDS
Reteach oh, open, gone, don't

FLUENCY
Expression

GRAMMAR/WRITING
Reteach Describing Words: How Many

Materials Needed:

Photo
Cards

Word Builders
and Word
Builder Cards

Write-On/
Wipe-Off
Boards

What a Thrill!
Student Edition
pp. 46–52

Happy Landings
Student Edition
pp. 24–25

Practice
Book
p.83

Practice
Book

Spelling Words

1. came	6. take
2. game	7. day
3. gate	8. play
4. late	9. four
5. lake	10. place

 Have children practice writing spelling words on their *Write-on/Wipe-off Boards.*

LESSON 21

30+ Minutes

Phonemic Awareness

Phoneme Isolation Display *Photo Cards rain* and *road*. Have children say the picture names after you and listen for the /ā/ sound. Say: ***Rain, road.* Which picture name has the /ā/ sound?** *Rain* has the /ā/ sound. **Now you try.** Repeat with *Photo Cards stage* and *rose; toad* and *cake*.

RETEACH

Phonics and Spelling

Long Vowel /ā/a-e
Word Building Place the *Word Builder Cards c, a, m,* and *e* in the *Word Builder*. Ask children to say each letter name and the sound it stands for. Slide your hand under the letters as you blend the sounds—/kāāmm/. Then read the word naturally—*came*. Have children repeat the process. Ask:

- **Which letter should I change to make *came* become *game*?** (Change *c* to *g*.)
- **Which letters should I change to make *game* become *gate*?** (Change *m* to *t*.)
- **Which letters should I change to make *gate* become *late*?** (Change *g* to *l*.)

Continue with the words *lake* and *take*.

Read Words in Context Write the following sentences on chart paper. Have children read each sentence silently. Then track the print as children read the sentences aloud. Finally, point to the underlined words at random and have children read them. *My four friends will play the game. Don't be late on the day we go to the lake. Dad came to paint the gate. He will take you to a nice place.*

PRETEACH

Comprehension

Problem/Solution Tell children that many stories begin with a problem the characters have to solve. The rest of the story tells how the characters fix the problem. Have children turn to "Where Is Tom?" in *Heading Out*. Say: **In the beginning of the**

story, a family is missing a doll, a ball, and a shoe. When I read the rest of the story I find out that the pet dog, Tom, has been taking these things. When the family finds Tom, they also find their things and the problem is solved. Have children recall a familiar story such as "The Three Little Pigs." Help them identify the problem and solution in this story.

High-Frequency Words

 pp. 24–25

Write the words *oh, open, gone,* and *don't* on the board.

- Point to and read *oh*. Repeat, having children say *oh* with you.
- Say: *Oh*, look at that cute puppy!
- Repeat *oh* and point to each letter as you spell it. Then have children say and spell *oh* with you. Have children reread the word.

Repeat for *open, gone,* and *don't*. Use the following sentences: *Leave the window* open. *My hamster is* gone! Don't *be late for lunch.*

Have children turn to page 24 of *Happy Landings* and have them read aloud the words at the top of the page. Talk about the illustrations. Then guide children in choosing and writing the word that names each picture. (4. *lake,* 5. *gate,* 6. *plane*) Have children read aloud each word in the list on page 25. Ask volunteers to read the sentences aloud. Then have children choral-read the sentences. Guide them to read and circle the word that completes each sentence. (1. *open,* 2. *Oh,* 3. *don't,* 4. *gone*)

Grammar/Writing

 Practice Book p.83

Describing Words: How Many   Write this poem on chart paper.

> Five little birds in the big
> oak tree,

Remind children that some describing words tell how many. Read the poem aloud while tracking the print. Have children echo-read each line. Have them identify the word that tells how many little birds are in the poem. (*five*)

Tell children you are going to change the describing word. Write the word *two* on a self-stick note and place it over *five*. Reread the poem and ask what word tells how many now.

Ask children to think of other things that might live in the tree. Invite children to name these things and tell how many there are. For example: *three little squirrels, ten honey bees, one woodpecker.* Complete *Practice Book* page 83 together.

High-Frequency Words

oh	gone
open	don't

Fluency

Expression   Remind children that good readers use expression when they read. Model reading aloud "First Snow" in *What a Thrill!* while children follow along. Read with expression. Point out the different end marks and how you raise your voice at the end of a question and use excitement for an exclamation. Read the story again and have children echo-read.

DAY AT A GLANCE

Day 2

PHONEMIC AWARENESS
Phoneme Blending

PHONICS AND SPELLING
Reteach Long Vowel /ā/*a-e*

HIGH-FREQUENCY WORDS
Reteach *around, found, near, tired, might, open, gone, hears, oh, don't*

FLUENCY
Expression

READING
"Max Is Missing!"

BUILD ROBUST VOCABULARY
Preteach *alarmed, mysterious, overjoyed*

GRAMMAR/WRITING
Reteach Describing Words: How Many

Materials Needed:

Word Builders and Word Builder Cards

Practice Book p.84

Lesson 21 High-Frequency Word Cards

Heading Out Student Edition pp. 56–62

Happy Landings Student Edition pp. 26–33 pp. 16–22

High-Frequency Words

around	open
found	gone
near	hears
tired	oh
might	don't

30+ Minutes

Phonemic Awareness

Phoneme Blending   Tell children they are going to play a guessing game. Then say: **I'm thinking of a word that is something people might eat on their birthday. It is /k/ /ā/ k/. What's my word? The word is** *cake.* **Now you try.** Continue with clues for the words: /r/ /ā/ /s/ (*race*), /b/ /ā/ /k/ (*bake*), /l/ /ā/ /t/ (*late*), /p/ /l/ /ā/ /n/ (*plane*), /l/ /ā/ /k/ (*lake*).

RETEACH

Phonics and Spelling

 Practice Book p.84   **Long Vowel /ā/*a-e***
Word Building   Use *Word Builders* and *Word Builder Cards* and have children repeat each step after you. Build the word *can.* Blend the sounds to read the word—/kaann/. Then say the word naturally—*can.* Have children do the same. Then have children add final *e* and read the new word, *cane.* Lead children in building and reading new words. Say:

- **Change *c* to *pl*. Read the word.** (*plane*)
- **Take away the *l*. Read the word.** (*pane*)
- **Take away the *e*. Read the word.** (*pan*)

Continue with the following words: *tap-tape-cape-cap; skat-skate-gate.*

Read Words in Context   Ask children to turn to *Practice Book* page 84. Read each sentence aloud and have children echo-read. Ask volunteers to read each sentence aloud. Ask: **What will Jake's class have?** (a sale) **What has Jane made?** (a cake) **What will Wade sell?** (games) **What will the children do with the money?** (save it) Call on volunteers to frame and read the long *a* words. Then have them circle words with the long *a* sound.

RETEACH

High-Frequency Words

Copying Masters 81–82   Display the *High-Frequency Word Cards* for *around, found, near, tired, might, open, gone, hears, oh,* and *don't.* Point to each card and read the word. Distribute cards to children and have them work in pairs. Have children take turns reading a word on one of the cards for the partner to find and read.

Reading

pp. 26–33

Build Background: "Max Is Missing!"

Read the title with children. Ask children if they have a pet and if the pet was ever lost. Have them tell what they did to find it. Tell children they will be reading about a lost pet.

Monitor Comprehension: "Max Is Missing!"

Have children turn to the first page of the story. Ask a volunteer to reread the title. Point out that this story is a play. Help children read the names of the characters. Explain how a character's name appears each time that character speaks. Then ask children to look at the picture on page 26 and think about what the characters might do to find their pet. Then guide children through the story as they read.

pp. 26–27

Say: **I see a woman calling someone. I also see a gate is open. Let's read to find out who is missing.**

After reading the pages, ask: **Who is missing?** (Max, the pet cat is missing.) **Note Details**

Ask: **Do you think this is a problem? Why?** (Possible response: Yes, because I think the gate is usually closed to keep Max in.) **Problem/Solution/Make Inferences**

Ask: **Who does Mom ask first about the cat? Frame and read the name.** (Kate) **Sequence/Apply Phonics**

pp. 28–29

Say: **Kate begins to look for Max. Let's read to find out what she does to find her cat.**

After reading the pages, ask: **What does Kate do to find the cat?** (She calls the cat.) **Problem/Solution**

Ask: **Who is the next person to be asked about Max? Frame and read his name.** (Dave) **Sequence/Apply Phonics**

Ask: **Do you think Dave was home when Max disappeared? Why or why not?** (Possible response: No, because I see Dave on a bike and I think he was riding it) **Make Inferences**

Ask: **Who does Dave ask about the cat?** (Dad) **Note Details**

Fluency

Expression Remind children that punctuation marks are clues to let you know how to read each sentence. Have children turn to "The Map at Camp" in *Heading Out.* Model reading sentences that end with a period, a question mark, and an exclamation point. Have children follow your model and echo-read each sentence using the same expression.

Say: **Look at the pictures on the pages. What do you think the family will plan to do next?** (Possible response: I see a can of cat food. They will put food out for the cat.) **Let's read to find out if you are right.** **MAKE PREDICTIONS**

After reading the pages, ask: **Who has the first plan to get Max to come back?** (Kate) **What is Kate's plan?** (to make a path with bits of fish) **PROBLEM/SOLUTION**

Ask: **Do you think this will work? Why or why not?** (Possible response: It might work because cats like fish.) **DRAW CONCLUSIONS**

Ask: **What does Dave think will work?** (open a can of cat food) **PROBLEM/SOLUTION**

Do you think this will work? Why? (Possible response: Yes, because when my cat hears a can open, she knows it's time to eat) **DRAW CONCLUSIONS**

 Say: **Look at the picture on this page. What do you think happened?** (Possible response: I think Dave's plan worked.) **MAKE PREDICTIONS**

After reading the page, ask: **Did Dave's plan work?** (Yes, Max is back.)  **PROBLEM/SOLUTION**

Ask: **What does the family do after Max returns?** (They close the gate.) **What word has the long _a_ sound on this page?** (gate) **SEQUENCE/ APPLY PHONICS**

Answers to _Think Critically_ Questions

Help children read and answer the _Think Critically_ questions on page 33. Answers are shown below.

1. ‹_missing cat_› **CHARACTER**

2. ‹_front yard_› **SETTING**

3. ‹_open a can_› **PROBLEM/SOLUTION**

VOCABULARY
Student-Friendly Explanations

alarmed If you are alarmed, you feel scared or worried.

mysterious If something is mysterious, it is strange or puzzling.

overjoyed When you are overjoyed, you are very, very happy.

PRETEACH
Build Robust Vocabulary

Introduce Robust Vocabulary   Read the student-friendly explanation for each word. Then discuss each word using the following examples.

Say: **I get alarmed when I lose my keys. Would you feel alarmed if you lost your pet or if a friend came to visit?**

Say: **What would seem mysterious to you—a get-well card from a friend or a friendly letter from someone you don't know?**

Say: **Would you be overjoyed if you were going on a family vacation or if you were helping to clean out the garage or a messy room?**

RETEACH
Grammar/Writing

Describing Words: How Many   Have children turn to "In Each Place" in *Happy Landings*. Have them take a picture walk through the story and describe what they see using words that tell how many. Record their sentences on the board.

> I see three men on camels.
>
> I see many people on the beach.
>
> I see two hikers.
>
> I see six people in a family.
>
> I see many people outside in the snow.
>
> I see three people sitting on a hill.
>
> I see two polar bears.
>
> I see two more hikers.
>
> I see two boats in the water.

Read each sentence as you track the print. Ask a volunteer to underline the describing word that tells how many.

LESSON 21

DAY AT A GLANCE

Day 3

PHONEMIC AWARENESS
Phoneme Segmentation

PHONICS
Preteach Phonograms -ake, -ate

PHONICS AND SPELLING
Reteach Long Vowel /ā/a-e

HIGH-FREQUENCY WORDS
Reteach oh, open, gone, don't

FLUENCY
Expression

COMPREHENSION
Reteach Problem/Solution

GRAMMAR/WRITING
Reteach Play

Materials Needed:

Write-On/
Wipe-Off
Boards with
Phonemic
Awareness
Disks

Photo
Cards

Word Builders
and Word
Builder Cards

Copying
Masters
83–84

Lesson 21
Story Strips

Happy Landings
Student Edition
pp. 26–32

What a Thrill!
Student Edition
pp. 26–32

Spelling Words

1. came	6. take
2. game	7. day
3. gate	8. play
4. late	9. four
5. lake	10. place

Phonemic Awareness

Phoneme Segmentation   Have children use the three boxes on the *Write-on/Wipe-off Boards*. Remind children that the boxes stand for sounds in words. Show *Photo Card* *cake* and ask: **What is the first sound in *cake*?** (/k/) Have children place a disk in the first box along with you. Have them name the second sound in *cake* (/ā/) and place a disk in the second box. Then have them identify the last sound in *cake* (/k/) and place a disk in the third box. Point to each box in sequence as children say the word. Ask: **How many sounds do you hear in *cake*? I hear three.** Repeat with *Photo Cards rain, rose, head, night, farm, sack.*

PRETEACH

Phonics

Phonograms -ake, -ate   Write the words *bake, lake,* and *rake* on the board. Point to and read each word. Explain that the phonogram *-ake* stands for /āk/ and that the final *e* is silent. Read the remaining words, emphasizing /āk/ and underlining *ake*. Lead children in reading all three words.

Follow the same procedure to teach the phonogram *-ate*, using *date, late,* and *gate*.

RETEACH

Phonics and Spelling

 Long Vowel /ā/a-e

Build Words   Use *Word Builders* and *Word Builder Cards* to form words. Have children listen to your directions and change letters in each word to spell a spelling word. Form *same* and have children read the word. Ask: **Which spelling word can you make by changing the first letter?** (*came*)

Follow a similar procedure with the following words: *tale* (*take*), *say* (*day*), *name* (*game*), *game* (*gate*), *lace* (*late*), *rake* (*lake*), *slay* (*play*).

Remind children that there are some other words they have to remember how to spell. Have children say *four*. Have them put *Word Builder Cards* *f, o, u, r* in their *Word Builders*, picture the word *four* in their minds, and build the word. Write the word on the board. Follow the same procedure with *place*.

RETEACH

High-Frequency Words

 Duplicate and distribute *Copying Masters* 83–84 to each child. Explain that the sentences tell the story "Max Is Missing!" but some have missing words.

List the words *oh, open, gone,* and *don't* on the board. Have children read aloud each story strip sentence and name the correct word on the board that makes sense in the sentence. Have children write the missing words in the blanks and read the completed sentences aloud. Help children cut apart the strips, read the completed sentences, and arrange them in story order.

RETEACH

Comprehension

 Problem/Solution Remind children that a problem is something that makes things difficult for characters and the solution is how they solve, or fix, the problem. Revisit "Tom's Books" in *What a Thrill!* Read the story together and look for examples of problem/solution. For example: Tom does not know how to read. (problem) Tom learns his letters and words. (solution) Tom wants more books. (problem) He goes to the library. (solution) Record children's ideas in a chart. Create two columns labeled: *Problem* and *Solution*. Read the chart together.

RETEACH

Grammar/Writing

Play Write the following text on the board. Tell children that this is a short play. Read the play aloud, then lead children in a choral reading of the play. Have boys read the part of Shane and girls read the part of Kate.

> Shane: What do you want to play?
>
> Kate: How about tag?
>
> Shane: We played that yesterday.
>
> Kate: Let's play kickball! We can have two teams.
>
> Shane: Great idea! Let's go!

Explain to children that a play has a setting and characters. Point out the setting and characters in this short play. Circle *Shane:* in the first line and say: **Each line in a play starts with a character's name and a colon. This shows us which character is talking.** Then point out how the characters in a play tell a story.

High-Frequency Words

oh	gone
open	don't

Fluency

Expression Remind children that good readers sound as if they are talking when they read aloud. They let their voices rise and fall to read with expression. They read a little faster and louder when they are excited.

Read aloud some of the dialogue from "Max Is Missing!" in *Happy Landings* to demonstrate reading fluently with expression. Then have children rotate reading the parts of the characters to practice reading with expression.

LESSON 21

30+ Minutes

PHONEMIC AWARENESS
Phoneme Blending

PHONICS
Preteach Phonograms -ane, -ade

PHONICS AND SPELLING
Reteach Long Vowel /ā/a-e

HIGH-FREQUENCY WORDS
Reteach around, found, near, tired, might, open, gone, hears, oh, don't

FLUENCY
Expression

COMPREHENSION
Reteach Problem/Solution

GRAMMAR/WRITING
Reteach Play

Materials Needed:

Photo Cards | Practice Book | Lesson 21 High-Frequency Word Cards

Happy Landings Student Edition pp. 6–12 pp. 26–32

Spelling Words

1. came	6. take
2. game	7. day
3. gate	8. play
4. late	9. four
5. lake	10. place

Phonemic Awareness

Photo Card

Phoneme Blending   Tell children that together you are going to play a game of "Fix It." Tell them you are going to say some picture names that are broken and they will put together sounds to figure out the picture names. Display *Photo Cards stage, leaves, lunch, cake, farm,* and *snow.* Say: **What picture name does /s/ /t/ /ā/ /j/ say? /s/ /t/ /ā/ /j/ says** *stage.* **Now you try.** Continue with: /l/ /ē/ /v/ /z/ (*leaves*), /l/ /u/ /n/ /ch/ (*lunch*), /k/ /ā/ /k/ (*cake*), /f/ /är/ /m/ (*farm*), /s/ /n/ /ō/ (*snow*).

Phonics

Phonograms -ane, -ade   Write the words *pane, vane,* and *cane* on the board. Read *pane* and underline *ane.* Explain that the phonogram *-ane* stands for /ān/ and that the final *e* is silent. Read the remaining words with children, emphasizing /ān/ and underlining *ane.* Follow the same procedure to teach the phonogram *-ade,* using the words *made, wade,* and *shade.*

Phonics and Spelling

Practice Book p.85

Long Vowel /ā/a-e
Direct children's attention to page 85 of their *Practice Books.* Complete the page together.

Assess children's progress using the following sentences.

1. came   I'm glad Gram **came** to the play.
2. game   Let's play a new **game.**
3. gate   Close the **gate** when you leave the yard.
4. late   Meg was **late** for school.
5. lake   Let's go fishing at the **lake.**
6. take   My mom will **take** us to soccer practice.

Review

7. day   Tomorrow is a special **day.**
8. play   Jack will **play** the part of the troll.

High-Frequency

9. four   I have **four** new pencils.
10. place   Let's sit in this shady **place.**

RETEACH

High-Frequency Words

Copying Masters 81–82 Display *High-Frequency Word Cards* for this lesson's words—*around, found, near, tired, might, open, gone, hears, oh, don't*—and the previously learned high-frequency words. Point to words at random and ask children to read them.

RETEACH

Comprehension

 Problem/Solution Review that a problem is something story characters must solve, and a solution is the way they solve it. Draw a chart like the one below. Have children turn to "Max Is Missing" in *Happy Landings*. Review its problem and solution and write them in the chart. Do a picture walk through "Frog and Rabbit" in *Happy Landings*. Help children find the problem and solution in "Frog and Rabbit." Record their responses on the chart.

	Problem	Solution
"Frog and Rabbit"	Frog wants to win the race, but he is slower than Rabbit.	Frog tells himself he can win and he keeps trying until he does.
"Max Is Missing"	Max, the cat, is missing.	The family opens up a can of cat food and Max comes back.

RETEACH

Grammar/Writing

Photo Card **Play** Review with children the characteristics of a play.

> **Play**
>
> It has a setting and characters.
> Each line starts with a character's name and a colon.
> The characters tell the story.

Tell children that you will write a short play together. Work with children to select a topic, a story to tell, the names of characters, and which character speaks first. Have children dictate play lines. Track the print and read the play with children as you point out its characteristics.

High-Frequency Words

around	open
found	gone
near	hears
tired	oh
might	don't

Fluency

 Expression Have children work in groups of four. Ask them to take on the roles of the four characters in "Max Is Missing!" in *Happy Landings*. Have them read aloud the play.

Remind children to read aloud just like they think the character would speak, changing their voices to ask a question or express excitement. Listen as children read to one another. Provide feedback to help them improve their expression.

30+ Minutes

DAY AT A GLANCE

Day 5

HIGH-FREQUENCY WORDS
around, found, near, tired, might, open, gone, hears

PHONEMIC AWARENESS
Onset and Rime

PHONICS AND SPELLING
Preteach Long Vowel /ī/*i-e*

BUILD ROBUST VOCABULARY
Preteach *incident, gradual, downpour*

GRAMMAR/WRITING
Preteach Describing Words: Feelings

Materials Needed:

Lesson 21 High-Frequency Word Cards

Sound/ Spelling Card *Ii*

Word Builders and Word Builder Cards

Practice Book

Write-On/ Wipe-Off Boards

Happy Landings Student Edition pp. 26–32

High-Frequency Words

around	might
found	open
hear	gone
tired	hears

High-Frequency Words

Copying Masters 81–82 Display *High-Frequency Word Cards* for *around, found, near, tired, might, open, gone, hears,* and the other previously learned high-frequency words. Say the word *around,* ask a volunteer to point to *around,* and have children read the word aloud. Continue with the remaining high-frequency words. Repeat this activity several times to reinforce instant recognition.

Phonemic Awareness

Onset and Rime Tell children you are going to say some words, but you will say them in parts. Have children listen to see if they can figure out the word. Say: **Listen as I say this word in parts. /r/-ide—the word I said was** *ride.* **Now you try some: /l/-ike, /m/-ile, /p/-ine, /sm/-ile, /k/-ite.**

PRETEACH

Phonics and Spelling

Sound/ Spelling Card **Long Vowel /ī/*i-e***
Connecting Letter to Sound Say the words *kite, hide,* and *line* and have children repeat the words. Explain that all three words have the /ī/ sound. Have children say /ī/ several times. Display *Sound Spelling Card Ii.* Say the letter name and identify the picture. Tell children that *i* can stand for the sound /ī/, the sound they hear in the middle of *kite.* Remind children that this is the "long *i* sound." Point to the letter several times as children say /ī/.

Say: **When I say a word with /ī/ in the middle, raise your hand and say /ī/. When I say a word that does not have /ī/ in the middle, put your hand behind your back.** Say these words: *five, bite, mitt, side, fine, zip, pipe.*

 Word Blending Demonstrate each step with *Word Builder Cards* and a *Word Builder* and have children repeat each step after you. Hold up *k* and say /k/. Hold up *i* and say /ī/. Hold up *t* and say /t/.

- Slide *i* next to *k.* Run your hand under the letters as you blend the sounds, elongating them—/ki/.

- Point to *t* and say /t/.

- Slide *t* next to *ki.* Run your hand under *kit* as you blend the sounds, elongating them—/kit/. Read *kit* naturally.

- Add *e* to *kit* to form *kite.* Explain that the final *e* is silent; it is a clue that the *i* stands for the long *i* sound, /ī/. Slide your hand under *kite* as you blend the sounds, elongating them—/kīt/. Read *kite* naturally. Remove and replace the *e* several times as children read *kit* and *kite.*

k i t

k i t

k i t e

Follow the same procedure with the words *rid-ride, dim-dime,* and *bit-bite.*

  Word Building Place the *Word Builder Cards l, i, k,* and *e* in the *Word Builder* and have children do the same. Slide your hand under the letters as you slowly blend the sounds to read the word /līk/. Then read the word naturally—*like.* Have children build and read new words. As they build each word, write it on the board. Say:

- **Change *k* to *n*. What word did you make?** (*line*)
- **Change *l* to *n*. What word did you make?** (*nine*)

Continue with the words *mine, mile,* and *while.* Then have children read the words on the board. Direct children's attention to page 86 of their *Practice Books.* Complete the page together.

PRETEACH

Build Robust Vocabulary

Introduce Robust Vocabulary Read the student-friendly explanation for each word. Then discuss each word using the following examples.

Say: **There was an incident in the cafeteria when two students dropped their trays. Describe an incident you might see on the playground.**

Say: **When I learned Spanish, it was gradual. It took me months of work. When you learned to ride a bike, was it a gradual change or did you learn everything all at once?**

Say: **If you were caught in a downpour, would you just stand there or would you run for cover? Explain.**

PRETEACH

Grammar/Writing

Describing Words: Feelings Remind children that a describing word tells more about something. Today they will learn about describing words that tell about feelings. Say: **I feel happy today. How do you feel?** Repeat describing words children use to describe how they feel. Then have children turn to the story "Max Is Missing!" in *Happy Landings.* Guide children to suggest words that name how the characters are feeling throughout the story. (Possible responses: *worried, sad, upset, happy*)

Spelling Words

1. like	6. while
2. line	7. take
3. nine	8. came
4. mine	9. gone
5. mile	10. near

Have children practice writing spelling words on their *Write-on/Wipe-off Boards.*

VOCABULARY

Student-Friendly Explanations

incident An incident is something unusual that happens and often is an accident.

gradual If something happens in a gradual way, it happens slowly.

downpour A downpour is a large amount of rain that falls in a short time.

LESSON 22

The Picnic Plan

DAY AT A GLANCE

Day 1

PHONEMIC AWARENESS
Phoneme Isolation

PHONICS AND SPELLING
Reteach Long Vowel /ī/*i-e*

COMPREHENSION
Reteach Problem/Solution

HIGH-FREQUENCY WORDS
Reteach *right, nice, found*

FLUENCY
Expression

GRAMMAR/WRITING
Reteach Describing Words: Feelings

Materials Needed:

Word Builders and Word Builder Cards

Write-On/Wipe-Off Boards

Happy Landings Student Edition pp. 26–32 pp. 34–35

Practice Book p.87

Practice Book

Spelling Words

1. like	6. while
2. line	7. take
3. nine	8. came
4. mine	9. gone
5. mile	10. near

Have children practice writing spelling words on their *Write-on/Wipe-off Boards.*

Phonemic Awareness

Phoneme Isolation Tell children to listen for the /ī/ sound as you say two words. Say: *mine, mitt.* **Which word has the /ī/ sound?** *Mine* **has the /ī/ sound. Now you try.** Repeat with the words: *sit/bite, smile/six, time/mine, spill/spine, dime/wig, ice/itch, skit/pipe, ride/grin.*

RETEACH

Phonics and Spelling

Long Vowel /ī/*i-e*
Word Building Place the *Word Builder Cards l, i, k,* and *e* in the *Word Builder.* Ask children to say each letter name and the sound it stands for. Slide your hand under the letters as you blend the sounds—/līk/. Then read the word naturally—*like.* Have children repeat the process. Ask:

- **Which letter should I change to make *like* become *line*?** (Change *k* to *n*.)

 l i k e

- **Which letter should I change to make *line* become *nine*?** (Change *l* to *n*.)

l i n e

- **Which letter should I change to make *nine* become *mine*?** (Change *n* to *m*.)

n i n e

Continue with the words *mile* and *while.*

Read Words in Context Write the following sentences on chart paper. Have children read each sentence silently. Then track the print as children read the sentences aloud.

 m i n e

Finally, point to the underlined words at random and have children read them. *Stand in a line near the door. Your coat is like mine. We will walk a mile at nine. It will take a while to play. Dad came to my room. My pet is gone.*

RETEACH

Comprehension

Problem/Solution Tell children that many stories begin with a problem the characters must solve. The rest of the story tells how the characters fix the problem. Guide children to recall the problem in "Max Is Missing!" in *Happy Landings.* Say: **What problem does the family have in this story?** (Max, the pet cat, is missing.)

How is the problem finally solved? (Max comes back when a can of cat food is opened.) Have children recall another familiar story such as "Goldilocks and the Three Bears." Help them identify the problem and solution in this story.

RETEACH

High-Frequency Words

pp. 34–35 Write the words *right, nice,* and *found* on the board.

- Point to and read *right.* Repeat, having children say *right* with you.
- Say: **My picture does not look *right.***
- Repeat the word and point to each letter as you spell it. Then have children say and spell *right* with you. Have children reread the word.

Repeat for *nice* and *found.* Use the following sentences: *It's a* nice *day for a swim. I* found *my lost library book.*

Have children turn to page 34 of *Happy Landings* and have them read aloud the words at the top of the page. Talk about the illustrations. Then guide children in choosing and writing the word that names each picture. (4. *nine,* 5. *line,* 6. *pile*) Have children read aloud each word in the list on page 35. Ask volunteers to read the sentences aloud. Then have children choral-read the sentences. Guide them to choose and circle the word that completes each sentence. (1. *nice,* 2. *right,* 3. *found*)

RETEACH

Grammar/Writing

Practice Book p.87 **Describing Words: Feelings** Write the following poem on chart paper.

> I feel happy when I play with you.
> I feel excited on a trip to the zoo.
> I feel hungry when it's time to eat.
> I feel surprised when I get a sweet treat.

Read the poem while tracking the print. Ask children to name the describing words that tell about feelings. Guide children to underline the words *happy, excited, hungry,* and *surprised.* Then write the sentence frame: *I feel ___ when ____.* Help children use describing words to describe their thoughts, and feelings. Complete *Practice Book* page 87 together.

High-Frequency Words

right	nice
found	

Fluency

Expression Remind children that good readers use expression when they read. Have children turn to "Max Is Missing!" in *Happy Landings.* Read aloud with expression. Point out end marks. Remind children that an exclamation point is used to show strong feeling. Read the story again and have children echo-read.

Materials Needed:

Word Builders and Word Builder Cards

Practice Book p.88

Practice Book

Copying Masters 85–86

Lesson 22 High-Frequency Word Cards

What a Thrill! Student Edition pp. 46–52

Happy Landings Student Edition pp. 36–43

High-Frequency Words

right	light
those	nice
walked	found
because	

30+ Minutes

Phonemic Awareness

Phoneme Blending   Tell children they are going to play a guessing game. Then say: **I'm thinking of a word that names one more than four. It is /f/ /ī/ /v/. What's my word? The word is** *five.* **Now you try.** Continue with clues for the words: /h/ /ī/ /v/ (*hive*), /s/ /l/ /ī/ /d/ (*slide*), /d/ /ī/ /m/ (*dime*), /b/ /ī/ /k/ (*bike*), /v/ /ī/ /n/ (*vine*).

RETEACH

Phonics and Spelling

Long Vowel /ī/*i-e*

Word Building   Use a *Word Builder* and *Word Builder Cards* and have children repeat each step after you. Build the word *line.* Blend the sounds to read the word—/līn/. Then say the word naturally—*line.* Remind children that in words with the consonant-vowel-consonant *e* pattern, the vowel sound is often long. Ask them what vowel sound they hear in the word. (/ī/; long *i*) Lead children in building and reading new words. Say:

- **Change *i* to *a*. Read the word.** (*lane*)
- **Change *l* to *p*. Read the word.** (*pane*)
- **Change *a* to *i*. Read the word.** (*pine*)

Continue with the following words: *mile-male-tale-tile, line-lane-lake-like.* Remind children that the vowel sound /ī/ can be spelled *i* with final *e.*

Read Words in Context   Ask children to turn to *Practice Book* page 88. Read each sentence aloud and have children echo-read. Ask volunteers to read each sentence aloud. Ask: **What does Spike look like?** (black and white with a stripe) **Where does Spike hide?** (in the pine trees) **What does Spike like to eat?** (vines) **What kind of animal is Spike?** (one fine little skunk) Guide children to frame and read the long *i* words. Have them circle words with the long *i* sound.

RETEACH

High-Frequency Words

Copying Masters 85–86

Display the *High-Frequency Word Cards* for *right, those, walked, because, light, nice,* and *found.* Point to each card and read the word. Distribute cards to children. Say: **I'm thinking of a word that rhymes with** *night.* **What is my word?** Have children find the word card and hold it up for you to see. Then read the word together. Repeat with a clue for each word.

Reading

 pp. 36–43

Build Background: "The Picnic Plan"

Read the title with children. Ask children about picnics they have been on. Talk about what you need to plan before going, such as food and supplies to take. Tell children they will be reading about three friends who make a plan for their own picnic.

Monitor Comprehension: "The Picnic Plan"

Have children turn to the first page of the story. Ask a volunteer to reread the title. Ask children to look at the picture on page 36 and think about what the selection will be about. Ask children to identify the animals they see. (fox, skunk, duck) Explain that they are friends. Guide children through the story as they read.

 pp. 36–37

Say: **Three friends are planning something. Let's read to find out what it is.**

After reading the pages, ask: **What are the three friends planning?** (a picnic) **Note Details**

Ask: **What is the first thing they need to decide?** (what food to bring) **Sequence**

Ask: **What does Duck decide to bring?** (a pile of nuts) **Why does Duck choose nuts?** (because she likes them) **Characters' Motivations**

Say: **Frame and read the words with long *i* sound.** (*nice, like, pile*) **Apply Phonics**

 pp. 38–39

Say: **We know that Duck is planning to bring nuts for the picnic. Let's read to find out what Fox and Skunk plan to bring.**

After reading the pages, ask: **Which friend brings peaches?** (Fox) **What does Skunk bring?** (apples) **What kind of apples does Skunk bring? Frame and read the word.** (*ripe*) **Note Details/Apply Phonics**

Ask: **Why do you think they choose peaches and apples?** (Possible response: because they like them) **Characters' Motivations**

Fluency

Expression Remind children that good readers read with expression. Read aloud the first few pages of "Paint Your Dog!" in *What A Thrill!* to demonstrate how to read in a way that sounds natural and to show emotion by changing the pace of the reading or the pitch of your voice. Have children follow your model to echo-read each sentence using the same expression.

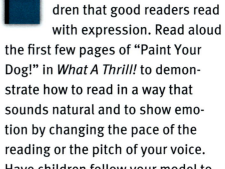

Ask: Do you see any other animals in the pictures? (some squirrels)
What do you think they are doing by the tree? (Possible response:
They are watching the three friends plan their picnic. Maybe they
want to come too.) **MAKE INFERENCES**

 **pp.
40–
41**

Say: **There is a problem in the picture. Let's read to find out what
the problem is.**

After reading the pages, ask: **What did Duck, Fox, and Skunk forget
to bring?** (dishes and cups) **NOTE DETAILS**

Ask: **What problem happened when they left to get them?** (The food
was taken.) **PROBLEM/SOLUTION**

Ask: **What do you think happened to the nuts, peaches, and apples?**
(Possible response: Maybe the squirrels took them.) **Why do you
think this?** (because they are the only other animals around) **DRAW
CONCLUSIONS**

Ask: **Which friend do you think will solve the problem first? Tell why.**
(Possible response: I think Duck will because she sees the squirrels.)
MAKE PREDICTIONS

**page
42**

Say: **Look at the picture on this page. I wonder if the problem will be
solved. Let's read to find out.**

After reading the page, ask: **Where did the friends find their food?**
(The squirrels took it.) **NOTE DETAILS**

Ask: **Do you think Duck, Fox, and Skunk will share their picnic with
the squirrels? Why or why not?** (Possible response: Yes, because
there is a lot of food.) **PERSONAL RESPONSE**

**page
43**

Answers to *Think Critically* Questions

Help children read and answer the *Think Critically* questions on page
43. Answers are shown below.

1. ‹*it's a nice day*› **CAUSE AND EFFECT**

 2. ‹*take the food*› **PROBLEM/SOLUTION**

 3. ‹*Duck*› **PROBLEM/SOLUTION**

VOCABULARY

Build Robust Vocabulary

PRETEACH

Introduce Robust Vocabulary   Read the student-friendly explanation for each word. Then discuss each word using the following examples.

Say: **When I seek a new sweater, I go to my favorite store. Where would you seek for a good book to read?**

Say: **Would you probably be oblivious if a family member took your favorite toy or a toy you never play with? Explain.**

Say: **Would you be indecisive if you had to choose between going to the beach or going to a theme park? Explain.**

RETEACH

Grammar/Writing

Describing Words: Feelings   Write these sentences on the board.

> We were excited to go to the zoo.
>
> We were worried that it would rain, but then the sun came out.
>
> We were surprised at all the different animals we saw.
>
> One polar bear looked lonely sitting by himself.
>
> We were very pleased with our class trip.

Read each sentence as you track the print. Guide children to identify describing words that tell about feelings. Ask volunteers to underline the words *excited, worried, surprised, lonely,* and *pleased.* Invite children to choose a word to use in sentence about themselves, for example *I feel excited when I get a gift.* Write their sentences on the board, then read them with children.

VOCABULARY

Student-Friendly Explanations

seek When you seek something, you look for or try to find it.

oblivious If you are oblivious to something, you do not see it or realize it is happening.

indecisive When you are indecisive, you cannot make up your mind about something.

LESSON 22

30+ Minutes

DAY AT A GLANCE

Day 3

PHONEMIC AWARENESS
Phoneme Segmentation

PHONICS
Preteach Inflections *-ed, -ing* (drop final *e*)

PHONICS AND SPELLING
Reteach Long Vowel /ī/*i-e*

HIGH-FREQUENCY WORDS
Reteach *right, nice, found*

FLUENCY
Expression

COMPREHENSION
Reteach Problem/Solution

GRAMMAR/WRITING
Reteach Description of a Memory

Materials Needed:

Write-On/
Wipe-Off
Boards with
Phonemic
Awareness
Disks

Photo
Cards

Word Builders
and Word
Builder Cards

Copying
Masters
87–88

Lesson 22
Story Strips

Happy Landings
Student Edition
pp. 36–42

Spelling Words

1. like	6. while
2. line	7. take
3. nine	8. came
4. mine	9. gone
5. mile	10. near

Phonemic Awareness

Phoneme Segmentation   Have children use the three boxes on the *Write-on/Wipe-off Boards*. Remind children that the boxes stand for sounds in words. Show *Photo Card* *night* and ask: **What is the first sound in *night*?** (/n/) Have children place a disk in the first box along with you. Have them name the second sound in *night* (/ī/) and place a disk in the second box. Repeat for the last sound in *night*. (/t/) Point to each box in sequence as children say the word. **How many sounds do you hear in *night*? I hear three.** Repeat with *Photo Cards* *ice, gift, hen, snow, fish, pie.*

PRETEACH

Phonics

Inflections *-ed, -ing* (drop final *e*)   Write the following on the board: *hike + ed = hiked, pile + ed = piled, rake + ed = raked.* Read each root word with children. Say: **When a verb ends in *e*, drop the *e* before adding *-ed*.**

Repeat with: *hike + ing = hiking, pile + ing = piling, rake + ing = raking.* Say: **When a verb ends in *e*, drop the *e* before adding *-ing*.** Guide children to help you add *-ed* and *-ing* to the root words *smile, slice,* and *tape.* (*smiled, smiling; sliced, slicing, taped, taping*)

RETEACH

Phonics and Spelling

Long Vowel /ī/*i-e*
Build Words   Use *Word Builder Cards* and a *Word Builder* to form words. Have children listen to your directions and change letters in each word to spell a spelling word. Form *life* and have children read the word. Ask: **Which spelling word can you make by changing *f* to *k*?** (*like*)

Follow a similar procedure with the following words: *bake* (*take*), *cave* (*came*), *pine* (*line, nine, mine*), *male* (*mile*), and *white* (*while*).

Remind children that there are some other words they have to remember how to spell. Have children say *gone.* Have them put *Word Builder Cards* *g, o, n, e* in their *Word Builders,* picture the word *gone* in their minds, and build the word. Write the word on the board. Follow the same procedure with *near.*

RETEACH
High-Frequency Words

 Duplicate and distribute *Copying Masters* 87–88 to each child. Explain that the sentences tell about the story "The Picnic Plan" but some have missing words.

List the words *right, nice,* and *found* on the board. Have children read aloud each story strip sentence and name the correct word on the board that makes sense in the sentence. Have children write the missing words in the blanks and read the completed sentences aloud. Help children cut apart the strips, read the completed sentences, and arrange them in story order.

RETEACH
Comprehension

  Problem/Solution   Review how to identify problem and solution. Guide children to identify the main problem and solution in "The Picnic Plan." (Problem: The squirrels take the friends' food. Solution: The friends see the squirrels and find their food.) Read the following to children: **Think about what might happen after "The Picnic Plan" ends. When the friends get their food back, they invite the squirrels to have some. There are enough nuts, but there are not enough apples and peaches for everyone.** Guide children to identify the problem. (There is not enough food to share.) Ask them to suggest a possible solution. (Possible responses: They can cut the fruit in half. They can get more fruit. The squirrels can bring some food of their own to share.)

RETEACH
Grammar/Writing

Description of a Memory   Read the following sentences to children, and talk about the feelings being described. Explain that these sentences describe an experience someone had.

> I felt very happy today! I went on a picnic with my friends. I was excited to see what foods everyone planned to bring. We got worried when the food was missing. Then I heard rustling up the tree. I saw squirrels with our food! We were pleased when the squirrels gave the food back. We had fun.

Point out that the sentences describe an experience and that they have words that describe feelings. Reread the sentences, and have children raise their hands when they hear words that describe feelings. Tell them that descriptions should help them form a picture in their minds.

High-Frequency Words

right	found
nice	

Fluency

 Expression   Remind children that good readers want to sound like the characters who are talking in a story when they read aloud. They let their voices rise and fall to read with expression. They read a little faster and louder when they are excited. Read aloud "The Picnic Plan" to demonstrate reading fluently with expression. Then have children reread parts of the story to practice reading with expression.

LESSON 22

30+ Minutes

PHONEMIC AWARENESS
Phoneme Blending

PHONICS
Reteach Inflections -ed, -ing (drop final e)

PHONICS AND SPELLING
Reteach Long Vowel /ī/i-e

HIGH-FREQUENCY WORDS
Reteach right, those, walked, because, light, nice, found

FLUENCY
Expression

COMPREHENSION
Reteach Problem/Solution

GRAMMAR/WRITING
Reteach Description of a Memory

Materials Needed:

Photo Cards

Practice Book
p.89

Copying Masters 85–86
Lesson 22 High-Frequency Word Cards

Happy Landings Student Edition pp. 26–32 pp. 36–42

Spelling Words

1. like	6. while
2. line	7. take
3. nine	8. came
4. mine	9. gone
5. mile	10. near

Phonemic Awareness

Photo Card

Phoneme Blending Tell children that they are going to play a game of "Fix It." Tell them you are going to say some picture names that are broken and they will put together sounds to figure out the picture names. Display *Photo Cards ice, king, hen, night, path,* and *toad*. Say: **What picture name does /ī/ /s/ say? /ī/ /s/ says ice. Now you try.** Continue with: /n/ /ī/ /t/ (*night*), /t/ /ō/ /d/ (*toad*), /k/ /i/ /ng/ (*king*), /p/ /a/ /th/ (*path*), /h/ /e/ /n/ (*hen*).

RETEACH

Phonics

Inflections -ed, -ing Remind children that endings can be added to a root word to make new words. Write *smile, smiled, smiling*. Say: **You can make *smiled* and *smiling* by dropping e and adding -ed or -ing.** Then write: *stay, stays, stayed, staying*. Say: **You can make new words by adding -s, -ed, or -ing with no spelling change.** Write *wipe, wiped, wiping; dine, dined, dining;* and *save, saved, saving* on the board. Guide children to read the words, underline the root words, and circle the endings.

RETEACH

Phonics and Spelling

Practice Book **p.89**

Long Vowel /ī/i-e Direct children's attention to page 89 of their *Practice Books*. Complete the page together.

Assess children's progress using the following sentences.

1. like — We **like** to go hiking.
2. line — We walk on a path in a **line**.
3. nine — We went **nine** miles today!
4. mine — Dad lost his compass, but I have **mine**.
5. mile — Just one more **mile** to the lake!
6. while — It takes a **while** to get there.

Review

7. take — We will **take** another path back.
8. came — Good thing we **came** with snacks!

High-Frequency

9. gone — We will have **gone** a long time without eating.
10. near — Soon we will be **near** a place to rest and eat.

RETEACH

High-Frequency Words

Copying Masters 85–86

Display *High-Frequency Word Cards* for this lesson's words—*right, those, walked, because, light, nice, found*—and the previously learned high-frequency words. Point to words at random and ask children to read them.

RETEACH

Comprehension

Problem/Solution   Remind children that most stories have a problem of some kind that must be solved before the end of the story. Draw a chart like the one below. Review with children the problem and solution in "The Picnic Plan" and record the information on the chart. Then have children do a picture walk through "Max is Missing" in *Happy Landings*. Guide children to point out the problem and solution. Record their responses on the chart.

	"The Picnic Plan"	"Max Is Missing!"
Problem	The food is missing from the picnic.	Max, the pet cat, is missing.
Solution	The friends find the food and invite new friends to the picnic.	A can of cat food is opened and *Max* comes back.

RETEACH

Grammar/Writing

Description of a Memory   Review with children the characterstics of a description of a memory.

Description of a Memory

The sentences describe an experience.
The sentences have words that describe feelings.
The description helps me form a picture in my mind.

Have children think of an activity they have experienced together as a class. Prompt them to recall details about the activity. Guide them to use descriptive words that help their readers see, hear, smell, feel, or taste what is happening. Record their responses. Then read their description together.

High-Frequency Words

right	light
those	nice
walked	found
because	

Fluency

Expression   Have partners read "The Picnic Plan" in *Happy Landings* aloud three or four times. Remind them to look at end marks for clues about reading with expression. Listen to partners read, giving them feedback about their expression and about improving their fluency.

DAY AT A GLANCE

Day 5

30+ Minutes

HIGH-FREQUENCY WORDS
right, those, walked, because, light

PHONEMIC AWARENESS
Onset and Rime

PHONICS AND SPELLING
Preteach Long Vowel /ō/o-e

BUILD ROBUST VOCABULARY
Preteach *asserted, offended, retorted*

GRAMMAR/WRITING
Preteach Describing Words: *-er* and *-est*

Materials Needed:

Lesson 22 High-Frequency Word Cards

Sound/Spelling Card *Oo*

Word Builders and Word Builder Cards

Write-On/Wipe-Off Boards

Practice Book

High-Frequency Words

right	light
those	
walked	
because	

High-Frequency Words

Copying Masters 85–86 Display *High-Frequency Word Cards* for *right, those, walked, because, light,* and the other previously learned high-frequency words. Say the word *right,* ask a volunteer to point to *right,* and have children read the word aloud. Continue with the remaining high-frequency words. Repeat this activity several times to reinforce instant recognition.

Phonemic Awareness

Onset and Rime   Tell children you are going to say some words, but you will say them in parts. Have children listen to see if they can figure out the word. Say: **Listen as I say this word in parts. /r/-ose—the word I said was *rose*. Now you try some: /b/-one, /h/-ose, /r/-ope, /sm/-oke, /n/-ose.**

PRETEACH

Phonics and Spelling

 Sound/Spelling Card **Long Vowel /ō/o-e**
Connecting Letter to Sound   Say the words *nose, hole,* and *code* and have children repeat the words. Explain that all three words have the /ō/ sound. Have children say /ō/ several times. Display *Sound/Spelling Card Oo.* Say the letter name and identify the picture. Tell children that *o* can stand for the long *o* sound, the sound they hear in the middle of *nose.* Point to the letter several times as children say /ō/.

Give children *o* and *e Word Builder Cards.* Remind children that when *e* comes at the end of the word it is silent. Explain that *o* and *e* together make the long *o* sound in words. Say: **When I say a word with /ō/ in the middle, hold up the *o* and *e* cards. If the word has the /o/ sound, hold up just the *o* card.** Say these words: *hose, bone, mop, hole, rode, hot, mole.*

 Word Blending   Demonstrate each step with *Word Builder Cards* and a *Word Builder.* Have children repeat each step after you. Hold up *h* and say /h/. Hold up *o* and say /o/. Hold up *p* and say /p/.

- Place the letters *h, o, p* in the Word Builder.
- Point to *h.* Say /h/. Point to *o* and say /o/. Point to *p* and say /p/. Prompt children to repeat after you.
- Slide *o* next to *h.* Run your hand under the letters as you blend the sounds, elongating them—/ho/.
- Point to *p* and say /p/.
- Slide *p* next to *ho.* Run your hand under *hop* as you blend the sounds, elongating them—/hop/. Read *hop* naturally.

- Add *e* to *hop* to form *hope*. Explain that the final *e* is silent; it is a clue that the *o* stands for the long *o* sound, /ō/. Slide your hand under *hope* as you blend the sounds, elongating them—/hŏp/. Read *hope* naturally. Remove and replace the *e* several times as children read *hop* and *hope*.

Follow the same procedure with these words: rod-rode, not-note, cop-cope.

  Word Building Place the *Word Builder Cards h, o, m,* and *e* in the *Word Builder* and have children do the same. Slide your hand under the letters as you slowly blend the sounds to read the word /hōm/. Then read the word naturally—*home*. Have children build and read new words. As they build each word, write it on the board. Say:

Practice Book p.90

- **Change *m* to *p*. What word did you make?** (*hope*)
- **Change *h* to *r*. What word did you make?** (*rope*)

Continue with the words *rode, rose,* and *those*. Then have children read the words on the board. Complete *Practice Book* page 90 together.

PRETEACH

Build Robust Vocabulary

Introduce Robust Vocabulary Read the student-friendly explanation for each word. Then discuss each word using the following examples.

Say: **I asserted that it was important to read something new each week. When would you assert your feelings—if something is important to you or if something is not important?**

Say: **I would be offended if someone took my bag. Would you be offended if someone shared with you or took away your favorite dessert?**

Say: **Would you retort angrily if a friend gave you a compliment or hurt your feelings by saying something mean? Explain.**

PRETEACH

Grammar/Writing

Describing Words: *-er* and *-est* Remind children that they have been learning about different kinds of describing words. Write these sentences on the board: *The peach is sweeter than the apple. The berries are the sweetest of all.* Read them aloud as you track the print. Guide children to identify the describing words. (*sweeter, sweetest*) Write the words and underline *er* and *est*. Explain: **Describing words that end with *-er* and *-est* are used to compare things.** Ask children to look around the room to compare things using the words *bigger, biggest; longer, longest; darker, darkest; louder, loudest; smaller, smallest; taller, tallest.*

Spelling Words

1. home	6. those
2. hope	7. like
3. rope	8. nine
4. rode	9. right
5. rose	10. walk

Have children practice writing spelling words on their *Write-on/Wipe-off Boards.*

VOCABULARY
Student-Friendly Explanations

asserted If you asserted something, you said in a strong way what you believe.

offended If you feel offended, you feel hurt or upset by something someone did or said.

retorted If you retorted, you replied in an angry way to something someone else said.

LESSON 23

School Day

DAY AT A GLANCE

Day 1

PHONEMIC AWARENESS
Phoneme Isolation

PHONICS AND SPELLING
Reteach Long Vowel /ō/o-e

COMPREHENSION
Preteach Draw Conclusions

HIGH-FREQUENCY WORDS
Reteach *hello, about, would, Mr.*

FLUENCY
Punctuation

GRAMMAR/WRITING
Reteach Describing Words: *-er* and *-est*

Materials Needed:

Photo
Cards

Word Builders
and Word
Builder Cards

Write-On/
Wipe-Off
Boards

Happy Landings
Student Edition
pp. 6–12
pp. 36–42
pp. 44–45

Practice
Book
p.91

Practice
Book

Spelling Words

1. home	6. those
2. hope	7. like
3. rope	8. nine
4. rode	9. right
5. rose	10. walk

Have children practice writing
spelling words on their
Write-on/Wipe-off Boards.

Phonemic Awareness

Phoneme Isolation   Display *Photo Cards rose* and *rain.* Tell
children to listen for the /ō/ sound as you say the two words. Say:
***rose, rain.* Which picture name has the /ō/ sound? *Rose* has the /ō/
sound. Now you try.** Repeat with the words: *tone/time, ripe/rope, smile/
smoke, pole/pile, mile/mole.*

RETEACH

Phonics and Spelling

d o t   **Long Vowel /ō/o-e**
Word Building   Place the *Word Builder Cards h, o, m,* and *e* in
the *Word Builder.* Ask children to say the name and the sound of each letter.
Then read the word naturally—*home.* Have children do the same. Ask:

- **Which letter should I change to make *home*
  become *hope*?** (Change *m* to *p*.)

- **Which letter should I change to make *hope*
  become *rope*?** (Change *h* to *r*.)

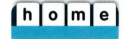

Continue with the words *rode, rose,* and *those.*

Read Words in Context   Write the following sentences
on chart paper. Have children read each sentence
silently. Then track the print as children read the sentences aloud. Finally,
point to the underlined words at random and have children read them.
*Please, be <u>home</u> at <u>nine</u>. I <u>hope</u> Dan will help us pull the <u>rope</u>. I <u>rode</u> my new
bike. <u>Walk</u> down the street and then turn <u>right</u>. Mom will like the yellow <u>rose</u>.
<u>Those</u> are the two books I <u>like</u> the best.*

PRETEACH

Comprehension

Draw Conclusions   Remind children that an author
does not always tell everything and can use clues in a
story to help readers draw conclusions and fill in missing
pieces of information. Review "Frog and Rabbit" in *Happy Landings.* Say: **I
can draw the conclusion that Rabbit feels very proud of himself and likes to
brag. He was so sure that he would win. The story didn't tell me this exactly,
but I can figure it out. The biggest clue was when Rabbit took a nap.** Guide

children to look at the last picture in the story and tell what conclusions they can draw about Rabbit now. (Possible response: Rabbit is angry with himself for thinking he could win without really trying.)

RETEACH

High-Frequency Words

 pp. 44–45

Write the words *hello, about, would,* and *Mr.* on the board.

- Point to and read *hello.* Repeat, having children say *hello* with you.
- Say: **I say "*hello*" to my neighbor every day.**
- Repeat the word and point to each letter as you spell it. Then have children say and spell *hello* with you. Have children reread the word.

Repeat for the remaining words. Use the following sentences: *We read* about *whales in class. I* would *like to go with you to the park.* Mr. *Murphy is our librarian.*

Have children turn to page 44 of *Happy Landings* and have them read aloud the words at the top of the page. Talk about the illustrations. Then guide children in choosing and writing the word that names each picture. (4. *hole,* 5. *rope,* 6. *home*) Have children read aloud each word in the list on page 45. Ask volunteers to read the sentences aloud. Then have children choral-read the sentences. Guide them to read and circle the word that completes each sentence. (1. *Mr.,* 2. *hello,* 3. *would,* 4. *about*)

RETEACH

Grammar/Writing

 Photo Card   Practice Book p.91

Describing Words: -er and -est   Display *Photo Cards ocean, snow, ice, bridge, path, road.* Write the following sentences on the board and read them aloud:

> The ocean is cold. Snow is colder. But ice is the coldest one of all.
>
> The bridge is long. The path is longer. But the road is the longest one of all.

Guide children to name the describing words used. Have them point to the corresponding *Photo Card* as each word is named. (*cold, colder, coldest; long, longer, longest*) Have volunteers underline *er* and *est.* Remind children that these describing words are used to compare two or more things. Complete *Practice Book* page 91 together.

High-Frequency Words

hello	**would**
about	**Mr.**

Fluency

Punctuation   Have children turn to "The Picnic Plan" in *Happy Landings* and track the print as you read aloud. Point out punctuation marks. Remind children to pause at a comma and stop at a period. Show how their voices should rise at the end of a question and how to express excitement when they see an exclamation point. Model reading fluently and have children echo-read.

LESSON 23

DAY AT A GLANCE
Day 2

30+ Minutes

PHONEMIC AWARENESS
Phoneme Blending

PHONICS AND SPELLING
Reteach Long Vowel /ō/o-e

HIGH-FREQUENCY WORDS
Reteach brown, hello, loudly, city, love, pulled, about, would, Mr.

FLUENCY
Punctuation

READING
"School Day"

BUILD ROBUST VOCABULARY
Preteach congenial, congregate, cheerful

GRAMMAR/WRITING
Reteach Describing Words: -er and -est

Materials Needed:

Word Builders and Word Builder Cards | Practice Book | Lesson 23 High-Frequency Word Cards

Practice Book p.92

Copying Masters 89–90

Happy Landings Student Edition pp. 26–32 pp. 46–53

High-Frequency Words

brown	pulled
hello	about
loudly	would
city	Mr.
love	

Phonemic Awareness

Phoneme Blending   Tell children they are going to play a guessing game. Then say: **I'm thinking of a word that names something you wear over pajamas. It is /r/ /ō/ /b/. What's my word? The word is** robe. **Now you try.** Continue with clues for the words: /h/ /ō/ /m/ (home), /r/ /ō/ /p/ (rope), /n/ /ō/ /z/ (nose), /n/ /ō/ /t/ (note), /k/ /ō/ /n/ (cone).

RETEACH

Phonics and Spelling

Long Vowel /ō/o-e
   Word Building   Use a Word Builder and Word Builder Cards and have children repeat each step after you. Build the word mop and have children read it. Point out the spelling pattern and the short o vowel sound. Add e to mop to form mope. Ask children what this spelling pattern tells about the vowel sound. (The final e is "silent." It is a clue that the o will probably stand for the long o sound.) Then have children read the word.

Have children build and read the following words: hop, hope, not, note, rod, rode.

Practice Book p.92   **Read Words in Context**   Ask children to turn to Practice Book page 92. Read each sentence aloud and have children echo-read. Ask: **Where did Rose go?** (to the apple grove) **What did Rose do there?** (chose her apples and rode home) **Where did Rose put her cake?** (on the stove) **How did Rose test her cake to see if it was done?** (She poked a hole in it.) Guide children to underline words with /ō/.

RETEACH

High-Frequency Words

Copying Masters 89–90   Display the High-Frequency Word Cards for brown, hello, loudly, city, love, pulled, about, would, and Mr. Point to each card and read the word. Have children repeat. Distribute cards to children. Then point to the High-Frequency Word Card for brown, say the word, and have children hold up the matching card. Repeat with the remaining words and continue the activity until children respond quickly and accurately.

Reading

pp. 46–53

Build Background: "School Day"

Read the title with children. Ask children to recall their first day of school. Talk about how they felt, how they got ready, and what it was like to be back in school again. Tell children they will be reading about one boy's first day of school.

Monitor Comprehension: "School Day"

Have children turn to the first page of the story. Ask a volunteer to reread the title. Ask children to look at the picture on page 46 and think about what the selection will be about and what the character is doing. Guide children through the story as they read.

pp. 46–47

Say: **I see a boy just first waking up. Let's read to find out what he needs to get ready to do.**

After reading the pages, ask: **Who is this boy? Frame and read his name.** (*Cole*) CHARACTERS/APPLY PHONICS

Ask: **Why does Cole have to get out of bed?** (It is time to get up.) NOTE DETAILS

Ask: **What does Cole do after he is up?** (He eats breakfast.) **What does Cole eat for breakfast?** (toast and eggs) SEQUENCE/NOTE DETAILS

Ask: **Do you think Cole has any brothers or sisters? Why do you think this?** (Possible response: No, because he is the only child eating with his parents.) DRAW CONCLUSIONS

pp. 48–49

Say: **We see Cole leaving for school. Let's read to see what he finds out when he gets there.**

After reading the pages, ask: **How does Cole get to school?** (on a school bus) **Who is Mr. Mills?** (the bus driver) NOTE DETAILS/CHARACTER

Ask: **What does Cole discover he likes once school begins?** (He likes art and math.) NOTE DETAILS

Ask: **What did Cole learn in math that day?** (how to add numbers) NOTE DETAILS

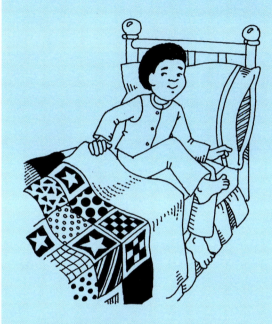

Fluency

Punctuation Read aloud the first few pages of "Max Is Missing!" ignoring all punctuation marks. Ask children if they noticed anything different about your reading. Then read the pages normally, with attention to punctuation.

Explain that good readers pay attention to commas, periods, question marks, and exclamation marks. These marks signal when to pause, stop, or change the sound of your voice. Have children follow your model to echo-read each sentence paying close attention to punctuation.

pp. 50–51

Say: **Cole seems to have made a new friend. Let's read to find out who it is.**

After reading the pages, ask: **Who does Cole sit next to at lunch? Frame and read the name.** (*Hope*) **CHARACTERS/APPLY PHONICS**

What kind of girl is Hope? (friendly, happy) **Why do you think so?** (She smiles and likes to tell jokes.) **DRAW CONCLUSIONS**

Ask: **What does Cole do after lunch?** (He reads a book.) **Does Cole's classmate seem interested in the book too? How do you know?** (Yes, because he is looking at it too.) **NOTE DETAILS/** **DRAW CONCLUSIONS**

Ask: **What kinds of things has Cole done in school today?** (art, math, read a book) **SUMMARIZE**

 page 52

Say: **Cole is waving to his friends and the school bus is there. I wonder what time of the day it is. Let's read to find out.**

Ask: **What time do you think it is now?** (Possible response: It's time to go home.) **MAKE PREDICTIONS**

After reading the page, ask: **What time it is now?** (It is time to go home.) **CONFIRM PREDICTIONS**

Ask: **Why does Cole feel fine about going home?** (because he knew he would be back again the next day) **CHARACTER'S MOTIVATIONS**

Ask: **Do you think Cole liked school? Give a reason for your answer.** (Possible response: Yes, because he looked happy all day long. He liked what he did and he was glad to be going back again.) **MAKE JUDGMENTS**

 page 53

Answers to *Think Critically* Questions

Help children read and answer the *Think Critically* questions on page 53. Answers are shown below.

1. ‹*bats*› **MAKE INFERENCES**
2. ‹*said hello*› **DRAW CONCLUSIONS**
 3. ‹*got up*› **SEQUENCE**

PRETEACH
Build Robust Vocabulary

Introduce Robust Vocabulary   Read the student-friendly explanation for each word. Then discuss each word using the following examples.

Say: **Would you act congenial toward a neighbor if you smiled and said hello or if you turned the other way and did not speak?**

Say: **Some students congregate at the swings on the playground. What is a place your friends like to congregrate?**

Say: **I feel cheerful after reading a funny book. Would you be more cheerful on a sunny day or on a rainy day? Explain.**

RETEACH
Grammar/Writing

Describing Words: *-er* and *-est*   Write this advertisement on the board:

> The Whirl and Twirl is the fastest spinning toy.
> It's faster than the older Spin Around and
> smaller and easier to use.
> For the greatest fun you'll ever have, buy
> one today!

Read aloud each sentence as you track the print. Ask children how many toys are being compared. (two) Then guide them to identify describing words with *-er* and *-est*. (*fastest, faster, older, smaller, easier, greatest*) Invite children to add a few more ideas to the ad using words with *-er* or *-est*, such as *cheaper, cheapest, newer, newest, quicker, quicker, brighter, brightest* .

VOCABULARY
Student-Friendly Explanations

congenial   A congenial person is very nice and friendly.

congregate   When people congregate at a place, they gather there and spend time there.

cheerful   When you are happy and smiling, people say you are cheerful.

PHONEMIC AWARENESS
Phoneme Segmentation

PHONICS
Preteach Phonograms -ose, -oke

PHONICS AND SPELLING
Reteach Long Vowel /ō/o-e

HIGH-FREQUENCY WORDS
Reteach hello, about, would, Mr.

FLUENCY
Punctuation

COMPREHENSION
Reteach Draw Conclusions

GRAMMAR/WRITING
Reteach Descriptive Poem

Materials Needed:

Write-On/ Wipe-Off Boards with Phonemic Awareness Disks

Word Builders and Word Builder Cards

Happy Landings Student Edition pp. 46–52

Copying Masters 91–92

Lesson 23 Story Strips

Spelling Words

1. home	6. those
2. hope	7. like
3. rope	8. nine
4. rode	9. right
5. rose	10. walk

Phonemic Awareness

 Phoneme Segmentation Have children use the three boxes on the *Write-on/Wipe-off Boards*. Remind children that the boxes stand for sounds in words. Show *Photo Card rose* and ask: **What is the first sound in *rose*? It is /r/.** Have children place a disk in the first box along with you. Have them name the second sound in *rose* (/ō/) and place a disk in the second box. Then have them identify the last sound in *rose* (/z/) and place a disk in the third box. Point to each box in sequence as children say the word. **How many sounds do you hear in *rose*? I hear three.** Repeat with the *Photo Cards road, cake, ice, snow, toad, queen, rain.*

PRETEACH

Phonics

Phonograms -ose, -oke Display these words and read them with children: *rose, nose, hose.* Ask: **How are the words the same?** (They all end in -ose; they rhyme.) Underline -ose and say: **At the end of a word, -ose can be pronounced /ōz/ or /ōs/.** Point to *close* and say the word with each pronunciation. Display and read *smoke, poke, woke.* Ask: **How are the words the same?** (They all end in -oke; they rhyme.) Underline -oke and say: **At the end of a word, -oke is pronounced /ōk/.** Guide children to write words with -ose and -oke. Read the words together.

RETEACH

Phonics and Spelling

 **Long Vowel /ō/o-e**
Build Words Use *Word Builders* and *Word Builder Cards* to form words. Have children listen to your directions and change letters in each word to spell a spelling word. Form *home* and have children read the word. Ask: **Which spelling word can you make by changing *m* to *p*?** (*hope*)

h	o	m	e

Follow a similar procedure with the following words: *hope* (*rope*), *rope* (*rode*), *rode* (*rose*), *rose* (*those*), *Mike* (*like*), *fine* (*nine*).

h	o	p	e

Remind children that there are some other words they have to remember how to spell. Have children say *right*. Have them put *Word Builder Cards r, i, g, h, t* in their *Word Builders,* picture the word *right* in their minds, and build the word. Write the word on the board. Follow the same procedure with *walk.*

RETEACH
High-Frequency Words

 Duplicate and distribute *Copying Masters* 91–92 to each child. Explain that the sentences tell about the story "School Day" but some have missing words.

List the words *hello, about, would,* and *Mr.* on the board. Have children read aloud each story strip sentence and name the correct word on the board that makes sense in the sentence. Have children write the missing words in the blanks and read the completed sentences aloud. Help children cut apart the strips, read the completed sentences, and arrange them in story order.

RETEACH
Comprehension

 Draw Conclusions Review with children that writers do not always include every detail. Readers use clues from the story and what they already know to better understand a story. Have children reread "School Day" in *Happy Landings*. Ask: **How do you know Cole and Hope are friends?** (They eat together. They are laughing and smiling so they look like they like being together. Cole says good-bye to Hope at the end of the day. If I like someone, I spend time with that person.) Then ask: **What makes you think Cole likes school?** (He liked the things he learned, he made new friends, he looks happy to go back again the next day. If I like school, I want to go back too.)

RETEACH
Grammar/Writing

Descriptive Poem Write the following poem on the board and read it aloud.

> A black-and-white face peeks through the branches of a tree.
>
> I stand very still so he won't see me.
>
> He chews and chews, munch, crunch, munch, crunch.
>
> Eating sticks of bamboo for his lunch.
>
> Round, chunky panda happy as can be.

Explain to children that this is a descriptive poem, a poem that gives details about a subject. Talk about the words used to describe the panda and explain that descriptive poems use words that tell about the subject's size, shape, color, smell, or texture. Ask: **What words describe the way the panda looks?** (*black-and-white, round, chunky*) **How does the panda act?** (*happy*) **What sound words tell what is heard?** (*crunch, munch*)

High-Frequency Words

hello	would
about	Mr.

Fluency

Punctuation Guide children to understand that good readers use capitalization and punctuation to understand what they read. They stop at a period. Their voice rises at the end of a question. They read with emotion when they see an exclamation point.

Model how to read sentences, questions, and exclamations. Then have children turn to "School Day" in *Happy Landings* and read the story with a partner. Offer feedback to help children improve their fluency.

LESSON 23

DAY AT A GLANCE

Day 4

30+ Minutes

PHONEMIC AWARENESS
Phoneme Blending

PHONICS
Reteach Phonograms -one, -ole

PHONICS AND SPELLING
Reteach Long Vowel /ō/o-e

HIGH-FREQUENCY WORDS
Reteach brown, hello, loudly, city, love, pulled, about, would, Mr.

FLUENCY
Punctuation

COMPREHENSION
Reteach Draw Conclusions

GRAMMAR/WRITING
Reteach Descriptive Poem

Materials Needed:

Practice Book

Lesson 23 High-Frequency Word Cards

Happy Landings Student Edition pp. 36–42 pp. 46–52

Photo Cards

Spelling Words

1. home	6. those
2. hope	7. like
3. rope	8. nine
4. rode	9. right
5. rose	10. walk

RETEACH

Phonemic Awareness

Phoneme Blending   Tell children that they are going to play a game of "Fix It." Tell them you are going to say some picture names that are broken and they will put together sounds to figure out the picture names. Display *Photo Cards rose, road, cake, rain, stage, bug,* and *snow.* Say: **What picture name does /r/ /ō/ /z/ say? /r/ /ō/ /z/ says *rose.* Now you try.** Continue with: /s/ /t/ /ā/ /j/ (*stage*), /r/ /ō/ /d/ (*road*), /b/ /u/ /g/ (*bug*), /k/ /ā/ /k/ (*cake*), /s/ /n/ /ō/ (*snow*), /r/ /ā / /n/ (*rain*).

RETEACH

Phonics

Phonograms -*one*, -*ole*   Tell children that word families help them read words. Then write the following words on the board: *cone, stone, phone.* Read the words and have children repeat. Ask: **How are the words the same?** (They all end in -*one*; they rhyme.) Say: **In these words, the letters *o-n-e* are pronounced /ōn/.** Then write: *mole, hole, stole.* Ask: **How are the words the same?** (They all end in -*ole*; they rhyme.) Say: **In these words, the letters *o-l-e* are pronounced /ōl/.** Display a two-column chart with the headings -*one* and -*ole.* Have children add beginning sounds to the phonograms to create words.

RETEACH

Phonics and Spelling

Practice Book p.93

Long Vowel /ō/o-e

Direct children's attention to page 93 of their *Practice Books.* Complete the page together.

Assess children's progress using the following sentences.

1. home   I go to Gramp's **home** each summer.
2. hope   I **hope** we can go fishing this year.
3. rope   Gramp made me a **rope** swing.
4. rode   We **rode** in a hay wagon.
5. rose   Latrice has a big **rose** garden.
6. those   **Those** are Gram's favorite flowers.

Review

7. like   I **like** going to Gramp's.
8. nine   He has **nine** cows.

High-Frequency

9. right   The barn is **right** by the house.
10. walk   We **walk** there to feed and milk the cows.

RETEACH
High-Frequency Words

Copying Masters 89–90

Display *High-Frequency Word Cards* for this lesson's words—*brown, hello, loudly, city, loved, pulled, about, would, Mr.,* and previously-learned high-frequency words. Point to words at random and ask children to read them.

RETEACH
Comprehension

Draw Conclusions   Ask children what they do when they draw a conclusion. (figure something out using clues in a story and what I already know) Draw a chart like the one below. Model drawing a conclusion about something in "The Picnic Plan" and write it on the chart. Then have children do a picture walk through "School Day" in *Happy Landings*. Ask volunteers to suggest what to write. Record their responses on the chart.

Title	Conclusion	Clues/What I know
"The Picnic Plan"	The squirrels took the food for the picnic.	the food was missing no one was around except for the squirrels
"School Day"		

RETEACH
Grammar/Writing

Descriptive Poem   Review with children the characteristics of a descriptive poem.

Descriptive Poem

Gives details about the subject.
Uses words that tell about the subject's size shape, color, smell, and texture.
Creates pictures in readers' minds.

Invite children to think of an animal they would like to describe in a poem. Have them help you write a poem about it, using as many describing words as possible. Read the poem together.

High-Frequency Words

brown	pulled
hello	about
loudly	would
city	Mr.
love	

Fluency

Punctuation   Have children work with partners to take turns reading pages from "School Day" in *Happy Landings*. Remind them to pay attention to the different types of punctuation as they read and to use expression to sound like the characters talking. Listen to partners read and provide feedback and support. Invite groups to read the story to the class.

30+ Minutes

DAY AT A GLANCE

Day 5

HIGH-FREQUENCY WORDS
brown, hello, loudly, city, love, pulled

PHONEMIC AWARENESS
Onset and Rime

PHONICS AND SPELLING
Preteach Consonants /s/*c;* /j/*g, dge*

BUILD ROBUST VOCABULARY
Preteach *pleased, joy, stammered*

GRAMMAR/WRITING
Preteach Troublesome Words: Multiple Meaning Words

Materials Needed:

Lesson 23 High-Frequency Word Cards

Sound/ Spelling Cards *Ss, Jj*

Word Builders and Word Builder Cards

Write-On/ Wipe-Off Boards

Practice Book
p.94

Practice Book

Happy Landings Student Edition p. 51

High-Frequency Words

brown	city
hello	love
loudly	pulled

High-Frequency Words

 Display *High-Frequency Word Cards* for *brown, hello, loudly, city, love, pulled,* and the other previously learned high-frequency words. Say the word *brown,* ask a volunteer to point to *brown,* and have children read the word aloud. Continue with the remaining high-frequency words. Repeat this activity several times to reinforce instant recognition.

Phonemic Awareness

Onset and Rime   Tell children that you are going to say some words, but you are going to say them in parts. Have children listen to see if they can figure out the word. Demonstrate by saying: **/m/-ice—The word I said was** *mice.* **Now you try some: /f/-ace, /br/-idge, /h/-edge, /b/-adge, /r/-ace, /n/-ice.**

PRETEACH

Phonics and Spelling

 Consonants /s/*c;* /j/*g, dge*
Connecting Letter to Sound   Say the words *rice, cent,* and *brace.* Say: **These words have the same sound—/s/ In these words, this sound is called soft** *c.* Have children say /s/ several times. Say the words *ledge, bridge,* and *cage.* Ask: **What sound is the same in all these words?** (/j/) **This sound is called soft** *g.* Have children say /j/ several times.

Display *Sound/Spelling Card Ss,* say the letter name, and identify the picture. Remind children that the letter *s* usually stands for the /s/ sound. Then point to the *ce* and *ci* and explain that when the letter *c* is followed by an *e* or an *i* it can stand for the /s/ sound. Explain that this sound is called the "soft c sound." Have children say /s/ several times as you touch the letters *ce* and *ci.*

Display *Sound/Spelling Card Jj,* say the letter name, and identify the picture. Remind children that the letter *j* usually stands for the /j/ sound. Then follow the same procedure to introduce the "soft g sound."

Word Blending   Demonstrate each step with *Word Builder Cards* and a *Word Builder* and have children repeat each step after you. Hold up *r* and say /r/. Hold up *a* and say /ā/. Hold up *c* and say /s/. Now add an *e.* Read the word: *race.* Remind children that this final *e* is silent. It tells you that the *a* in *race* is a long *a.*

- Place the letters *r, a, c, e* in the *Word Builder.*
- Point to *r.* Say /r/. Point to *a* and say /ā/. Prompt children to repeat.

- Slide *a* next to *r.* Run your hand under the letters as you blend the sounds, elongating them—/rā/. Have children repeat.

- Point to *c* and say /s/. Prompt children to repeat after you.

- Slide *c* next to *ra*. Then add *e* at the end. Run your hand under *race* as you blend the sounds by elongating them: /rās/. Have children repeat.

- Read *race* naturally.

Follow the same procedure with these words: *rice, edge, face*.

  Word Building   Place the *Word Builder Cards i, c,* and *e* in the *Word Builder* and model how to blend *ice*. Slide your hand under the letters as you slowly blend the sounds—/īs/. Then read the word naturally—*ice*. Have children build and read new words. As they build each word, write it on the board. Say:

- **Add an *n* to the beginning of *ice*. What word is it?** (*nice*)

- **Change *n* to *r* and change *i* to *a*. What word is it?** (*race*)

Continue with the words *page, large,* and *edge*. Direct children's attention to page 94 of their *Practice Books*. Complete the page together.

PRETEACH

Build Robust Vocabulary

Introduce Robust Vocabulary   Read the student-friendly explanation for each word. Then discuss each word using the following examples.

Say: **I was pleased when I finished my painting. I liked it. Tell about a time when you were pleased with something.**

Say: **You might feel joy if you see a friend you have not seen for a long time. What else makes you feel joy?**

Say: **Once when I was very excited I stammered when I tried to talk and my friends didn't understand me. Have you ever stammered? When?**

PRETEACH

Grammar/Writing

Troublesome Words: Multiple Meaning Words   Tell children that they will be learning about words with more than one meaning. Read aloud and show page 51 of "School Day" in *Happy Landings*: ***Cole chose a book about bats.*** Ask children what a bat is in this sentence. (an animal) Then write this sentence on the board. *I play with a bat and ball.* Elicit from children that in this sentence *bat* means something you play ball with. Then write these words on the board: *left, sink, tag, well*. Guide children to take turns using the words in sentences to show their different meanings.

Spelling Words

1. ice	6. large
2. nice	7. home
3. race	8. those
4. page	9. love
5. edge	10. hello

 Have children practice writing spelling words on their *Write-on/Wipe-off Boards.*

VOCABULARY

Student-Friendly Explanations

pleased   When you are pleased with something, you are happy with it.

joy   When you feel joy, you feel very happy.

stammered   If I stammered, I had a hard time speaking. I kept stopping and repeating the same sounds without even knowing it.

LESSON 24

Day at a Glance

PHONEMIC AWARENESS
Phoneme Isolation

PHONICS AND SPELLING
Reteach Consonants /s/c; /j/g, dge

COMPREHENSION
Reteach Draw Conclusions

HIGH-FREQUENCY WORDS
Guided Practice talk, listen, were, four

FLUENCY
Punctuation

GRAMMAR/WRITING
Reteach Troublesome words: Multiple Meaning Words

Materials Needed:

Word Builders and Word Builder Cards

Write-On/ Wipe-Off Boards

Practice Book p.95

Practice Book

Shooting Star Student Edition pp. 56–62

Happy Landings Student Edition pp. 46–52 pp. 54–55

Spelling Words

1. ice	6. large
2. nice	7. home
3. race	8. those
4. page	9. love
5. edge	10. hello

 Have children practice writing spelling words on their *Write-on/Wipe-off Boards*.

Phonemic Awareness

Phoneme Isolation Say the word *page* aloud and have children repeat it. Tell children to listen to the /j/ **sound at the end of *page*.** Then say the words *rack* and *edge*. Ask: **Which of these words has the /j/ sound you hear at the end of *page*? I hear it in *edge*.** Continue with: *cage, hedge, sing; bridge, budge, berries; ice, race, clue; huge, giant, night.*

RETEACH

Phonics and Spelling

 Consonants /s/c; /j/g, dge
Word Building Place the *Word Builder Cards i, c, e* in the *Word Builder*. Ask children to say the name and sound of each letter. Then read the word naturally—*ice.* Have children do the same. Ask:

- **Which letter should I add to *ice* to make *nice*?** (*n*)
- **Which letters should I change to make *nice* become *race*?** (Change *n* to *r* and *i* to *a*.)

i c e

n i c e

r a c e

Continue with *page, edge,* and *large.* Have children repeat each step after you and then read the words.

Read Words in Context Write the following sentences on chart paper. Have children read each sentence silently. Then track the print as children read the sentence aloud. *His home is nice. Is there ice in that glass? I will race you to the large rock. Let me say hello to them. You can hold the edge of the page to tell your place. I love those cats!*

RETEACH

Comprehension

 Draw Conclusions Tell children that an author may not always tell every detail in a story. Readers can use clues in the story to draw conclusions and fill in missing pieces of information. Read aloud this excerpt from "School Day" in *Happy Landings.* Say: **It was time to go home. But that was fine. Cole would be back at school the next day.** Explain that a reader could draw the conclusion that Cole likes school, because he is happy knowing he will be back the next day. Read this passage from "School Day" in *Happy Landings: Cole said hello to Mr. Mills. Then he got on the bus.* Ask what students can conclude about how Cole gets to school from what they read. (Cole gets to school by bus.)

RETEACH

High-Frequency Words

pp. 54–55

Write the words *talk, listen, were,* and *four* on the board.

- Point to and read *talk.* Repeat, having children say *talk* with you.
- Say: **I *talk* softly in the library.**
- Repeat the word and then point to each letter as you spell it. Then have children say and spell *talk* with you. Have children reread the word.

Repeat for the remaining words. Use the following sentences: Were *there toys in the box? I will* listen *to Mrs. Jackson. We have* four *balls.*

Have children turn to page 54 of *Happy Landings* and have them read aloud the words at the top of the page. Talk about the illustrations. Then guide children in choosing and writing the word that names each picture. (4. *page,* 5. *bridge,* 6. *race*) Have children read aloud each word in the list on page 55. Ask volunteers to read the sentences aloud. Then have children choral-read the sentences. Guide them to choose and circle the word that completes each sentence. (I. *were,* 2. *talk,* 3. *Listen,* 4, *four*)

RETEACH

Grammar/Writing

Practice Book p.95

Troublesome Words: Multiple Meaning Words   Tell children that they will listen to sentences with words that have more than one meaning. Say: **Listen to the word *bank* in these sentences. We sat on the *bank* of the river. Take your money to the *bank*.** Explain the meaning of the word *bank* in each sentence using context clues. Say: **A *bank* of a river is the side of the river. A *bank* is also a place to put money.** Then write these sentences on the board: *We play with blocks. The bed blocks the window.* Ask volunteers to tell the meaning of *blocks* in each sentence, explaining how he or she used context clues. (*Blocks* are a toy in the first sentence, since we play with them. *Blocks* means to be in the way in the second sentence.) Then complete *Practice Book* page 95 together.

High-Frequency Words

talk	were
listen	four

Fluency

Punctuation   Have children open to page 60 of "The Water Dish" in *Shooting Star* and track the print as you read: **Splash! She could drop shells in!** Remind children that an exclamation point is used to show strong feeling. Read the line with expression. Read aloud the story, one page at a time, and model responding to punctuation. Have children echo-read.

PHONEMIC AWARENESS
Phoneme Blending

PHONICS AND SPELLING
Reteach Consonants /s/c; /j/g, dge

HIGH-FREQUENCY WORDS
Reteach eyes, listen, visitor, remembered, become, talk, busy, high, were, four

FLUENCY
Punctuation

READING
"Under a Bridge"

BUILD ROBUST VOCABULARY
Preteach puzzling, probing, unrelenting

GRAMMAR/WRITING
Reteach Troublesome Words: Multiple Meaning Words

Materials Needed:

Word Builders and Word Builder Cards

Practice Book p.96
Practice Book

Copying Masters 93–94
Lesson 24 High-Frequency Word Cards

Shooting Star Student Edition pp. 36–42

Happy Landings Student Edition pp. 56–63

High-Frequency Words

eyes	talk
listen	busy
visitor	high
remembered	were
become	four

30+ Minutes

Phonemic Awareness

Phoneme Blending   Tell children that they are going to be detectives and use clues to find the word you have in mind. Then say: **I'm thinking of a word that means a sweet treat to eat. It is /f/ /u/ /j/. My word is** *fudge.* Continue with the following words: /b/ /r/ /i/ /j/ (*bridge*), /m/ /ī/ /s/ (*mice*), /b/ /a/ /j/ (*badge*), /k/ /ā/ /j/ (*cage*).

Phonics and Spelling

Consonants /s/c; /j/g, dge
Word Building   Use a *Word Builder* and *Word Builder Cards* and have children repeat each step after you. Build the word *ice.* Have children read the word naturally—*ice.* Lead children in building and reading new words. Say:

- **Add r before i. Read the word.** (*rice*)
- **Change i to a. Read the word.** (*race*)
- **Change r to l. Read the word.** (*lace*)

Continue in a similar manner to have children build and read these words: *edge, hedge.*

When building words with *dge,* point out that *dge* also has the sound of /j/. The vowel before *dge* has a short vowel sound.

Read Words in Context   Ask children to turn to *Practice Book* page 96. Read each sentence aloud and have children echo-read. Then ask volunteers to read each sentence aloud. Ask: **Where are the children?** (on a bridge) **Why do they stay by the edge?** (There is no ice there.) **Where will they rest?** (over the bridge) **What will they do next?** (race to the huge ridge) Then, guide children to underline words that have the soft *c* sound and circle words with the soft *g* sound.

High-Frequency Words

Copying Masters 93–94   Write the words *eyes, listen, visitor, remembered, become, talk, busy, high, were,* and *four* on the board. Give each child a set of *High-Frequency Word Cards* and have children spread the cards out in front of them. Read the following sentence and have children hold up the card that completes the sentence. *I like to _____ when she sings.* (*listen*) Compose a sentence for each word and read the sentence without the word, pausing for children to hold up the card that completes the sentence.

Reading

pp. 56–63

Build Background: "Under a Bridge"

Read the title with children. Ask if children have ever heard an echo under a bridge, in a tunnel, or in a cave. Ask children to tell what the echo sounded like. Tell children that they will be reading about friends who hear echoes.

Monitor Comprehension: "Under a Bridge"

Have children turn to the first page of the story. Ask a volunteer to reread the title. Guide children to look at the pictures on pages 56 and 57 and ask children what they think will happen. Then guide children through the story as they read.

pp. 56–57

Say: **I can see two children on these pages. Let's read to find out what they are doing.**

After reading the pages, ask: **What are the children doing?** (The children are talking to a bridge.) **Note Details**

Ask: **Where are the children?** (under a bridge) **Setting**

Ask: **Why is the bridge saying "Hello!" back?** (Possible response: The bridge is making an echo.) 🔵 **Draw Conclusions**

Ask: **Which word on these pages has the soft *c* sound?** (*Grace*) **Which word on these pages has the soft *g* sound?** (*bridge*) **Apply Phonics**

pp. 58–59

Say: **We found out what the children are doing under the bridge. Let's read on to find out what they'll do next.**

After reading the pages, ask: **How many children are there now? Who do you think the new children are?** (There are four children. Possible response: The new children are friends of the other children.) **Characters**/ 🔵 **Draw Conclusions**

Ask: **How does James show the bridge can talk?** (He yells, "Hello!") **Note Details**

Fluency

Punctuation Have children open to "Ben" in *Shooting Star* and invite a volunteer to name the end punctuation for each sentence. Guide children to recognize how readers use punctuation to comprehend. Explain that when readers see an exclamation mark they should read with strong feeling.

Model reading *"Your legs are so strong, Ben!"* with expression. Remind children to look at the end punctuation to help them figure out how to read each sentence. Have children choral-read "Ben" with expression. After they read, provide feedback and encouragement.

Ask: **What word on these pages has the soft _g_ sound?** (_bridge_) APPLY PHONICS

 Say: **Let's read on to find out what will happen next under the bridge.**

After reading the pages, ask: **What do the children under the bridge do now?** (They start to sing.) NOTE DETAILS

Ask: **What happens when Roger and the children sing?** (They hear singing coming back from under the bridge.) CAUSE AND EFFECT

Ask: **Who is singing back? How do you know?** (A dog is singing back. I see him in the picture.) DRAW CONCLUSIONS

Say: **What has happened in the story so far?** (Possible response: Some children are making echoes under a bridge, then two more children come and do it, too. Next, two more children come and start singing. They hear someone sing back.) SUMMARIZE

Ask: **Which child has a name with the soft _g_ sound?** (Roger) APPLY PHONICS

 Say: **The children say someone is singing back. Let's read on to find out more.**

After reading the page, ask: **Who is singing back to the children?** (the dog) NOTE DETAILS

Ask: **Do you think the children believe that the bridge is really singing?** (Possible response: No, they are pretending that the bridge is singing.) PERSONAL RESPONSE

 Answers to _Think Critically_ Questions

Help children read and answer the _Think Critically_ questions on page 63. Answers are shown below.

1. ‹_the bridge_› NOTE DETAILS

2. ‹_a dog sings back_› PLOT

 3. ‹_an echo_› DRAW CONCLUSIONS

PRETEACH

Build Robust Vocabulary

Introduce Robust Vocabulary   Read the student-friendly explanation for each word. Then discuss each word using the following examples.

Say: **The math problem was puzzling and I couldn't figure it out. Tell about a time something puzzled you.**

Say: **I was probing for answers when I wrote a research report. Would you probe about sports or about music? Why?**

Say: **Someone who is unrelenting doesn't give up. Which of these is unrelenting: the person who kept digging a hole or the person who stopped digging the hole when it got hot outside?**

RETEACH

Grammar/Writing

Troublesome Words: Multiple Meaning Words   Remind children that the same word can have different meanings, depending on how it is used in a sentence. Work with children to dictate sentences about things they do outside. Write the following multiple-meaning words on the board and guide children to include them in their sentences:

> fish, land, pet, park, trip

Then guide children to explain the different meanings of the words in their sentences.

VOCABULARY

Student-Friendly Explanations

puzzling   When something is puzzling, it is confusing.

probing   When you are probing, you are searching for answers.

unrelenting   When you are unrelenting, you do not give up until you do what you wanted to do.

DAY AT A GLANCE
Day 3

PHONEMIC AWARENESS
Phoneme Segmentation

PHONICS
Preteach Contractions *'s, n't, 'll*

PHONICS AND SPELLING
Reteach Consonants /s/*c*; /j/*g, dge*

HIGH-FREQUENCY WORDS
Reteach *talk, listen, were, four*

FLUENCY
Punctuation

COMPREHENSION
Reteach Draw Conclusions

GRAMMAR/WRITING
Reteach Rhyming Poem

Materials Needed:

Write-On/
Wipe-Off
Boards with
Phonemic
Awareness
Disks

Photo
Cards

Word Builders
and Word
Builder Cards

Copying
Masters
95–96

Lesson 24
Story Strips

Shooting Star
Student Edition
pp. 56–62

Happy Landings
Student Edition
pp. 56–62

Spelling Words

1. ice	6. large
2. nice	7. home
3. race	8. those
4. page	9. love
5. edge	10. hello

30+ Minutes

Phonemic Awareness

Phoneme Segmentation   Distribute the four-box papers to children. Tell them that the boxes stand for sounds in words. Display *Photo Card stage* and say: **Listen as I say this word:** *stage*. **The first sound I hear is /s/, so I place a disk in the first box. The next sound in *stage* I hear is /t/, so I put a disk in the second box. The next sound in stage is /ā/, so I put a disk in the third box. The last sound I hear is /j/, so I put a disk in the fourth box. I hear four sounds in *stage*.** Follow the procedure with the *Photo Cards lunch, bridge, gift,* and *school*.

PRETEACH

Phonics

Contractions *'s, n't, 'll*   Display and say these sentences: *She's set to go. We can't wait. He'll stay home.* Ask: **How are the underlined words the same?** (They are contractions.) **A contraction is a shorter way of saying two words. Let's say these sentences again, replacing the contractions with the words they represent.** (*She is set to go. We can not wait. He will stay home.*) Write and read the sentences below. Guide children to underline each contraction and name the words it stands for. *We'll jog with her. You'll get dressed. We can't go that way. He's on the bus.*

RETEACH

Phonics and Spelling

Consonants /s/*c*; /j/*g, dge*
Build Words   Use *Word Builders* and *Word Builder Cards* to form words. Have children listen to your directions and change one letter in each word to spell a spelling word. Form *mice* in the *Word Builder* and have children read it. Ask: **Which spelling word can you make by taking away a letter?** (*ice*)

Follow a similar procedure with the following words: *rage* (*race*), *pace* (*page*), *nine* (*nice*), *hedge* (*edge*), *charge* (*large*), *hose* (*home*), *nose* (*those*).

Remind children that there are some other words they have to remember how to spell. Tell children that *love* is one such word. Tell them to put *Word Builder Cards l, o, v, e* in their *Word Builders,* picture the word *love* in their minds, and build the word. Write the word on the board. Follow this procedure with the word *hello*.

RETEACH

High-Frequency Words

 Duplicate and distribute *Copying Masters 95–96* to each child. Explain that the sentences tell the story "Under a Bridge" but some have missing words.

List the words *talk, listen, were,* and *four* on the board. Have children read aloud each story strip sentence and name the correct word on the board that makes sense in the sentence. Have children write the missing words in the blanks and read the completed sentences aloud. Help children cut apart the strips, read the completed sentences, and arrange them in story order.

RETEACH

Comprehension

 Draw Conclusions   Review with children how to draw conclusions about a story. Explain that writers don't always tell us everything we need to know. We can use clues from the story. Figuring things out this way is called drawing conclusions. Have children turn to "The Water Dish" in *Shooting Star* and guide them to draw a conclusion about why the bird is interested in the water. (The bird is thirsty.) Then ask children to turn to page 60 and draw a conclusion about why the bird is putting shells into the glass. (She is trying to make the water high enough to drink.)

RETEACH

Grammar/Writing

Rhyming Poem   Write the following poem on the board and read it aloud:

Roses are red,
Violets are blue.
Sugar is sweet,
And so are you.

Ask children which words in the poem rhyme. (blue, you) Point out that this poem has four lines and there are rhyming words at the end of every other line. Explain that in rhyming poems, some lines end with rhyming words, it has a rhythm, and it is enjoyable to read and listen to. Have children experiment with changing the words, beginning with changing the rhyming words. For example, show how changing words can lead to this poem: *The wind is up, / the sky is blue. / We have a kite / to fly with you!*

High-Frequency Words

talk	were
listen	four

Fluency

Punctuation   Remind children that good readers pay attention to punctuation as they read. Have children turn to "Under a Bridge" in *Happy Landings*. Say: **I'm going to read "Under a Bridge" one page at a time. I'm going to pay attention to the punctuation. If I see a period, I will stop. If I see a comma, I will pause. I will use my voice to make it sound as if I'm talking. Read each page after me, just the way I read it.**

PHONEMIC AWARENESS
Phoneme Blending

PHONICS
Reteach Contractions *'s, n't, 'll*

PHONICS AND SPELLING
Reteach Consonants /s/*c*;
/j/*g, dge*

HIGH-FREQUENCY WORDS
Reteach *eyes, listen, visitor, remembered, become, talk, busy, high, were, four*

FLUENCY
Punctuation

COMPREHENSION
Reteach Draw Conclusions

GRAMMAR/WRITING
Reteach Rhyming Poem

Materials Needed:

Copying Masters 93–94	Practice Book p.97	
Lesson 24 High-Frequency Word Cards	Practice Book	*Happy Landings* Student Edition pp. 46–52 pp. 56–62

Spelling Words

1. ice	6. large
2. nice	7. home
3. race	8. those
4. page	9. love
5. edge	10. hello

Phonemic Awareness

Phoneme Blending   Tell children that together you are going to play a game of "Fix It." Tell them that you are going to say some words that are broken and they should listen to see if they can put them back together to figure out the word. Say: **Listen: /l/ /e/ /j/. What word does /l/ /e/ /j/ say? It says *ledge*. Now you try with these sounds:** /ī/ /s/ (*ice*), /b/ /u/ /j/ (*budge*), /r/ /ā/ /s/ (*race*), /b/ /r/ /i/ /j/ (*bridge*), /s/ /t/ /ā/ /j/ (*stage*).

RETEACH

Phonics

Contractions *'s, n't, 'll*   Display and say these sentences: *He is my dad.* *They will be here first. We will not eat that.* Say: **Let's replace the underlined words with contractions. Contractions are a shorter way to say or write two words.** Guide children to write the rephrased sentences. (*He's my dad.* *They'll be here first. We won't eat that.*)

RETEACH

Phonics and Spelling

Consonants /s/*c*; /j/*g, dge*
Direct children's attention to page 97 of their *Practice Books.* Complete the page together.

Assess children's progress using the following sentences.

1.	ice	Look at the **ice** on the lake.
2.	nice	It's a **nice** time of day.
3.	race	He wants to **race** me.
4.	page	We read that **page** of the book.
5.	edge	Stay away from the **edge**.
6.	large	That house is **large**.

Review

7.	home	I want to go **home** now.
8.	those	**Those** mittens are mine.

High-Frequency

9.	love	We **love** to run in the snow.
10.	hello	Can we say **hello** to them?

RETEACH

High-Frequency Words

Display *High-Frequency Word Cards* for this lesson's words—*eyes, listen, visitor, remembered, become, talk, busy, high, were,* and *four*—and the previously learned high-frequency words. Point to words at random and ask children to read them.

 **RETEACH**

Comprehension

Draw Conclusions   Ask children what they do when they draw a conclusion. (figure something out using clues in a story) Draw a chart on the board like the one below. Have children turn to "Under a Bridge" in *Happy Landings*. Discuss conclusions they drew from the story. Then do a picture walk with children through "School Day" in *Happy Landings*. Guide children to draw conclusions from the story and record their responses. Suggest that children look at the illustrations to help them draw conclusions.

	"Under a Bridge"	"School Day"
Conclusion	The bridge makes an echo.	Cole likes bats.
Clues I used	When they talk under the bridge, they hear what they say back.	In the library, he chooses a book about bats.

RETEACH

 ## Grammar/Writing

Rhyming Poem   Review with children the characteristics of a rhyming poem.

Rhyming Poem

Some lines end with rhyming words.

It has a title.

It has a rhythm.

It is enjoyable to read and listen to.

Tell children they are going to write a rhyming poem together. Display a variety of *Photo Cards* and have children choose one to write about. Then guide children through the steps of writing a rhyming poem with the characteristics you discussed above. Read the poem together and point out the characteristics.

High-Frequency Words

eyes	talk
listen	busy
visitor	high
remembered	were
become	four

Fluency

Punctuation   Remind children that good readers pay attention to punctuation as they read. They stop when they get to a period. Their voice rises at the end of a question. They read text within quotation marks as if someone were talking.

Model how to read dialogue, read questions, and read exclamations. Have partners read "Under a Bridge" in *Happy Landings* aloud three or four times. Remind them to look at punctuation for clues. Listen to partners read, giving them feedback about their expression and guidance for improving their fluency.

DAY AT A GLANCE
Day 5

HIGH-FREQUENCY WORDS
eyes, listen, visitor, remembered, become, talk, busy, high

PHONEMIC AWARENESS
Onset and Rime

PHONICS AND SPELLING
Preteach Long Vowel/(y) o͞o/u-e

BUILD ROBUST VOCABULARY
Preteach *deserve, usually, peaceful*

GRAMMAR/WRITING
Preteach Verbs

Materials Needed:

Lesson 24 High-Frequency Word Cards

Sound/ Spelling Card *Uu*

Word Builders and Word Builder Cards

Photo Cards

Write-On/ Wipe-Off Boards

Practice Book

Happy Landings Student Edition pp. 6–12

High-Frequency Words

eyes	become
listen	talk
visitor	busy
remembered	high

High-Frequency Words

Display *High-Frequency Word Cards* for *eyes, listen, visitor, remembered, become, talk, busy, high,* and the other previously learned high-frequency words. Say the word *eyes,* ask a volunteer to point to *eyes,* and have children read the word aloud. Continue with the remaining high-frequency words. Repeat this activity several times to reinforce instant recognition.

Phonemic Awareness

Onset and Rime   Have children name the words as you say them in parts. Model the first one. **Listen as I say this word in parts /k/-ute—The word I said was *cute*. Now you try some: /t/-ube, /t/-une, /d/-uke, /h/-uge, /k/-ube, /r/-ule, /d/-ude, /m/-ule.**

PRETEACH

Phonics and Spelling

Long Vowel /yo͞o/u-e
Connecting Letter to Sound   Say the words *unit, unique,* and *universe* and have children repeat the words. Explain that all three words begin with the /yo͞o/ sound. Have children say /yo͞o/ several times. Display *Sound/Spelling Card Uu.* Say the letter name and point to *u-e.* Tell children the letter *u* can stand for the sound /yo͞o/, the sound at the beginning of *unit.* It can also stand for the /o͞o/ sound in the middle of words such as *flute* and *rude.* Have children repeat the sound several times as you touch *u-e* on the card. Give each child a *u* *Word Builder Card.* Say: **When I say a word that begins with /yo͞o/ or /o͞o/, hold up your card and say the sound. When I say a word that does not begin with /yo͞o/ or /o͞o/, hold the card behind your back.** Say these words: *use, ate, eat, unicorn, useful, oak.* Tell children that some words have the /yo͞o/ or /o͞o/ sound in the middle. Show *Photo Card cube* and say *cube,* elongating the /yo͞o/ sound. Tell children that *cube* has /yo͞o/ in the middle. Follow the same procedure for the medial position with the following words: *cute, bun, rule, hut, tube, mule.*

Word Blending   Demonstrate each step with *Word Builder Cards* and a *Word Builder* and have children repeat each step after you. Hold up *c* and say /k/. Hold up *u* and say /u/. Hold up *b* and say /b/.

- Place the letters *c, u, b* in the *Word Builder.*
- Point to *c.* Say /k/. Point to *u* and say /u/. Point to *b* and say /b/. Prompt children to repeat after you.

- Slide *u* next to *c*. Run your hand under the letters as you blend the sounds, elongating them—/ku/.

- Point to *b* and say /b/.

- Slide *b* next to *cu*. Run your hand under *cub* as you blend the sounds, elongating them—/kub/. Read *cub* naturally.

- Add *e* to *cub* to form *cube*. Remind children that the final *e* is silent; it is a clue that *u* stands for the long *u* sound, /yōō/. Slide your hand under *cube* as you blend the sounds, elongating them—/kyōōb/. Read *cube* naturally. Remove and replace the *e* several times as children read *cub* and *cube*.

Follow the same procedure with these words: *tube, cute, huge*.

  Word Building Place the *Word Builder Cards u, s,* and *e* in the *Word Builder* and have children do the same. Ask children to say each letter name and the sound it stands for. Then read the word naturally—*use*. Have children build and read new words. As they build each word, write it on the board. Say:

- **Add a *c* at the beginning. Change *s* to *t*. What word is it?** (*cute*)

- **Change *t* to *b*. What word is it?** (*cube*)

Continue with the words *tube, tune,* and *rule*. Then have children read the words on the board. Complete *Practice Book* page 98 together.

PRETEACH

Build Robust Vocabulary

Introduce Robust Vocabulary Read the student-friendly explanation for each word. Then discuss each word using the following examples.

Say: **I worked hard all week, so I deserve to enjoy the weekend. When have you gotten something you deserved? Explain.**

Say: **I usually eat a sandwich for lunch. What do you usually eat?**

Say: **I like to go to the lake because it is very peaceful and I can relax there. What do you think is peaceful—a crowded store or a quiet forest?**

PRETEACH

Grammar/Writing

Verbs Read aloud the following sentences from "Frog and Rabbit" in *Happy Landings*: **Rabbit ran so fast. Frog passed by Rabbit.** Point out that *ran* and *passed* are verbs. Explain that each word names an action that an animal did. Write the sentences on the board without the verbs. Read the sentences with children then ask children to suggest a verb to complete the sentence. Reread the sentence with the new verb.

Spelling Words

1. use	6. rule
2. cute	7. nice
3. cube	8. large
4. tube	9. hear
5. tune	10. talk

Have children practice writing spelling words on their *Write-on/Wipe-off Boards.*

VOCABULARY

Student-Friendly Explanations

deserve If you deserve something, you have worked hard to get it.

usually If you usually do something, you almost always do it.

peaceful When something is peaceful, it is calm and quiet.

DAY AT A GLANCE

Day 1

30+ Minutes

LESSON 25

Animals Eat

PHONEMIC AWARENESS
Phoneme Isolation

PHONICS AND SPELLING
Reteach Long Vowel /(y)o͞o/u-e

COMPREHENSION
Preteach Alphabetize

HIGH-FREQUENCY WORDS
Reteach kinds, other, only

FLUENCY
Intonation

GRAMMAR/WRITING
Reteach Verbs

Materials Needed:

Photo Card

Word Builders and Word Builder Cards

Write-On/ Wipe-Off Boards

Photo Cards

Practice Book
p.99

Sweet Success Student Edition pp. 4–5

Happy Landings Student Edition pp. 46–52

Practice Book

Spelling Words

1. use	6. rule
2. cute	7. nice
3. cube	8. large
4. tube	9. hear
5. tune	10. talk

 Have children practice writing spelling words on their *Write-on/Wipe-off Boards.*

Phonemic Awareness

Phoneme Isolation   Say the word *mule* and have children repeat it. Have children listen for other words with the /yo͞o/ or /o͞o/ sound. Say the words *cage* and *cute*. Say: **Which of these words has the /yo͞o/ sound?** *Cute* **has this sound. Now you try some.** Continue with: *cube, huge, yarn; Luke, dune, sky; brute, June, fudge.*

RETEACH

Phonics and Spelling

d o t   **Long Vowel /(y)o͞o/u-e**
Word Building   Place the *Word Builder Cards u, s,* and *e* in the *Word Builder.* Ask children to say the name and sound of each letter. Remind children that the final *e* is silent and is a clue that *u* stands for the long *u* sound. Then read the word naturally—*use.* Have children do the same. Ask:

- **Which letter should I add and which should I change to make *use* become *cute*?** (Add *c* at the beginning. Change *s* to *t*.)

- **Which letters should I change to make *cute* become *cube*?** (Change *t* to *b*.)

Continue with the words *tube, tune,* and *rule.*

u s e

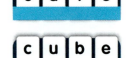
c u t e

c u b e

Read Words in Context   Write the following sentences on chart paper. Have children read each sentence silently. Then track the print as children read the sentences aloud. Finally, point to the underlined words at random and have children read them. *Brad can use that. Lin looks cute in that dress. I can play a tune on the flute. Let's take the large tube to the lake. The ice cube melts when it is hot. Sam had a nice time at the beach. Can I hear that song again? Please read each class rule. I talk to my friend at school.*

PRETEACH

Comprehension

Alphabetize   Remind children that alphabetical order will help them to do many things. Explain that anything that is arranged in alphabetical order is placed in the same order as the alphabet beginning with *a* and ending with *z*. Show *Photo Cards cake,*

house, and *rose,* and write the names of each on the board. Ask a volunteer to place the cards in alphabetical order. Choose three other *Photo Cards* and follow the same procedure.

RETEACH
High-Frequency Words

pp. 4–5

Write the words *kinds, other,* and *only* on the board.

• Point to and read *kinds.* Repeat, having children say *kinds* with you.

• Say: **There are all *kinds* of flowers.**

• Repeat the word and then point to each letter as you spell it. Then have children say and spell *kinds* with you. Have children reread the word.

Repeat for the remaining words. Use the following sentences: *The* other *children go to school, too. There is* only *one apple left.*

Have children turn to page 4 of *Sweet Success* and have them read aloud the words at the top of the page. Talk about the illustrations. Then guide children in choosing and writing the word that names each picture. (4. *huge,* 5. *tune,* 6. *mule*) Have children read aloud each word in the list on page 5. Ask volunteers to read the sentences aloud. Then have children choral-read the sentences. Guide them to choose and write the word that completes each sentence. (1. *kinds,* 2. *Only,* 3. *Other*)

RETEACH
Grammar/Writing

Practice Book
p.99

Verbs   Remind children that verbs are words that show action. Then read the following paragraph, telling children to listen for verbs.

> There are many children at the school. Some children read a book in class. Others write stories or solve math problems. Some are in the yard. In the yard, children kick the ball. Some jump rope, while others slide down the slide.

Read the story again, and guide children to identify and count how many verbs they can hear. Point out the verbs. Read the sentences again and have children pantomime the action each time they hear a verb. Complete *Practice Book* page 99 together.

Fluency

Intonation   Remind children that good readers make their voices rise and fall as they read so that the reading sounds like natural speech. Explain that this helps listeners better understand and appreciate the story or selection.

Model for children how to read with proper intonation by reading "School Day" from *Happy Landings.* Have children follow along and echo-read.

DAY AT A GLANCE

Day 2

PHONEMIC AWARENESS
Phoneme Blending

PHONICS AND SPELLING
Reteach Long Vowel /(y)o͞o/u-e

HIGH-FREQUENCY WORDS
Reteach clear, color, kinds, good-bye, hair, only, toes, others

FLUENCY
Intonation

READING
"Animals Eat"

BUILD ROBUST VOCABULARY
Preteach variety, incredible, typical

GRAMMAR/WRITING
Reteach Verbs

Materials Needed:

Word Builders and Word Builder Cards

Practice Book p.100
Practice Book

Copying Masters 97–98
Lesson 25 High-Frequency Word Cards

Sweet Success Student Edition pp. 6–13

Happy Landings Student Edition pp. 56–62

High-Frequency Words

clear	hair
color	only
kinds	toes
good-bye	other

Phonemic Awareness

Phoneme Blending Tell children that they are going to be detectives and find the word you are thinking about. Say: **I'm thinking of a word that means something very large. A cow is big, but a whale is /h/ /yo͞o/ /j/. The word is huge.** Continue with the following: /k/ /yo͞o/ /t/ (*cute*), /d/ /o͞o/ /n/ (*dune*), /r/ /o͞o/ /d/ (*rude*), and /yo͞o/ /z/ /d/ (*used*).

RETEACH

Phonics and Spelling

 Long Vowel /(y)o͞o/u-e
Word Building Use a *Word Builder* and *Word Builder Cards* and have children repeat each step. Build the word *Luke*. Have children name each letter and tell whether it is a consonant or a vowel. Remind children that in words with the consonant-vowel-consonant-*e* pattern, the *e* is silent and signals a long-vowel sound. Then say the word naturally—*Luke*. Lead children in building and reading new words by saying:

- **Change *u* to *a*. Read the word.** (*lake*)
- **Change *a* to *i*. Read the word.** (*like*)

Continue in a similar manner to have children contrast vowel sounds in the following words: *tune/tone; mute/mate; Bruce/brace.*

Practice Book p.100
Read Words in Context Ask children to turn to *Practice Book* page 100. Read the sentences aloud and have children echo-read. Then ask volunteers to read each sentence aloud. Ask: **What does Jude play?** (a flute) **Who plays the drums?** (June) **Who likes their music?** (the cute birds) After reading, have children find and circle words that have the long *u* sound.

RETEACH

High-Frequency Words

Copying Masters 97–98
Display the *High-Frequency Word Cards* for *clear, color, kinds, good-bye, hair, only, toes,* and *other*. Point to each card and read the word. Have children repeat. Then randomly point to the words, and ask children to read each one. Distribute cards to children and have them work with partners. Tell children to turn the cards over and shuffle them. Then have them play a memory game with the cards.

Reading

pp. 6–13 **Build Background: "Animals Eat"**
Read the title with children. Ask them to name their favorite animals. Then ask them if they know what types of food animals eat. Tell children they will be reading about what animals eat.

Monitor Comprehension: "Animals Eat"
Have children turn to the first page of the selection. Ask a volunteer to reread the title. Guide children to look at the picture on page 6. Guide children to think about what the selection will be about. Then guide children through the selection as they read.

pp. 6–7 Say: **There is an illustration of a mule and photographs of mules. Let's read to find out about mules.**

After reading the pages, ask: **What do mules eat?** (grass and hay) **What do they use to mash up food?** (their back teeth) NOTE DETAILS

Ask: **Who is telling this story?** (a narrator) POINT OF VIEW

Ask: **Which words on these pages have the long _u_ sound? Find and frame the words.** (*mule, use*) APPLY PHONICS

pp. 8–9 Say: **What do you see on these pages? What do you think we'll find out on these pages? Let's read to find out.**

After reading the pages, ask: **What do birds use to eat?** (beaks) **If birds don't have teeth how do you think they eat?** (Possible response: Some may swallow their food whole, others may use their beaks to mash the food and swallow it.) NOTE DETAILS/DRAW CONCLUSIONS

Ask: **Look at the pictures on page 9. How are the birds the same and how are they different?** (Possible response: They both have wings and beaks. The bird on the left has a small, thin beak. The other bird has a large, long beak.) COMPARE AND CONTRAST

Ask: **Which word on page 9 begins with the long _u_ sound?** (*use*) APPLY PHONICS

Fluency

Intonation Have children open to pages 56–57 of "Under a Bridge" in *Happy Landings*. Read the page in monotone with no stress placed on any words. Then read the pages with proper intonation. Point out the exclamation mark and demonstrate how to read an exclamatory sentence.

Have children work with a partner. Have each pair read the story with proper intonation. Give children feedback by describing what the reader did well as he or she reads.

Say: **Look at the pictures on these pages. What do you think we may learn on these pages? Let's read to find out.**

After reading the pages, ask: **How do whales like the one in the top photo catch fish?** (They use their teeth.) **How do whales like the one in the bottom photo catch fish?** (They gulp down little animals they find in the water.) **GRAPHIC AIDS/NOTE DETAILS**

Ask: **Why do you think the author wrote this selection?** (Possible response: to inform the reader of facts about animals and what they eat) **AUTHOR'S PURPOSE**

Ask: **Which words on these pages have the long *u* sound? Frame and read the long *u* words.** (*huge, use*) **APPLY PHONICS**

 Say: **There are several animals on this page. What are they all doing? Let's read to find out.**

After reading the pages, ask: **How are all the animals on this page the same?** (Possible response: They are all eating.) **Are they all eating the same thing? Explain what some of the animals are eating.** (No. Possible response: The gorilla is eating some type of leaf and the bear is eating a fish.) **COMPARE AND CONTRAST**

Ask: **Which sentences tell what the selection is about.** (*There are all kinds of animals. And they all need to eat.*) **SUMMARIZE**

Ask: **Which animals on this page are big?** (the bear and gorilla) **Which are small?** (the iguana and hamster) **CLASSIFY/CATEGORIZE**

 Answers to *Think Critically* Questions

Help children read and answer the *Think Critically* questions on page 13. Answers are shown below.

1. ‹*teeth*› **DETAILS**

2. ‹*beaks*› **COMPARE AND CONTRAST**

3. ‹*they are so big*› **MAKE INFERENCES**

PRETEACH

Build Robust Vocabulary

Introduce Robust Vocabulary   Read the student-friendly explanation for each word. Then discuss each word using the following examples.

Say: **There was such a variety of donuts at the donut shop that I had a hard time choosing which one I wanted. Tell about a place where there is a variety of items.**

Say: **I think a bird that can talk is incredible. Tell about something that you think is incredible.**

Say: **On a typical day I go to work and the gym. Do you think it is typical to see snow in the summer or to see snow in the winter?**

RETEACH

Grammar/Writing

Verbs   Ask children to think about what they did over the weekend. Have them to dictate sentences about what they did as you record them. Read the sentences and have volunteers identify the verbs. Then write the following sentence frames on the board. Read them with children and guide them to suggest a verb that best completes each one.

> Bill _____ a sandwich.
>
> The bee _____ in the air.
>
> We _____ our bikes to the park.
>
> I _____ one inch this year.

VOCABULARY

Student-Friendly Explanations

variety If there is a variety of something, there are many different kinds.

incredible If something is incredible, it is so amazing that it's hard to believe.

typical If something is typical, it usually happens this way.

LESSON 25

DAY AT A GLANCE

Day 3

PHONEMIC AWARENESS
Phoneme Segmentation

PHONICS
Preteach Inflections -ed, -ing

PHONICS AND SPELLING
Reteach Long Vowel /(y)oo̅/u-e

HIGH-FREQUENCY WORDS
Reteach kinds, other, only

FLUENCY
Intonation

COMPREHENSION
Reteach Alphabetize

GRAMMAR/WRITING
Reteach Research Report

Materials Needed:

Write-On/ Wipe-Off Boards with Phonemic Awareness Disks

Word Builders and Word Builder Cards

Lesson 25 Story Strips

Sweet Success Student Edition pp. 6–12

Happy Landings Student Edition pp. 56–62

Photo Cards

Spelling Words

1. use	6. rule
2. cute	7. nice
3. cube	8. large
4. tube	9. hear
5. tune	10. talk

30+ Minutes

Phonemic Awareness

Phoneme Segmentation Have children use the three boxes on the *Write-on/Wipe-off Boards.* Tell children that the boxes stand for the sounds in words. Have children repeat each step with their *Write-on/Wipe-off Boards.* Say: *Mule.* **The first sound I hear in *mule* is /m/.** Model placing a disk in the first box. Use this procedure for the second sound in *mule* (/yoo̅/) placing a disk in the second box, and the last sound in *mule* (/l/) placing a disk in the third box. Point to each box in sequence as children say the word. **How many sounds do you hear in *mule*? I hear three.** Repeat this procedure with: *hat, nine, sock, rake.*

PRETEACH

Phonics

Inflections -*ed*, -*ing* Write the following words on the board: *close, closed, closing.* Read the words, having children say each word after you. Point out the -*ed* and -*ing* endings. Remind children that in root words such as *close,* which ends with *e,* the final *e* is dropped when -*ed* or -*ing* is added. Review the sounds that -*ed* can stand for: /d/ in *moved,* /t/ in *raced,* and /əd/ in *rated.* Guide children to build new words with -*ed* and -*ing* using the following root words: *use, lose, jump.*

RETEACH

Phonics and Spelling

Long Vowel /(y)oo̅/u-e
Build Words Use *Word Builders* and *Word Builder Cards* to form words. Have children listen to your directions and change a letter in each word to spell a spelling word. Form *us* and have children read the word. Ask: **Which spelling word can you make by adding a letter to the end?** (*use*)

Follow a similar procedure with the following words: *tube* (*cube*), *role* (*rule*), *cure* (*cute*), *tub* (*tube*), *tone* (*tune*), *ice* (*nice*), *barge* (*large*).

Remind children that there are some other words they have to remember how to spell. Have children say *hear.* Tell them to put *Word Builder Cards* *h, e, a, r* in their *Word Builders,* picture the word *hear* in their minds, and build the word. Write the word on the board. Follow the same procedure with *talk.*

High-Frequency Words

kinds	**only**
other	

RETEACH

High-Frequency Words

Duplicate and distribute *Copying Masters* 99–100 to each child. Explain that the sentences tell about the selection "Animals Eat" but some have missing words.

List the words *kinds, other,* and *only* on the board. Have children read aloud each story strip sentence and name the correct word on the board that makes sense in the sentence. Have children write the missing words in the blanks and read the completed sentences aloud. Help children cut apart the strips, read the completed sentences, and arrange them in story order.

RETEACH

Comprehension

Alphabetize Remind children that some books in libraries are arranged in alphabetical order and information in encyclopedias is also arranged in alphabetical order. Review the animals that are presented in the story "Animals Eat" in *Sweet Success*. Write the animal names on the board. Display a beginner's encyclopedia and show children how the information is arranged. Ask children which animal would appear first in the encyclopedia. Guide children to find the animals in the encyclopedia.

RETEACH

Grammar/Writing

Research Report Write the following research report on the board.

> ### Fish Facts
>
> Fish are interesting animals. They are animals which live and breathe in water. All fish have a backbone. They breathe through gills. They have fins and scales.

Show *Photo Card fish* and explain that this is a research report about fish. Explain that a research report gives facts about something. Read the report to children. Then point out that research reports, like this one, have a title. Explain that the first sentence tells the main idea. Then explain how the other sentences in the report tell facts that support the main idea. Display *Photo Card flower*. Have children tell what they know about flowers. Elicit from children facts rather than opinions.

Fluency

Intonation Remind children that good readers stress certain words and make their voices rise and fall as they read so that it sounds like natural speech. Have children turn to "Under a Bridge" in *Sweet Success*.

Say: **I'm going to read some pages from "Under a Bridge." I am not going to read every word exactly the same. It sounds better if I read some words a little bit louder and with more expression than other words.** Have children echo-read "Under a Bridge" as you model reading with appropriate intonation.

LESSON 25

30+ Minutes

DAY AT A GLANCE

Day 4

PHONEMIC AWARENESS
Phoneme Blending

PHONICS
Reteach Inflections -ed, -ing

PHONICS AND SPELLING
Reteach Long Vowel /(y)ōō/u-e

HIGH-FREQUENCY WORDS
Reteach clear, color, kinds, good-bye, hair, only, toes, other

FLUENCY
Intonation

COMPREHENSION
Reteach Alphabetize

GRAMMAR/WRITING
Reteach Research Report

Materials Needed:

Practice Book

Lesson 25 High-Frequency Word Cards

Photo Cards

Sweet Success Student Edition pp. 6–12

Spelling Words

1. use	6. rule
2. cute	7. nice
3. cube	8. large
4. tube	9. hear
5. tune	10. talk

Phonemic Awareness

Phoneme Blending Tell children that together you are going to play a puzzle game. Tell them that you are going to say some words in pieces and they should listen to see if they can put the puzzle pieces together to figure out the word. Say: /r/ /ōō/ /l/. **What word does /r/ /ōō/ /l/ say? It says** *rule.* Continue with the following words: /k/ /yōō/ /b/ (*cube*), /h/ /e/ /j/ (*hedge*), /b/ /r/ /e/ /d/ (*bread*), /b/ /r/ /ōō/ /t/ (*brute*), /k/ /yōō/ /t/ (*cute*), /h/ /e/ /v/ /ē/ (*heavy*).

RETEACH

Phonics

Inflections -ed, -ing Remind children that endings can be added to a root word to make new words. Write *live.* Say: **Live ends in** *e* **so** *lived* **and** *living* **are made by dropping the final** *e* **and then adding** *-ed* **or** *-ing.* Write *lived* and *living.*

Write *pat.* Say: **Pat has a short vowel followed by one consonant, so** *patted* **and** *patting* **are made by doubling the final consonant** *t* **and then adding** *-ed* **or** *-ing.* Write *patted* and *patting.* Write the words *stop, blame, close,* and *pop* on the board. Work with children to add *-ed* and *-ing* to make new words by following the rules. Then read all the words together.

RETEACH

Phonics and Spelling

 Long Vowel /(y)ōō/u-e
Direct children's attention to page 101 of their *Practice Books.* Complete the page together.

Assess children's progress using the following sentences.

1.	use	My dad can **use** that tool.
2.	cute	Your dog has a **cute** name.
3.	cube	Mom put an ice **cube** in my glass.
4.	tube	Dad got a new **tube** of toothpaste.
5.	tune	Do you know the **tune** I played?
6.	rule	The **rule** is "No yelling."

Review

7.	nice	My family had a **nice** time at the beach.
8.	large	A ship is a very **large** boat.

High-Frequency

9.	hear	I can **hear** the phone ring.
10.	talk	Vince and Todd **talk** on the telephone.

High-Frequency Words

clear	hair
color	only
kinds	toes
good-bye	other

RETEACH

High-Frequency Words

Copying Masters 97–98

Display *High-Frequency Word Cards* for this lesson's words—*clear, color, kinds, good-bye, hair, only, toes, other*—and the previously learned high-frequency words. Point to words at random and ask children to read them.

RETEACH

Comprehension

Alphabetize Remind children that many things are arranged in alphabetical order, such as some books in the library and information in encyclopedias. Learning about alphabetical order will help them to find information. Write the following titles on three separate sentence strips and tape them to the board: *"Frog and Rabbit," "School Day,"* and *"Animals Eat."* Remind children that these are three selections that they have read. Ask a volunteer to arrange the titles in alphabetical order.

"Frog and Rabbit"

"Animals Eat"

"School Day"

Then distribute 4–6 *Photo Cards* to children and have them work in pairs to alphabetize their set.

RETEACH

Grammar/Writing

Research Report Review with children characteristics of a research report.

Research Report

A research report has a title.

The title tells what the report is about.

The first sentence tells the main idea.

The other sentences tell facts.

Display the research report from Day 3 and read it to children. Guide children through the characteristics of a research report, pointing out that there is a title that tells what the report is about. Point out that the first sentence is the main idea and the other sentences tell facts. Have children choose an animal, and guide them in writing questions they want to investigate about the animal they chose.

Fluency

Intonation Have partners reread "Animals Eat" in *Sweet Success* aloud three or four times. Coach children to read aloud with fluency in a manner that sounds like natural speech. Remind them to place stress on some words and to make their voices rise and fall as they read each sentence.

Listen to partners read, giving them feedback about their intonation and guidance for improving their fluency.

DAY AT A GLANCE
Day 5

HIGH-FREQUENCY WORDS
clear, color, kinds, good-bye, hair, only, toes

PHONEMIC AWARENESS
Onset and Rime

PHONICS AND SPELLING
Preteach Long Vowel /ī/ *y, ie, igh*

BUILD ROBUST VOCABULARY
Preteach *fondly, pale, shadowy*

GRAMMAR/WRITING
Preteach Verbs That Tell About Now

Materials Needed:

Lesson 25
High-Frequency
Word Cards

Sound/
Spelling
Card *Ii*

Word Builders
and Word
Builder Cards

Write-On/
Wipe-Off
Boards

Practice
Book

High-Frequency Words

clear	hair
color	only
kinds	toes
good-bye	

High-Frequency Words

Display *High-Frequency Word Cards* for *clear, color, kinds, good-bye, hair, only, toes* and the other previously learned high-frequency words. Say the word *clear,* ask a volunteer to point to *clear,* and have children read the word aloud. Continue with the remaining high-frequency words. Repeat this activity several times to reinforce instant recognition.

Phonemic Awareness

Onset and Rime   Have children name the words as you say them in parts. Model the first one: **Listen as I say this word in parts. /s/-igh—The word I said was *sigh.* Now you try some: /fr/-y, /wh/-y, /t/-ight, /p/-ies, /h/-igh.**

PRETEACH

Phonics and Spelling

Long Vowel /ī/y, ie, igh
Connecting Letter to Sound   Say the words *my, lie,* and *sigh* and have children repeat the words. Explain that all three words end with the /ī/ sound. Have children say /ī/ several times. Display *Sound/Spelling Card Ii*. Point to *i-e* and remind children that they have learned that these letters stand for the long *i* sound. Tell children that they are going to learn three more spellings for the long *i* sound. Point to *y* on *Sound/Spelling Card Ii* and tell children that the letter *y* can stand for the sound /ī/, the sound in *my*. Have children say /ī/ several times as you touch the *y*. Point to *ie*. Explain that the letters *i* and *e* together can stand for /ī/, the long *i* sound in *lie*. Then point to *igh*. Explain that the letters *i, g,* and *h* together can stand for /ī/, the long *i* sound in *sigh*.

Say: **When I say a word with /ī/ in the middle, raise your hand and say /ī/. An example of this would be *fight*. When I say a word that does not have /ī/ in the middle, put your hand behind your back.** Say these words: *tries, tree, light, rug, fried, sight.*

Tell children that some words, like *my,* have the sound /ī/ at the end. Follow the same procedure for the final position with the following words: *by, do, tie, high, sky, you.*

Word Blending   Demonstrate each step with *Word Builder Cards* and a *Word Builder*. Have children repeat each step after you. Hold up *t* and say /t/. Hold up *i* and *e* together and say /ī/. Hold up *d* and say /d/.

- Place the letters *t, i, e, d* in the *Word Builder.*

- Point to *t*. Say /t/. Point to *i* and *e* together and say /ī/. Prompt children to repeat after you.

- Slide *ie* next to *t*. Run your hand under the letters as you blend the sounds, elongating them—/tī/.

- Point to *d* and say /d/.

- Slide *d* next to *tie*. Run your hand under *tied* as you elongate and blend the sounds—/tīd/. Read *tied* naturally.

Follow the same procedure with these words: *my, dries, might.*

  Word Building   Model how to blend *my.* Place the *Word Builder Cards m* and *y* in the *Word Builder* and have children do the same. Slide your hand under the letters as you slowly blend the sounds to read the word /mmī/. Then read the word naturally—*my.* Have children build and read new words. As they build each word, write it on the board. Say:

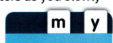

- **Change *m* to *tr*. What word did you make?** (*try*)

- **Change *y* to *ie* and add *d* at the end. What word did you make?** (*tried*)

Continue with *ties, light,* and *might.* Have children read the words. Direct children to page 102 of their *Practice Books.* Complete the page together.

PRETEACH

Build Robust Vocabulary

Introduce Robust Vocabulary   Read the student-friendly explanation for each word. Then discuss each word using the following examples.

Say: **I pet my cat fondly when I go home from school. Whom do you treat fondly? What do you do?**

Say: **Dark clothes can get pale if washed a lot. What do you have that is pale in color?**

Say: **My bedroom looks shadowy when I turn out the light at night. What would be shadowy—a dark forest or a beach?**

PRETEACH

Grammar/Writing

Verbs That Tell About Now   Remind children that verbs are action words. Write these sentences on the board: *Mice run fast. A bird flies fast.* Track the print as you read them aloud. Underline *run* in the first sentence. Explain that it is a verb that tells what mice do right now. Help children find the verb that tells what a bird does right now (*flies*). Explain that if these verbs did not tell about something happening right now, they would be *ran* and *flew.*

Spelling Words

1. my	6. might
2. try	7. use
3. tried	8. rule
4. ties	9. hair
5. light	10. color

 Have children practice writing spelling words on their *Write-on/Wipe-off Boards.*

VOCABULARY

Student-Friendly Explanations

fondly When something is done fondly, it is done in a caring, loving, or tender way.

pale If something is pale, it is very light or without much color.

shadowy If a place is shadowy, it is not in the light; it is shady.

DAY AT A GLANCE
Day 1

PHONEMIC AWARENESS
Phoneme Isolation

PHONICS AND SPELLING
Reteach Long Vowel /ī/y, ie, igh

COMPREHENSION
Reteach Story Elements

HIGH-FREQUENCY WORDS
Reteach mouse, mother, should, thought

FLUENCY BUILDER
Intonation

GRAMMAR/WRITING
Reteach Verbs That Tell About Now

Materials Needed:

Word Builders and Word Builder Cards

Write-On/ Wipe-Off Boards

Practice Book p.103

Happy Landings Student Edition pp. 36–42

Sweet Success Student Edition pp. 14–15

Photo Cards

Spelling Words

1. my	6. might
2. try	7. use
3. tried	8. rule
4. ties	9. hair
5. light	10. color

 Have children practice writing spelling words on their *Write-on/Wipe-off Boards.*

LESSON 26

Phonemic Awareness

Phoneme Isolation Say the word *why* and have children repeat it. Have children listen for other words with the /ī/ sound. Say the words *how* and *shy*. Say: **Which of these words has the /ī/ sound?** *Shy* **has this sound. Now you try some.** Continue with: *sky, try, found; slight, might, loud; my, bell, fry; pie, by, green; bright, tight, home.*

RETEACH

Phonics and Spelling

 **Long Vowel /ī/y, ie, igh**
Word Building Place the *Word Builder Cards* m and y in the *Word Builder.* Ask children to say each letter name and the sound it stands for. Then read the word naturally—*my.* Have children do the same. Ask children which letter you should change to make *my* become *try.* (Change *m* to *tr.*) Continue by asking them:

- **Which letter should I change to make *try* become *tried*?** (Change *y* to *ied.*)
- **Which letters should I change to make *tried* become *ties*?** (Take away *r.* Change *d* to *s.*)

Continue with the words *light* and *might.*

Read Words in Context Write the following sentences on chart paper. Have children read each sentence silently. Then track the print as children read the sentences aloud. Finally, point to the underlined words at random and have children read them. *Jack <u>tried</u> to ride my sled. I will <u>try</u> to come. I <u>might</u> be sick. Will <u>ties</u> the bow. Plants <u>use</u> <u>light</u> from the sun. <u>My</u> <u>hair</u> <u>color</u> is black. Cleaning after playtime is a <u>rule</u>.*

302 Lesson 26 • Sweet Success

RETEACH

Comprehension

Story Elements   Review with children that the people or animals in a story are called characters. Where and when a story takes place is the setting, and what happens is the plot. Have children turn to "The Picnic Plan" in *Happy Landings*. Tell children that the characters in this story are animals. Have children tell what kind of animals are in the story. (a duck, a fox, a skunk, and squirrels) Guide children to look at the pictures to identify the setting. (under a tree) Then do a picture walk through the story and have children point out the events of the story.

RETEACH

High-Frequency Words

pp. 14– 15

Write the words *mouse, mother, should,* and *thought* on the board.

- Point to and read *mouse*. Repeat, having children say *mouse* with you.
- Say: **The *mouse* was gray.**
- Repeat the word and then point to each letter as you spell it. Then have children say and spell *mouse* with you. Have children reread the word.

Repeat for the remaining words. Use the following sentences: *My* mother *takes care of me at home. I* should *brush my teeth every day. Tyrone* thought *about trying out for the team.*

Have children turn to page 14 of *Sweet Success* and have them read aloud the words at the top of the page. Talk about the illustrations. Then guide children in choosing and writing the word that names each picture. (4. *ties,* 5. *sky,* 6. *flight*) Have children read aloud each word in the list on page 15. Ask volunteers to read the sentences aloud. Then have children choral-read the sentences. Guide them to choose and write the word that completes each sentence. (1. *mouse,* 2. *thought,* 3. *mother,* 4. *should*)

RETEACH

Grammar/Writing

Verbs That Tell About Now   Remind children that verbs are words for actions and that some verbs tell about what is happening right now. Display *Photo Cards octopus* and *hen.* Write the following sentence frames on chart paper and read them aloud: _____ *waves its arms.* _____ *pecks in the yard.* Have children paperclip the correct animal to each sentence frame. Point out the verbs in the sentences. (*waves, pecks*) Explain that if these verbs told about the past they would be *waved* and *pecked.* Complete *Practice Book* page 103 together.

High-Frequency Words

mouse	**should**
mother	**thought**

Fluency

Intonation   Remind children that good readers make their voices rise and fall as they read. This makes reading sound like talking. Explain that this helps listeners understand and appreciate the story and its characters.

Read aloud each page of "The Picnic Plan" in *Happy Landings*. Model appropriate intonation and have children echo-read.

DAY AT A GLANCE

Day 2

PHONEMIC AWARENESS
Phoneme Blending

PHONICS AND SPELLING
Reteach Long Vowel /ī/*y, ie, igh*

HIGH-FREQUENCY WORDS
Reteach *climbed, earth, fooling, thought, table, mouse, mother, should*

FLUENCY
Punctuation

READING
"The Flight"

BUILD ROBUST VOCABULARY
Preteach *imaginative, similar, affectionate*

GRAMMAR/WRITING
Reteach Verbs That Tell About Now

Materials Needed:

Word Builders and Word Builder Cards

Practice Book p.104
Practice Book

Copying Masters 101–102
Lesson 26 High-Frequency Word Cards

Happy Landings Student Edition pp. 6–12

Sweet Success Student Edition pp. 16–23

High-Frequency Words

climbed	table
earth	mouse
fooling	mother
thought	should

Phonemic Awareness

Phoneme Blending   Tell children that they are going to be detectives and find the word you are thinking about. Say: **I'm thinking of a word that means the opposite of wet. The word is /d/ /r/ /ī/. The word is *dry*.** Continue with the following words: /t/ /ī/ (*tie*), /h/ /ī/) (*high*), /b/ /ī/ (*by*), /m/ /ī/ (*my*), /sh/ /ī/ (*shy*).

RETEACH

Phonics and Spelling

Long Vowel /i/*y, ie, igh*
Word Building   Use a *Word Builder* and *Word Builder Cards* and have children repeat each step after you. Build the word *my*. Blend the sounds to read the word—/mmī/. Then say the word naturally—*my*. Have children do the same. Lead children in building and reading new words by saying:

- **Change *y* to *e*. Read the word.** (*me*)
- **Change *e* to *ay*. Read the word.** (*may*)

Continue with the following words: *by-be-bay, night-neat, try-tray-tree.*

Read Words in Context   Ask children to turn to *Practice Book* page 104. Read each sentence aloud and have children echo-read. Then ask volunteers to read each sentence aloud. Ask: **What are the lights like?** (bright) **What does Dwight have?** (a tray) **What does Bea try?** (Lee's pie) **What might Elaine eat?** (fries) Call on volunteers to frame and read long *i* words. Have children find and circle all the long *i* words.

RETEACH

High-Frequency Words

Copying Masters 101–102   Display the *High-Frequency Word Cards* for *climbed, earth, fooling, thought, table, mouse, mother,* and *should*. Point to each card and read the word. Have children repeat. Then have children sit in a circle and give each child a card. In random order, ask an individual to stand and hold up his or her card. Have the group read the card in unison. Continue with the remaining words.

Reading

Build Background: "The Flight"

pp. 16–23

Read the title with children. Ask them what *fly* means. Have them pretend to be planes and act out flying. Help them connect the word *flight* with *fly.* Ask them to tell about any experiences they have flying in an airplane. Tell them they will read a story about a mouse who wants to fly into space.

Monitor Comprehension: "The Flight"

Have children turn to the first page of the story. Ask a volunteer to reread the title. Guide children to look at the picture on page 16. Encourage children to predict whom the story will be about and what that character might want to do. Then guide children through the story as they read.

pp. 16–17

Say: **The mouse has a spaceship and he looks like he is getting ready for a trip. Let's read to find out where he wants to go.**

After reading the pages, ask: **What is Little Mouse looking at? Frame and read the word that tells.** (*sky*) **What has he made?** (a spaceship) **APPLY PHONICS/NOTE DETAILS**

Ask: **Why do you think Little Mouse might want to go into space?** (Possible response: He thinks it will be exciting.) **CHARACTERS' MOTIVATIONS**

Ask: **What does his mother want him to do first?** (eat lunch) **SEQUENCE**

pp. 18–19

Say: **We know that Little Mouse wants to go into space, but in the picture he is going to bed. Let's read to find out more.**

After reading the pages, ask: **Does Little Mouse still want to go into space? How do you know?** (Yes. He says, "I will fly into space.") **NOTE DETAILS**

Ask: **Why do you think Little Mouse thinks it is a good idea to sleep before his trip?** (Possible response: If he is rested, he will do a good job of flying his spaceship.) **CAUSE AND EFFECT**

Ask: **Do you think his mother wants him to go on a trip into space? Explain your answer.** (Possible response: No, she tries to get him to think about other things so he will forget about wanting to fly into space.) **DRAW CONCLUSIONS**

pp. 20–21

Say: **Look at the pictures on these pages. We see Little Mouse in space. Let's find out if he really went into space.**

Fluency

Punctuation Have children turn to "Frog and Rabbit" in *Happy Landings.* Point out an example of each of the following: period, question mark, quotation mark, and comma.

Explain that the quotation marks surround the words that Frog and Rabbit say. Have children find other examples of the punctuation marks you have identified for them.

Explain that punctuation marks are clues that help them know how to read so that their reading sounds like natural speech. Model how to make your voice rise and fall as you read aloud the story. Then have children practice reading aloud paying attention to punctuation marks.

After reading the pages, ask: **Is Little Mouse really in space? Explain.** (No, he is just dreaming.) **DRAW CONCLUSIONS**

Ask: **How do you know that Little Mouse is dreaming?** (We see him still in bed. The cloud shows what he is dreaming.) **NOTE DETAILS**

Ask: **How does the author describe the stars? Frame and read the word that tells.** (*bright*) **APPLY PHONICS**

page 22 Say: **Little Mouse had a dream about going into space. Let's read the ending of the story to see if he still wants to take a trip in a spaceship.**

After reading the pages, ask: **Do you think Little Mouse wants to go on a real space trip after his dream? Why or why not?** (Possible response: No, he wouldn't want to go because he decided he likes being home with his mother more.) **EXPRESS PERSONAL OPINIONS**

Ask: **Why does Little Mouse's mother look surprised?** (Possible response: She is surprised that Little Mouse hugs her so hard. She does not know about his dream. She does not know that his dream made him feel lonely.) **CAUSE AND EFFECT**

Ask: **Did the story change your mind about whether you would want to go into space?** (Possible response: Yes, because I thought it would be exciting, but I would miss my family, too. No, I would still like to go, but I would take Dad with me.) **PERSONAL RESPONSE**

page 23 **Answers to *Think Critically* Questions**
Help children read and answer the *Think Critically* questions on page 23. Answers are shown below.

 1. ‹fly into space› **CHARACTERS**

 2. ‹a forest› **SETTING**

 3. ‹home› **BEGINNING, MIDDLE, END**

PRETEACH

Build Robust Vocabulary

Introduce Robust Vocabulary Read the student-friendly explanation for each word. Then discuss each word using the following examples.

Say: **People who write music are imaginative. What other kind of people are imaginative?**

Say: **A dog is similar to a wolf. What other animals are similar? Do you think a lion is similar to a tiger or a bear?**

Say: **Giving a hug is a way to be affectionate. What are some other ways to be affectionate?**

RETEACH

Grammar/Writing

Verbs That Tell About Now Write the following sentences on the board.

Mouse sits in a box.

Mother and mouse talk.

Read them aloud. Have children read them. Circle the verb *sits* in the first sentence. Say: **This is a verb. It tells about an action that happens now.** Guide children to find and circle the verb that tells about now in the second sentence. *(talk)*

Point out that *sits* tells about one character. There is an *-s* at the end of the verb. *Talk* tells about two characters. There is no *-s* at the end. Guide children to look at the other pictures in the book and dictate sentences about what is happening in each.

VOCABULARY

Student-Friendly Explanations

imaginative If you are imaginative, you are good at coming up with ideas and picturing things in your mind.

similar If two things are similar, they are alike in some ways.

affectionate If you are affectionate, you like to show you love someone by hugging or cuddling.

30+ Minutes

PHONEMIC AWARENESS
Phoneme Segmentation

PHONICS
Preteach Contraction *'d*

PHONICS AND SPELLING
Reteach Long Vowel /ī/*y, ie, igh*

HIGH-FREQUENCY WORDS
Reteach *mother, mouse, should, thought*

FLUENCY
Intonation

COMPREHENSION
Reteach Story Elements

GRAMMAR/WRITING
Reteach Research Reports

Materials Needed:

Write-On/
Wipe-Off
Boards with
Phonemic
Awareness
Disks

Word Builders
and Word
Builder Cards

Copying Masters 103-104

Lesson 26
Story Strips

Sweet Success
Student Edition
pp. 16–22

Spelling Words

1. my	6. might
2. try	7. use
3. tried	8. rule
4. ties	9. hair
5. light	10. color

Phonemic Awareness

Phoneme Segmentation Have children use the three boxes on the *Write-on/Wipe-off Boards.* Tell children that the boxes stand for the sounds in words. Have children repeat each step with their *Write-on/Wipe-off Boards.* Say: *Cry.* **The first sound I hear in *cry* is /k/.** Model placing a disk in the first box. Use this procedure for the second sound in *cry* (/r/), placing a disk in the second box, and the last sound in *cry* (ī), placing a disk in the third box. Point to each box in sequence as children say the word. **How many sounds do you hear in *cry*? I hear three.** Repeat this procedure with: *fly, light, fried, sky, right.*

PRETEACH

Phonics

Contraction *'d* Write on the board: *I had worked hard. I'd worked hard.* Read the sentences and then have children echo them. Underline *I had* and *I'd.* Point out that *I'd* is a contraction—a shorter way of saying *I had.* Have children name the letters that were dropped from *I had* to form *I'd.* (ha) Point to the apostrophe. Explain that this mark shows that letters were left out. Use the same process with the following sentences: *We would* help you; *We'd* help you. (woul) *She had* stayed too late; *She'd* stayed too late. (ha)

RETEACH

Phonics and Spelling

Long Vowel /ī/*y, ie, igh*

Build Words Use *Word Builder Cards* and a *Word Builder* to form words. Have children listen to your directions and change a letter in each word to spell a spelling word using their *Word Builder Cards* and *Word Builders.* Form *by* and have children read the word. Ask: **Which spelling word can you make by changing *b*?** (my)

Follow a similar procedure with the following words: *my* (try), *try* (tried), *toes* (ties), *night* (light, might), *mule* (rule, use).

Remind children that there are some other words they have to remember how to spell. Have children say *hair.* Tell them to put *Word Builder Cards h, a, i, r* in their *Word Builders,* picture the word *hair* in their minds, and build the word. Write the word on the board. Follow the same procedure with the word *color.*

RETEACH

High-Frequency Words

Copying Masters 103–104

Duplicate and distribute *Copying Masters* 103–104 to each child. Explain that the sentences tell the story "The Flight" but some have missing words.

List the words *mother, mouse, should,* and *thought* on the board. Have children read aloud each story strip sentence and name the correct word on the board that makes sense in the sentence. Have children write the missing words in the blanks and read the completed sentences aloud. Help children cut apart the strips, read the completed sentences, and arrange them in story order.

RETEACH

Comprehension

Story Elements   Remind children that characters are the animals or people in a story. Have them recall the characters in "The Flight" in *Sweet Success.* Remind them that the setting is where a story happens. Ask children to point to and name the settings in "The Flight." Point out that children have learned that the plot is what happens in a story. Ask them to revisit the pictures and retell what happens during each part of the story.

RETEACH

Grammar/Writing

Research Reports   Remind children that they have talked about research reports in the past. Write the following beginning of a research report on chart paper. Ask children to tell what they recall about research reports.

All About Mice

Mice are interesting little animals. They have small bodies with long tails. Is there only one kind of mouse? No, there are many kinds of mice. Some are grasshopper mice, jumping mice, and harvest mice.

Remind children that a research report has a title. Explain to children that the first sentence tells the main idea of the report. Explain that the other sentences tell facts. Point out how they support the main idea.

High-Frequency Words

mouse	should
mother	thought

Fluency

Intonation   Point out that good readers make their voices rise and fall in pitch as they read so that it sounds like talking. Explain that they can also use their voices to show what is happening and how characters feel.

Reread aloud "The Flight" from *Sweet Success,* and have children echo-read. Show children how to use their voices to show surprise, wonder, and other emotions as characters speak.

DAY AT A GLANCE

Day 4

PHONEMIC AWARENESS
Phoneme Blending

PHONICS
Reteach Contractions *'d, 've, 're*

PHONICS AND SPELLING
Reteach Long Vowel /ī/y, *ie, igh*

HIGH-FREQUENCY WORDS
Reteach *climbed, earth, fooling,
thought, table, mouse, mother, should*

FLUENCY
Intonation

COMPREHENSION
Reteach Story Elements

GRAMMAR/WRITING
Reteach Research Reports

Materials Needed:

Practice
Book

Lesson 26
High-Frequency
Word Cards

Sweet Success
Student Edition
pp. 16–22

Happy Landings
Student Edition
pp. 56–62

Spelling Words

1. my	6. might
2. try	7. use
3. tried	8. rule
4. ties	9. hair
5. light	10. color

Phonemic Awareness

Phoneme Blending Tell children that you are going to say some words in pieces and they should listen to see if they can put the pieces together to figure out the word. **Say: /s/ /p/ /ī/. What word does /s/ /p/ /ī/ say? It says *spy*.** Continue with the following words: /hw/ /ī/ (*why*), /t/ /r/ /ī/ /d/ (*tried*), /t/ /ī/ (*tie*), /n/ /ī/ /t/ (*night*), /m/ /ī/ /t/ (*might*), /b/ /ī/ (*by*).

RETEACH

Phonics

Contractions *'d, 've, 're* Remind children that a contraction is a word made up of two words. An apostrophe takes the place of the missing letters. Write *he had* and *he'd*. Say: **The word *he'd* comes from *he had*. The letters *ha* were dropped. We put an apostrophe in their place.** Use the same procedure with *they would* (*they'd*) and *we have* (*we've*).

RETEACH

Phonics and Spelling

Practice Book p.105

Long Vowel /ī/ *y, ie, igh* Direct children's attention to page 105 of their *Practice Books*. Complete the page together.

Assess children's progress using the following sentences.

1. my — Would you like to see **my** bike?
2. try — I will **try** hard.
3. tried — Have you **tried** to ride a bike?
4. ties — I gave Dad two new **ties**.
5. light — Please turn on that **light**.
6. might — We **might** go to the store.

Review

7. use — May I **use** your red crayon?
8. rule — The **rule** is "Stop at the stop sign."

High-Frequency

9. hair — I combed my **hair**.
10. color — Blue is his favorite **color**.

RETEACH

High-Frequency Words

Copying Masters 101–102

Display *High-Frequency Word Cards* for this lesson's words—*climbed, earth, fooling, thought, table, mouse, mother,* and *should*—and the previously learned high-frequency words. Point to words at random and ask children to read them.

Comprehension

Story Elements   Ask children to tell what story elements are and explain each one. (character—people and animals in a story; setting—where and when a story takes place; plot—what happens)

Draw a three-column chart on the board labeled with "The Flight" and "Under a Bridge." Guide children to point out the main characters, the setting, and plot of "The Flight" in *Sweet Success*. Walk children through "Under a Bridge" in *Happy Landings* and have volunteers dictate the main characters, the setting, and plot of each story as you record their responses on the chart.

Story Elements	"The Flight"	"Under a Bridge"
Characters	Little Mouse, his mother	
Setting	Little Mouse's home; space	
Plot	Little Mouse wants to fly into space.	

Grammar/Writing

Research Report   Review characteristics of well-reports.

> **Research Report**
>
> A research report has a title.
> The first sentence tells the main idea.
> The other sentences tell facts.

Lead children in looking back at the example report on mice from Day 3. Point out the title, main idea sentence, and fact sentences. Have children think of another kind of animal. Ask them to tell facts they know about the animal. Write the facts on chart paper. Lead children in deciding on a main idea statement about the animal. Help children arrange the main idea and facts into a short report. Read the report with children.

High-Frequency Words

climbed	table
earth	mouse
fooling	mother
thought	should

Fluency

Intonation   Reread "The Flight" from *Sweet Success*, modeling fluent reading. Point out how you made your voice sound like talking. Remind children that good readers make their voices rise and fall in pitch to help listeners understand. Have children practice rereading the story for fluency.

DAY AT A GLANCE
Day 5

HIGH-FREQUENCY WORDS
climbed, earth, fooling, thought, table

PHONEMIC AWARENESS
Onset and Rime

PHONICS AND SPELLING
Preteach Vowel Diphthong /ou/*ow, ou*

BUILD ROBUST VOCABULARY
Preteach *quivered, wailed, scattered*

GRAMMAR/WRITING
Preteach Using *Am, Is,* and *Are*

Materials Needed:

Lesson 26
High-Frequency
Word Cards

Sound/
Spelling
Card *ou*

Word Builders
and Word
Builder Cards

Write-On/
Wipe-Off
Boards

Practice
Book

High-Frequency Words

climbed	thought
earth	table
fooling	

High-Frequency Words

Display *High-Frequency Word Cards* for *climbed, earth, fooling, thought, table,* and the other previously learned high-frequency words. Say the word *climbed,* ask a volunteer to point to *climbed,* and have children read the word aloud. Continue with the remaining high-frequency words. Repeat this activity several times to reinforce instant recognition.

Phonemic Awareness

Onset and Rime Have children name the words as you say them in parts. Model the first one. **Listen as I say this word in parts. /s/-outh—The word I said was** *south.* **Now you try some: /sh/-out, /n/-ow, /sp/-out, /k/-ow, /kl/-oud.**

PRETEACH

Phonics and Spelling

 Vowel Diphthong /ou/*ow, ou*
Connecting Letter to Sound Say the words *out, owl,* and *ouch* and have children repeat the words. Say: **The words** *out, owl,* **and** *ouch* **begin with the /ou/ sound.** Have children say /ou/ several times. Display *Sound/Spelling Card /ou/,* say the letter names, and identify the picture. Explain that the letters *ow* and *ou* can stand for /ou/, the vowel sound in *ouch.* Have children say /ou/ several times as you touch the letters.

Say: **When I say a word that begins with /ou/, clap your hands and say /ou/. When I say a word that does not begin with /ou/, keep your hands on your lap.** Say these words: *oak, out, octopus, ounce, oven, owl.* Tell children that some words have the sound /ou/ in the middle. Say *couch,* elongating the /ou/ sound. Tell children that *couch* has /ou/ in the middle. Then follow the same procedure for the medial position with the following words: *down, found, soap, south, trot, sound.* Say: **Some words have the sound /ou/ at the end. The word** *how* **has /ou/ at the end.** Follow the same procedure for the final position with the following words: *how, allow, jump, meow, find.*

Word Blending Demonstrate each step with *Word Builder Cards* and a *Word Builder* and have children repeat each step after you. Hold up *d* and say /d/. Hold up *o* and *w* together and say /ou/. Hold up *n* and say /nn/.

- Place the letters *d, o, w, n* in the *Word Builder.* Make sure the letters *o* and *w* touch.

- Point to *d.* Say /d/. Point to *o* and *w* together and say /ou/. Prompt children to repeat after you.

- Slide *ow* next to *d*. Run your hand under the letters as you blend the sound by elongating them—/dou/.

- Point to *n* and say /n/.

- Slide *n* next to *dow*. Run your hand under the letters as you blend the sounds by elongating them—/doun/. Read *down* naturally.

Follow the same procedure with these words: *pout, howl, our*.

  Word Building   Place the *Word Builder Cards h, o, w* in the *Word Builder* and have children do the same. Slide your hand under the letters as you slowly blend the sounds /hhou/. Then read *how* naturally. Have children build and read new words. As they build each word, write it on the board. Say:

Practice Book **p.106**

- **Change *h* to *c*. What word did you make?** (*cow*)

- **Change *c* to *d* and add *n* at the end. What word is it?** (*down*)

Continue with the words *out, found,* and *round*. Have children read the words on the board. Complete *Practice Book* page 106 together.

PRETEACH
Build Robust Vocabulary

Introduce Robust Vocabulary   Read the student-friendly explanation for each word. Then discuss each word using the following examples.

Say: **I would quiver if I were in the woods and saw a bear or if I were in my house and heard a strange sound. What might make you quiver?**

Say: **Sometimes babies wail if they don't get what they want. I would wail if something heavy fell on my toe. What would make you wail?**

Say: **When we play hide and seek, we scatter to look for the person who is hiding. When is a time that you were in a group that scattered?**

PRETEACH
Grammar/Writing

Using *Am, Is,* and *Are*   Remind children that they have learned some verbs that tell about now. Explain that this week they will learn about the words *am, is,* and *are,* which are also verbs that tell about now. Write on the board the following sentences: *It is the cat. It is the clown. I am a grown up. You are children.* Read them aloud. Tell children that *is* tells about one person, thing, or animal. Point out that the word *am* is used to tell about yourself. *Are* is used to tell about more than one person, thing, or animal.

Spelling Words

1. how	6. round
2. cow	7. try
3. down	8. light
4. out	9. earth
5. found	10. table

Have children practice writing spelling words on their *Write-on/Wipe-off Boards*.

VOCABULARY
Student-Friendly Explanations

quivered If something quivered, it shook, shivered, or trembled rapidly.

wailed If you wailed, you let out a long loud cry because you were upset about something or in pain.

scattered If things or people scattered, they separated and went off in different directions.

LESSON 27

Helping Baby Bird

Materials Needed:

Word Builders and Word Builder Cards

Write-On/Wipe-Off Boards

Practice Book p.107
Practice Book

What a Thrill! Student Edition pp. 56–62

Sweet Success Student Edition pp. 24–25

Spelling Words

1. how	6. round
2. cow	7. try
3. down	8. light
4. out	9. earth
5. found	10. table

 Have children practice writing spelling words on their *Write-on/Wipe-off Boards.*

Phonemic Awareness

Phoneme Isolation   Say the word *plow* and have children repeat it. Have children listen for other words with the /ou/ sound. Say the words *cow* and *face.* Say: **Which of these words has the /ou/ sound?** *Cow* **has this sound. Now you try some.** Continue with: *crowd, line, trout; pound, spout, vet; owl, foul, trap.*

RETEACH

Phonics and Spelling

 Vowel Diphthong /ou/*ow, ou*
Word Building   Place the *Word Builder Cards h, o, w* in the *Word Builder.* Read the word naturally—*how.* Have children do the same. Ask:

Which letter should I change to make *how* become *cow?* (Change *h* to *c*.)

Which letters should I change and add to make *cow* become *down?* (Change *c* to *d*. Add *n* at the end.)

Continue with the words *out, found,* and *round.*

Read Words in Context   Write the following sentences on chart paper. Have children read each sentence silently. Then track the print as children read the sentences aloud. Finally, point to the underlined words at random and have children read them. *How did my cow get out? The tube I found is round. I will try to climb down the rope. The sun's light heats our earth. I put a cup on the table.*

RETEACH

Comprehension

 Story Elements   Review with children that the characters in a story are the people and animals who take part in the action. The setting is where and when the story happens. The plot of a story is what happens. A plot usually has a beginning, a middle (when most of the action takes place), and an ending. Say: **Turn to the story**

we read called "The First Snow" in *What a Thrill!* The characters in the story are Meg and Tim. The setting where the story happens is a snowy day. At the beginning of the story, it snows. In the middle, Meg and Tim play in the snow. At the end, they go inside to get warm. Have children select a previously read story, and guide them to point to and name the characters, identify the setting, and tell what happens at the beginning, middle, and ending.

RETEACH

High-Frequency Words

pp. 24–25

Write the words *baby, house, carry,* and *together* on the board.

- Point to and read *baby.* Repeat with children.
- Say: **My *baby* brother is tiny.**
- Repeat the word and then point to each letter as you spell it. Have children say and spell *baby* with you. Have children reread *baby.*

Repeat for the remaining words. Use the following sentences: *Let's play at my* house! *Will you* carry *this box? We worked* together *to make a card.* Have children turn to page 24 of *Sweet Success* and read aloud the words at the top of the page. Talk about the illustrations. Then guide children in choosing and writing the word that names each picture. (4. *ground,* 5. *cow,* 6. *crown*) Have children read aloud each word in the list on page 25. Ask volunteers to read the sentences aloud. Then have children choral-read the sentences. Guide them to choose and circle the word that completes each sentence. (1. *house,* 2. *baby,* 3. *carry,* 4. *together*)

RETEACH

Grammar/Writing

Practice Book
p.107

Using *Am, Is,* and *Are* Remind children that *am, is,* and *are* are verbs that tell about now. Write the following adaptation of the song "If You Are Happy and You Know It" on the board.

> *I am happy and I know it.*
> *I clap my hands.*
> *He is happy and he knows it.*
> *He claps his hands.*
> *She is happy and she knows it.*
> *She claps her hands.*
> *We are happy and we know it.*
> *We clap our hands.*

Underline each instance of *am, is,* and *are.* Point out that these are verbs that tell about now. Have children echo each sentence with an underlined word after you, and guide them to tell how many people each sentence tells about.

Complete *Practice Book* page 107 together.

High-Frequency Words

baby	carry
house	together

Fluency

Accuracy Tell children that good readers read words correctly so that a story makes sense. Have children turn to "First Snow" in *What a Thrill!* Read aloud the story, one page at a time, modeling how to read with accuracy and having children echo-read.

LESSON 27

30+ Minutes

PHONEMIC AWARENESS
Phoneme Blending

PHONICS AND SPELLING
Reteach Vowel Diphthong
/ou/ *ow, ou*

HIGH-FREQUENCY WORDS
Reteach *answered, baby, heard, pools, done, pushed, together, house, carried*

FLUENCY
Accuracy

READING
"Helping Baby Bird"

BUILD ROBUST VOCABULARY
Preteach *lonesome, elated, hopeless*

GRAMMAR/WRITING
Reteach Using *Am, Is,* and *Are*

Materials Needed:

Word Builders and Word Builder Cards

Practice Book p.108
Practice Book

Copying Masters 105–106
Lesson 27 High-Frequency Word Cards

Sweet Success Student Edition pp. 16–22 pp. 26–33

Photo Card
Photo Cards

High-Frequency Words

answered	pushed
baby	together
heard	house
pools	carried
done	

Phonemic Awareness

Phoneme Blending Tell children that they are going to play a guessing game. Say: **I'm thinking of a word that tells the shape of a circle. The word is /r/ /ou/ /n/ /d/. The word is** *round.* **Now you try some.** Continue with: /f/ /ou/ /n/ /d/ (*found*), /m/ /ou/ /th/ (*mouth*), /k/ /r/ /ou/ /d/ (*crowd*), and /p/ /l/ /ou/ (*plow*).

RETEACH

Phonics and Spelling

 Vowel Diphthong /ou/*ow, ou*
Word Building Use a *Word Builder* and *Word Builder Cards* and have children repeat each step after you. Build the word *loud.* Then have children read the word naturally—*loud.* Lead children in building and reading new words. Say:

- **Take away** *l.* **Add** *pr* **before** *oud.* **Read the word.** (*proud*)
- **Change** *p* **to** *c.* **Change** *u* **to** *w.* **Read the word.** (*crowd*)
- **Change the** *c* **to** *g.* **Change** *d* **to** *l.* **Read the word.** (*growl*)

Continue in a similar manner to have children build and read these words: *scowl/scout/spout/pout* and *ground/around/drown.*

Practice Book p.108 **Read Words in Context** Ask children to turn to *Practice Book* page 108. Read each sentence aloud and have children echo-read. Then ask volunteers to read each sentence aloud. Ask: **Who is sniffing?** (the hound) **What is he looking under?** (the couch) **What has he found?** (a toy cow) **How does he feel?** (proud) After reading, have children find and circle words with the vowel diphthong /ou/.

RETEACH

High-Frequency Words

Copying Masters 105–106 Display the *High-Frequency Word Cards* for *answered, baby, heard, pools, done, pushed, together, house,* and *carried.* Point to each card and read the word. Have children repeat. Give each child a set of word cards and have children spread the cards out in front of them. Randomly call out one of the words, and have children hold up the matching card, repeating the word aloud. Continue until they can respond quickly and accurately.

Reading

pp. 26–33

Build Background: "Helping Baby Bird"

Invite children to tell about baby birds they have seen in nature, in books, or in the media. Encourage them to tell how baby birds look compared to adult birds. Ask them to share what they know about where baby birds live and who takes care of them.

Monitor Comprehension: "Helping Baby Bird"

Ask children to look at the first page of the story. Have a volunteer read the title. Then have children look at the picture on page 27 and make predictions based on the title and the illustration. Guide children through the story as they read.

pp. 26–27

Say: **I can see a girl pointing to a baby bird. Let's read to find out why she is pointing.**

After reading the pages, ask: **Why is the girl pointing to the bird?** (She is worried that it is out of its nest.) NOTE DETAILS

Ask: **Who are the characters in the story so far?** (Ann, Jim, baby bird) STORY ELEMENTS (CHARACTERS)

Ask: **What kind of girl do you think Ann is? Why?** (Possible response: She cares about the bird, so she is caring.) CHARACTER TRAITS

Ask: **What words do you see on pages 26 and 27 that have the sound /ou/? Frame and read the words.** (sound, ground, house)

pp. 28–29

Say: **It looks like a cat has come into the yard. Let's read to find out why Ann is picking up the cat.**

After reading the pages, ask: **Why does Ann pick up the cat?** (Possible response: Jim was afraid it would hurt the bird.) CAUSE AND EFFECT

Ask: **Who do you think the cat belongs to? Why?** (The cat belongs to Ann and Jim. That is why Ann puts the cat in the house.) MAKE INFERENCES

Fluency

Accuracy Remind children that good readers are careful not to skip, add, or misread words. Have children open up to "The Flight" in *Sweet Success* and follow along as you model reading with accuracy. As you read, omit a sentence from the text, mispronounce a few words and add a few words. After reading, ask: **Did I read with accuracy?** Point out your mistakes to children and have them choral-read the story.

Ask: **What do you think will happen next?** (Possible response: Ann and Jim will try to help the bird.) **Make Predictions**

Say: **Let's say the sound /ou/ together. (/ou/) What word do you see on page 29 that has the sound /ou/ spelled *o-w*?** (now)

pp. 30–31 Say: **Ann and Jim are talking to a man. Let's read to find out what they are talking about.**

After reading the pages, ask: **What new characters do we meet on these pages?** (Dad, the vet) **Story Elements (Characters)**

Ask: **What do the children ask Dad?** (They ask him what they should do to help the baby bird.) **Note Details**

Ask: **Why do you think the vet said to wait to see if the mother bird came back first?** (Possible response: because the mother bird can take better care of the baby bird) **Use Prior Knowledge**

Ask: **Why is it a good idea to wash your hands after touching an animal?** (Possible response: so you don't get sick if the animal is sick) **Draw Conclusions**

Say: **What words have the sound /ou/ on page 30?** (found, out) **Apply Phonics**

page 32 Say: **We see that everyone is smiling. Let's read to find out why they are smiling.**

After reading the pages, ask: **Why is everyone smiling and happy?** (The baby bird is back safely in its nest.) **Cause and Effect**

Ask: **Did the mother bird come back to put the bird in the nest? How do you know?** (She didn't. The story says the children waited but then they put the bird in the nest.) **Note Details**

Ask: **Why do you think the author wrote this story?** (Possible response: I think the author wrote this story to teach a lesson.) **Author's Purpose/Point of View**

page 33 ### Answers to *Think Critically* Questions
Help children read and answer the *Think Critically* questions on page 33. Answers are shown below.

1. ‹Jim› **Characters**

2. ‹on the ground› **Setting**

3. ‹put the bird in the nest› **Beginning, Middle, Ending**

Build Robust Vocabulary

Introduce Robust Vocabulary Read the student-friendly explanation for each word. Then discuss each word using the following examples.

Say: **Sometimes, people feel lonesome when they are sick and have to stay in bed while everyone else is having a good time. Tell about a time you felt lonesome.**

Say: **Some people are elated when they get a good grade. Friends are elated when they have fun together.** Show *Photo Cards gift* and *rain*. Say: **Which of these might make you feel elated?**

Say: **Someone might feel hopeless if he or she has a lot of work to do and not enough time to do it. What else might make someone feel hopeless?**

Grammar/Writing

Using *Am, Is,* and *Are* Write *am, is,* and *are* on the board. Remind children that these are verbs that tell about now. Write a sentence on the board about what you are doing: *I am teaching you.* Ask children to notice what they are doing right now and what their classmates are doing. Then have children dictate sentences about the activities. Write their sentences on the board. Intentionally make some errors.

> What We Are Doing
>
> Ms. Jones is teaching us. We is sitting. Pete am smiling. Leah is looking around. We are learning. I are happy.

Read the sentences aloud while tracking the print. Explain to children that there are some errors in the sentences. Guide children to correct the sentences using *am, is,* or *are* correctly. Then read the corrected sentences and have children echo-read.

VOCABULARY

Student-Friendly Explanations

lonesome If you are lonesome, you feel lonely and want company.

elated If you are elated, you are very happy and excited about something.

hopeless If something seems hopeless, you feel as if there is no chance that what you want to happen will happen.

LESSON 27

30+ Minutes

DAY AT A GLANCE

Day 3

PHONEMIC AWARENESS
Phoneme Segmentation

PHONICS
Preteach Phonograms -out, -ow

PHONICS AND SPELLING
Reteach Vowel Diphthong /ou/ow, ou

HIGH-FREQUENCY WORDS
Reteach baby, carry, house, together

FLUENCY
Accuracy

COMPREHENSION
Reteach Story Elements

GRAMMAR/WRITING
Reteach Book Review

Materials Needed:

Copying Masters 107–108

Write-On/ Wipe-Off Boards with Phonemic Awareness Disks

Word Builders and Word Builder Cards

Lesson 27 Story Strips

Photo Card

Photo Cards

Happy Landings Student Edition pp. 36–42

Sweet Success Student Edition pp. 26–32

Spelling Words

1. how	6. round
2. cow	7. try
3. down	8. light
4. out	9. earth
5. found	10. table

Phonemic Awareness

Phoneme Segmentation   Have children use the three boxes on the *Write-on/Wipe-off Boards.* Tell children that the boxes stand for the sounds in words. Have children repeat each step with their *Write-on/Wipe-Off Boards.* Say the word *plow.* Say: **The first sound I hear in plow is /p/.** Model placing a disk in the first box. Use this procedure for the second sound in *plow* (/l/), placing a disk in the second box and the third sound in *plow* (/ou/), placing a disk in the third box. Point to each box in sequence as children say the word. **How many sounds do you hear in plow? I hear three.** Repeat with: *down, shout, house, loud,* and *gown.*

PRETEACH

Phonics

Phonograms -out, -ow   Say the words *shout* and *snout.* Ask children how the words are the same. (They both end with /out/; they rhyme.) Using the words *scout, shot, pout,* and *boat,* have children motion "thumbs up" when they hear a word that rhymes with *shout.*

Say the words *now* and *pow.* Ask how these words are the same. (They both end with /ou/; they rhyme.) Have children show "thumbs up" when they hear a word that rhymes with *now.* Say the words *cow, vow, shy, how,* and *show.*

RETEACH

Phonics and Spelling

Vowel Diphthong /ou/ow, ou
Build Words   Use *Word Builders* and *Word Builder Cards* to form words. Have children listen to your directions and change and/or add a letter in each word to spell a spelling word using their *Word Builder Cards* and *Word Builders.* Form *hot* and have children read the word. Ask: **Which spelling word can you make by changing the last letter?** (how)

h o t

h o w

Follow a similar procedure with the following words: *how* (*cow*), *cow* (*down*), *sound* (*found, round*), *toy* (*try*), and *right* (*light*).

Remind children that there are some other words they have to remember how to spell. Tell them that *earth* is one such word. Have children say *earth.* Tell them to put *Word Builder Cards e, a, r, t, h* in their *Word Builders,* picture the word *earth* in their minds, and build the word. Write the word on the board. Follow the same procedure with *table.*

RETEACH

High-Frequency Words

 Copying Masters 107–108 Duplicate and distribute *Copying Masters* 107–108 to each child. Explain that the sentences tell about the story "Helping Baby Bird" but some have missing words.

List the words *baby, carry, house,* and *together* on the board. Have children read aloud each story strip sentence and name the correct word on the board that makes sense in the sentence. Have children write the missing words in the blanks and read the completed sentences aloud. Help children cut apart the strips, read the completed sentences, and arrange them in story order.

RETEACH

Comprehension

  Story Elements Review with children that stories have a plot, setting, and characters. Help them recall that the plot is the events that happen at the beginning, middle, and end of a story. Model identifying these elements in "Helping Baby Bird" in *Sweet Success*. Then have children turn to "The Picnic Plan" in *Happy Landings*. Walk children through the story and guide them to identify the plot, setting, and characters.

RETEACH

Grammar/Writing

Book Review Tell children that you are going to give a book review. Say: **I read *Charlotte's Web*. The author is E.B. White. The story is about a little girl, a pig, and a spider who are friends. The spider and the little girl save the pig's life in different ways. It is a great story about friendship.** Point out that in a book review, you name the title and author of the book. Then point out how you told what the book is about without telling the ending. Then point out how you told what you liked about the book. Have children think of a favorite story they have read recently and share what they liked about the story with a partner.

High-Frequency Words

baby	house
carry	together

Fluency

Accuracy Remind children that when good readers read a passage, it makes sense and sounds as if they are talking. Good readers recognize and read words automatically and correctly. Have children turn to "Helping Baby Bird" in *Sweet Success*.

Say: **I'm going to read "Helping Baby Bird" one page at a time. As I read each page, I will try to say the words in the sentences correctly and automatically, without having to stop to figure out the sounds that the letters stand for in each word. Read each page after me, just the way I read it.**

LESSON 27

30+ Minutes

DAY AT A GLANCE

Day 4

PHONEMIC AWARENESS
Phoneme Blending

PHONICS
Reteach Phonograms *-own, -ound*

PHONICS AND SPELLING
Reteach Vowel Diphthong /ou/*ow, ou*

HIGH-FREQUENCY WORDS
Reteach *answered, baby, heard, pools, done, pushed, together, house, carried*

FLUENCY
Accuracy

COMPREHENSION
Reteach Story Elements

GRAMMAR/WRITING
Reteach Book Review

Materials Needed:

Practice
Book

Lesson 27
High-Frequency
Word Cards

Sweet Success
Student Edition
pp. 16–22
pp. 26–32

Photo
Cards

Spelling Words

1. how	6. round
2. cow	7. try
3. down	8. light
4. out	9. earth
5. found	10. table

Phonemic Awareness

Phoneme Blending Tell children that together you are going to play a game of "Fix It." Tell them that you are going to say some words that are all broken and they should listen to see if they can put the sounds together to fix the word. Say: **/f/ /ou/ /n/ /d/. What word does /f/ /ou/ /n/ /d/ say? It says** *found.* Continue with the following words: **/h/ /ou/ /s/** (*house*), **/m/ /ou/ /th/** (*mouth*), **/s/ /ou/ /n/ /d/** (*sound*), **/sh/ /ou/ /t/** (*shout*).

RETEACH

Phonics

Phonograms *-own, -ound* Say the words *clown* and *drown*. Ask children how the words are the same. (Both end with /oun/ and rhyme.) Have children show "thumbs up" when they hear a word that rhymes with *clown*. Say these words: *town, tame, frown, brown, tin.*

Then say *found* and *ground*. Ask how these words are the same. (Both end with /ound/ and rhyme.) Have children show "thumbs up" when they hear a word that rhymes with *found*. Say these words: *sound, round, mind, hound, grind.*

RETEACH

Phonics and Spelling

Vowel Diphthong /ou/*ow, ou*
Direct children's attention to page 109 of their *Practice Books*. Complete the page together.

Assess children's progress using the following sentences.

1.	how	I know **how** to play the flute.
2.	cow	Have you ever seen a **cow**?
3.	down	We ran **down** the path.
4.	out	Can you come **out** of the house?
5.	found	I **found** a penny.
6.	round	The moon has a **round** shape.

Review

7.	try	**Try** this cake I made.
8.	light	The sun's **light** helps plants.

High-Frequency

9.	earth	The machine took **earth** out of the ground.
10.	table	Dad put dishes on the **table**.

RETEACH

High-Frequency Words

Copying Masters 105–106

Display *High-Frequency Word Cards* for this lesson's words—*answered, baby, heard, pools, done, pushed, together, house, carried*—and the previously learned high-frequency words. Point to words at random and ask children to read them.

RETEACH

Comprehension

Story Elements Elicit from children that characters are people and animals in a story, setting is when and where a story takes place, and plot is what happens. Draw a three-column chart on the board like the one below. Walk children through the stories and guide children to point out the characters, setting, and plot. Record their responses on the chart.

	"Helping Baby Bird"	"The Flight"
characters	Ann, Jim, bird, Dad, vet	Little Mouse, his mother
setting	backyard, one sunny day	Little Mouse's home; bedtime
plot	Jim and Ann find a baby bird and rescue it.	Little Mouse dreams about flying in space, then realizes it's good to be home.

RETEACH

Grammar/Writing

Book Review Review with children characteristics of a book review.

Book Review

The title and the author of the book are given.
The review tells what the book is about.
It tells what I think about the book.

Tell children that you will write a book review together. Brainstorm some familiar titles, and then have volunteers dictate their sentences as you write them on the board or on chart paper. Then track the print and read the book review with children.

High-Frequency Words

answered	pushed
baby	together
heard	house
pools	carried
done	

Fluency

Accuracy Have children practice reading "Helping Baby Bird" aloud three or four times. Remind them to use their blending skills and remember words they have learned as they read. Listen to children read, providing feedback about their accuracy and guidance for improving their fluency.

DAY AT A GLANCE
Day 5

HIGH-FREQUENCY WORDS
answered, baby, heard, pools, done, pushed, together

PHONEMIC AWARENESS
Onset and Rime

PHONICS AND SPELLING
Preteach Long Vowel /ē/y, ie

BUILD ROBUST VOCABULARY
Preteach arrived, familiar, properly

GRAMMAR/WRITING
Preteach Verbs That Tell About the Past

Materials Needed:

Lesson 27
High-Frequency
Word Cards

Sound/
Spelling Cards
Yy, Ii, Ee

Word Builders
and Word
Builder Cards

Write-On/
Wipe-Off
Boards

Practice
Book

High-Frequency Words

answered	done
baby	pushed
heard	together
pools	

High-Frequency Words

Copying Masters 105–106

Display *High-Frequency Word Cards* for *answered, baby, heard, pools, done, pushed, together,* and the other previously learned high-frequency words. Say the word *answered,* ask a volunteer to point to *answered,* and have children read the word aloud. Continue with the remaining high-frequency words. Repeat this activity several times to reinforce instant recognition.

Phonemic Awareness

Onset and Rime Tell children that you will say some words, but you will say them in parts. Have children listen to see if they can figure out the word. Say: /k/- country –What word did I say? I said *country.* **Now you try some:** /pr/-etty, /s/-afely, /k/-ookie, /d/-uty, /st/-ories.

> **PRETEACH**

Phonics and Spelling

Sound/Spelling Card

Long Vowel /ē/y, ie
Connecting Letter to Sound Say the words *silly, easy,* and *cookie* and have children repeat the words. Say: **The words *silly, easy,* and *cookie* all have the /ē/ sound.** Have children say /ē/ several times. Display *Sound/Spelling Card Yy.* Tell children that the letter *y* can stand for the sound /ē/, the sound at the end of *easy.* Have children say the sound /ē/ as you touch the letter. Display *Sound/Spelling Cards Ii* and *Ee,* and say the letter names. Tell children that the letters *i* and *e* together can also stand for the /ē/ sound, the sound at the end of *cookie.*

Give children each a *y Word Builder Card.* Say: **When I say a word that ends with /ē/, hold up your card and say /ē/. When I say a word that does not end with /ē/, hold your card behind your back.** Say these words: *baby, study, play, lady, copy, try.* Tell children that some of the following words also have the /ē/ sound, but that it is spelled with *ie.* Have them raise their hands when they hear the /ē/ sound. Use these words: *Marie, too, marries, worried.*

Word Blending Demonstrate each step with *Word Builder Cards* and a *Word Builder.* Have children repeat each step after you. Hold up *b* and say /b/. Hold up *u* and say /u/. Hold up *nn* and say /n/. Hold up *y* and say /ē/.

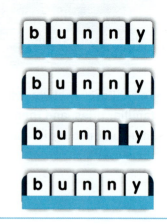

- Place the letters *b, u, n, n, y* in the *Word Builder.*
- Point to *b.* Say /b/. Point to *u* and say /uu/.
- Slide *u* next to *b.* Run your hand under the letters as you blend the sounds, elongating them—/buu/.

- Point to *nn* and say /n/. Hold up *y* and say /ē/. Slide *nn* next to *bu*. Slide your hand under *bunn* as you blend the sounds, elongating them—/bun/. Have children repeat.

- Finally, slide *y* next to *bunn*. Run your hand under *bunny* as you blend the sounds, elongating them—/bunē/. Have children repeat. Read *bunny* naturally and repeat with children.

Follow the same procedure with these words: *funny, penny, dirty.*

  Word Building   Place the *Word Builder Cards f, u, n, n,* and *y* in the *Word Builder* and have children do the same. Ask children to say each letter name and the sound it stands for. Read the word naturally— *funny.* Have children build and read new words. As they build each word, write it on the board. Say: **Change *f* to *h* and each *n* to an *r*. What word did you make?** (*hurry*)

Continue with the words *hurried, happy, story,* and *stories.* Then have children read the words on the board. Complete *Practice Book* page 110 together.

Practice Book p.110

PRETEACH

Build Robust Vocabulary

Introduce Robust Vocabulary   Read the student-friendly explanation for each word. Then discuss each word using the following examples.

Say: **I arrived at 7:30 today. What time was it when you arrived?**

Say: **I am familiar with a story called *Paddington Bear*. What is the title of a story you are familiar with?**

Say: **I know how to write all the letters of the alphabet properly. What is something you know how to do properly?**

PRETEACH

Grammar/Writing

Verbs That Tell About the Past   Remind children that they have already learned about verbs that tell about now. Explain that today they will learn some verbs that tell about the past. Write the following sentences on the board: *The children <u>worked</u> hard. They <u>learned</u> a lot.* Explain that these sentences tell about something that happened in the past. Ask children what is the same about the underlined words. (Both end with *ed.*) Ask children how the words would be changed to tell about now. (They would take off the *ed.*)

Spelling Words

1. funny	6. hurried
2. happy	7. how
3. story	8. out
4. stories	9. baby
5. hurry	10. done

Have children practice writing spelling words on their *Write-on/Wipe-off Boards.*

VOCABULARY

Student-Friendly Explanations

arrived If you arrive at a place, you have come to that place.

familiar If something is familiar, it is something you know very well.

properly If you do something properly, you do it the right way.

LESSON 28

PHONEMIC AWARENESS
Phoneme Isolation

PHONICS AND SPELLING
Reteach Long Vowel /ē/y, ie

COMPREHENSION
Preteach Note Details

HIGH-FREQUENCY WORDS
Reteach blue, color, great, our

FLUENCY
Accuracy

GRAMMAR/WRITING
Reteach Verbs That Tell About the Past

Materials Needed:

Photo Cards

Word Builders and Word Builder Cards

Write-On/Wipe-Off Boards

Sweet Success Student Edition pp. 16–22 pp. 34–35

Practice Book

Happy Landings Student Edition pp. 56–62

Spelling Words

1. funny	6. hurried
2. happy	7. how
3. story	8. out
4. stories	9. baby
5. hurry	10. done

Have children practice writing spelling words on their *Write-on/Wipe-off Boards.*

Phonemic Awareness

Phoneme Isolation Show *Photo Card factory.* Say the word *factory* aloud, and have children repeat it. Tell children to listen to the /ē/ sound at the end of *factory.* Then say the words *quarry* and *girl.* Have children repeat both words. Ask: **Which word has the same /ē/ sound you hear at the end of *factory*? *Quarry* does. Now you try some.** Continue with the words *pony, track, empty; army, only, feet; hurry, hard, bubbly.*

RETEACH

Phonics and Spelling

Long Vowel /ē/y, *ie*
Word Building Place the *Word Builder Cards f, u, n, n, y* in the *Word Builder.* Ask children to say the name of each letter and the sound it stands for. Then read the word naturally—*funny.* Remind children that the letter *y* and the letters *i* and *e* together can stand for the /ē/ sound. Ask:

- **Which letters should I change to make *funny* become *happy*?** (Change *f, u, n, n* to *h, a, p, p.*)

- **Which letters should I change to make *happy* become *story*?** (Change *h, a, p, p* to *s, t, o, r.*)

Continue with the words *stories, hurry,* and *hurried.*

Read Words in Context Write the following sentences on chart paper. Have children read each sentence silently. Then track the print as children read the sentences aloud. Finally, point to the underlined words at random and have children read them. *Mom read the baby a story. I am not happy when I have to hurry. All the stories were funny. I wondered how soon lunch would be done. I hurried out to the kitchen to eat it.*

PRETEACH

Comprehension

Note Details Tell children that details tell little bits of information about a character, place, or event. Say: **Details help readers picture in their minds what is happening.** Details can tell what something looks like, how it sounds, or what it does. Details help us answer *Who? What? Where?* and *When?* They help us better understand what we read.

Read aloud the following excerpt from "Under a Bridge" in *Happy Landings:* ***Six kids and a dog were under the bridge. They all sang. And the bridge sang back.*** Then model how to recognize details. Say: **I know that there are six kids. I know there is a dog, too. I know they are all under a bridge. What detail tells what the kids did?** (They sang.)

High-Frequency Words

color	great
blue	our

RETEACH

High-Frequency Words

Write the words *color, blue, great,* and *our* on the board.

- Point to and read *color.* Repeat, having children say *color* with you.
- Say: *My favorite* **color** *is red.*
- Repeat the word and then point to each letter as you spell it. Have children say and spell *color* with you and reread the word.

Repeat for the remaining words. Display *Photo Cards sky, cake,* and *school.* Use the following sentences: *The sky is* blue. *Cake tastes* great. *This is* our *school.*

Have children turn to page 34 of *Sweet Success* and have them read aloud the words at the top of the page. Talk about the illustrations. Then guide children in choosing and writing the word that names each picture. (4. *field,* 5. *happy,* 6. *stories*) Have children read aloud each word in the list on page 35. Ask volunteers to read the sentences aloud. Then have children choral-read the sentences. Guide them to choose and circle the word that completes each sentence. (1. *blue,* 2. *color,* 3. *our,* 4. *great*)

RETEACH

Grammar/Writing

Verbs That Tell About the Past Write the following poem on the board. Tell children to listen for words that tell about the past as you read it. Read the poem aloud a few times, emphasizing the verbs.

I used a pencil to draw my cat Gene.
I painted his eyes bright green.
I glued gold glitter on his fur.
I showed him the picture, and he purred.

After reading the poem, say: ***Used* is a verb that tells about the past.** Guide children to identify the verbs that tell about the past in the poem. (*painted, glued, showed, purred*) Complete *Practice Book* page 111 together.

Fluency

Accuracy Have children open to "The Flight" in *Sweet Success.* Model how to read the first page with accuracy. Ask children to track the print as you read aloud. Remind children that it is important to read each word carefully and to read the words in the order they appear in the story. Read aloud the rest of the story, one page at a time. Read with accuracy and have children echo-read after you.

DAY AT A GLANCE

Day 2

PHONEMIC AWARENESS
Onset and Rime

PHONICS AND SPELLING
Reteach Long Vowel /ē/ *y, ie*

HIGH-FREQUENCY WORDS
Reteach *great, took, poured, almost, traveled, blue, able, color, our*

FLUENCY
Accuracy

READING
"Do You Know Me?"

BUILD ROBUST VOCABULARY
Preteach *anticipate, numerous, vibrant*

GRAMMAR/WRITING
Reteach Verbs That Tell About the Past

Materials Needed:

Practice Book p.112	**Copying Masters** 109–110	

Word Builders and Word Builder Cards | Practice Book | Lesson 28 High-Frequency Word Cards

Sweet Success Student Edition pp. 36–43 | *Happy Landings* Student Edition pp. 26–32 | Photo Cards

High-Frequency Words

great	blue
took	able
poured	color
almost	our
traveled	

Phonemic Awareness

Onset and Rime Tell children that they will play a guessing game. Say: **I'm thinking of a word that describes something that makes you laugh. It is /f/-unny. What's my word? My word is** *funny*. **Now you try some.** Continue with /s/-/illy (*silly*), /h/-urries (*hurries*), and /pr/-etty (*pretty*).

RETEACH

Phonics and Spelling

Long Vowel /ē/ *y, ie*
Word Building Use a *Word Builder* and *Word Builder Cards* and have children repeat each step with their *Word Builders* and *Word Builder Cards*. Build the word *party* and read it aloud with children. Lead children in building and reading new words. Say:

- **Take away the** *y*. **Read the word.** (*part*)
- **Change** *pa* **to** *di*. **Read the word.** (*dirt*)

Continue with the following words: *dirty, hurry, hurries, scurries, scurry*. Point out that you changed *y* to *ie* when you added *-s*.

Read Words in Context Ask children to turn to *Practice Book* page 112. Then ask volunteers to read each sentence aloud. Ask: **What is Marie?** (a bunny) **What does she plan for her friends?** (a party) **What do the bunnies do at the party?** (tell funny jokes) **What do the bunnies eat at the party?** (jelly cookies) After reading, guide children to circle all the long *e* words.

RETEACH

High-Frequency Words

Copying Masters 109–110 Write *great, took, poured, almost, traveled, blue, able, color,* and *our* on the board. Point to and read each word. Give each child a set of *High-Frequency Word Cards,* and have children spread the cards out in front of them. Call on volunteers to hold up a card. Have the rest of the children hold up the matching card and say the word with you. Assess how well children are able to identify the words, and repeat until they can respond quickly and accurately without you saying the word with them.

Reading

pp. 36–43

Build Background: "Do You Know Me?"

Invite children to talk about art materials they have used. Ask: **What do you use to draw? What do you use to color your drawings? What do you use to cut things apart and put things together?** Ask children to tell about art projects they have done at home and in school. Ask volunteers to identify particular materials and tools they used.

Monitor Comprehension: "Do You Know Me?"

Ask children to look at page 36 in *Sweet Success*. Read the title and have children repeat it. Have children look at the pictures, identify the characters, and tell what they think this selection will be about. Then guide children through the selection as they read.

pp. 36–37

Say: **I see a pencil with a face. The pencil looks like it is talking. Let's read to find out what the pencil is saying.**

After reading the pages, ask: **What does the pencil say it can do?** (make lines, shapes, and letters) NOTE DETAILS

Ask: **Point to the word *fancy*. What is the last sound in the word? What letter makes the sound?** (/ē/, *y*) APPLY PHONICS

Display *Photo Cards gold, crayon,* and *school.* Ask: **Which card is most like the characters on page 37? What can they do?** (crayon; fill in spaces, make lines) CHARACTERS' TRAITS

Ask: **How does the pencil say he is different from his friends?** (he is black or gray, but his friends are many colors.) COMPARE AND CONTRAST

Ask: **Remember that *y* can make the sound /ē/. Say the sound. What words do you see on page 37 that end with a *y* that make the sound /ē/?** (many, pretty) **Let's read the words together.** APPLY PHONICS

pp. 38–39

Say: **These pages show two more characters. Let's read to find out what they can do.**

After reading the pages, ask: **Who are these characters?** (paintbox, brush) **What can they do?** (paint splashes of color) NOTE DETAILS

Why do the paint and brush need water to do their job? (Possible response: Paints need to be wet so we can get them on a paintbrush.) MAKE INFERENCES

Fluency

Accuracy Reread "Max is Missing" from *Happy Landings* aloud, demonstrating accuracy. Have children track the print. Next, reread the selection but reverse the order of some words, or skip a line. Mispronounce some words. Have children talk about the difference between the readings and decide which was easier to understand. Remind children that it is important to read with accuracy.

Ask: **What is something you could use the characters on these pages to paint?** (Possible response: a bird, a car, a person) **PERSONAL RESPONSE**

pp. 40–41

Say: **I see two more characters on these pages. They look familiar. Let's read to find out who they are.**

After reading the pages, ask: **What do these pages tell about?** (scissors, glue) **NOTE DETAILS**

Say: **Scissors cut things apart. How is that different from what glue does?** (Glue puts things together.) **COMPARE AND CONTRAST**

Ask: **What else could scissors cut?** (Possible answer: cut red paper into apples, cut white paper into clouds) **USE PRIOR KNOWLEDGE**

Ask: **Find the word** *stick* **on page 41. Point to the word. What letter would we have to add to turn the word into** *sticky?* (*y*) **APPLY PHONICS**

page 42

Say: **We see a girl showing us a picture. Let's read to find out about the picture.**

After reading the pages, ask: **Who probably made the picture?** (the girl) **What did she probably use to make the picture?** (the art tools we read about) **MAKE INFERENCES**

Ask: **Do you like to make art? Why or why not?** (Possible response: Yes, because it is fun.) **PERSONAL RESPONSE**

Ask: **Why do you think the author wrote this selection?** (Possible response: to teach about different art tools, to make children want to do art projects) **AUTHOR'S PURPOSE**

page 43

Answers to *Think Critically* Questions

Help children read and answer the *Think Critically* questions on page 43. Answers are shown below.

1. ‹pencils› **DRAW CONCLUSIONS**
2. ‹glue› **SETTING**
 3. ‹paint› **NOTE DETAILS**

PRETEACH

Build Robust Vocabulary

Introduce Robust Vocabulary Read the student-friendly explanation for each word. Then discuss each word using the following examples.

Say: I **anticipate** my birthday each year. What special events or holidays do you **anticipate**?

Say: I have **numerous** things on my desk. Do we have **numerous** books in our classroom? Explain.

Say: Red is my favorite color. It is **vibrant**. What is your favorite color? Is it **vibrant**? Point to something **vibrant** in the room.

RETEACH

Grammar/Writing

Verbs That Tell About the Past Have children recall a recent class activity. Have them dictate sentences that tell about things they did during the activity. Ask them to include verbs that tell about the past. Include some sentences of your own with errors to be corrected later.

> ### Our Cookie Bake
> We baked cookies yesterday. We collect flour, sugar, butter, milk, and eggs. Then we mix them together. We dropped the dough on a pan. Our teacher placed them in the oven. When they were done, we cool them. Then we gobbled them up.

Read the dictated sentences to children as you track the print. Guide children to correct errors with verbs by saying: **The word *collect* tells what is happening now. Because the sentence tells what happened in the past, I know to add -*ed* to *collect*.** Repeat with *mix* and *cool*.

VOCABULARY

Student-Friendly Explanations

anticipate When you anticipate a party, you look forward to it.

numerous If you have numerous toys, you have many toys.

vibrant If your shirt is vibrant, it has bright or bold colors.

LESSON 28

DAY AT A GLANCE

Day 3

PHONEMIC AWARENESS
Phoneme Blending

PHONICS
Preteach Inflections -ed, -er, -est, -es

PHONICS AND SPELLING
Reteach Long Vowel /ē/y, ie

HIGH-FREQUENCY WORDS
Reteach blue, color, great, our

FLUENCY
Accuracy

COMPREHENSION
Reteach Note Details

GRAMMAR/WRITING
Reteach How-to Paragraph

Materials Needed:

Word Builders
and Word
Builder Cards

Copying
Masters
111–
112

Lesson 28
Story Strips

Sweet Success
Student Edition
pp. 36–42

Photo
Card

Photo
Cards

Spelling Words

1. funny	6. hurried
2. happy	7. how
3. story	8. out
4. stories	9. baby
5. hurry	10. done

30+ Minutes

Phonemic Awareness

Phoneme Blending   Tell children that they are going to be builders and put together pieces of words to make whole words. Say: **This is good on toast. It is /j/ /e/ /l/ /ē/. What word did I say? I said** *jelly.* **Now, you try some.** Continue with the words: /m/ /e/ /s/ /ē/ (*messy*), /t/ /ī/ /n/ /ē/ (*tiny*), /b/ /u/ /g/ /ē/ (*buggy*).

PRETEACH

Phonics

Inflections -ed, -er, -est, -es   Write on the board *hurry + es = hurries; hurry + ed = hurried; funny + er = funnier; funny + est = funniest.* Point to the root word *hurry.* Point to the -es on *hurries,* and tell children that this ending tells the reader that something is happening now. Point to the -ed on *hurried.* Explain that this ending tells that something happened in the past. Use the same procedure to point out the root and endings for *funny.* Have children read all the words with you.

RETEACH

Phonics and Spelling

d o t   **Long Vowel /ē/y, ie**
Build Words   Use *Word Builders* and *Word Builder Cards* to form words. Have children listen to your directions and change a letter in each word to spell a spelling word using their *Word Builder Cards* and *Word Builders.* Form *hurry* and have children read the word. Ask:

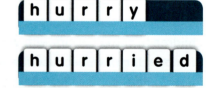

- **Which spelling word can you make by changing the *y* to *i* and adding -ed?** (*hurried*)

- Form *story.* Ask: **Which spelling word can you make by changing *y* to *i* and adding -es?** (*stories*)

Follow a similar procedure with the following words: funny (*funnier*), happy (*happier*), now (*how*), oat (*out*).

Remind children that there are some other words they have to remember how to spell. Have children say *baby.* Tell them to put *Word Builder Cards* b, a, b, y in their *Word Builders,* picture the word *baby* in their minds, and build the word. Write the word on the board. Follow the same procedure with *done.*

RETEACH
High-Frequency Words

Copying Masters 111–112

Duplicate and distribute *Copying Masters* 111–112 to each child. Explain that the sentences tell the selection "Do You Know Me?" but some have missing words.

List the words *color, blue, great,* and *our* on the board. Have children read aloud each story strip sentence and name the correct word on the board that makes sense in the sentence. Have children write the missing words in the blanks and read the completed sentences aloud. Help children cut apart the strips, read the completed sentences, and arrange them in story order.

RETEACH
Comprehension

Note Details Review how to identify details in a selection. Ask children to tell what details are. (little bits of information about a character, place, or event in a story)

Tell children they are going to listen to "Do You Know Me?" in *Sweet Success.* Ask them to close their eyes and imagine the details as you read. Pause after each sentence, allowing children an opportunity to visualize the selection details. Encourage them to discuss what they visualize.

RETEACH
Grammar/Writing

Photo Card

How-to Paragraph Display *Photo Card pie.* Write the following paragraph on the board:

> First, roll out the crust. Put the bottom crust in a pan. Next, put the filling in the crust. Put on a top crust. Last, bake the pie.

Explain that this is a how-to paragraph about how to make a pie. Read the paragraph aloud as you track the print and talk about how the directions help us know how to make a pie. Tell children that how-to paragraphs must tell the directions in order. The directions must be written clearly. Point out that how-to paragraphs include words such as *first, next, after,* and *last.*

High-Frequency Words

color	great
blue	our

Fluency

Accuracy Remind children that good readers read with accuracy to understand a selection. Say: **I am going to read "Do You Know Me?" one page at a time. I will listen to myself read to be sure all the words make sense. If I do not understand something, I can reread aloud to help me understand. Read each page after me, just the way that I read.**

LESSON 28

30+ Minutes

DAY AT A GLANCE

Day 4

PHONEMIC AWARENESS
Phoneme Blending

PHONICS
Reteach Inflections -ed, -er, -est, -es

PHONICS AND SPELLING
Reteach Long Vowel /ē/y, ie

HIGH-FREQUENCY WORDS
Reteach great, took, poured, almost, traveled, blue, able, color, our

FLUENCY
Accuracy

COMPREHENSION
Reteach Note Details

GRAMMAR/WRITING
Reteach How-to Paragraph

Materials Needed:

Practice Book

Lesson 28 High-Frequency Word Cards

Happy Landings Student Edition pp. 6–12

Sweet Success Student Edition pp. 36–42

Spelling Words

1. funny	6. hurried
2. happy	7. how
3. story	8. out
4. stories	9. baby
5. hurry	10. done

Phonemic Awareness

Phoneme Blending   Tell children that together you are going to play a puzzle game. Tell them that you will say some words in pieces like a puzzle and they should listen to see if they can put the puzzle pieces together to figure out the word. Say: /kw/ /är/ /ē. **What word does /kw/ /är/ /ē/ say? It says** *quarry.* **Now you try some.** Continue with the following words: /g/ /u/ /m/ /ē/ (*gummy*), /r/ /oo/ /k/ /ē/ (*rookie*), /s/ /ā/ /f/ /t/ /ē/ (*safety*), /ē/ /z/ /ē/ (*easy*).

RETEACH

Phonics

Inflections -ed, -er, -est, -es   Remind children that endings can be added to a root word to make new words. Write *funny, funnier, funniest.* Say: **Make** *funnier* **and** *funniest* **by adding** *-er* **and** *-est* **to** *funny.* **Change the** *y* **to** *i* **before adding** *-er* **or** *-est.*

Write *worry, worries, worried.* Say: **Make new words by adding** *-es* **or** *-ed* **to** *worry.* **Change the** *y* **to** *i* **before adding** *-es* **or** *-ed.* Guide children in adding endings to *easy, angry, marry,* and *carry.*

RETEACH

Phonics and Spelling

Practice Book p.114

Long Vowel /ē/y, ie

Direct children's attention to page 114 of their *Practice Books.* Complete the page together.

Assess children's progress using the following sentences.

1.	funny	Fuzz is a **funny** cat.
2.	happy	I was **happy** to see my dad.
3.	story	The teacher told us a good **story.**
4.	stories	My grandpa reads us silly **stories.**
5.	hurry	**Hurry** so we will not be late.
6.	hurried	Lilly **hurried** to catch the bus.

Review

7.	how	Do you know **how** to make pizza?
8.	out	Go **out** to the yard.

High-Frequency

9.	baby	My **baby** brother is very little.
10.	done	I am **done** with all my chores!

RETEACH

High-Frequency Words

Copying
Masters
109–110

Display *High-Frequency Word Cards* for this lesson's words—*great, took, poured, almost, traveled, blue, able, color,* and *our*—and the previously learned high-frequency words. Point to words at random and ask children to read them.

RETEACH

Comprehension

  Note Details Help children recall what details are. (little bits of information in a story or selection) Draw a chart on the board like the one below. Have children look at the stories "Frog and Rabbit" in *Happy Landings* and "Do You Know Me?" in *Sweet Success.* Write details that answer each question in the first column from "Frog and Rabbit." Guide children to identify details from "Do You Know Me?" Record their responses in the chart.

	"Frog and Rabbit"	**"Do You Know Me?**
Who?	Frog, Rabbit	pencil, crayons, paints, brush, scissors, glue
What?	run a race	make art
When?	day time	anytime
Where?	outside	in school, at home

RETEACH

Grammar/Writing

How-to Paragraph Review characteristics of how-to paragraphs.

> ### How-to Paragraph
> Gives directions in order.
> Sentences should be clearly written.
> Includes words such as *first, next, after,* and *last.*

Write the following paragraph on the board: *First, get out your paints, brush, and paper. Next, put water in a can. Dip the brush into the water. Then rub the wet brush on the paint. Paint with light colors first. After you put on the light colors, use dark colors. Last, let your painting dry.* Read the paragraph aloud, tracking the print. Say: **This paragraph tells us how to paint with watercolors.** Guide children to dictate a paragraph about how to do a different art project, such as making a greeting card. Record their sentences on chart paper. Choral-read the paragraph with children.

High-Frequency Words

great	blue
took	able
poured	color
almost	our
traveled	

Fluency

Accuracy Remind children that good readers read with accuracy. Have children turn to "Do You Know Me?" in *Sweet Success.* Ask them to follow along as you read the pages aloud and check to see that you read every word correctly. After reading, ask: **Did I read each word correctly? Did I skip any words? Did I add any words?** Have children choral-read the selection with accuracy.

DAY AT A GLANCE
Day 5

HIGH-FREQUENCY WORDS
great, took, poured, almost, traveled, blue, able

PHONEMIC AWARENESS
Onset and Rime

PHONICS AND SPELLING
Preteach Vowel Variant /o͞o/*oo, ew*

BUILD ROBUST VOCABULARY
Preteach *wriggle, prickly, interested*

GRAMMAR/WRITING
Preteach Using *Was* and *Were*

Materials Needed:

Lesson 28
High-Frequency
Word Cards

Sound/Spelling
Card *Uu*

Word Builders
and Word
Builder Cards

Write-On/
Wipe-Off
Boards

Practice
Book

Photo
Cards

High-Frequency Words

great	traveled
took	blue
poured	able
almost	

30+ Minutes

High-Frequency Words

Copying Masters 109–110 Display *High-Frequency Word Cards* for *great, took, poured, almost, traveled, blue, able,* and the other previously learned high-frequency words. Say the word *able,* ask a volunteer to point to *able,* and have children read the word aloud. Continue with the remaining high-frequency words. Repeat this activity several times to reinforce instant recognition.

Phonemic Awareness

Onset and Rime Tell children you are going to say some words, but you are going to say them in parts. Have children listen to see if they can figure out the word. Say: **Listen as I say this word in parts: /h/-oop–The word I said was** *hoop.* **Now, you try it. /f/-ood, /b/-oost, /br/-oom, /l/-oop, /bl/-ew, /r/-oom, /sp/-oon, /d/-ew, /r/-ooster**

PRETEACH

Phonics and Spelling

Vowel Variant /o͞o/*oo, ew*
Connecting Letter to Sound Say the word *tooth.* Have children say the word. Repeat for the words *booth, loop,* and *few.* Have children say /o͞o/ several times. Display *Sound/Spelling Card Uu* and say the letter name. Point to *u_e* and remind children that they have already learned that words with *u* followed by a consonant and the letter *e* have the long *u* sound as in the word *blue.* Then point to *oo* and *ew* and explain that they are going to learn two more spellings for the long *u* sound. Say *boots,* elongating the /o͞o/ sound. Tell children that *boots* has /o͞o/ in the middle. Give each child two *o Word Builder Cards.* Say: **When I say a word with /o͞o/ in the middle, hold up your cards and say /o͞o/. When I say a word that does not have /o͞o/ in the middle, hold your cards behind your back.** Say these words: *moon, top, roof, cup, root, boat.* Say *stew,* elongating the /o͞o/. Tell children that *stew* has /o͞o/ at the end. Follow the same procedure for the final position with the following words: *knew, flew, pea, moo, jump, drew.*

Word Blending Demonstrate each step with *Word Builder Cards* and a *Word Builder* and have children repeat each step after you. Hold up *r* and say /r/. Hold up *oo* and say /o͞o/. Hold up *m* and say /m/.

- Place the letters *r, o, o, m* in the *Word Builder.*
- Point to *r.* Say /r/. Point to *oo* and say /o͞o/. Prompt children to repeat after you.

- Slide *oo* next to *r.* Run your hand under the letters as you blend the sounds, elongating them—/ro͞o/.

- Point to *m* and say /m/.
- Slide *m* next to *roo*. Run your hand under *room* as you blend the sounds, elongating them—/r$\overline{oo}$m/. Read *room* naturally.

Follow the same procedure with these words: *food* and *mood*. Then repeat the activity using *Word Builder Cards e* and *w* together to stand for the /$\overline{oo}$/ sound in the words *new, blew,* and *chew*.

  Word Building   Place the *Word Builder Cards b, o, o,* and *t* in the *Word Builder* and have children do the same. Ask children to say each letter name and the sound it stands for. Then read the word naturally—*boot*. Have children do the same. Have children build and read new words. As they build each word, write it on the board. Say:

- **Change *b* to *t* and add *h* at the end. What word did you make?** (*tooth*)

- **Change *t* to *s* and *th* to *n*. What word did you make?** (*soon*)

Continue with the words *noon, new,* and *grew*. Have children read the words on the board. Direct children's attention to page 114 of their *Practice Books*. Complete the page together.

PRETEACH

Build Robust Vocabulary

Photo Card   **Introduce Robust Vocabulary**   Read the student-friendly explanation for each word. Display *Photo Cards fish, rose, porcupine.* Then focus on the appropriate card and discuss each word using the following examples:

Say: **A fish can wriggle through the water. What other animals can wriggle?**

Say: **The thorns on a rose bush are prickly. What else in nature is prickly?**

Say: **I am interested in learning more about porcupines. What are you interested in learning about?**

PRETEACH

Grammar/Writing

Using *Was* and *Were*   Explain that *was* and *were* are used to tell about things that happened in the past. Display the following sentences: *Juan was playing in the yard. His friends were playing with him.* Place a self-stick note over *was* and write *is* on it. Read the sentence and tell children that it tells about now. Remove the word *is* and read the sentence. Tell children that this sentence tells about the past. Follow the same procedure with the second sentence.

Spelling Words

1. boot	6. grew
2. tooth	7. story
3. soon	8. hurry
4. noon	9. great
5. new	10. took

Have children practice writing spelling words on their *Write-on/Wipe-off Boards.*

VOCABULARY

Student-Friendly Explanations

wriggle   When you wriggle, you move your body back and forth, as you do when you are squirming.

prickly   Something that is prickly is sharp and hurts to touch.

interested   When you are interested in something, you want to do it or learn more about it.

30+ Minutes

LESSON 29

PHONEMIC AWARENESS
Phoneme Isolation

PHONICS AND SPELLING
Reteach Vowel Variant /o͞o/*oo, ew*

COMPREHENSION
Preteach Note Details

HIGH-FREQUENCY WORDS
Reteach *pulled, boy, building, tomorrow*

FLUENCY
Reading Rate

GRAMMAR/WRITING
Reteach Using *Was* and *Were*

Materials Needed:

Word Builders and Word Builder Cards

Write-On/ Wipe-Off Boards

Practice Book p.115

Happy Landings Student Edition pp. 46–52

Sweet Success Student Edition pp. 36–42 pp. 44–45

Practice Book

Spelling Words

1. boot	6. grew
2. tooth	7. story
3. soon	8. hurry
4. noon	9. great
5. new	10. took

Have children practice writing spelling words on their *Write-on/Wipe-off Boards.*

Phonemic Awareness

Phoneme Isolation   Say the word *soon*. Tell children to listen to the /o͞o/ sound in the middle of the word *soon*. Then say the words *bread* and *boot*. Have them repeat the words aloud. Ask: **Which of these words has the /o͞o/ sound you hear in soon?** *Boot* has the /o͞o/ sound. Continue with the words *tooth, zoom, badge; spool, piece, broom; stew, brew, rope.*

RETEACH

Phonics and Spelling

Vowel Variant /o͞o/*oo, ew*

Word Building   Place the *Word Builder Cards b, o, o,* and *t* in the *Word Builder*. Ask children to say the name and sound of each letter. Then read the word naturally—*boot*. Have children do the same. Ask:

- **Which letters should I change to make *boot* become *tooth*?** (Change *b* to *t* and add *h* at the end.)

- **What letters should I change to make *tooth* become *soon*?** (Change *t* to *s* and *th* to *n*.)

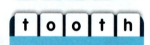

Continue with the words *noon, new,* and *grew.*

Read Words in Context   Write the following sentences on chart paper. Have children read each sentence silently. Then track the print as children read the sentences aloud. Finally, point to the underlined words at random and have children read them. *You took my boot! That story was great! I will hurry and get home by noon. I have a new tooth. Soon a plant grew from the seed.*

PRETEACH

Comprehension

Note Details   Remind children that details are pieces of information in a story. Explain that identifying details can help readers answer the questions *Who? What? When? Where?* and *How?* Read aloud the following excerpts from "School Day" in *Happy Landings*: **It was time for lunch. Cole sat next to Hope. She knows good stories.**

Then model for children how to identify details. Say: **Cole and Hope are sitting together. This is an important detail because it shows that they are friends.** Have children tell another important detail from the page. (One reason they are friends is because Hope knows jokes. That makes her fun.)

High-Frequency Words

Write the words *pulled, boy, building,* and *tomorrow* on the board.

- Point to and read *pulled*. Repeat, having children say *pulled* with you.

- Say: **The girl *pulled* the wagon.**

- Repeat the word and then point to each letter as you spell it. Then have children say and spell *boy* with you. Have children reread the word.

Repeat for the remaining words. Use the following sentences: *A* boy *is a young man. I like* building *sand castles. I will wake up early* tomorrow *morning.*

Have children turn to page 44 of *Sweet Success* and have them read aloud the words at the top of the page. Talk about the illustrations. Then guide children in choosing and writing the word that names each picture. (4. *threw,* 5. *boots,* 6. *scoop*) Have children read aloud each word in the list on page 45. Ask volunteers to read the sentences aloud. Then have children choral-read the sentences. Guide them to write the word that completes each sentence. (1. *boy,* 2. *building,* 3. *pulled,* 4. *tomorrow*)

Grammar/Writing

Practice Book p.115

Using *Was* and *Were* Read aloud the following poem and have children echo-read.

> Dad was reading a book.
> Mom and Jan were wading in the brook.
> Jack and Dan were playing ball.
> It was a perfect day for all!

Then ask children if it tells about something that is happening now or something that happened in the past. (in the past) Ask them how they know. (Words like *was* and *were* tell about the past.) Help children identify and circle *was* and *were* each time they appear. Complete *Practice Book* page 115 together.

High-Frequency Words

pulled	building
boy	tomorrow

Fluency

Reading Rate Remind children that good readers read at just the right speed, not too fast and not too slow. Good readers slow down when they are having trouble understanding something. Revisit page 37 of "Do You Know Me?" in *Sweet Success.*

Say: **I slowed down the first time I read this page. I didn't know what friends the pencil was talking about. I slowed down and figured it out.**

Discuss with children places they might have to slow down while reading this selection.

DAY AT A GLANCE

Day 2

PHONEMIC AWARENESS
Phoneme Blending

PHONICS AND SPELLING
Reteach Vowel Diphthong /o͞o/ *oo, ew*

HIGH-FREQUENCY WORDS
Reteach *boy, building, tomorrow, toward, welcoming, pulled*

FLUENCY
Reading Rate

READING
"Snow Fort"

BUILD ROBUST VOCABULARY
Preteach *cooperative, construct, assist*

GRAMMAR/WRITING
Reteach Using *Was* and *Were*

Materials Needed:

Word Builders
and Word
Builder Cards

Practice
Book

Lesson 29
High-Frequency
Word Cards

Happy Landings
Student Edition
pp. 16–22
pp. 46–52

Sweet Success
Student Edition
pp. 46–53

Photo
Cards

High-Frequency Words

boy	toward
building	welcoming
tomorrow	pulled

Phonemic Awareness

Phoneme Blending Tell children that they are going to play a guessing game and find the word you have in mind. Then say, **I'm thinking of a word that means something you can use to clean a floor. You use it to sweep things, and it is called a /b/ /r/ /o͞o/ /m/. My word is broom.** Have children guess the following words: /s/ /p/ /o͞o/ /n/ (*spoon),* /l/ /o͞o/ /p/ /s/ (*loops),* /f/ /l/ /o͞o/ (*flew),* /t/ /o͞o/ /th/ (*tooth),* /b/ /l/ /o͞o/ /m/ (*bloom).*

RETEACH

Phonics and Spelling

 Vowel Variant /o͞o/*oo, ew*

Word Building Use a *Word Builder* and *Word Builder Cards* and have children repeat each step after you. Build the word *new.* Then have children say the word naturally—*new.* Lead children in building and reading new words by saying:

- **Change *n* to *fl*. Read the word.** (*flew*)
- **Change *ew* to *ow*. Read the word.** (*flow*)
- **Change *f* to *b*. Read the word.** (*blow*)

Continue with the following words: *snow, school, spool, boot, boat.*

Read Words in Context Ask children to turn to *Practice Book* page 116. Read each sentence aloud and have children echo-read. Then ask volunteers to read each sentence aloud. Ask: **What did Lew eat?** (food) **What did he do?** (he grew) **What did he grow out of?** (a few boots) **What did he need to buy?** (new boots) Guide children to circle all the words with *oo.* Then guide children to underline the words with *ew.*

RETEACH

High-Frequency Words

Display the *High-Frequency Word Cards* for *boy, building, tomorrow, toward, welcoming,* and *pulled.* Point to each card and read the word. Have children repeat. Then randomly point to the words, and ask children to read each one. Distribute cards to children and have them work with partners to play a game. Tell children to turn the cards over and shuffle them. Then have them play a memory game with the cards.

Reading

pp.
46–
53

Build Background: "Snow Fort"

Read the title with children. Ask them to tell how they play in the snow. Ask: **How do you play in the snow? Do you make things with snow? What?** If they live in an area where it doesn't snow, have children tell what they know about snow from books, television, and films. Tell children they will be reading about some children who play outside on a snowy day.

Monitor Comprehension: "Snow Fort"

Have children turn to the first page of the story. Ask a volunteer to reread the title. Have children look at the picture on page 46. Ask children to think about what the story will be about and what the characters will be doing. Then guide children through the selection as they read.

pp.
46–
47

Say: **We see a boy looking at the snow. Let's read to find out if he goes outside.**

After reading the pages, ask: **Does the boy go outside? Why does he put on a coat, mittens, and boots?** (yes; because it is cold outside when it snows) CAUSE AND EFFECT

Ask: **Did Jack make the snow fort by himself? Explain.** (No, a boy came by and helped.) NOTE DETAILS

Ask: **Is a snow fort more like a house or a person? Explain.** (It is more like a house because it is something you can get inside of.) GENERALIZE

Ask: **Which word on these pages has the /o͞o/ sound?** (boots, scooped, soon) APPLY PHONICS

pp.
48–
49

Say: **I see a girl in these pictures. Let's find out who she is.**

After reading the pages, ask: **Who else came by to help?** (a girl) NOTE DETAILS

Ask: **What kind of children do you think the boy and girl who stopped by are?** (friendly, helpful, fun) CHARACTERS' TRAITS

Ask: **Which words on these pages have the /o͞o/ sound?** (grew, soon) APPLY PHONICS

Fluency

Reading Rate Have children turn to "In Each Place" in *Happy Landings*.

Say: **This is a selection of true facts. It tells about some places that you may not know much about. Some of the places are different from where we live. That makes it a little harder to read. How should we read this section—slow or quickly? I think we should read it slowly to make sure we understand everything.**

Then display "School Day" in *Happy Landings*. Say: **This book tells about school. We know a lot about school. How would you read this book?** (a little more quickly)

Ask: **What do you think will happen next?** (The children will make snowballs.) **MAKE PREDICTIONS**

pp. 50–51

Say: **We see Jack's dad. Let's read on to find out if he will help.**

After reading the pages, ask: **How does Jack tell his dad he can help? What does this mean?** (Jack says Dad can be "It." It means they are going to play a game of tag.) **NOTE DETAILS/USE PRIOR KNOWLEDGE**

Ask: **How are snow forts and snowballs alike?** (They are both made of snow. They can both be stacked. They both can be used for outdoor play.) **COMPARE AND CONTRAST**

Ask: **What do you think the children may do with the fort and the snowballs?** (They might have a snowball fight.) **What do you think will happen to the snow fort? Why?** (It might fall down if some of the snowballs hit it.) **MAKE PREDICTIONS**

page 52

Say: **Look at the picture. What do you think the children and Dad are doing? Let's read to find out.**

After reading the pages, ask: **What do the children and Dad do?** (play tag, jump on the fort, throw snowballs) **NOTE DETAILS**

Ask: **Why do the children have to make a new fort tomorrow?** (The one they made fell down because they jumped on it and hit it with snowballs.) **CAUSE AND EFFECT**

Ask: **Do you think Dad and the children had fun? Explain.** (Yes because they are smiling and because they want to do it again tomorrow.) **MAKE INFERENCES**

Ask: **Which words on this page have the /o͞o/ sound?** (*threw, soon, new*) **APPLY PHONICS**

page 53

Answers to *Think Critically* Questions

Help children read and answer the *Think Critically* questions on page 53. Answers are shown below.

1. ‹*snowballs*› **DETAILS**

2. ‹*the kids jump on it*› **CAUSE AND EFFECT**

3. ‹*build another fort*› **MAKE INFERENCES**

PRETEACH

Build Robust Vocabulary

 Introduce Robust Vocabulary   Read the student-friendly explanation for each word. Then discuss each word using the following examples.

Say: **You cooperate when you follow directions for me.** Show *Photo Cards* *queen* and *ice*. **Which of these could cooperate? Explain.**

Say: Show *Photo Cards bridge, factory,* and *school*. **These are all things that people can construct. What are other things that people construct?**

Say: **I need someone to assist me when I lift something very heavy. Would you be more likely to need someone to assist you to play or to reach something on a high shelf? Explain.**

RETEACH

Grammar/Writing

Using *Was* and *Were*   Recall with children something that happened at school in the past. Guide them to dictate a message about it as you write it on the board. Make a few usage errors to be corrected later on. Ask children to include *was* and *were* in the message.

> A cat came into our classroom. She was lost. Our teacher was trying to catch the cat. We was trying to help. The cat was hiding under a desk. Our teacher got the cat and found her owner. We was happy the cat got back to her home. Our teacher was happy, too.

Read the dicated message to children and invite them to read along. As you read, lead children to spot and correct errors.

VOCABULARY
Student-Friendly Explanations

cooperative   A cooperative person works with others in a helpful way to complete a task.

construct   When I construct something, I build or make it.

assist   When I assist someone, I help them do something.

PHONEMIC AWARENESS
Phoneme Segmentation

PHONICS
Preteach Phonograms *-ool, -ew*

PHONICS AND SPELLING
Reteach Vowel Variant /o͞o/ *oo, ew*

HIGH-FREQUENCY WORDS
Reteach *pulled, boy, building, tomorrow*

FLUENCY
Reading Rate

COMPREHENSION
Reteach Note Details

GRAMMAR/WRITING
Reteach Story

Materials Needed:

Write-On/
Wipe-Off
Boards with
Phonemic
Awareness
Disks

Photo
Cards

Word Builders
and Word
Builder Cards

Copying
Masters
115–116

Lesson 29
Story Strips

Happy Landings
Student Edition
pp. 36–42

Sweet Success
Student Edition
pp. 46–52

Spelling Words

1. boot	6. grew
2. tooth	7. story
3. soon	8. hurry
4. noon	9. great
5. new	10. took

Phonemic Awareness

Phoneme Segmentation Distribute the four-box papers to children. Tell them that the boxes stand for sounds in words. Show *Photo Card igloo* and ask: **What is the first sound we hear in *igloo*? We hear /i/.** Have children place a disk in the first box to represent this sound. Then guide them to name the second sound (/g/) and place a second disk on the paper. Then help them identify the third and fourth sounds in *igloo* (/l/ and /o͞o/) and place a disk on the paper for each sound. Point to the disks in sequence as children say the word with you. Say: ***Igloo* has four sounds.** Repeat with *Photo Cards moon* and *school.*

PRETEACH

Phonics

Phonograms *-ool, -ew* Display and say these words: *cool, stool, drool.* Ask: **How are these words the same?** (They all end in *-ool.* They rhyme.) Underline *-ool* and say: **o-o-l at the end of a word is pronounced /o͞ol/.** Display and say these words: *few, brew, new.* Ask: **How are these words the same?** (They all end in *-ew.* They rhyme.) Underline *-ew* and say: **e-w at the end of a word is pronounced /o͞o/.** Guide children to sort and say: *tool, spool, blew, screw, school.* Write the words on the board and help children underline the phonograms.

RETEACH

Phonics and Spelling

Vowel Variant /o͞o/ *oo, ew*
Build Words Use *Word Builders* and *Word Builder Cards* to form words. Have children listen to your directions and change a letter in each word to spell a spelling word. Form *hoot* and have children read the word. Ask: **Which spelling word can you make by changing the first letter?** (*boot*)

Follow a similar procedure with the following words: *tool* (*tooth*), *sun* (*soon*), *soon* (*noon*), *dew* (*new*), *grow* (*grew*), *stork* (*story*), *flurry* (*hurry*).

Remind children that there are some other words they have to remember how to spell. Tell them that *great* is one such word. Have children picture the word and then write it. Continue with *took.*

RETEACH

High-Frequency Words

 Copying Masters 115–116

Duplicate and distribute *Copying Masters* 115–116 to each child. Explain that the sentences tell the story "Snow Fort" but some have missing words.

List the words *pulled, boy, building,* and *tomorrow* on the board. Have children read aloud each story strip sentence and name the correct word on the board that makes sense in the sentence. Have children write the missing words in the blanks and read the completed sentences aloud. Help children cut apart the strips, read the completed sentences, and arrange them in story order.

RETEACH

Comprehension

Note Details Review with children how to recognize details in a story. Ask them what questions details can help them answer about a story. (Who? What? When? Where?) Have children turn to "The Picnic Plan" in *Happy Landings*. Reread the first page aloud and identify details that answer the questions *Who? What? When? Where?* (three friends, a picnic, a nice day, outside) Then guide children to identify details for the rest of the story.

RETEACH

Grammar/Writing

 Photo Card

Story Display *Photo Cards king, queen, island, sandcastle, ocean, fish, ant, octopus*. Use the cards to tell a story.

Say: **A New Castle. A king and queen lived on an island. They built a beautiful sandcastle. One day, the ocean waves got so big that they washed the castle away. The king and queen needed a new house fast. Fish offered to help, but he didn't have hands to build with. Ant offered to help, but he was too small to make a big castle. At last, Octopus came to help. He used his eight arms to build fast. Soon, the king and queen had a beautiful new home.**

Help children identify that the story has a title, characters, setting, beginning, middle, ending, and a plot.

High-Frequency Words

pulled	building
boy	tomorrow

Fluency

Reading Rate Remind children that good readers read at just the right speed, not too slowly and not too fast. Model how to slow down when you don't understand something and read at the proper rate.

Say: **I'm going to read "Snow Fort" one page at a time. I'm going to read at just the right speed, not too slowly and not too fast. If I come to a part that I don't understand, I'm going to read a little bit slower. Read each page after me, just the way I read it.**

LESSON 29

DAY AT A GLANCE
Day 4

30+ Minutes

PHONEMIC AWARENESS
Phoneme Blending

PHONICS
Reteach Contractions *'d, 've, 're, 's, n't, 'll*

PHONICS AND SPELLING
Reteach Vowel Variant /o͞o/*oo, ew*

HIGH-FREQUENCY WORDS
Reteach *boy, building, tomorrow, toward, welcoming, pulled*

FLUENCY
Reading Rate

COMPREHENSION
Reteach Note Details

GRAMMAR/WRITING
Reteach Story

Materials Needed:

Practice Book
p.117

Copying Masters 113–114

Practice Book

Lesson 29 High-Frequency Word Cards

Photo Card

Sweet Success Student Edition pp. 26–32 pp. 46–52

Photo Cards

Spelling Words

1.	boot	6.	grew
2.	tooth	7.	story
3.	soon	8.	hurry
4.	noon	9.	great
5.	new	10.	took

Phonemic Awareness

Phoneme Blending   Tell children that together you are going to play a game of "Fix It." Tell them that you are going to say some words that are all broken and they should listen to see if they can put the sounds together to figure out the word. Say: **Listen: /f/ /o͞o/ /l/. What word does /f/ /o͞o/ /l/ say? It says** *fool.* **Now, you will try some.** Continue with the following words: /s/ /t/ /o͞o/ /l/ (*stool*), /b/ /r/ /o͞o/ /m/ (*broom*), /s/ /t/ /o͞o/ (*stew*), /b/ /r/ /o͞o/ (*brew*), /m/ /o͞o/ /n/ (*moon*).

RETEACH

Phonics

Contractions *'d, 've, 're, 's, n't, 'll*   Remind children that a contraction is a shorter way to write two words. Apostrophes in contractions stand for the missing letters. Write the following sentences on the board: *We are in first grade. There is our classroom. You will like it. We would like you to visit. We have learned a lot. I will show you how I can read. It is fun.* Read each sentence and work with children to replace the underlined words with contractions. Have children identify the missing letters in each contraction.

RETEACH

Phonics and Spelling

Practice Book
p.117

Vowel Variant /o͞o/*oo, ew*
Direct children's attention to page 117 of their *Practice Books.* Complete the page together.

Assess children's progress using the following sentences.
1. boot   The **boot** is too small.
2. tooth   He can wiggle his **tooth**.
3. soon   Mom will go out **soon**.
4. noon   I have lunch at **noon**.
5. new   My **new** coat is red.
6. grew   This bean plant **grew** from a seed.

Review
7. story   Please tell us a **story**.
8. hurry   I'll **hurry** so I won't miss the bus.

High-Frequency
9. great   She had a **great** idea.
10. took   I **took** my book back to the library.

RETEACH

High-Frequency Words

Copying Masters 113–114

Display *High-Frequency Word Cards* for this lesson's words—*boy, building, tomorrow, toward, welcoming, pulled*—and the previously learned high-frequency words. Point to words at random and have children read them.

RETEACH

Comprehension

Note Details Ask children what questions details can help them answer about a story. (Who? What? When? Where?) Draw a three-column chart on the board like the one below. Have children turn to "Helping Baby Bird" and "Snow Fort" in *Sweet Success*. Walk children through both stories to answer the questions in the first column. Record their responses.

	"Helping Baby Bird"	"Snow Fort"
Who?	Ann, Jim, Ginger, Dad, bird, vet	Jack, boy, girl, Dad
What?	helping a bird	playing in the snow
When?	one day	a snowy day
Where?	yard	outdoors

RETEACH

Grammar/Writing

Photo Card

Story Review with children the characteristics of stories.

Story

It has a title.
It has a character and a setting.
It has a beginning, a middle, and an ending.
It has a plot.

Remind children of the story you told about the king and queen and their sandcastle. Display a selection of *Photo Cards* that show animals and people. Have children pick two as story characters. Also display the *Photo Cards* that show places such as *factory* and *library*. Have children pick one as a story setting. Guide children in brainstorming what could happen to the characters in the setting. Encourage them to dictate a story with a beginning, middle, and ending. Record their ideas. Guide them in selecting a title. Read the story aloud and help children match its parts to the characteristics.

High-Frequency Words

boy	toward
building	welcoming
tomorrow	pulled

Fluency

Reading Rate Read aloud "Snow Fort" in *Sweet Success* one page at a time. Have children mimic your reading rate as they choral-read each page after you. Next, have each child select a page and practice reading it to themselves at an appropriate reading rate. Then invite volunteers to read their pages for the class.

DAY AT A GLANCE
Day 5

HIGH-FREQUENCY WORDS
boy, building, tomorrow, toward, welcoming

PHONEMIC AWARENESS
Onset and Rime

PHONICS AND SPELLING
Preteach Long Vowels /ī/*i*, /ō/*o*

BUILD ROBUST VOCABULARY
Preteach *seized, tiresome, tremendous*

GRAMMAR/WRITING
Preteach Using *Go* and *Went*

Materials Needed:

Lesson 29
High-Frequency
Word Cards

Sound/
Spelling
Cards *Ii, Oo*

Word Builders
and Word
Builder Cards

Write-On/
Wipe-Off
Boards

Practice
Book

High-Frequency Words

boy	toward
building	welcoming
tomorrow	

High-Frequency Words

 Display *High-Frequency Word Cards* for *boy, building, tomorrow, toward, welcoming,* and the other previously learned high-frequency words. Say the word *boy,* ask a volunteer to point to *boy,* and have children read the word aloud. Continue with the remaining high-frequency words. Repeat this activity several times to reinforce instant recognition.

Phonemic Awareness

Onset and Rime   Tell children you are going to say some words, but you are going to say them in parts. Have children listen to see if they can figure out the word. Say: **/w/-ild—The word I said was** *wild.* **Now you try some: /ch/-ild, /p/-ost, /k/-old, /m/-ind, /bl/-ind.**

PRETEACH

Phonics and Spelling

Long Vowels /ī/*i*, /ō/*o*
Connecting Letter to Sound   Say the word *icy.* Have children repeat it. Say: **The word** *icy* **begins with the /ī/ sound.** Have children say /ī/ several times. Display *Sound/Spelling Card Ii.* Say the letter name, and identify the picture. Tell children that the letter *i* can stand for the sound /ī/, the sound at the beginning of *icy.* Have children say /ī/ several times as you touch the letter. Repeat this activity for the long *o* sound using *Sound/Spelling Card Oo* and the word *oak.* Give each child an *i* and an *o* *Word Builder Card.* Say: **When I say a word that begins with /ī/, hold up your** *i* **card and say /ī/. When I say a word that begins with /ō/, hold up your** *o* **card and say /ō/.** Say these words: *obey, ocean, idea, ivory, item, odor.* Tell children that some words have the sounds /ī/ and /ō/ in the middle. Say *wild,* elongating the /ī/ sound. Tell children that *wild* has the /ī/ sound in the middle. Repeat for *most.* Then say the following words, elongating the medial sound: *mild, post, hind, gold, bolt.*

Word Blending   Demonstrate each step with *Word Builder Cards* and a *Word Builder,* and have children repeat each step after you. Hold up *m* and say /mm/. Hold up *i* and say /ī/. Hold up *n* and say /nn/. Hold up *d* and say /d/.

- Place the letters *m, i, n, d* in the *Word Builder.*

- Point to *m.* Say /m/. Point to *i* and say /ī/. Prompt children to repeat after you.

- Slide *i* next to *m.* Run your hand under the letters as you blend the sounds, elongating them—/mī/.

- Point to *n* and say /n/.
- Slide *n* next to *mi*. Run your hand under the letters are you blend the sounds, elongating them—/mīn/.
- Slide *d* next to *min*. Run your hand under *mind* as you blend the sounds, elongating them—/mīnd/.
- Read *mind* naturally.

Follow the same procedure with these words: *wild, fold, hold*.

  Word Building   Place the *Word Builder Cards f, i, n,* and *d* in the *Word Builder* and have children do the same. Ask children to say each letter name and the sound it stands for. Then read the word naturally—*find*. Have children do the same. Have children build and read new words. As they build each word, write it on the board. Say:

- **Change *f* to *m*. What word did you make?** (*mind*)
- **Change *n* to *l*. What word did you make?** (*mild*)

Continue with the words *cold, fold,* and *most*. Have children read the words on the board. Direct children's attention to page 118 of their *Practice Books*. Complete the page together.

PRETEACH

Build Robust Vocabulary

Introduce Robust Vocabulary   Read the student-friendly explanation for each word. Then discuss each word using the following examples.

Say: **My dog seized my slipper. What else might a dog seize? Have you ever seized something you really wanted? When?**

Say: **I think it is tiresome to wash lots of dishes. Which chores do you think are tiresome? Why?**

Say: **I would not like to have a tremendous dog for a pet. Why do you think I say that? Do you agree?**

PRETEACH

Grammar/Writing

Using *Go* and *Went*   Write on the board and read aloud the following sentences tracking the print: *I go to my friend's house after school. Then we go to the park to play*. Explain that the sentences tell what is happening now. Have a volunteer underline *go*. Tell children that *go* is a verb that can be used to tell about now. Then replace the word *go* in both sentences with *went* and read the sentences aloud. Explain that *went* tells about something that has already happened. Invite volunteers to tell about their after school activities. Encourage them to use *go* and *went*.

Spelling Words

1. find	6. most
2. mind	7. soon
3. mild	8. new
4. cold	9. boy
5. fold	10. building

Have children practice writing spelling words on their *Write-on/Wipe-off Boards*.

VOCABULARY

Student-Friendly Explanations

seized If you seized something, you grabbed it in a sudden strong way.

tiresome If something is tiresome, it is boring.

tremendous If something is tremendous, it is very large and great.

30+ Minutes

LESSON 30

PHONEMIC AWARENESS
Phoneme Isolation

PHONICS AND SPELLING
Reteach Long Vowels /ī/*i*, /ō/*o*

COMPREHENSION
Reteach Alphabetize

HIGH-FREQUENCY WORDS
Reteach *love, ready, sorry*

FLUENCY
Reading Rate

GRAMMAR/WRITING
Reteach Using *Go* and *Went*

Materials Needed:

Word Builders and Word Builder Cards

Write-On/ Wipe-Off Boards

Photo Cards

Happy Landings Student Edition pp. 36–42

Sweet Success Student Edition pp. 54–55

Practice Book

Spelling Words

1. find	6. most
2. mind	7. soon
3. mild	8. new
4. cold	9. boy
5. fold	10. building

Have children practice writing spelling words on their *Write-on/Wipe-off Boards.*

Phonemic Awareness

Phoneme Isolation Tell children to listen to the /ī/ sound in the middle of the word *kind*. Then say the words *mild* and *sail*. Ask: **Which word has the /ī/ sound we hear in *kind*? *Mild* has the /ī/ sound.** Have children identify which of the following have the /ī/ sound: *child, grind, hand; wild, blind, bone; kind, whale, child.* Repeat the process with the word *post* to introduce /ō/. Then have children identify the long *o* words in the following: *fold, troll, drop; most, mile, hold; scold, grind, bolt.*

RETEACH

Phonics and Spelling

 Long Vowels /ī/*i*, /ō/*o*
Word Building Place the *Word Builder Cards f, i, n,* and *d* in the *Word Builder.* Ask children to say the name and sound of each letter. Then read the word naturally—*find*. Have children do the same. Continue building new words by asking children:

- **Which letter should I change to make *find* become *mind*?** (Change *f* to *m*.)

- **What letter should I change to make *mind* become *mild*?** (Change *n* to *l*.)

Continue with the words *cold, fold,* and *most*.

Read Words in Context Write the following sentences on chart paper. Have children read each sentence silently. Then track the print as children read the sentences aloud. Finally, point to the underlined words at random and have children read them. *The new boy will find our classroom soon. Most rooms in the school building are cold. Jack has a mild sunburn on his arms. Do you mind if I fold your newspaper?*

RETEACH

Comprehension

  Alphabetize Put *Photo Cards house, arm, shoes, night,* and *house* in a pocket chart. Rearrange them as you model. Say: **I want to put these words in alphabetical**

order. I'll put *fish* after *arm* because *fish* begins with *f* and *arm* begins with *a*. I'll put *house, night,* and *shoes* next because *h* comes before *n* and *n* comes before *s* in the alphabet. Now the words are in alphabetical order: *arm, fish, house, night, shoes—a, f, h, n, s.*

RETEACH

High-Frequency Words

pp. 54–55

Write the words *love, ready,* and *sorry* on the board.

- Point to and read *love.* Repeat, having children say *love* with you.
- Say: **Parents *love* their children.**
- Repeat the word and then point to each letter as you spell it. Then have children say and spell *love* with you. Have children reread the word.

Repeat for the remaining words. Use the following sentences: *I am* ready *for school. I am* sorry *that I bumped into you.*

Have children turn to page 54 of *Sweet Success* and have them read aloud the words at the top of the page. Talk about the illustrations. Then guide children in choosing and writing the word that names each picture. (4. *find,* 5. *blinds,* 6. *open*) Have children read aloud each word in the list on page 55. Ask volunteers to read the sentences aloud. Then have children choral-read the sentences. Guide them to choose and circle the word that completes each sentence. (1. *ready,* 2. *love,* 3. *sorry*)

RETEACH

Grammar/Writing

Practice Book
p.119

Using *Go* and *Went* Tell children that they will listen to a poem that has sentences with *go* and *went.* Write the poem on the board and track the print as you read aloud.

> All morning, we drove in the car.
> We left the city. We went far.
> Finally we get to the park and stop.
> "Now, let's go!" say Mom and Pop.
> We go sit under the trees.
> And share our lunch with the ants and bees.

Ask children to underline the words *go* and *went.* Say: **The words *all morning* are a clue that the action happened in the past. The word *went* tells about an action in the past. The word *now* is a clue that the action is happening now. The word *go* tells about an action that is happening now.**

Complete *Practice Book* page 119 together.

High-Frequency Words

love	**sorry**
ready	

Fluency

Reading Rate Have children turn to "The Picnic Plan" in *Happy Landings* and track the print as you read aloud with expression. Remind children that they may be able to speed up their reading rate since they are already familiar with the story. Suggest that they move at a speed where their words flow smoothly, making it interesting for the listener.

LESSON 30

DAY AT A GLANCE

Day 2

PHONEMIC AWARENESS
Phoneme Blending

PHONICS AND SPELLING
Reteach Long Vowels /ī/i, /ō/o, /ō/o-e

HIGH-FREQUENCY WORDS
Reteach *any, front, nothing, ready, sorry, love*

FLUENCY
Reading Rate

READING
"Garden List"

BUILD ROBUST VOCABULARY
Preteach *exhausted, outrageous, patient*

GRAMMAR/WRITING
Reteach Using *Go* and *Went*

Materials Needed:

Word Builders and Word Builder Cards

Practice Book
p.120

Lesson 30 High-Frequency Word Cards

Happy Landings Student Edition pp. 56–62

Sweet Success Student Edition pp. 56–63

High-Frequency Words

any	ready
front	sorry
nothing	love

Phonemic Awareness

Phoneme Blending   Tell children that they are going to play a guessing game. Then say, **I'm thinking of a word that tells about some kinds of animals. Animals like lions and tigers are not tame. They are /w/ /ī/ /l/ /d/. The word is *wild*.** Continue with the following words: /m/ /ī/ /n/ /d/ (*mind*), /m/ /ō/ /s/ /t/ (*most*), /ch/ /ī/ /l/ /d/ (*child*), /t/ /r/ /ō/ /l/ (*troll*).

RETEACH

Phonics and Spelling

 Long Vowels /ī/i, /ō/o
Word Building   Use a *Word Builder* and *Word Builder Cards* and have children repeat each step after you. Build the word *mile*. Then have them say the word naturally—*mile*. Lead children in building and reading new words by saying:

- **Change *e* to *d*. Read the word.** (*mild*) **Note that both words have the sound /ī/ but have different spellings. Both *i-e* and *i* can stand for the sound /ī/.**

- **Change *mi* to *ho*. Read the word.** (*hold*)

- **Change *d* to *e*. Read the word.** (*hole*) **Note that both words have the sound /ō/ but have different spellings. Both *o* and *o-e* can stand for the sound /ō/.**

Continue with the following words: *pole, pile, file, fold, told, tile.*

 Read Words in Context   Ask children to turn to *Practice Book* page 120. Read each sentence aloud and have children echo-read. Then ask volunteers to read each sentence aloud. Guide children to read this page. Ask: **Who had a plan?** (a child) **What kind of plan did she have?** (bold) **What did she want to find?** (gold) **What did she tell her pal to do?** (hold a bag) Guide children to circle all the words with /ī/ and underline the words with /ō/.

RETEACH

High-Frequency Words

 Display the *High-Frequency Word Cards* for *any, front, nothing, ready, sorry,* and *love*. Point to each card and read the word. Have children repeat. Then randomly point to the words, and ask children to read each one. Distribute cards to children and have them work with partners. Tell children to turn the cards over and shuffle them. Then have them play a memory game with the cards.

Reading

pp. 56–63

Build Background: "Garden List"

Read the title with children. Ask them to tell what they like to put in a salad. Encourage them to tell where they get the things to put into a salad. Tell children they will be reading about some animals that make a salad. Then ask children if they have ever helped make a list. Have them tell what lists are used for.

Monitor Comprehension: "Garden List"

Have children turn to the first page of the selection. Ask a volunteer to reread the title. Have children look at the picture on page 56. Encourage children to think about what the selection will be about and what the characters will be doing. Then guide children through the selection as they read.

pp. 56–57

Say: **We see two rabbits. One has a list. Let's read to find out what is on the list.**

After reading the pages, ask: **What are the rabbits going to make?** (a salad) **What kinds of things do you think they might write on their list?** (Possible response: lettuce, carrots, tomatoes) NOTE DETAILS/ MAKE PREDICTIONS

Ask: **Where do radishes grow? What story clue lets you know?** (They grow in the ground. The rabbits had to dig them out of the ground.) MAKE INFERENCES

Ask: **Which word on these pages has the /ī/ sound?** (kind, find) APPLY PHONICS

pp. 58–59

Say: **We see Rex and Penny with other vegetables. Let's find out what else they put in their salad.**

After reading the pages, ask: **What is in the salad so far? Which vegetable went in first, second, and third?** (radishes, beans, carrots) NOTE DETAILS/SEQUENCE

Ask: **Do you like the same vegetables that Rex and Penny like?** (Possible answer: I like carrots and beans, but I don't like radishes.) PERSONAL RESPONSE

Ask: **Which words have the /ō/ sound?** (those, bowl) APPLY PHONICS

Fluency

Reading Rate Tell children that sometimes they need to change their reading speed. If they come across unfamiliar words or long sentences, they need to slow down. If they are reading short sentences and words they know, they can speed up.

Have them open to the story "Under a Bridge" in *Happy Landings*. Read aloud page 57. Then turn to page 59 and read it aloud. Point out that you can speed up your reading for this page because it is the same as page 57, so you know what the words are.

Day 2

 pp. 60–61

Say: **We see Rex and Penny finishing their salad. Let's see what they do last.**

After reading the pages, ask: **What is the last thing they put into the salad?** (nuts) **Why does the author say, "Crack, crack, crack" when he tells about the nuts.** (because nuts have hard shells that must be cracked open) NOTE DETAILS/USE PRIOR KNOWLEDGE

Ask: **The story says the rabbits *dig, snap, crack,* and *pluck.* Put those words in ABC order.** (crack, dig, pluck, snap) ALPHABETIZE

Ask: **Why did Rex and Penny wash the things for their salad?** (because the things were from the ground so they might have dirt on them) CAUSE-AND-EFFECT

Ask: **Which words have the /ō/ sound?** (those, opened, bowl) APPLY PHONICS

page 62

Say: **Look at the faces of the rabbits on this page. Let's read to find out why they look that way.**

After reading the pages, ask: **How do Rex and Penny feel at the end of the story? Why?** (Possible response: surprised and upset because they forgot to put greens in the salad) CHARACTERS' EMOTIONS

Ask: **What do you think the rabbits will do now?** (Possible responses: get some greens; eat the salad without greens) MAKE PREDICTIONS

Ask: **Which words have the /ō/ sound on this page?** (Oh, no, so, most) APPLY PHONICS

page 63

Answers to *Think Critically* Questions

Help children read and answer the *Think Critically* questions on page 63. Answers are shown below.

1. ‹radishes and carrots› NOTE DETAILS
2. ‹lunch› PLOT
3. ‹forget the greens› SUMMARIZE

PRETEACH

Build Robust Vocabulary

Introduce Robust Vocabulary   Read the student-friendly explanation for each word. Then discuss each word using the following examples.

Say: **Taking a long hike would make me exhausted. What makes you exhausted?**

Say: **I think it would be outrageous to see an elephant on a city street. Do you think it would be more outrageous if it snowed or rained in June? Why?**

Say: **I have to be patient when I am trying to buy something in the grocery store and there is a long line. Tell about a time you were patient.**

RETEACH

Grammar/Writing

Using *Go* and *Went*   Revisit "Garden List" with children. Tell children you will pretend to be one of the rabbits and write sentences that tell what you are doing. Have children look at page 57. Say: ***I go to the field.*** Look at page 61. ***I go to the kitchen.*** Look at page 62. ***I go to the dining room.*** Write the sentences on the board. Have a volunteer underline *go* and remind children that it tells about now. Then change *go* to *went* and write those sentences on the board. Ask: **Does *went* tell about now or the past?** (the past)

I <u>go</u> to the field.	I <u>went</u> to the field.
I <u>go</u> to the kitchen.	I <u>went</u> to the kitchen.
I <u>go</u> to the dining room.	I <u>went</u> to the dining room.

VOCABULARY

Student-Friendly Explanations

exhausted If you are exhausted, you are so tired you can hardly move.

outrageous If something is outrageous, it is different in a shocking way.

patient If you are patient, you put up with things without complaining.

LESSON 30

PHONEMIC AWARENESS
Phoneme Segmentation

PHONICS
Preteach Phonograms -ind, -ild

PHONICS AND SPELLING
Reteach Long Vowels /ī/i, /ō/o

HIGH-FREQUENCY WORDS
Reteach love, ready, sorry

FLUENCY
Reading Rate

COMPREHENSION
Reteach Alphabetize

GRAMMAR/WRITING
Reteach Writing a Story

Materials Needed:

Write-On/
Wipe-Off
Boards with
Phonemic
Awareness
Disks

Photo
Cards

Word Builders
and Word
Builder Cards

Copying
Masters
119–120

Lesson 30
Story Strips

Sweet Success
Student Edition
pp. 56–62

Spelling Words

1. find	6. most
2. mind	7. soon
3. mild	8. new
4. cold	9. boy
5. fold	10. building

Phonemic Awareness

Phoneme Segmentation   Distribute the four-box papers to children. Tell them that the boxes stand for sounds in words. Show *Photo Card gold* and say: **The first sound we hear in *gold* is /g/.** Guide children in placing a disk in the first box. Then identify the second sound in *gold* (/ō/) with children and place a second disk on the paper. Continue this procedure with the third (/l/) and fourth sounds (/d/). Point to the disks in sequence and say the word with children. Say: **How many sounds do you hear in *gold*? I hear four.** Repeat with the following words: *sold, host, child, rind.*

Phonics

Phonograms -ind, -ild   Say *kind* and *bind* and ask children how the words are the same. (They both end with /īnd/. They rhyme.) Using the words *hind, tin, mend,* and *rind,* have children point to their heads when they hear a word that rhymes with *mind.*

Then say *child* and *mild.* Ask how these words are the same. (They both end with /īld/. They rhyme.) Have children point to themselves when they hear a word that rhymes with *child.* Say *wild, time, mild, lid.* Write *kind, bind, hind, rind, mind, wild, mild,* and *child* on the board. Have children underline *-ind* and *-ild.*

Phonics and Spelling

Long Vowels /ī/i, /ō/o
Build Words   Use *Word Builder Cards* and a *Word Builder* to form words. Have children listen to your directions and change a letter in each word to spell a spelling word. Form *kind* and have children read the word. Ask: **Which spelling words can you make by changing the first letter?** (*find, mind*)

Follow a similar procedure with the following words: *milk* (*mild*), *host* (*most*), *sold* (*cold, fold*), *moon* (*soon*), *net* (*new*).

Remind children that there are some other words they have to remember how to spell. Have children say *boy.* Tell them to put *Word Builder Cards b, o, y* in their *Word Builders,* picture the word *boy* in their minds, and build the word. Write the word on the board. Follow the same procedure with the word *building.*

RETEACH

High-Frequency Words

 Copying Masters 119–120 Duplicate and distribute *Copying Masters* 119–120 to each child. Explain that the sentences tell the story "Garden List" but some have missing words.

List the words *love, ready,* and *sorry* on the board. Have children read aloud each story strip sentence and name the correct word on the board that makes sense in the sentence. Have children write the missing words in the blanks and read the completed sentences aloud. Help children cut apart the strips, read the completed sentences, and arrange them in story order.

RETEACH

Comprehension

Alphabetize   Review with children how to alphabetize words. Write the words *radish, bean, carrot, nut,* and *greens* on the board, then have children copy them on index cards. Have children work with the cards and arrange them in ABC order. Then have them shuffle the cards and repeat several times.

RETEACH

Grammar/Writing

Writing a Story   Remind children that they learned about stories last week. Help children recall the important parts they learned that stories have. (title, characters, setting, beginning, middle, ending, plot) Guide children to identify each of those parts in "Garden List." Then work with children to brainstorm ideas for a story that you can write together. Help them think of a title, characters, and a time and place for the story to take place. Save their ideas for Day 4.

High-Frequency Words

love	sorry
ready	

Fluency

Reading Rate   Remind children that when good readers read, it sounds like talking. Tell children that they want to be careful not to read the story too fast or too slow. Show children how to read at a steady pace. Also, demonstrate how to slow down for sections that are harder to read.

Say: **I will read "Garden List" one page at a time. I will stop for a moment after each sentence but not after each word. I want my voice to sound like someone is talking to me and telling the story. Read each page after me, just the way I read it.**

LESSON 30

DAY AT A GLANCE
Day 4

30+ Minutes

PHONEMIC AWARENESS
Phoneme Blending

PHONICS
Preteach Phonogram *-old*

PHONICS AND SPELLING
Reteach Long Vowels /ī/*i*, /ō/*o*

HIGH-FREQUENCY WORDS
Reteach *any, front, nothing, ready, sorry, love*

FLUENCY
Reading Rate

COMPREHENSION
Reteach Alphabetize

GRAMMAR/WRITING
Reteach Writing a Story

Materials Needed:

Practice Book
p.121

Practice Book

Copying Masters 117–118

Lesson 30 High-Frequency Word Cards

Sweet Success Student Edition pp. 36–42 pp. 56–62

Photo Card

Photo Cards

Spelling Words

1. find	6. most
2. mind	7. soon
3. mild	8. new
4. cold	9. boy
5. fold	10. building

Phonemic Awareness

Phoneme Blending   Tell children that together you are going to play a building sound-by-sound game. Tell them that you are going to say some words and they should listen to see if they can put the sounds together to figure out the word. Say: **/f/ /ō/ /l/ /d/. The word is *fold*. Now, you try some.** Continue with the following words: /ch/ /ī/ /l/ /d/ (*child*), /p/ /ō/ /s /t/ (*post*), /m/ /ī/ /n/ /d/ (*mind*), /k/ /ō/ /l/ /t/ (*colt*).

PRETEACH

Phonics

Phonogram *-old*   Say *told* and *cold* and ask children how the words are the same. (They both end with /ōld/. They rhyme.) Using the words *hold, bold, bad, scold, hole,* have children hold up their right arm when they hear a word that rhymes with *told*. Have children say words that rhyme with *told*.

RETEACH

Phonics and Spelling

Practice Book p.121

Long Vowels /ī/*i*, /ō/*o*
Direct children's attention to page 121 of their *Practice Books.* Complete the page together.

Assess children's progress using the following sentences.

1. find — Please help me **find** my lost cat.
2. mind — Use your **mind** to figure out the answer.
3. mild — I like **mild,** dry weather.
4. cold — I don't like **cold** winter weather.
5. fold — The teacher asked us to **fold** the paper.
6. most — Our team won the game with the **most** goals.

Review

7. soon — The bus will leave the station **soon.**
8. new — I wore my **new** jeans to the party.

High-Frequency

9. boy — Luis is the **boy** who sits behind me.
10. building — The library **building** has lots of shelves.

RETEACH

High-Frequency Words

Copying Master 117–118

Display *High-Frequency Word Cards* for this lesson's words—*any, front, nothing, ready, sorry,* and *love*—and the previously learned high-frequency words. Point to words at random and ask children to read them.

Comprehension

Alphabetize Ask children how we alphabetize. *(Look at the first letter of each word and arrange the words in the same order as the letters of the alphabet.)* Draw a three-column chart on the board like the one below. Have children write the names of characters in each story and then alphabetize them.

	"Do You Know Me?"	"Garden List"
Characters	pencil, crayons, brush, scissors, glue	Rex, Penny
Characters in ABC Order	brush crayons glue pencil scissors	Penny Rex

Grammar/Writing

Photo Card

Writing a Story Review with children characteristics of stories.

Story

It has a title.

It has a character and a setting.

It has a beginning, middle, and ending.

It has a plot.

Use *Photo Cards ant, berries, cake,* and *pie* as visuals and tell children the following story: **"Pie or Cake?" Once a greedy ant went to a party. The host asked him if he would like pie or cake. "I want pie *and* cake," the ant said. All the animals warned him that this would be too much food, but he gobbled up four pieces of each. Then it was time for him to go back into his ant hole. He didn't fit! He had to jog around his hole for days before he could fit in. The next time, he went to a party and the host asked what he wanted, he said, "Just one berry, please."** Help children identify the characteristics of a story in "Pie or Cake?" Display children's story ideas from Day 3. Work with children to write a short story and identify the characteristics you discussed.

High-Frequency Words

any	ready
front	sorry
nothing	love

Fluency

Reading Rate Tell children that sometimes they need to change their reading speed. If they come across unfamiliar words or long sentences, they need to slow down. If they are reading parts of stories that have patterns, they can read more quickly.

Read pages 57–60 of "Garden List." Point out the pattern and discuss with children how the pattern makes it easy to read the pages quickly.

HIGH-FREQUENCY WORDS
Review *any, front, nothing, ready, sorry*

PHONEMIC AWARENESS
Phoneme Blending

PHONICS AND SPELLING
Review Long Vowels /ī/*i*, /ō/*o*

BUILD ROBUST VOCABULARY
Review *seized, tiresome, tremendous, exhausted, outrageous, patient*

Materials Needed:

Copying Masters 117–118
Lesson 30 High-Frequency Word Cards

Word Builders and Word Builder Cards

Photo Card
Photo Cards

High-Frequency Words

any	ready
front	sorry
nothing	

30+ Minutes

REVIEW
High-Frequency Words

Copying Masters 117–118 Display *High-Frequency Word Cards* for *any, front, nothing, ready, sorry* and the other previously learned high-frequency words. Say the word *any,* ask a volunteer to point to *any,* and have children read the word aloud. Continue with the remaining high-frequency words. Repeat this activity several times to reinforce instant recognition.

Phonemic Awareness

Phoneme Blending Tell children that they are going to listen to clues and guess words. Then say: **I'm thinking of a word that tells what you are. You are a /ch/ /ī/ /l/ /d/. The word is *child.*** Continue with the following words: /s/ /ō/ /l/ /d/ (*sold*), /p/ /ō/ /s/ /t/ (*post*), /d/ /r/ /o͞o/ (*drew*), /b/ /r/ /o͞o/ /m/ (*broom*), /h/ /a/ /p//ē/ (*happy*).

RETEACH
Phonics and Spelling

Long Vowels /ī/*i*, /ō/*o*
Word Building Place the *Word Builder Cards k, i, n,* and *d* in the *Word Builder* and have children do the same. Ask children to say each letter name and the sound it stands for. Then read the word naturally—*kind.* Have children do the same. Have children build and read new words. As they build each word, write it on the board. Say:

- **Change *k* to *m.* What word did you make?** (*mind*)
- **Change *ind* to *oon.* What word did you make?** (*moon*)

Continue with the words *mew, chew,* and *child.* Have children read the words.

Word Blending Demonstrate each step with *Word Builder Cards* and a *Word Builder.* Have children repeat each step after you. Hold up *w* and say /w/. Hold up *i* and say /ī/. Hold up *l* and say /l/. Hold up *d* and say /d/.

- Place the letters *w, i, l, d* in the *Word Builder.*
- Point to *w.* Say /w/. Point to *i* and say /ī/. Prompt children to repeat after you.
- Slide *i* next to *w.* Run your hand under the letters as you blend the sounds, elongating them—/wī/.

- Point to *l* and say /l/.
- Slide *l* next to *wi.* Run your hand under *wil* as you blend the sounds, elongating them—/wīl/.

- Slide *d* next to *wil*. Run your hand under *wil* as you blend the sounds, elongating them—/wīld/.
- Read *wild* naturally.

Follow the same procedure with these words: *gold, boot, blew, bunny,* and *babies.*

 Build Spelling Words   Use *Word Builder Cards* and a *Word Builder* to form words. Have children listen to your directions and change a letter in each word to spell a spelling word using their *Word Builder Cards* and *Word Builders.* Form *rind* and have children read the word. Ask:

- **Which two spelling words can you make by changing the first letter?** (*find, mind*)

Follow a similar procedure with the following words: wild (*mild*), fold (*cold, fold*), post (*most*), moon (*soon*), net (*new*). After children build each spelling word, see if they can think of another word they could form by changing the first letter. Help them form the words.

REVIEW

Build Robust Vocabulary

Photo Card **Review Robust Vocabulary**   Read the student-friendly explanation for each word. Review the words using the following examples.

Say: **I would seize a fork from a baby so she didn't hurt herself.** Show *Photo Card porcupine.* **Would you want to try to seize one of these? Why or why not?**

Say: **I think it would be tiresome to watch the same movie three days in a row. What do you think would be tiresome to do three days in a row?**

Say: **The sky is tremendous.** Show *Photo Cards ocean, ant, leaves.* **Which of these is tremendous? Explain.**

Say: **Raking leaves all day would make me feel exhausted. Would you be more likely to be exhausted from watching television all day or from playing soccer all day? Why?**

Say: **It would be outrageous to see a cake as big as a car.** Show *Photo Cards queen* and *toad.* **It would be outrageous if which one of these said, "Hello?"**

Say: **My dog is not patient when he wants to eat and I am busy. Would a baby or an adult be more likely to be patient? Explain.**

VOCABULARY

Student-Friendly Explanations

seized   If you seized something, you grabbed it in a sudden strong way.

tiresome   If something is tiresome, it is boring.

tremendous   If something is tremendous, it is very large and great.

exhausted   If you are exhausted, you are so tired you can hardly move.

outrageous   If something is outrageous, it is different in a shocking way.

patient   If you are patient, you put up with things without complaining.